方显廷文集

第 6 卷

方显廷 著

《方显廷文集》编辑委员会委员

主　编：厉以宁　熊性美

副主编：方惟琳

编　委：穆家修　常绍民　叶　坦　纪　辛
　　　　张世荣　方露茜　方菊龄(Julie Thomas)
　　　　方　郁　魏　玥　关永强

方 显 廷

(1903—1985)

1942年方显廷访问哈佛。

1944年春,自美国归来。摄于重庆沙坪坝新生照相馆。

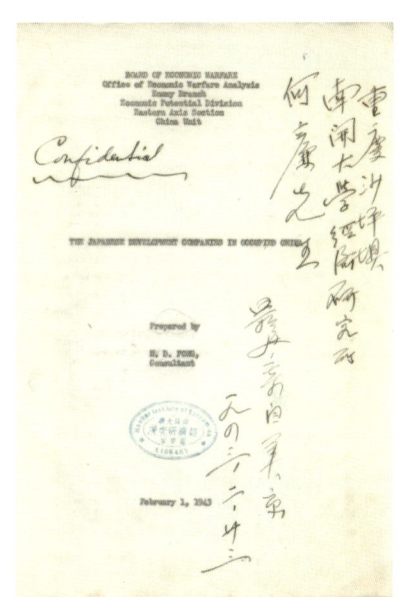

英文版《沦陷区之日本开发公司》书影（南开大学图书馆藏）

英文版《战后工业化》书影（南开大学图书馆藏）

本卷部分著述文章书影(南开大学图书馆藏)

总　　序

厉以宁

我是1951年9月进入北京大学经济系的，1955年毕业，毕业后留校工作至今。陈振汉先生是我的老师，也是我研究经济史的领路人。从1951年我进入北大到2008年陈振汉先生逝世，我们作为师生和同事相处了58年之久。陈振汉先生毕业于南开大学经济系，方显廷先生长期执教于南开大学，是陈振汉先生的老师。

我没有见过方显廷先生，但我不仅从陈振汉先生那里了解到南开大学经济研究所和方显廷先生的学术成就，而且也了解到方显廷先生的人品和治学态度，使我很早就对方显廷先生十分仰慕。商务印书馆在2006年出版《方显廷回忆录》之后，立即准备出版6卷本的《方显廷文集》，原来是请陈振汉先生撰写序言的，但陈振汉先生这时已卧病在家（2006年他94岁高龄了），他嘱咐我代为执笔，我应允了。这篇序言，既可表达我对方显廷先生这样一位学术界前辈的崇敬与仰慕，又可作为我对我的老师陈振汉先生的纪念与追思。

方显廷先生的早年生活是很艰苦的。据他在回忆录（商务印书馆2006年出版）中的记述，他原籍浙江宁波，1906年他3岁时家里遭了一场大火，一切尽化为灰烬。1910年他7岁时，父亲病故，

i

家业衰败。他在家乡只受过初等教育。14岁那年(1917年)经亲戚介绍来到上海厚生纱厂当了学徒。厚生纱厂的经理是著名民族企业家穆藕初先生,他同时也是学徒们的师傅。由于方显廷先生刻苦学习英语,英语程度较高,所以只做了半年学徒,就被调到办公室工作。他工作出色,得到穆藕初先生赏识。1921年,方显廷先生18岁,在穆藕初先生资助下,赴美国继续学习,先后在美国威斯康辛大学读预科,在纽约大学读完本科,获学士学位,再进入耶鲁大学攻读经济学,1928年获哲学博士学位。这一年他25岁。第二年(1929年)他回国任教于南开大学。陈振汉先生是1931年考进南开大学经济系,1935年毕业的,在这段时间内受业于方显廷先生。

陈振汉先生多次和我谈起,方显廷先生的治学方法有着明显的特点,可以归结为经济理论、经济史研究、统计学三者并重和交融。经济理论被认为是经济研究的基础,如果经济理论缺乏深厚的功底,研究难以深入,更难以有新的见解。经济史研究,是指研究者应当具备广博的经济史知识,因为现实经济中的重大问题绝不是凭空出现的,总有其历史的渊源以及其产生、发展、演变的过程。脱离历史背景去进行研究,往往难以认清规律,难以作出清晰的判断。而统计学,则被认为是一种必不可少的方法论基础,如果不能运用科学的统计方法,结论通常是缺乏依据的,或者会误导研究者得出错误的结论。陈振汉先生自称他在治学方法上受到了方显廷先生的影响,所以多年来一直强调把经济理论、经济史研究和统计学三者结合在一起的必要性。陈振汉先生还说,这也是南开大学经济系和南开大学经济研究所多年坚持的治学方法。从方显廷先生的著作中,我们可以处处看到经济理论、经济史研究和统计学三者的融合。

方显廷在纽约大学和耶鲁大学学习期间,受过严格的西方经济学训练,功底十分深厚。他在耶鲁大学的博士论文,题为《英格兰工厂制度之胜利》,赢得了国外学术界的好评。据方显廷先生在回忆录中所述,十九世纪中期前后的英国工厂组织,传统的分类方法是按照个体手工工匠、家庭作坊制和工厂制度来划分的,而方显廷先生在博士论文中则按照另一种划分方法,即按照手工艺人、商人雇主和工厂制度分类,这种分类主要突出了商人雇主在工业化初期的作用,工厂制度的胜利实际上也就是工厂组织取代商人雇主制度的胜利。[①] 这篇博士论文不仅可以看成是工业经济史研究的成果,而且也可以看成是企业组织理论的一项突破。

方显廷先生回国以后,除了对欧洲经济史继续进行研究以外,他的主要研究领域转入了中国近代工业史和中国近代地区经济发展史。在这次出版的6卷本的《方显廷文集》中,至少有一半以上的内容是中国近代工业史和中国近代地区经济发展史方面的著作。1934年由国立编译馆出版的《中国之棉纺织业》,是方显廷先生的力作,也是第一本对中国棉纺织业进行系统研究的学术著作,资料翔实,分析透彻,尤其是在该书中专门论及中国棉纺织业发展中所遇到的阻力以及今后的发展前途等章节,反映了方显廷先生对国民经济中这一重要产业的远见卓识。

在有关中国近代地区发展史方面,方显廷先生由于长期执教于南开大学,所以把华北地区的经济发展作为研究重点。他所撰

[①] 参看方显廷著,方露茜译:《方显廷回忆录》,商务印书馆2006年版,第47、135页。

写的《天津地毯工业》、《天津织布工业》、《天津针织工业》、《天津棉花运销概况》、《华北乡村织布工业与商人雇主制度》等，都是在广泛社会经济调查的基础上完成的。方显廷先生在回忆录中写道："我发现为三、四年级学生讲授好3小时的经济史课程不难，但是要充分准备一份关于天津地毯工业的报告却需要投入大量的时间。"①尽管这项研究在方显廷先生从事之前已由南开大学的其他研究人员做过，方显廷先生认为："但是所收集到的情况完全不够充分。我不得不多少重新开始这一工作。首先，对这一工业进行概括的了解；然后，到天津不同地区亲自去参观那些用手工编织地毯的作坊。"②正因为有了详细而认真的调查，才完成了《天津地毯工业》这样一本专著(1929年出版)。

对于华北的乡村工业发展，方显廷先生选择了河北省高阳的织布业作为研究对象，题目定为《华北乡村织布工业与商人雇主制度》。这是同方显廷先生的博士论文《英格兰工厂制度之胜利》有相当密切的联系的，因为正如前面已经提到的，在那篇博士论文中，方显廷先生用商人雇主制度作为工业化初期的分类形式之一代替了传统的分类方法中的家庭作坊制。商人雇主制度使工业化初期的商人雇主的作用更加突出，反映了商人资本在活跃城乡经济和以供给工具和原料、订货和包销等手段成为乡村工业的实际控制者，从而说明了华北地区的乡村工业距工厂制度的建立还存在一定的差距。

在方显廷先生的经济研究中还有一个重要领域，这就是对抗

---

① 方显廷著，方露茜译：《方显廷回忆录》，第71页。
② 同上。

日战争胜利之后中国经济建设途径的探讨。方显廷先生早就认为日本必败,中国必胜,对前途充满信心。1941年至1943年,他受美国洛克菲勒基金会的邀请,到美国进行访问,访问期间先在哈佛进行研究,半年后去华盛顿的战时经济委员会(后改称国外经济管理局,以后又改称国外开发总署)做研究工作。据方显廷先生在回忆录中所述,这是一个庞大的组织,拥有好几百名雇员,其中包括一些专家,调查分析研究亚洲国家经济状况。战后中国经济如何重建,是该组织研究项目之一。① 在这期间,即1943年12月4日至14日,方显廷先生由美国去加拿大魁北克参加太平洋国际学会第八届会议。与会者有来自美国、英国、苏联、荷兰、加拿大、澳大利亚、中国、印度和泰国的150位代表。② 这次会议对中国在过去六年来(1937—1943)抵抗日寇侵略战争之举表达敬佩之意,会议一致同意有必要废除自鸦片战争以来中国同西方列强签署的不平等条约,一致赞成将台湾归还中国,允许朝鲜独立,惩罚日本战争罪犯,解除日本武装并支付战争赔款等。③

关于抗日战争结束后中国的经济重建问题,方显廷的经济观点和政策建议,见于文集的第3卷(《中国战后经济问题研究》等)、第5卷(《现代中国的经济研究》、《中国经济危机及其挽救途径》、《胜利后的中国经济》等)。他的基本思路依然是中国必须早日实现工业化。20世纪30年代他是这样主张的,20世纪40年代后半期他仍坚持这一观点。

---

① 参看方显廷著,方露茜译:《方显廷回忆录》,第138—139页。
② 同上书,第141页。
③ 同上。

把凯恩斯经济学介绍给中国学术界，是方显廷先生20世纪40年代的贡献之一。这同他自1939年起在南开大学经济研究所主持工作和1941年在哈佛大学进行访问、研究有关。凯恩斯的代表作《就业、利息和货币通论》出版于1936年2月。凯恩斯在这部著作中系统阐述了自己的宏观经济学理论，对西方国家的经济政策的制定有着深远的影响。西方经济学界普遍认为这是一场"凯恩斯革命"，但又是双重意义上的"凯恩斯革命"，即一方面是经济理论的革命（以有效需求不足理论代替了新古典经济学的均衡论），另一方面是政策意义上的革命（以国家对经济调节的政策代替传统的政府不干预经济的政策）。① 方显廷先生抗战期间在重庆南开大学经济研究所主持工作，他在回忆录中写道："研究所之所以将培训研究生的方向选定为经济理论和货币问题，是受到1936年2月英国经济学家凯恩斯议员出版《货币通论》之后兴起的'凯恩斯革命'的影响。"② 稍后，方显廷先生到了美国，他在哈佛大学进行访问和研究时，同一些美国经济学家接触，更深入地了解到"凯恩斯革命"的影响。他在美国设法为研究所通过海运，并通过滇缅通道运来一批关于"凯恩斯革命"的最新书籍。20世纪40至50年代，南开大学能成为国内在研究当代西方经济学方面处于前列的高等学府之一，同方显廷先生的功绩是分不开的。

1947年，方显廷先生应联合国的聘请，在联合国及亚洲远东经济委员会（ECAFE）工作，任调查研究室主任，具体任务是研究亚洲及远

---

① 参看厉以宁：《宏观经济学的产生和发展》，湖南出版社1977年版，第109—119页。

② 方显廷著，方露茜译：《方显廷回忆录》，商务印书馆2006年版，第111页。

东地区各国的经济状况和发展趋势,编辑《亚洲及远东经济年鉴》。该委员会原在上海,1949年1月迁往曼谷,那年方显廷先生46岁。1964年他61岁时从联合国机构退休。但紧接着又担任了亚洲经济发展及计划研究院副院长。这是一个由联合国开发计划署主要提供资金的、以研究亚洲经济发展和培训亚洲及远东地区各国企业家、银行家和政府官员为宗旨的机构。方显廷先生在这里工作一年后便离去,过着自己向往的清闲退休生活。但不久他又被聘为新加坡南洋大学客座教授,1971年再度退休,从此去瑞士定居,安度晚年。

从1947年进入联合国机构工作起,到1971年自新加坡南洋大学退休为止,将近25年的国外生活,使方显廷先生的研究方向发生了一个转折,即从专心致志研究中国工业化转而关注东南亚经济发展。在这些年内,他撰写了一些有关东南亚国家的经济发展的文章,收集到这部文集的有:《太平洋各国经济问题》《新加坡的小型工业》《新加坡经济发展的策略》《亚洲及远东地区工业品出口的发展》等。但他更多的精力和时间放在编辑历年的《亚洲及远东经济年鉴》之上。这套年鉴很有价值,它见证了这一地区的发展中国家在第二次世界大战结束后是如何一步步从衰退趋于复苏,再迈向成长和繁荣的。

方显廷先生是一位爱国者。即使他在联合国机构中工作多年,后来又在新加坡南洋大学任教,但他始终忘不了祖国的工业化,忘不了祖国大陆的经济建设。据方显廷先生在回忆录中所述,《亚洲及远东经济年鉴》的内容自1953年起有所改动,即"《年鉴》对于中国大陆的发展给予更为透彻的报导"。[①] 此外,1953年11月出版的《亚洲

[①] 方显廷著,方露茜译:《方显廷回忆录》,商务印书馆2006年版,第175页。

及远东经济季刊》（这是联合国亚洲及远东经济委员会下设的刊物，创刊于1950年）上，发表了方显廷先生撰写的《1949—1953年中国大陆的经济发展》一文，引起了国外经济界的注意。方显廷先生在这篇文章中引用了中国政府公布的许多数字，他用这些数字说明中国经济恢复的速度是惊人的。文章中写道："生产的恢复受益于多种因素，而其中最为重要的一个，无疑是和平与秩序的恢复。"[①]文章还肯定了中华人民共和国成立初期制度变革的积极作用："毋庸置疑，制度的改变对于自1949年以来经济的恢复也是一个重要方面，因而关于在过去几年过程中，中国经济框架的改变对生产的恢复起到了一定作用这一判断应当是中肯的。"[②]

6卷本的《方显廷文集》出版了。这里记录下方显廷先生一生的主要论著。国内人士尽管过去对方显廷先生的学术贡献了解得不多，但我深信，历史是公平的、公正的，只要认真阅读了《方显廷文集》中各个时期的著述，就一定会了解方显廷先生为人处世的原则、他的治学方法、他的学术成就，以及他在经济学和经济史领域所作出的贡献。

2009年6月2日于北京大学光华管理学院

---

① 方显廷：《1949—1953年中国大陆的经济发展》，"引言"，载联合国《亚洲及远东经济季刊》，1953年11月；另见方显廷著，方露茜译：《方显廷回忆录》，第286页。
② 方显廷著，方露茜译：《方显廷回忆录》，第286页。

本卷说明

本卷收录了方显廷先生著述 15 种，分为两编。

第一编战前中国经济：《中国乡村工业的出路》，刊载于《国货》月刊 1935 年第 4 期；《中国棉纺织业之危机》，刊载于《纺织周刊》1933 年第 3 卷第 20 期；《中国工业之现况与展望》，刊载于《南大半月刊》1934 年第 16 期；《中国工业发展的前途》，方显廷、陈振汉著，刊载于《纺织周刊》1933 年第 3 卷第 47 期；《中外棉花交易所之比较》，刊载于《天津棉鉴》1930 年 8 月第 1 卷第 3 期；《我国工厂法与纱厂业之关系》，刊载于《纺织周刊》1933 年第 3 卷第 48 期；《国民经济建设之途径》，刊载于《信托》（季刊）1937 年第 2 卷第 2 期；《工业经济与国货》，刊载于《国货与实业》1941 年创刊号。

第二编战时经济与区域经济：*The Post-War Industrialization of China*，南开大学 1942 年版；"The Japanese Development Companies in Occupied China"，1943 年 2 月，原件为打印件，现藏于南开大学图书馆古籍部；"War-Time Economic Reconstruction in China"，刊载于 *Nankai Social and Economic Quarterly*, Vol. XI, 1943；《今日西南各省之衣的问题》，方显廷、毕相辉著，刊载于《新经济》1939 年第 2 卷第 6 期；《论粮食统制》，刊载于《生力》（半月刊）1941 年第 3 卷第 24 期；《川康棉纺织工业之固有基础》，刊载于《农本》1942 年第 57 期；"The Prospect for China's Industrialization"，刊载于 *Pacific Affair*, Vol.

15，No.1，May，1942。

  本卷收录的方显廷先生中英文著作,均经方显廷先生手订。本次出版,除将繁体字转为简体字,并修订明显讹误外,译名(人名、地名)术语、数字用法与今不一致者,均一仍其旧,个别因原件不清无法辨识的字用"□"代替。

目 录

第一编 战前中国经济

中国乡村工业的出路 …………………………………… 3
中国棉纺织业之危机 …………………………………… 11
中国工业之现况与展望 ………………………………… 23
中国工业发展的前途 ……………………… 方显廷 陈振汉 37
中外棉花交易所之比较 ………………………………… 57
我国工厂法与纱厂业之关系 …………………………… 77
国民经济建设之途径 …………………………………… 93
工业经济与国货 ………………………………………… 101

第二编 战时经济与区域经济

THE POST-WAR INDUSTRIALIZATION OF CHINA …………… 111
THE JAPANESE DEVELOPMENT COMPANIES IN
　　OCCUPIED CHINA …………………………………… 267
WAR-TIME ECONOMIC RECONSTRUCTION IN CHINA ………… 421

今日西南各省之衣的问题 …………………… 方显廷　毕相辉　439
论粮食统制 ……………………………………………………… 451
川康棉纺织工业之固有基础 …………………………………… 459
THE PROSPECT FOR CHINA'S INDUSTRIALIZATION ………… 473

第一编

战前中国经济

中国乡村工业的出路

现代的经济组织,是以全世界为单位的,任何国家的经济组织的变迁,多少是要受其他国家的经济组织变迁的影响的,这个道理,在我们这经济落后的国家,更觉得显明,所以我们要谈到中国乡村工业的出路,必须连带谈到世界各国一般的乡村工业的出路。

　　现在世界各国工业制度的趋势,最显明的就是从集中而分散,从竞争而合作,这两种趋势,和乡村工业的发展,是有很重大的关系的,所以我们在没有讨论"中国乡村工业的出路"以前,附带的先来说明(一)一般工业的趋势——分散化,及(二)乡村工业的一个新制度,说完这两点之后,再去说第二点:"中国乡村工业的出路"。

一、一般工业的趋势——分散化

　　自从十八世纪初叶,工业革命在英国发生以来,在这过去的一百六十年里,世界工业发展的趋势,是"集中化",工业集中在大的城市里,因此城市很发达。可是近几年来,工业发达的趋向改变了,从"集中化"而变为"分散化"了,从城市里而回到乡村里去了。改变的原因,可以从三方面来解释:

第一方面是经济的原因——自从一九二九年世界经济恐慌开始以来,世界各国没有一国不被波及的。经济恐慌的结果,失业人口增加。失业人口的增加,城市里不能生活,因此人口又都返回乡村去。据美国农业统计局白克(Baker)先生的报告,美国从一九二〇年到一九二九年,平均每年由乡村移到城市去的人口,大约有一百九十四万,从城市移到乡村去的人口,大约有一百三十一万。结果平均每年由乡村移到城市去的人口有六十三万。一九三〇年是经济恐慌的第一年,那一年从乡村移到城市的人口,和从城市移到乡下去的人口,多二十万,一九三二年多到五十万。美国农业发达的程度,已经不能再容纳工作的人了,所以只有提倡乡村工业,去吸收这些因失业而又跑回乡村去的人。因此工作有"分散化"的必要和趋势。

第二方面是政治的原因——工业集中城市,城市因之而发展,交通便利,街道整洁,设备完美,生活上感到舒适,因此城市愈发达,乡村的人口愈往城市里跑。结果城市里人口拥挤得厉害,可是乡下,缺少耕地的人,以致农业衰落。像这种高度工业化的国家,倘使一旦发生战争,就有粮食和原料被人断绝供给的危险。所以国家地位,颇受动摇,一般的政治家,也就感觉到复兴农村的重要,不使乡下人往城里跑。但是,要使乡下人不往城市里跑,那只有设法改善乡下人的生活。假若乡下也能得到舒适的生活,乡下人自然不会往城市里跑,办法就是使乡村工业化。那就是在乡村提倡小工业,也就是工业分散化。乡村和城市,都在常态之下发展,社会是稳固的,社会稳固,政治上自然不会有什么问题发生。

第三方面是工业技术进步的原因——工业之所以集中城市,是因为城市有交通、金融、工人、运输、动力和原料的便利。可是现在交通、运输都大有进步,乡村金融,亦渐发展,并且现在工业所用的动力多半是电,电可以从电线上送到任何地方去。因此乡下和城市差不多。打破了以前集中化的条件,工业要"分散化"了。

二、乡村工业的一个新制度

提倡乡村工业,首先当顾到剥削和摧残乡村工业的敌人。剥削乡村工业的是通行的"商人雇主制度",摧残乡村工业的是大量出产的城市工业。

什么是"商人雇主制度"?商人雇主制度,或者叫作"散工制度",那是由商人发给原料,由乡村里农人,以每家为单位,去制造,制造出来的东西再交给发原料的商人去卖。农人所得到的,只是一点点工资,乡下人多半是没有高深的智识,对于买原料,卖货物的情形,一点不懂,因此只好受商人的剥削。在剥削的状况之下,乡村工业自然不会发达的。所以要想发展乡村工业,必须设法打倒商人雇主的制度。

第二个摧残乡村工业的,是大量出产的城市工业,因为用机器制造,一天可出几千件,几万件,出货多成本自然低,成本低,自然可以和乡村工业的出品相竞争,乡村工业品,竞争不过,只有消灭。比仿:以前中国农家,差不多都有一张织布机,自己纺纱,自己织布,可是自从新式的纺纱厂织布厂设立了以后,乡下的纺纱机和织布机,一天比一天少了。这就是一个很好的例子。所以要想发展乡村工业,必须想出方法来,能和这种大规模生产的工业抵抗。

抵抗以上这两个敌人的最好方法,是采用合作制度,换句话说：就是组织合作社。大家合作起来直接的去购买原料,去办理运销,就无须乎用中间人,可以免去中间人的剥削,这一来商人雇主制度,将要不打自倒。用机器大规模制造出来的货品,价钱贱是贱,可是有的东西,总不如手做出来的好。况且乡村的劳工,到了农闲的时候,差不多是不值钱的。所以乡村工业,可以用这一点来抵抗。再说,假若大家合作起来,用团体的信用,去向银行借款,自然能够多借款项,少付利息,同样的用团体的名义,去购买原料,自然数量要大,价格要低,利息低,原料贱,那就可以减轻不少的成本负担,更加上大家自己去销售,用费省,货物的定价自然可以低的。所以,我们可以说,"合作制度",是乡村工业抵抗商人雇主和大量生产二种敌人的好武器。在德国,在俄国,在日本,在印度,他们的乡村工业之所以发达,不能不归功于他们的合作制度。

德国是农村信用合作银行的发源地,一八五二年就实行了信用合作制度,农民和小手艺工人,得到不少的帮助。据一九二九年的统计,德国全国合作社联合会,共有信用合作社一,三八七社,其中一,二五四社,共有社员一,〇一七,一九三人,手艺工人占百分之二十五。此外手艺工人所办的供给和运销合作社有一,七〇一社。其中一,一五八社共有社员一七五,二九六人。

俄国的合作制度是政府从上面施下来的一种政策。据一九三〇年的统计,全俄国共有手艺工人合作社一八,三六三社,社员达二万人。其中百分之六十是住在乡下的小手艺工人。印度和日本自从采用合作制度之后,乡村工业大为发达,所以无论是在德国,在俄国,在日本,在印度,"合作制度"是一种辅助农民,发展乡村工业的好制度。

三、中国乡村工业的出路

　　中国的情形,和欧美各国迥乎不同,欧美各国的工业是先向一块儿集中,近几年来,发现集中化的弱点,才又向四处分散。中国的工业,压根儿就是分散的。所以无须乎学欧美先把工业集中起来,然后再分散开。中国的工业是分散的,比如:纺纱、织布、酿酒、榨油、制茶等等,中国乡村里,到处都有,但是近些年来,一方面因为商人雇主的剥削,一方面因为洋货的倾销,乡村工业消减了不少。大家知道:种地是靠天吃饭,因为气候的关系,农夫不能一年三百六十五天都在田里种地,换句话说:种地是一种有季节性的职业,所以一个农夫,一年里有不少天是无事可作。若不利用这些无事可作的工夫,让它白白的过去,那是多么可惜?假使提倡乡村工业,农民不种地的时候,可以作工,做出来东西,可以去换钱,所以乡村工业,可以增加农民的收入,也是复兴农村方法的一种。

　　要在中国发展乡村工业,自然也得设法抵抗摧残乡村工业的敌人。我们已经说过,抵抗摧残乡村工业的敌人唯一武器,是合作制度,所以要想发展中国的乡村工业,也得从采用合作制度着手。中国的农民,又穷又没有知识,提倡合作制度,起初自然不是一件容易的事,要想合作制度的成功,在中国现在的状况之下,须得几方面的援助。

　　第一,须银行出来向农村投资,帮助农人发展工业,因为中国的农民多半是穷的,素常没有储蓄,自然不会有钱作资本去办工业,所以希望银行肯向农村工业投资。

第二,发展乡村工业,技术也是一件很关重要的事,技术和工具,都得想法改良,这方法,我们希望全国经济委员会,农村复兴委员会和实业部等等政府机关负责去作。

第三,中国农民没有知识,提倡合作制度,创办合作社,因此不是一件容易的事,对合作知识的灌输,合作事业的办法,各方面都需人指导,所以在这方面都希望国里的三作团体、学术机关,负责去作。

假使这三方面都能够作到,中国的乡村工业,一定能够发展,中国的农村,也可以因之而复兴。

中国棉纺织业之危机

一、危机的严重

近来《津沪日报》给了我们一个惊人的消息,虽然并没有引起大家的注意,那就是中国棉业目前所遭遇的空前危机。大家都知道热河的陷落,农村的破产,然而没有人注意到中国唯一巨大的民族资本工业的将趋毁灭。

中国为世界上一个最大的农业国家,有众庶的人口,广博的富源,在这实业发达的时期,却没有一种在世界上占地位的工业。就是棉纺织业,在中国过去四十年中算是发达的最有成绩的,比起东西其他国家的重要实业来,还是瞠乎其后。欧战以后,中国的棉纺锤数增加极速,差不多增加现在的纺锤数之四分之三,然而拿纺锤数去与人口相比较,其比率在世界的棉纺业国家中还是最低的。英国最高,每千人有纺锤一,一九九锭,而中国则每千人只有九锭,仅当英国的百分之一的四分之三。中国的纺锤对人口之比率,就是比别的两大农业国家,俄国与印度,也是相形见绌。俄国每千人有四十八锭,印度有二十六锭,而中国则仅仅九锭。所以中国的棉纺织品产量,只供自己消费,尚感不足。譬如在民国十八年中国就运进值一八八,三八九,二五三海关两的棉货,约值进口总值的百分之十五(总值一,二六五,七七八,八二一两),在这种情形之下,目前棉纺织业所遭遇的危机,便尤其值得我们注意。现在的危机,固然不是一朝一夕所致,它的原因可以追溯到大战以前,特别是大战以后的不健全的发展。而现在严重的情形,我们比较一下上海纱市的棉纱批发市价,便可知道在去年第一星期人钟十六支纱每包现货价为一百六十八两五钱,自后即继续跌减,到了今年三月的最后一星期,跌到一百三十七两七钱五,一共跌了三十两七钱五,或百分之一八.二。而质地较高的纱,跌价愈厉害,譬如人钟四十二支纱在同样的一年多一点的期间,纱价从三百二十五两一包跌到二百〇六两一包,竟跌落一百十九两或百分之三十六.六。纱价这样狂跌,自然每个纱厂都亏本极大。据一个上海厂主的估计,每包十六支纱,要赔蚀十五两左右,在上海一个平均资本在一百五十万元,一年平均出纱一万七千五百包的纱厂,每年就要赔蚀二十六万二千五百两,折合银元三十六万五千元,计合资本的四分之一,这样,叫他们如何维持。所以上海纱厂联合会提议实行减工,每星期工作四日四夜,希望将原有生产减少三分之一,使得生产与消费能够互相适应,纱厂可以勉强维持下去。四月十日在上海举行联合会全体会员大会,集合上海、汉口、天津、无锡的各厂,共同议决,一致实行。致于以前轰传全国纱厂联合实行停工的传说,暂时虽不至于实行,但是如果现在的恶劣状况,继续深刻下去,未始不会见诸事实。我们所应注意的是这件事情意义的严重和关系的重大,这是一种空前的举动。从好的方面看,是中国的工厂已发达到需要一种彻底的改革的程度,去适应世界上的剧烈竞争。"合理化"已成了世界各种工业的警语,现在在远东也发生了影响,然而这不是宣导的结果,而是由于在一个技术与商业效力较高的场所竞争的需要。从坏的方面看,这却是中国民族资本工业在各国经济侵略下没落的先兆。以规模最大成绩最好的棉纺织业的命运尚且如此,其他各种工业的前途,更可想而知。现在在各方在设法积极的抵制日货,而尚不能以本国最有希望的棉纺织业去抵抗倾销最甚的日本棉纱,其他的一切也可设想了。至于减工以后,占最大部分的工人的生活问题,又会替社会增加了不少不安与扰乱,从天津方面的工人自得了减工的消息以后,即集议应付,这件事实上看来,可见我们的预料并不是杞忧。

二、纱业危机的外因

　　这次的危机,是内外两方面的原因造成的。外来的影响,虽然对各业都一样,而棉纺织业因为规模较大的缘故,所受的打击尤重。第一种外因,即是内战,民国以来,除了极少的几年以外,自相残杀的内战差不多是继续着,最近的实例便是四川的混战与江西、福建、两湖等省的剿共战役。内战对工商业的摧残有如下几方面,第一是阻碍交通,割断棉花供给的来源,同时又封闭纱布的市场,而且受到战祸的区域的人民购买力减低,纱布的销路势趋滞钝。内战的第二个影响是城市的过度繁荣与乡村的凋敝,因为战祸的频仍,税捐的苛重,乡间的富户,大都将田产完全变卖成现金运到城里去存储,或者迁移到城市里去居住,这样,乡村不但没有这些人的人力,就是信用积储也完全随之以俱去了。所以在乡间银根奇紧,利息高涨,而在城市情形却完全相反。乡间只有手纺织业,所以一向是各棉纺织生产品销售的尾间,而现在则因此而不能推销。所以近来在各棉纺织业中心的城市存货极多,中国一半以上棉纺织业集中在上海,所受内战的影响也特甚,据说上海棉纱存底已在十万包以上。

第二个外来的原因就是这一年多的中日纠纷。自九一八事变以后,东三省的广大市场就被日本的棉货独占,中国的棉纺织业就不得染指了。例如民国十八年大连和牛庄两埠就销进值二五,九〇九,七四一海关两的国产棉货,约值中国各埠运销国产棉货总值的百分之一三.五一,现在,这样广大的市场被日本攫去,中国棉纺织品就不能入口,即使让你入口,也多一笔关税的耗费。中日问题的另一个影响,便是日本在华所设的纱厂的倾销政策,给予我国纱厂颇不小的打击。九一八事变以后,我国对日货无论是在日本制造抑在中国制造的一致加以排斥,为抵御我们的抵货,日商在华所设的纱厂就采取倾销政策,廉价销售纱布。爱国心是极难持久的,时间一长,消费者的经济打算终究会胜过他的爱国热忱,日本纱货质地较高,如果再价钱便宜一点,在市场上自然占了优胜。倾销的程度究竟怎样,我们还不知道,不过由下面的事例我们可以知道竞争影响的重大。譬如高阳一县的土布业有二十多年的历史,而近来因山东潍县出品的竞争,一落千丈,潍县布业用的是青岛日商纱厂所纺的纱,价廉成本因之减轻,高阳的布业则是用高价购买天津石家庄华商纱厂的纱,因之不能和潍县的竞争,别的地方也必定有同样的情形。据说日商纱厂为减少抵货的效力起见,竟至于冒贴华商纱厂棉纱的商标,日人的没有商业道德,固然毫不足怪,然而华商纱厂要与其竞争,却多了一层困难。

第三种外因即是没有政府的保护。先说政府的税,虽然厘金已经废除,通行统税,各厂运出棉纱都只要付一定额的税,不必缴付许多次的地方通行税，然在中央政府势力没有达到的省份如四川、广东等省，还是须付变相的通行税。而且就是在中央直辖的省份，各厂运出棉纱各缴一定额的统税，这税率也不能对华商纱厂尽适当的保护。中国的棉纺织工业并不完全在中国人手内的，一部分是在外国人手内的，例如民十九全国的纺锤里面，只有百分之五五.二完全属于中国人的，其余的百分之四四.八，则差不多在日本人手里面，现在统一税规定二十三支及二十三支以下的棉纱每担纳税二元七角五，二十三支以上的棉纱，每担纳税三元七角五，就不足以保护竞争能力较低的华商纱厂，因为日商纱厂大抵都是专纺三十二支的纱，而中国纱厂则是多纺十支、十六支和二十支纱，这样自然是日商纱厂的负担较轻，还有现在华商纱厂所用的棉花，大部分是外来的，最大的原因就是政府不能利用改良棉种规定标准的方法去奖励棉花生产。至于频年内乱对于棉花生产影响，更不必说了。中国棉产最多的一年是民国八年，产棉共九，〇二八，三九〇担，以后就逐年减少，到了二十年，估计只有六，三九九，七八〇担了。本国棉产逐渐减少，自然进口棉花逐渐增加，在民国八年以前，中国的棉花贸易都是出超，从那年入超三〇二，〇六七担后，以后即一蹶不振，国内产量减少，需要增加，入超量也一年一年加多，到民国二十年，竟达三，四五六，四九四担之巨。值一三二，二五六，六六九海关两，十二年内增加了十一倍，不可谓不速了。

三、纱业危机的内因

上面的种种外因，我们希望不久都能消灭，对内对外的战争都能够停止，稳固有秩序的政府能够建立起来，至于内面的原因，已是根深蒂固了，除了于棉纺织业有利害关系的各方面都能够尽量实行大刀阔斧的改革，是不会有帮助的。内面的原因大概可分两方面，一方面是资本的不足，另一方面是技术人才，负责管理以及效力高的劳工的缺乏，我们现在就依次说明吧。

中国纱厂资本的缺乏，运用资金方法的幼稚，说起来是可惊人的。也许一个工厂刚开始设立就会遇到资金的困难，因为它是按照所招股本额拟定计划决定厂屋的大小、机器的多寡的，经董事会承认后，即进行订购机器，招标承建房屋，然而到了机器快要运到的时候，股本也许还没有收足，因为中国任何实业所认的股本照例不是一次付足的。一波未平一波又起，纱厂的固定资本额很大，又是经营者的一个困难，在有许多纱厂，固定资本往往会较已付的资本额大，因为它们的利润极大——在民国九年左右能够高到百分之五十至百分之一百，所得的利润，他们就用来购买新机器。当市面紧急时，这种厂家的金融周转还是一样的不灵活，虽然他们的资产增加了，换句话说，虽然他们的纺锤数目增加，他们的资金还是周转不灵。对于那些年数较长的老工厂，另有一个困难，即是他们没有相当的折旧资金准备，在平常他们都是在红利与公积金都规定了之后，才计算机器与房屋的折旧，蚀本的年头，便根本没有折旧的准备，就是有盈余的时候，折旧的准备额也都嫌太少，普通最低限度的折旧准备是百分之五，然而就作者研究过的工厂而论，便没有一家的准备超过这个限度的。其结果便是这些旧工厂的固定资产超过它们真正的市价，当一部分机器不能再修理的时候，便不能置换。因为资金的不足，便发生许多严重的结果，顶危险的，就是纱厂没有现金作为流动资本。在上海的纱厂，因为缺乏流动资本,用十天的期货棉花制成棉纱,差不多成为习惯。厂家赊得了棉花以后,即用最大的速率,夜以继日的将棉花在十天未到期以前纺成棉纱,再卖出棉纱以取得现金来偿付棉花的货价,有的时候因为纺工的关系,厂家须得买几等几样的棉花搀和起来,又因为手头没有现金,不得不在一个花商这里多赊几包十天的期货,然后把余多的卖出去,去交换另一等的棉花。这样他的流动债务就增加起来,所背的利息也比较高,而当偶然有事变发生的时候,纱厂只有停工,去年一·二八事变发生,即有不少厂家因之破产。当现在的危机,已经提议将作工时间从每周六天半减到每周四天,如果银行界不挺身出来以资金帮助,一定有不少纱厂会有同样的命运的。

资金不足及调剂金融的方法之幼稚,虽是最重要的内因,当然不是唯一的原因,其他内部的原因像技术人才的缺乏,不负责任的管理以及劳工效力的低下,也是极重要的。就是现在,中国棉纺织工业的技术方面差不多有百分之六十是中国工人自己管理的,他们只受过最粗浅的教育,在机器方面的一点训练,是由日本、英、美送到中国来装置机器的工程师那里学习来的。中国唯一的纺织专门学校南通纺织大学的毕业生及日本、英、美的留学生,虽然担任指导与监督在他们手下的工人,一向他们还是摆着书生架子,直到最近始知道自己去做管理与修理机械的工作,把这部分责任从不学无术的工人手里取出来。至于管理的状况,情形更是恶劣,因为管理纺织事业的差不多是对这方面绝对没有知识和训练的,中国纱厂十有八九都倒闭在经理者的无知,任用私人以及侵吞款项上面。特别是那些毫无经验只为贸利的人看到欧战及战后数年的兴旺,如夜蛾赴火似的都来经营纱厂,把整个几百万资本的工厂交与一个无纺织知识的大经理,普通大都是大股东的亲信,既不懂复杂的纺织机械,也不知道成本会计,资金调动,市场销售为何物的。他们又把实际上的责任推到属员的身上,只凭着运气赚钱。而这属员呢,像纺织部主任之类,普通又都是大股东或经理的亲信,只知道利用地位来吃饭,把实际上的职务又推到几个工头的身上去,他们只有利用机械的技术而没有什么科学的训练,于是结果弄到机器没有好好保管,工人没有选择和训练,出品质地日坏,而成本反而涨高。在欧战的时候,供给缺乏,赚钱很容易,这些缺点便不能觉察出来,一旦恢复了常态,外国纱厂用他们较大的资本,较好的技术,较有组织的市场来相竞争,中国纱厂焉能不一败涂地呢!

因了上述的原因,劳工效力的低下是自然而不可免的现象,因为工资极低,从前大家都说中国的劳工价廉,实际上这是倒因为果的说法,我国工人工资的低,至少有一部分的原因是因为劳工成本高,我们一比较国内日商纱厂与华商纱厂的劳工情形,就会明白,日商纱厂工人的工资较高,而华商纱厂工人的工资较低,然而华商纱厂每年每个工人所产的棉布只有二六一.七三匹,较之日商纱厂每人每年出产七八六.三八匹,低百分之二〇〇.四,差得实在可惊。

四、造成这次危机的近因

由上面分析,可以知道有二种不同的原因,造成这次中国纱厂的危机,纱厂不能用本身的能力去救济外因,内因却是可以纱厂自己的力量去除去的,现在我们的问题是这些原因在过去早已存在,为什么单单的在现在发生这样的危机,换句话说,就是这许多原因之中，那些是比较近的原因，那些是比较远的原因。这次危机的近因，完全可以追溯到日本在东北的侵略，日本割裂我们在东北的广大市场，日本在华的纱厂用倾销政策来抵抗我们排货，日本使得我们内地乡村的购买力减低，东北四省是我国纱厂销售出品的重要市场，然而被日本用武力轻轻攫去，他们在华的纱厂，资金势力比较大，技术与经理比较好，他们有政府的强有力的援助，他们有便易的运输工具，中国的航运大部操在他们手内，自然很容易把价格减得比成本还低，来推广销售。愚昧穷苦的民众，自然只知道价格的高低，经济的动机胜过了他们的爱国心。日本占领东北以后，农村的破产程度日甚，农民的购买力急剧减低，因为炫于价格的低廉，自然把仅有的一点购买力，都去购买货高价廉的日本货，对于货低价高的国货自然无力光顾了。上述的情形，它的影响是愈积愈大的，如果中日的纠纷这样继续下去，永远没有和平解决的希望，其危险将伊于无底。而现在如果工厂方面或者政府方面没有断然的处置，我们可以断然的说，危机只有更形严重，影响只有更加扩大。如果只靠减少生产以求价格的上涨，正和自己扼住自己的喉咙一样，无异自趋经济上的自杀，只有更增加外国人的竞争，和使得日本棉纱易于倾销，外国棉纱充斥市场。

（本文所用统计均详见拙著《中国棉纺织工业及棉纺织品贸易》上卷）

中国工业之现况与展望

一、导言

近年以来,中国之各种工业,咸遭困难,致皆濒于危机四伏,险象环生之境。查其所共同遭遇之困难,不外内在的及外袭的二种;而造成此两种困难之主因,复可归纳为政治的、社会的及经济的三项原因。中国过去政治上失败所遗留之种种钳制约束,与夫今日因政治混乱所生之种种恶果,皆为中国工业现有之困难。至积重难返之社会制度,中古式之经济制度与现象,以及原料与动力之缺乏等,亦为酿成今日工业危机之主因。兹分别缕述之。

二、工业现况之分析

(一)政治上之障碍,最显著者为内乱频仍,税捐繁重,以及不平等条约对工商业所加之绊缚。内战则可直接或间接对工商业有不良之影响,而苛捐杂税之种种摧残为尤甚。于此先就不平等条约之影响与范围,约略加以解述。

租借地，租界领事裁判权：租借地大都为我国地理上之重要港口，不特有关于国际贸易，即内地货物之散集，亦大都往往以此等口岸为吞吐地，是以租借地与内地之经济，有息息之相关，倘进出口业一旦为外人所劫持，则租借地即自然造成一特殊势力范围，如青岛之于山东，大连之于满洲是，而英国之据有香港，尤足以控制我国经济之命脉。复次，国内频年内战以及匪乱猖獗之结果，造成今日租界特殊之地位，现金源源流入，造成畸形之局部繁荣，而乡村及其他城镇经济反陷于枯竭之惨状。资金周转不灵，购买力日就萎缩，自然失去本国工商业之内国市场上之往昔景象。

外人在中国境内设立工厂，外人得在中国境内设立工厂经营制造业，始于清光绪二十一年（一八九五）之《中日马关新约》，自后外商工厂，遂先后在我国星罗棋布。单就纱厂论，根据二十一年华商纱厂联合会之调查，外人在华之纱厂势力，仅以日本一国计，上海一隅，已达三十厂！而散布各埠者，尚未计入！其势力之雄厚，可想而知。此外，英国之棉纺织业，在上海亦有相当之根据势力。要之，外商之在华设厂权，实为我国工商业之枷绊。

沿海与内河航权之丧失：自清咸丰八年，《中英天津条约》开放扬子江航运，许外人内河航行权及沿岸贸易权后，光绪二十四年复与各国修订修改《长江通商章程》、《华洋轮船驶赴内江章程》、《内港航轮章程续补》，我国门户，遂尔洞开。其结果不但使我国航业，惨遭竞争之打击，一蹶不振；即本国之工业亦直接感受恶劣之影响。根据海关华洋贸易报告册所载，民国十五年迄十九年中间进口及清卸船只，就吨位言，英国恒居首位，日本次之，本国船只，则列居第三。且外国船只进口及清卸吨数，近年来增加甚速，而我国船只吨位反而日见减落；民十九年我国轮船及帆船吨位合计，不及全额之三分之一！至于国外进去运输吨数，中国更无地位可述。以民国十九年作标准，英国第一，日本第二，其次即推美国与德国，而中国虽居第五位，所运输之货值，尚不及日本货值六分之一，进出口总值之十八分之一。内港之运输，中国船只虽占第二席，但远不及英国船运输值额之大，总计中国船只所运货物，只有全部货运之五分之一。航运如此，其对于工业之影响可以想见！

至于因内乱频仍与税捐繁重，工业上感到之影响，较前述之种种，更为綦重。如当内战方酣，各省军兴时期，军需上之支应，以及军事供款等悉取之于工商业者，此项额外负担，工商业者固可转嫁于消费者，但民众之购买力亦因匪乱而削弱，分担无力。因循退却，反予外货以进攻之机会，使国货之销源，更为缩小。他如割据军阀，威迫植烟，致使大好良田，竟不能供给原料及粮食之生产。总之，恶劣之政治，不特不能维护工商业之进展，反横加摧残，使已有之工业先后衰落，未兴之工业，萌芽无从，良可慨也！

（二）经济方面，可就下列分别述之：

交通阻滞：中国新式交通工具之缺乏，至为明显。中国面积大过美国三分之一，而铁路里数仅及美国四十分之一。以全国人口四八五兆之众，全国铁路只有一五，三〇〇公里，平均每百万人仅有三一八公里，而美国则在一九二〇年，每百万人有五，八六一公里，是则中国每人所有之铁路里数，仅及美国之一八六分之一。且事实上能利此区区一万余公里之铁路，只一小部分人民耳。请再论及公路。全国公路之建筑，近年来进展颇速，各重要省份，几皆有数百里之省道，但就实际论：车辆缺乏，运费昂贵，其对工商业之辅助殊微。至于水运，只局于沿海、长江流域及珠江流域之一隅。而全国大部分之交通工具，尚以木筏及驼重之牲畜是赖。工商业之不克发展,由于交通之阻滞者实多也。

币制混乱:我国乏完备之银行制度,而在废两改元之前,尤无所谓法定本位货币。就硬币论,银元之成色与重量,复各殊异,辅币则更形复杂不堪!复次,就纸币论,外国银行可以在中国滥发钞票,本国则上自银行下至杂货店,皆可自由发行纸币,甚至钱票一张,竟可撕为段片应用。而一地有一地之通货,由甲省至乙省,由甲县至乙县,无异由此国至彼国,须兑汇其本地通用之银钱。在此种状况之下,一般民众,已亏累不堪,况以货币为活动命脉之工商界乎?在银两尚未废除以前,在外汇上复倍受洋厘涨落,及金银汇价变动之亏损!

资本缺乏:资金之缺乏,为中国工业资本的最大之贫血症,兹在下列表内,足可窥见中国纱厂资本之薄弱,难足与英日在华纱厂抗衡之真情。

在华一二二纱厂资本额之比较(二十一年)

国别	纱厂数	资本及公积金总额(元)	每厂平均资本(元)
中	78	143,279,083.30	1,836,911.30
英	3	14,162,300.00	4,720,766.70
日	41	371,536,633.70	9,061,869.10
总计	122	528,978,017.00	4,335,885.40

原料不能自给:关于中国工业之原料供给,可就二方面论之:一方面为农产原料,一方面为矿产原料。就农产品原料而论,重要之工业原料,无论就量上言或就质上言,皆不能自给。自量上言之,近数来年,棉花进口,有急剧之增加。民十九进口棉花共三,四八一,二二四担,值一三三,一三五,五六七关平两;二十年增至四,六八八,〇八一担,值一八〇,三五七,八四四关平两;二十一年为

三，七一九，五二九担，值一一九，〇六一，四七一关平两，然是年之统计，仅包括前半年东三省之进口统计，故实际上，或不至减少。即以此年论，国内消费之棉花，其自外国输来者，约占三分之一。虽然，我国自产之棉花，亦有一部分，运往外洋，然决难与是年自外洋进口之数量相抵销。在过去三年中，棉花之出口仅二八二，七九四担，二九〇，三〇三担，及一四七，六二四担。复次，如烟叶自民国十九年至二十年，进口量亦有显著之增加，十九年为九六四，五九四担，值三二，七三六，九六二关平两；二十年增为一，二五六，六六七担，值四九，〇五九，五四二关平两；民二一年，为五八九，九九八担，值二四，五二五，六八八关平两（只包括东三省之半年进口量）。棉纺织业与卷烟业皆为今日中国规模较大之新工业。自棉花与烟草之进口量增加观之，可见此二种工业近年来颇有长足之发展，盖棉纱与棉布及卷烟之输入，业已减少。然他方面则可见本国自产原料之不足以应工业上急剧增加之需要也。

就矿产原料论，只煤一项，因国内消费量薄弱，每年尚有出超。其他重要矿产原料，如铁及石油，皆感不足，石油国内几无生产，故所消费之煤油（灯油）、汽油、机器油及燃料油，悉直接自外国输来。燃料油之输入，民国十九年为一五一，〇九三吨，值三，八七七，〇〇〇关平两，二十年为一一七，一一三吨，值五，〇五八，〇〇〇关平两；机器油之输入十九年为三一〇，二二〇桶，值六，三〇一，〇〇〇关平两，二十年为二五九，四三四桶，值八，八五四，〇〇〇关平两。二十年之入口量虽减，然入口值依然增加，此非由于国内之生产增加，实由于金价上涨所致。至于铁矿砂，国内所消费者极少，总计每年不过一百余万吨，仅及国内铁砂产量四分之三，其余四分之一，悉运往外国，而以运往日本者为最多。然仅就此一百余万吨言之,其为日商铁矿鞍山、本溪湖所消费者,已占大半,其余之五六十万吨,概系每年用土法炼铁之消费量。故中国工业所消费者,大部分为钢铁制成品,而所消费之钢铁品其直接自外国输入者,约占十分之六,其余十分之四为辽宁日商铁矿所供给。近年国内之钢铁消费量日有增加,故钢铁之输入量亦随之而增加!

外货竞争:在国外贸易市场上,日本已久为中国之劲敌。民二一年华丝国外市场最为恶劣,原因一方面由于世界不景气,另一方面则受日元跌落之影响。结果中国生丝出口,一年之内,竟较过去十年平均数量减低百分之七十五,中国工业在强邻经济压迫下之趋势于此可见。外国之竞争,不特为今日中国之致命伤,且为未来发展之最大障碍。吾人试一回想欧战时期中国工业之繁荣,当愈见今日中国工业之所以凋敝!

(三)社会的原因:我国教育之不普及,为中外共晓之事实。文盲占全国国民百分之九十五;而劳工阶级中之不识字者为尤多。文盲产生无智,亦发展劳工效率之最大障碍。盖劳力价值,固与数量有关,而尤与质量有关也。工人既缺乏教育,自然与机械之作用、出品之考求,毫无相当观念,只站在被动之地位,供给劳力而已。故就知识能力、工作效率、进取性、创造性各项言之,中国工人实不及西方工人。大家庭之生活,尊重祖制习惯,又常使中国人习于保守,不乐迁徙,因此中国人口虽多,但百分之七十五之农民,并不愿入新兴之工厂工作,依然不忘春耕秋获。今日若干地方之工厂劳工供给,皆有季节性,即为一例。

至于资本家之漠视技术与管理,亦关系綦重,单就中国纱厂而论,不少厂内管理人选,为大股东之亲信,既不洞悉纺织机械之复杂构造,复不明成本会计,对于资金调动、市场销售之精义等,尽皆茫然。只凭命运以卜前途,其不败也几难矣!

三、展望

关于一国工业发展之主要原素,当有两方面,即富源与环境。富源之最重要者为劳工供给、原料供给及动力供给。兹就各方面分别述之,以作我国工业前途之展望:

甲、劳工供给:中国人口过剩,生活程度极低,劳工廉贱,最适宜于发展工业。设工业能充分发展,使服役于工业之农民增加率,能较生长在乡间人口增加率为大,则不但农业与工业效率皆能增高,即中国之人口问题,亦可从此得到解决办法。然实际靠发展工业以吸收乡村人口,效力甚小,故若以发展工业解决中国之人口问题,此种愿望,颇难实现。须知在一农业国家,制造工业发展后,第一种反应,即人口之急剧增加也。

发展工业能吸收一部分人口,为暂时之现象。只有工业不断发展,始能继续吸收人口。否则,若一旦停顿,只维持现状而不继续扩张,则人口增加之速度又必增加。而大规模之工业,因实施合理化之结果,机械之利用,与纵横之联合,事实上可使生产效率增加,而工厂中,雇佣之工人减少。换言之,即大规模工业发达后,机器可以代替人工,造成工人失业。在英国工业革命之初期,纺织工人之暴乱,反对新式机器之使用,便为一例。职是之故,中国人口众多,固为初步工业发展之促进剂,然反言之,亦为大规模工业与工业极度发展之障碍。设吾人顾及大部分民众之生活及社会秩序与幸福之安全,则吾人之工业决不能使之全部合理化与机械化。

乙、原料供给：中国之农产物不足以供应自己消费，已为至显。至于金属原料，中国亦难称之为富足。其中最重要者为铁矿，根据地质调查所《第四次中国矿业纪要》所载，铁矿总储量为一，〇〇〇兆吨，而美国有九四，三二四兆吨，大于中国九十四倍，法国有十二，二五四兆吨，英国有一二，一六六兆吨，大于中国十二倍，按人口比较，则中国每人所有铁矿砂更属稀少，只两吨，而美国有七八九吨，大于中国约四百倍，法国有二九九吨，英国有二六七吨，大于中国约一百三四十倍。故吾国之铁矿砂，只可以对日人自傲，盖日本只有八千五百万吨之储量，平均每人只有一吨，日本每年之矿砂消费量为三百余万吨，以此计之，则日本之铁矿储量仅足三十余年之需，而中国以同等之消费量，却可支持三百余年。然中国之重要铁矿，为辽宁之鞍山及本溪湖等，此二矿之储量，达七八百兆吨，占全国铁矿砂总储量十分之七强。即在东北未沦亡前，矿产开采权业已操诸日人！故就中国之金属原料而论，姑不论目前生产之不足与运输之困难。单就储量而论，最重要之金属原料，铁矿贫乏，已感不足以应来日之用矣！

丙、动力供给：动力来源颇多，大致其主要者为煤炭、石油及水力。

中国煤矿储量，以前估计为九九六，〇〇〇兆吨，居世界第三位，仅次于美国与坎拿大；然据北京地质调查所比较可靠之估计，则为二四八，二八七兆吨。虽较前面之估计数量为少，更次于德国，然若将萨尔区域储量及上西来西亚之烟煤储量，自德国煤矿储量中除去，则中国仍居第三位。此只按其相对之重要而论。论实量，则美国有一，五五九，五九九兆吨，大于中国七倍，坎拿大以前之估计亦在一，〇〇〇，〇〇〇兆吨以上，大于中国六倍。以世界总储量计算，中国储量仅及百分之六，若按人口计算，中国每人应有煤储量约为五吨，而美国则每人有一万余吨，坎拿大每人十三万吨，英国四千吨，德国一千五百吨，中国均属瞠目不及。量既如此有限，矿质又劣，其可以供炼焦炭之用者，仅一部分耳。

中国煤矿之分布亦颇不平均。北方辽冀鲁豫诸省之储量确为不小，然多已被开发。南方之川湘滇黔诸省储量虽丰，然煤层极薄，煤质亦劣，山西虽为我国煤矿最富之省份，占全国储量百分之五十以上，然地势之不良与运输之困难，皆为开发之问题。

关于中国之石油储量。虽无精确估计，但据近二三年各方之调查，为量亦殊不多。石油因质地轻，运输便，且燃烧容易，在近代工业用途中，已有驾原煤而上之趋势。各种运输工具，如乘坐用之汽车，所需之燃料，为直接由石油炼出之汽油，然其他各种比较轻便之动力机械，亦莫不用内燃发动机而以石油为燃料。更因其为质地轻而富流动性，运输便装载易，石油在近代航轮与军舰中之用途，亦已大增，飞机中更非石油不可。因此各国对煤油之掠夺，不惜钩心斗角，演成伏尸流血之惨剧。中国虽有相当之储量，然只能供给一时之需要，若欲藉以发展大规模之工业，则殊未可凭赖也。

请进而论及水力。中国水力将来之利用，似不无乐观！据云长江之三峡，西江之伏波滩，及黄河之龙门，皆有富饶水力，足资利用。

综前所述，我国三种动力来源之供给，除水力外，均甚有限。煤矿之分布地位既劣，埋藏亦不丰富。设目前之消费额，增加五倍，尚可供给若干年，然须知今日之消费额，决不能藉以预卜来日之消费量。煤油储量，设美国技师之估计为确实，则中国所有者亦不为少，然只能供短时间之自给，若欲谋大规模工业发展，则尚有不足之虑。只有水力之供给，为吾人"取之不尽，用之不竭"之天赋动力，但能否利用，则须视乎今后之努力如何耳！

四、结语

我国今日工业之困难，与夫来日之展望，既经略述，兹再引申管见，以作结语：

溯英国工业之繁兴，远在欧洲各国五十年至一百年前，故一方面可以工业制造品换取原料，而另一方面英国有广大之殖民地，为其原料之供给地与制造品之销售市场，故各种无形与有形之收入，已足抵偿食物与原料之入超。而中国则不适合以上诸条件。复次，今日世界之市场与原料产地，几尽为各工业先进国所劫持或控制，殖民地之掠夺，已几告终了，各种经济上之剧烈倾轧，如倾销政策，报复关税，货币膨胀政策等，我国又何能置身其间！况我国本身即为一被控制与劫持下之国家乎？

就环境言，社会上、政治上、经济上各方面之障碍殊多，或谓此等障碍终有扫除之一日。但回想德国在一八七〇年以前，尚为一农业国家，有百分之七十人口为农民，政治上积弱与纷乱，几与我国今日之情形同，于一九一〇年，始一跃而为欧洲之霸主，其间经过已有四十年之悠长。以中国土地之大、人口之众，转变改革自匪易易，所须经过之辛苦与时间，自必较长，况欲摆脱各国政治经济上之牵制，则更为不易矣！

无论就富源言，或环境言，中国大规模工业极难发展，即欲发展，照原料与动力供给情形观之，至多不过称雄于东亚而已，若欲与英美等角逐于世界市场，则为期殊远也。故吾人以为现应从事发展者，非为重工业，乃轻工业——日用品工业——耳。一方面维持已有之轻工业，如棉纺织工业、缫丝工业、面粉工业、火柴工业等，另一方面则亟应提倡与奖励乡村工业，如织布、针织、编织、草帽辫、刺绣、花边、榨油、制酒、磨粉、造纸、锡箔、制伞、造扇、瓷器、罐头食品、鸡蛋等工业。盖发展乡村工业，为复兴农村之主要步骤之一，其裨益于农村者实多也。就经济方面言之，第一，能使农民利用农余之暇从事生产事业，中国之人口，有百分之七十五为农民，农业又大多系季节性，则一岁农暇时间，约有一百乃至三百天，故农余之暇更有利用之必要。第二，可以利用乡间自产之原料，如粮食、果实、毛皮、苎麻、草杆、泥土之类。第三，乡村工业可以增加农民之收入，减少灾害匪乱之危险。就社会方面言，乡村小工业，可以减少工厂机器产生对工人之种种恶劣影响，增加农民之生活趣味、智慧与进取心，及发展教育之机会，而尤以利用合作方法组织乡村工业，对于农民可施以种种社会式之教育。至于宜如何发展，问题极大，非本文所能详述。然无论如何，"和平"为经济发展之必要条件。其次如便利廉价之交通运输、统一之币制、教育之普及，及农事之改善等，在在与中国明日工业前途之发展有密切之关系也。

中国工业发展的前途

方显廷 陈振汉

中国现代工业比较现世各重要国家都为幼稚的事实，即无统计数字的证明，是谁也承认的。中国工业现在所遭遇的各种痛苦与困难之异甚，也是一般人所共见共闻的。只有对中国工业的前途，一般人的希望也许未免过奢，期待也许未免太大。普通人的见解，大概总以为中国地大物博，人口众庶，如果一旦政治能上轨道，工业的发展，一定可与欧美诸工业先进国并驾齐驱。事实上怎样呢？恐怕不能如此乐观，究竟中国工业能够发展到什么程度，和我们应循什么路线发展，是我们现在所待讨论的问题。

关系乎一国的工业发展的主要因子有两方面，即富源与环境，富源之最重要的是劳工的供给、原料的供给和动力的供给。环境则包含社会的环境、政治的环境，以及经济的环境。我们现在试分析这各方面的因子，对于中国工业的关系与影响：

一、劳工供给

中国人口众多，尽人皆知。人口的密度，以全国面积计算是每方哩一〇五人，不过实际上全国人口只集中于东南海滨及长江与黄河流域数省，蒙古高原、西藏高原那样广大的地域都是人口稀少，事实上也不适于居住的。根据翁文灏氏的区划，中国人口集中在五个区域：第一是华北平原，即华北白河、黄河、淮河一带，在河北、山东、河南、安徽诸省之间，人口每方哩有六百五十人；第二是扬子江区，包括扬子江中下游平原，及洞庭、鄱阳、安徽太湖等几个局部盆地，人口密度由每方哩八百五十人至一千人；第三是山东、江苏、安徽、江西、湖南诸省的丘陵地带，人口密度每方哩三五〇人；第四是浙江、福建、广东等海滨区域，人口密度也差不多。此外四川一区密度，达每方哩六百人，与华北区相似。这样，差不多全国百分之八十三的人口，集中在百分之十七的面积上面，平均密度为每方哩五百人。至于每人平均所有的可耕地及已耕地，则更有限。按照人口的密度计算，平均每人所有土地在华北平原是六亩，扬子江流域四.七亩，东南山区及海滨十一亩，四川平原六.五亩。自然，这些面积里面也含有山有水有住宅，并不是直接可用以农耕的，至于每人所有的已耕地面积，各家的估计稍有不同，平均起来，大概每人有三亩或半英亩之谱，这是很低的数目。因此，中国人口过剩，生活程度极低，劳工廉贱，很适宜于发展工业。如果工业能够充分的发展，使服役于工业的农民的增加率，能够比较生长在乡间的人口增加率为大，则不但农业与工业的效率都能增高，就是中国的人口问题，也从此得到解决。不过实际上靠发展工业来吸收乡村人口，效力是很小的，要以发展工业来解决中国人口问题，这种想望很难实现。因为我们知道，普通在一个农业国家里面，制造工业发展后的第一种反应，即是人口的急遽增加，死亡率减低，生育率增高，只在工业有非常的发展的时候，如同德国在一八七〇年至一九一〇年中间似的，工业的扩张或者足以吸收全部人口的增加。然而即在德国，无论他的经济变迁的速度如何惊人，实际从事于农业的实在人数,还是没有绝对的减少,只有比例的减少而已。在中国,工业发展的速度,当然要缓慢得多,最多我们只能希望工业的发展能够吸收一部分的人口增加;因此中国的乡村人口,除非用旁的方法来节制,或因旁的原因而减少,即在工业发展之后,也还是要继续增加的,不过增加得慢一点罢了。

发展工业能够吸收一部分的人口,不过这种现象是暂时的,只有工业不断的发展,才能继续的吸收人口。否则,要是一旦停顿,只是维持现状而不继续扩张,则人口增加的速度又要增加。而大规模的工业,因为合理化的结果,机械的利用,与纵横的联合,事实上可使得生产效率增高,工厂中雇用的工人减少。换言之,即是大规模工业发达以后,机器可以替代人工,造成失业。在英国工业革命的初期,纺织工人的暴乱,反对新式机器的使用,便是一例。当 Arkwright 发明棉纺织机的时候,英国即有五千二百纺工、二千七百织工的生活受到威胁。在引用动力机械之后有五万纺织工人濒于饥饿。今日英国的工业生产率已经落伍,生产机械与技术的陈旧,是酿成今日英国在经济上的危机的主因之一。因此全国有合理化的呼声,而唯一反对一切合理化计划的努力,便是几千万的劳工群众。一九二一年以来,英国的失业群众永远在一百万以上,纺织业工人的罢工,尤为政府最大的威胁。中国的工业革命方在开始,如果中国也同样的扩张大工业,则在达到一定的限度以后,必定将有同样的危机遭遇。中国现在的人口已患过剩,生活程度极低,如果在工业扩张的时候,吸收了一部分的增加人口,同时又促进总人口的增加,则在异日的人口问题,将更得不到解决。失业问题的严重,将远在今日各国之上。因此中国人口的众多,固是初步工业发展的促进剂,却是大规模工业与极度发展的障碍。如果我们顾忌大部分民众的生活以及社会秩序与幸福的安全，我们的工业决不能够全部的合理化与机械化。

二、原料的供给

中国自产农业原料之缺乏，间接的可从已耕地的稀少上看出来。在美国已耕地占可耕地的百分之三十九，在中国则不过百分之二十六；以人口平均计之，中国每人所有的耕地仅及美国的九分之一。因此即令所有的可耕地完全开垦了，也不及美国每人耕地的一半。耕地既如稀少，原料的生产与供给，自然极有限度。中国是一个农业国家，米麦和面粉是中国各省人民的主要食品，然而据海关报告，一九三二年输入米值一一九，二三二，〇〇〇关两，麦值五一，七六〇，〇〇〇关两，面粉三六，一七六，〇〇〇关两，总共二〇七，一六八，〇〇〇关两，占全国总进口额五分之一。在一九二八年，中国之饮食品、烟酒等输入额，占入口总额百分之二七.四四，而原料及半成品之输入额占百分之一九.二三，总计占全入口额百分之四六.六七。在一个工业国家，输入项目最大的应当是原料与食品，在一个农业国家，则这种现象是反常的，是不应当有的，像粮食的输入固然是由于国内运输便利的缺乏，以及各省当局的禁止粮食流通，分配不能均匀所致，但国内灾荒频仍，生产丰欠无定，也是极显著的现象。此外有许多项原料，也确实不敷自己的消费，例如棉花的入口，近年的增加更是可惊。根据海关报告，一九三二年进口棉花达一，二四一，〇〇〇包，每包五百磅，值一一九，八八五，〇〇〇关两，几乎占本国消费棉花的三分之一。此外烟叶是几乎各地都产的,然在一九三一年烟叶的入口达一六五,六〇九,〇〇〇磅,值四八,六一九,〇〇〇关两,一九三二年达七八,三五九,〇〇〇磅,值二三,七九一,〇〇〇关两,此外他项原料的输入也属不少。

至于金属原料中国也并不能算是富足。其中最重要的是铁矿砂。根据地质调查所《第四次中国矿业纪要》所载,铁矿总贮量为一,〇〇〇兆吨,而美国有九四,三二四兆吨,大于中国九十四倍,法国有一二,二五四兆吨,英国有一二,一六六兆吨,大于中国十二倍,按人口比较则中国每人所有铁矿砂更属稀少,仅只两吨,而美国有七八九吨,大于中国约四百倍,法国有二九九吨,英国有二六七吨,大于中国约一百三四十倍。所以我们的铁矿砂,在事实上只可以对日本人自傲,因为他们只有八千五百万吨的储量,平均每人只有一吨,每年消费矿砂却需三百余万吨,自己只能够供给二十余年,而中国以同等的消费量可支持三百多年。不过中国重要的铁矿,是辽宁的鞍山、本溪湖等,共占七八百兆吨,占全国铁矿砂十分之七强,即在东北没有沦陷以前,矿产开采权已操诸日人,内地铁矿砂仅占总贮量十分之二强,约二百余兆吨,如和日本同样速率的采用,便连二百年也支持不到了。

次于铁的重要金属原料为铜,铜为人类最早利用的金属,而自电器工业发达,各国竞相电气化以来,铜在工业上的用途,更有一日千里,不胫而走之势;但是不幸,中国的铜产额极少,贮量亦不丰,民十八、十九、二十三年的产量平均仅三百五十吨。而每年销费量当在此数的十倍以上。其他铅锌银等矿产也十分缺乏。虽然锑和锡的矿产在中国很为丰富,锑与钨的贮量在世界占第一位,这些终久只是辅助金属或次要金属,在制造工业上的地位并不重要。

43

所以就中国的金属原料而论,我们即不论现在的生产是怎样少,运输与交通是怎样不便,因为这些问题都是以后可以逐渐改善的;单于贮量而论,最重要的两项金属原料,铁与铜的贮量已很贫乏。矿产是不会生长的,虽然可以掠夺,却不能移植的,但我们能有力量,掠夺人家的矿产吗!

三、动力的供给

动力的来源有三种,即是黑色的煤,流动的石油,和白色的水力。

中国的煤矿贮量,以前的估计是九九六,〇〇〇兆吨,居世界第三位,仅次于美国与坎拿大,不过据北京地质调查所比较可靠的估计,则是二四八,二八七兆吨,虽然较前面的估计数量为小,且更次于德国,但如果把萨尔区域的储量及上西来西亚的烟煤储量,从德国矿储中除去,中国仍然占第三位。不过这只是按相对重要而论。论实量,则美国有一,五五九,五九九兆吨,大于中国七倍,坎拿大以前的估计亦在一,〇〇〇,〇〇〇兆吨以上,大于中国六倍。以世界总储量计算,中国储量仅及百分之六,若按人口计算,中国每人应有煤贮量约为五百吨,而美国则每人有一万余吨,坎拿大每人十三万吨,英国四千吨,德国一千五百吨,中国均属瞠目不及。量既如此有限,矿质也不很好,只有一部分是可以供炼焦炭之用的。

中国煤矿的分布很不均匀,在北方辽冀鲁豫诸省的,确是不小,只是已经开发的很多,南方的川湘滇黔虽然贮量也很丰富,但煤层极薄,煤质也劣。现在煤矿最富的是山西,占全国贮量百分之五十以上。地势的不好与运输的困难,想是以后可以克服的,只是增加成本罢了。还有一点值得欣幸的即是东三省的煤矿并不怎样重要,连热河在内,四省共占四千六百多兆吨,占总贮量百分之一.八四,而连年为日人所经营开采,所余也有限也。

关于中国的石油贮量,不特没有较为可靠的估计,并且连可资估计的资料都没有。民国三年至五年北京政府曾与美国美孚油公司合作,在陕西钻探,并派员到四川调查石油矿,大约即根据此项结果,美国地质调查所在民国九年发表中国石油储藏量为一,三七五兆桶(每七桶为一吨),如果以这数字作标准,再加上已勘测的油页岩油量一,八九九兆桶,则中国油储量当为三,二七四兆桶,占世界总贮量十五分之一,不及美国的一半,只是比印度与日本都来得多,在东亚可称首富。可惜其中油页岩完全在抚顺,已被日本人侵占去了。

石油因为质地轻运输方便而且燃烧容易,在近代工业用途中已有驾原煤而上的趋势,各种运输用的或乘坐用的汽车固然直接应用从石油提炼出来的汽油,其他各种比较轻便的动力机械,也莫不用内燃发动机以石油作燃料,更因为他的质地轻而流动,运输方便,装载较省地方,在近代航轮与军舰中的用途也已大增,飞机中更非石油不可,在将来的战争中,不能控制油矿贮的国家,必有败北的危险。因此各国今日的煤油争夺,常是各种政治斗争的背景,而差不多世界所有已发现油田,都已被几个重要的国家所捷足先登占据控制去了。中国虽然有相当的贮量,不过只能供给一时的需要,欲藉以发展大规模的工业,尚是不足用的。

第三种的动力来源是白色的煤(white coal),即是水力。中国可发展的水力(potential supply)有二千万马力,占世界第四位,次于美国、印度与巴西,但就已发展的说,占世界最末的一位,仅有一千马力。可利用的水力最大的所在是长江的三峡，西江的伏波滩和黄河龙门等。据说三峡水力，在巴县一带，低流时即有每秒钟四十三万马力，平流时四十四万马力，较之最著名的美国尼瓜拉瀑布多百分之三十。即此可以概见中国的水力供给在实量上说并不是贫弱的。不过以中国土地之大，人口之众，比较起来，其在将来工业中的效应，也属有限了。

在上我们约略的叙述了中国的三种动力来源的供给，煤矿的分布地位自然不好，矿藏也不丰富，如果照现在的消费额增加五倍，尚可供给一千余年，不过要知道现在的消费额真是微乎其微，民十七、十八、十九、二十四年，每年销煤仅二千余万吨，平均每人消费不过〇.〇五吨，所以如果工业有急剧的发展，煤矿的告竭是很迅速的。德国地质学家李希多芬（F. von Richthofen）在一八七〇年所说的山西省的煤矿"可以单独供给全世界几千年"已是过去了。煤油的贮量，如果美国技师的估计是确实的话，则中国也并不为少，不过也只能供短时间的自给，如果谋大规模的工业发展，则尚有不足之虞，只有水力的供给，是我们所可取之不尽用之不绝的。

就上列所论各种矿产的供给，无论是原料或是动力的来源，不论他们的贮量究有多少，是否足用，有一个问题，是须特别注意的，即是外资的控制，这些矿产大半在外人的手内。百分之五十六的煤之出产是由外国人经营的，而铁矿砂贮量虽少，却有百分之八十二在日人的掌握之内，因此一大半的出产矿砂都是输出到日本去的。我们应当知道这事情的意义的严重，在一个合理的世界这也许没有什么，但在现在这种各国经济斗争这样剧烈，掠夺原料与矿产如此激进的世界中，却不容我们忽视这情形的危险。如果我们不赶紧在政治上想办法，中国的工业也许永没有翻身的日子，虽有原料与矿产，不论是多少都是空的，更况所贮有的又不多呢。

四、社会环境

现在的中国是一个变乱的中国，我们所处的是一个在不绝变动的社会，昨日的社会可与今日的不同，影响于昨日社会的势力，在今天或者要失去他的效应，旧的社会制度习俗与风物，也许在明天就会失去它的存在，而产生新的社会制度与信仰。不过我们也应该知道，这种变迁是逐渐的缓慢的，而非一时的迅速的，是部分的而非整个的。比如贱视工商业心理，至少现在有一部分人已经没有了，至少政府不但已注意到工商业的发展上去，而且在积极提倡着，自己兴办着，像汉高祖的律令"贾人不得衣丝乘车"，惠帝之令"市井子孙，不得仕宦为吏"，隋制"工商不得仕进"，唐制"工商什类不得预于仕伍"，是不会再有的了。现在依然怀着这种观念的，大概只有毫无知识的乡农苦力，他们没有知道什么叫劳工神圣，依然迷信着士农工商的历阶，慨叹着自己的贫苦的运命，而惭愧不能把子孙送入庠学去为仕宦后进。然而他们占着中国人口的大部分，他们的潜势力很可以左右社会，他们的观念依然是工商业的障碍物。

最重要的问题，是中国的家庭问题，中国的家庭制度，实际上也即是社会制度，除了家庭，中国就没有社会，离开家庭的观念，中国人也就没有社会观念。现在旧式的大家庭制度虽在逐渐破坏，不过影响所及，还是表面的，部分的，即是不出都市范围，中国最大多数，或者可以说是全体的人民，还是这种大家庭的分子，还是大家庭制度的奴隶与牺牲者。大家庭制度之有障碍于工业的发展有两方面：第一，家庭的束缚太重，使个人志气销沉，怯于冒险，即使青年自身有志企图上进，也无如家庭大权，操在长者手里，他们往往不愿子孙远离，但希望能够子孙满堂，催促子孙早日完娶，这样便很容易把一个青年堆葬在家里面了。第二，大家庭制度容易养成依赖习性，便成一种家庭共产制度。普通一家里面，如果有一人发财，则全家都靠他衣食。所谓"一人成仙，鸡犬登天"了。而且壮年人例须供养年长者，否则即是不孝，凡此种种，都足以妨碍个人的发展，事业的成就。而大规模工业的进行，工厂制度的实施，遂感受人才乏缺，劳工不足，管理腐败等等恶劣影响了。

五、政治环境

内战以及因内战而起的政治上的不稳定的现状，政府力量薄弱，政府之不能予工商业以保护种种事实，其影响和对于工商业的障碍都是极显然的。此外，也是一时足以为本国工业发展的障碍的，是由于政治的失败而订下的种种丧权辱国的不平等条约。外人在华的银行，外人在华的建设工厂权，外人在华的航行权，半自主式的关税，外人开采的矿山，以及领事裁判权的存在，种种不平等的条约与规定，一时把中国工业的咽喉扼住了，把中国工业的四肢束缚住了。欲图复兴，非先有艰苦卓绝的努力，去了这层层的枷锁与桎梏不可。至于这种种受不平等条约保护的特权在经济上的影响，我们在下节再为讨论。

六、经济环境

中国交通的困难，运输便利的缺乏，金融组织的混乱，资本势力的微小，民众购买力的薄弱，这些都阻扰着今日的工业发展，不过这些都是一时内现象，不是根本的病症。如果我们有一个志愿，我们就可以有一条路去改良除芟的。因为这些都是我们自己的事，自己的病，其治疗与败坏，兴建与废除，都是我们自己的力量所能达到的。所可忧虑的，是外人的竞争。外人的竞争有三方面，在国内市场，有外国制造家来竞争以及外人在华工厂来竞争，在国外市场，则有中国货与外国货在国际市场的争衡。中国以其面积之广（四，二七八，三五二方哩），人口之众（四八五兆）自然是一个广大的市场，不过中国五分之四的人民只能购买最低限度的生活必需品，因此其购买力之低，也是极明显的事实。因为民众购买力低，自然看价格的高下买货，因此中国是一个道地的价格市场，而竞争的所以剧烈，这也是一个原因。这几年来因为世界经济倾跌的异甚，中国成为各国的倾销市场是无容否认的，我国只有入口而无出口，其原因有几方面：第一即是世界的生产过剩，只有到中国来找市场；第二是外人知道了中国是一个价格市场，特别跌价倾销；第三是我国关税之不能完全自主，特别是对日本的互惠条约，给予日本以低价畅销货物的机会；第四就是他们直接从本国运货来销售，以其生产成本低，金融运输便利广，推广销售方法成效大，也很可以战胜国货，几年来中国纸烟事业的渐趋销声匿迹，即是一例。至于国外市场的竞争，以中国本有地位的出品如丝茶之类尚且失败，欲同样以制造工业去争夺国际市场，除南洋一带因有华侨的推销尚有可能外，其余都很难插足。这几年来中国工商业在市场竞争中所遇的失败已很凄惨。在竞争国家之中，英日的势力最盛，而日本则更是中国的国内外贸易上的世仇。过去一年因为日本在中国的大量倾销棉货、煤、洋灰、纸等类物件，中国工业的损失极大，而从日本在华因避免关税而建的工厂，像棉纺织业、煤业、钢铁业等的活动继续增加上看，中国如果要发展同样的工业，也想同样大规模去发展，其艰苦与牺牲将倍形惨重了。在外贸易上，日本也是中国最大的劲敌。譬如丝业，在去年即因为世界市场的不景气与日元跌价的缘故，中国出口生丝值竟至减少三分之二。中国本有市场的工业，其市场尚被人所夺去，欲从别人手中去争夺市场，困难可知了。

在这里我们不得不沉痛的特别提出来说的，是东北的丧失对于我国工业前途上的影响。前面我们已经说过人口过剩将是中国工业前途的最大障碍，然而东北本是内地移民的唯一尾闾，是"天留给中国的新农区"，据翁文灏氏的估计，辽吉黑三省人口约计三千万人，平均密度仅每方哩八十人，大多数人口集中于松辽平原（嫩江、松花江及辽河的宽谷），在此平原上现已有人口约二千万人，平均密度约每方哩一百七十人。这平原的面积共有十二万方哩，和华北平原区面积相似，比扬子江平原区还大，而每年雨量有自二十时至三十余时，也和华北平原区相似。并且土壤肥沃，可以不假肥料植物自丰，许多且是未经开垦的处女地。虽然温度较低，但在农作物需要的时期天气甚热，稻米都能生长。按翁氏的估计，这一大平原每方哩可以增加一百七十人至三百五十人的人口，假定增加一百七十人，则十二万方哩可再容纳二千万人。假定这些人口全从华北平原区移植,则能使该区减少人口四分之一。然而这样辽阔丰肥的区域,这样大好的河山,现在竟被人轻轻用武力攫夺去了。

中国各省工业化程度之高,辽宁一省仅次于江苏,而占全国之第二位。在民十六年辽宁矿产占全国百分之二九.二,民十七年,辽宁之煤产占全国百分之三三.〇,铁产占全国三二.七。民十八年发电量占全国百分之二一.五,贸易值占总贸易值百分之一七.八,总对外贸易百分之二一.五。交通方面,辽宁一省铁路在民十三年即占全国百分之二一.七,汽车路在民十九年占百分之六.五,电报在民十七年占百分之三.八。

至于东北的富源,农产品方面,大豆是东北的特产,近年以来,豆及豆制品占出口贸易的首位,以豆为原料的工业是东北的主要经济活动。此外高粱、小米、麦子都有丰富的出产。东北的矿产,石油与铁不特是中国的命脉,并且是东亚的命脉。前面已经说过,东北的煤矿贮量并不甚多,在东亚各区的煤贮中,东北只占百分之四,中国本部的煤,大于东北的煤六十二倍。是以对将来的工业发展,东北的煤的损失并未有若何严重的影响,不过目前的供给,特别是抚顺煤在华中与华南的倾销,颇使我国的煤矿,蒙受不利。东北的铁矿贮量前面已经说过占全国总贮量的十分之七强,而大于日本的贮量将及九倍,南洋群岛的贮量十倍,所以在东亚,除印度外,东北铁矿,无有其匹。中国全部的铁矿贮量本来不过美国九十四分之一,英法的十二分之一,德国的四分之一,不足为将来建设大规模工业国家之恃,然而东北一去,则所剩更微乎其微了。东北的石油矿产,就已经知道的说,以抚顺的油页岩为主,矿石储藏量约五千五百兆吨,含油百分之五.五,可炼油约二.一〇九兆桶,此外满洲里贮有沥青,可炼油十余万桶,总计所储油量,在东亚已是第一,几乎有美或俄的三分之一,世界的二十分之一,而中国本部油藏,据美国人的估计,仅一.三七五兆桶,比东北要少三分之一,现在日本已开始炼制抚顺的油页岩,其计划为每年产油三十万吨,据说即使每年产油三百万吨,亦可供一百年之用。中国全部石油矿或者可以支持一些时候,供短时期的工业应用,现在既去其五之三,不特工业上的损失为莫可计算,即在国防上的影响也是十分严重的了。

中国的工业本没有多大的前途,而东北一失,则是把我们的一线希望完全遮断了。

七、结论

就中国的人工富源论,人口众庶,劳力过剩,本为发展工业之有利条件,然大规模工业发展之结果,以技术组织之改进,生产效力之增高,不特所吸收之新工人极有限度,反足使旧有工人失业,使人口益患过剩,人口问题愈无解决之途径。所以人口众多虽能帮助工业之初步发展,实足障碍大规模之经营,而使有效的生产,充分的机械化成为不可能。

就中国的自然富源论,农产原料无论自质的方面与量的方面言都患不足。而农民食物又且从外国运入,有不足之患,即使把未垦的土地尽量使用,生产食物的需要也比较生产食物原料的需要来得更殷切,是以即使我们要增加原料的生产,事实上也很困难。中国煤矿贮量虽居世界第三位,论实藏则仅及美国七分之一,坎拿大六分之一,全世界百分之六,而每人所有煤贮量仅五百吨。较之美国之一万余吨,坎拿大之十三万吨者无与伦比。铁矿贮量更属稀少,平均每人仅有铁矿砂二吨,如东北之矿砂除外,则平均每人所有不及半吨。现在美国每人每年钢铁消费率达四六八公斤,法国达二〇三公斤,英国二〇〇公斤,中国若有与英国同样之消费率,本部的铁矿尚不足一年之用,连东北铁矿在内,也仅能维持三年。石油贮量连东北计算在内较有可观,不过也不足为发展大规模工业之用。此外,铜铅锌银等矿都不足用,水力的发展固然很有可能,不过一时很不容易,而且也有藉于铜矿的供给,以为传电线之主要原料。所以就天然富源言,无论其为农产、矿产,都不能供给大规模的工业发展之用。本来一国的原料与动力都能自给固然很好,而且在现在这种经济倾轧的世界是必要的。不过上帝赋与人类往往没有这样的便利,譬如法国现在有铁而没有煤,德国则情形刚好相反,即如英国在从前工业革命时代的一个极大便利是煤铁都很丰富而且为极接近,但英国的棉纺织业完全依赖外来的原料以为供给,英国的毛织业也大半依赖外来的原料。所以在某种情形下,富源的缺乏并不一定是工业发展的障碍。不过中国的情形是与别国不同的,现在的时势也与往昔有异了,英国的工业革命比欧洲其他各国早上五十至一百年,所以可以拿工业制造品来换原料,英国的煤是极重要的出口品,也可以拿来换取食物与原料,同时,英国有广大的殖民地,能供给原料与作为生产品销售的市场,即在现在,英国也以其雄厚的资本势力控制各方面的富源,波斯的石油富源即为英国所攫取,而英国又是老大的商业国家,他的各种无形的收入,可以抵偿食物与原料的大超。中国却并不适合任一条件,在现在,各工业先进国也差不多已把所有的市场与原料出产地控制住了,殖民地的略夺也快告完工了,各种经济上的剧烈的倾轧,像倾销、报复关税、货币膨胀政策等等,中国何尝能够置身其间?更何况中国自身即是这样一个被控制与掠夺的国家!

就环境言,社会上政治上经济上各方面的障碍很多,虽然这些障碍终是可以扫除的。德国在一八七〇年以前还是一个农业国家,有百分之七十的人口是农民,政治上的积弱与纷乱,也不亚于今日的中国,但是到了一九一〇年,则已一跃而为欧洲的霸主了。不过其间已经历了四十年的长期。以中国土地之大,人口之众,转变与改革自然更不容易,所经过的苦辛与时间,大概得更多更长,而欲摆脱各国政治经济上的牵制,更为不易。

无论就富源言或环境言,中国的大规模工业极难发展,即欲发展,照原料与动力的供给情形看来,最多也只能称雄于东方,若欲和英美等角逐于世界市场,恐怕很少可能性。我们所应当从事发展的不是重工业,而是轻工业——日用品工业。一方面维持已有规模的轻工业,像棉纺织工业、缫丝工业、面粉工业、火柴工业等,另一方面则应当提倡与奖励乡村工业,像织布、针织、编织、发网、草帽辫、刺绣、花边、榨油、制酒、磨粉、造纸、锡箔、制伞、制扇、瓷器、罐头食品、鸡蛋等工业。而对于中国过去已有地位的工业,像丝、茶等尤须设法维持。我们所丰富的既是劳工,缺少的既是原料与动力,我们便应当奖励多多利用人工少用原料与动力的工业。而在国际市场中,中国大概也只有利用特殊的精细产品,方能夺得一席地位。以一部分自己的制造品代替原料与食物,去交换人家的制造品。还有,发展乡村工业是复兴农村的主要步筹之一。乡村工业的发展对农村有几方面的好处:就经济方面说,第一是能够使农民利用农余之暇从事生产事业。中国的人口,有百分之七十五是农民,而农业又大多是季节性的,一年中农闲的时间可以从一百天到三百天,可见有加以利用的必要。第二是可以利用乡间的原料与生产,如粮食、果实、毛皮、苎麻、草杆、泥土之类。第三,乡村工业可以增加农民的收入,减少灾害匪乱的危险。其他的好处像减少乡村社会内因货品进出口的损失,促进农事之利用机器等,都是极明显的。就社会方面说,乡村小工业可以减少工厂机器生产的种种对工人的恶劣影响,增加农民生活的趣味、智慧与进取性,以及发展教育的机会,特别是利用合作方法来组织乡村工业,对于农民可以施以种种社会式的教育。

　　至于怎样去发展,问题极大,非三两语所能尽。不过无论怎样,和平是经济发展的必要条件。其次是便利廉价的交通运输,即是发展乡村工业也非有便利的交通不行。统一的币制、教育的普及、农事的改良、金融制度与市场的改善、合作事业的普及等等,都是必要的步筹。如果能够循着这条路线进行,我们敢说至少对内可以相当的提高人民生活程度,增进人民的生产能力,对外可以因人民购买能力的增加,为过剩的世界生产,开辟一个广大的市场,缓和不景气的空气,减轻恐慌的程度。

中外棉花交易所之比较

绪论

　　交易所之组织,滥觞于巴黎。当十四世纪中叶,巴黎交易所已具雏形,至一七二六年重行改组,典制始较完备。一七七三年英国有伦敦证券交易所之创设,一八一七年美国又有纽约证券交易所之创设。自兹以往,交易所之组织,始为世界各国所公认。日本亦于明治四年,效颦西洋,设立交易所。我国光绪年间,梁启超倡议组织股份懋迁公司,实为中国交易所创议之嚆矢。惟以当时民气未开,商人泥守旧习,未知交易所之功用,视若无关重轻。是故交易所之事,空有其议,而实无其成。直至民国二年,农商部长刘揆一氏,目击当时内国商情,大有设立交易所之必要,乃召集全国工商巨子会于旧京,以讨论之。会议结果,公决在通商大埠酌情分设,以为之倡。民国三年,又有官商合办之提议,假定资本为百万元。嗣以时局不靖,当政者意见纷歧,此议亦成泡影。至五年冬,虞洽卿与孙中山先生,鉴于上海有设立交易所之必要,若我不自谋,人将庖代,乃有组织上海交易所股份有限公司之动议,并拟具章程,呈请农商部立案批准,数经周折,至民国八年六月,始有上海证券物品交易所之设立。次年九月，正式营业。中国交易所之创议，始于光绪年间，至此方见诸事实，其间酝酿，盖已二十年矣。此所成立以后，半年间获盈余五十余万元。于是人皆以为有利可图，华商证券交易所、面粉交易所、杂粮油豆饼业交易所、华商棉业交易所，相继成立，风起泉涌，市利倍蓰。民国十年夏秋之交，可谓交易所极盛时代，继起设立者，竟有百四十余家之多，定名离奇，交易物品应有尽有，交易所事业，转成一时之投机事业矣，卒以投机过甚，资金转运不灵，黑暗内幕暴露社会，因此停业者日有所闻，此民十上海交易所之风潮，亦我国交易所发展进程中一至有趣之事实也。

交易所之性质，大别为二，即证券交易、物品交易是。华商纱布交易所即物品交易所之一。我国现存较大交易所有六，即金业、面粉、杂粮、华商证券、中国证券物品，及华商纱布交易所是。六者之中，尤为华商纱布交易所最为重要。据一九二七年统计，世界棉产丰富国家，中国列为第三。其棉产交易之市场，则以华商纱布交易所为首屈一指，证券物品交易所次之。前者自一九二一年成立后，营业上进展颇速，故于一九二八年七月，有世界棉花交易所调查委员会之组织，调查各著名棉花交易所，计有大阪棉花交易所、纽阿林棉花交易所、纽约棉花交易所、利物浦棉花公会及东印度棉花公会五处，其他如德之不来梅及法之哈复尔二地，亦有美棉之定期交易，但其交易额无如利物浦与纽约二所之大，为调查之便利计，该会未往调查。至若亚力山渠之棉市，则专营埃及棉花定期交易，此种交易，利物浦亦兼营之，故该会亦未另行调查。该会调查之范围，大都限于各交易所之行政、组织，及交易之方法。而交易所与本国政府之关系，亦在调查之列。惟欧美各国，均采取放任主义。故二者间，关系殊浅。本文即根据该会调查所得分类述之如下：

生棉之定期交易

美国为世界产棉最富之国，故亦为棉花定期交易之最大市场。纽约棉花交易所在棉花市场上之地位尤为重要，其交易之棉花纯为美产，与人交易皆为定期，无现期之买卖。次于纽约棉花交易所者，则有纽阿林棉花交易所。此外芝加哥商务局从前专营大麦之定期交易，近年亦兼营棉花之定期交易。此三大交易所所经营之棉花多为美产，美国棉花除在上列交易所行销外，英之利物浦、德之不来梅、法之哈复尔及日之大阪各地棉花交易所，亦以美国棉花为定期交易之主要物品焉。除美国外，产棉最富者，当推印度。印花之定期交易，据全世界棉花定期交易市场之第二位，仅次于美国而已。大部分交易多在东印度棉花公会，但利物浦棉花公会亦有印花买卖。埃及棉花，大多销售于亚力山渠，有时亦至利物浦。至于中国国产棉花及棉纱定期交易，则惟恃华商纱布交易所及证券物品交易所而已。

交易所组织之类别

大概言之，交易所之组织可分为二类。中国与日本之棉花交易所多为私人集资所创办，目的重在谋利，此第一类也。欧美各国及印度之棉花交易所并非谋利机关,主理其事者均为交易所之会员,或商人或经纪人,此第二类也。纽约棉花交易所即为第二类交易所中之最著者,共有会员四百人,会中经费之来源有二:一为会员会金,一为特捐。除此机关外,在纽约城中,尚有一纽约棉花交易清算所,交易所中人加入此清算所者,约有九十人之多,每订定一定期交易契约,由纽约棉花交易所执行时,必先由纽约棉花交易清算所清算之。董其事者,必兼为交易所清算所之会员。其仅为交易所之会员而非清算所之会员者,计约三百人。凡清算交易契约时,必假手于其他九十人。是以会员四百人,又可别为二类,一为清算会员,一为非清算会员。以清算会员,除清算其自己之契约外,尚可清算非清算会员之契约,并可取其为人经纪商业所得佣金之半数焉。约言之,清算会员即为经纪人,而非清算会员大部为商人或投机者。其与人交易,亦无不以私利为前题也。

利物浦棉花公会,亦如纽约棉花交易所,其组织之目的,纯在图谋会员中相互贸易之便利。其机关成立之经费及日常开支,悉赖会员会费,如有不足,可以每年会员特捐补偿之。此会会员现约有三百人,但人数决无限制,可增可减,会员大都为棉纺绩家、运输商人、入口贸易商人及棉花商人,此等会员可以分为二类,一为正式会员,一为特别会员。正式会员可派代表直入交易所,立于叫卖环栅之下,直接交易,故谓为直接交易人。特别会员与人交易,必假手于正式会员,但所付佣金仅当非会员之半,此盖特别会员之权利也。

华商纱布交易所或大阪棉花交易所,与纽约棉花交易所或利物浦棉花公会绝对不同,华商纱布交易所为一谋利机关,其组织按中国商法为有限公司,资本为三百万元,该公司有理事会为主体,理事由股东选举之，三年一任，公司股东必须华籍商人，方为合格。理事会由股东互选十五人组织之，其被选资格，为股权至少须满二百，每权五十元，年龄必在二十五岁以上，尤以棉商之富于经验者为合适。此理事会之行使职权，大都与欧美各国或印度棉花公会相仿，但其活动范围，尚较后者为广。华商纱布交易所各种常务委员会之工作，皆为理事会会员雇用助理员帮同办理。各理事亦均在交易所，按月支薪。纽约棉花交易所则不然，其常务委员会如执行、财务、监察、规则、会员、统计及情报、贸易、堆栈及运输、分类、审判、仲裁、佣金、理诉、商务等委员会，各有专职也。

经纪人与交易所

中国（或日本）与其他各国之棉花交易所，尚有一不同之处，即经纪人与交易所之关系是。在欧美各国及印度之交易所中，经纪人即为交易所中人，为交易所之代表，并非与交易所分开者。华商纱布交易所则异是，经纪人皆受交易所节制，及经纪人公会规章之限制。此经纪人公会，由交易所准许之经纪人组织而成，同时又非其他任何棉花交易所中之会员，其入会非先得交易所同意，不能有效。交易所所以限制经纪人如此谨严者，亦有相当理由。盖交易所对于经纪人招徕之买卖皆订立契约，如有损差，在法律上均由交易所负责。是以经纪人为保证其各人信用计，必缴纳上海规银二万两于交易所，以为保证。此外每于交易所买卖遇有损失时，必为偿补。但对于所内会员遇有违法之举动时，其处置方法不如纽约棉花交易所之严厉。按纽约棉花交易所之规定，当一会员发生违法举动时,首由清算所将其在本所中之未清契约结算。结算损差,可先由清算所储集盈余弥补,如损差极巨,罄此盈余犹不足以弥补,则惟有暂取清算所之保证基金偿之。此保证基金有定额,若如此挪动,必须填补,填补之法,即视清算所中人在前九月内清算契约之多寡为标准,以募集此保证金亏空之数焉。

政府立法

中国(或日本)与其他各国棉花交易所之第三不同点,即为政府之立法。利物浦或东印度棉花公会,各有规章,政府并无法律限制。美国棉花交易所,虽受政府立法之限制,但其限制仅及于所中契约方面,而不及其行政。中国或日本,则情形大异,政府立法关系于棉花交易事项者,极为详尽,定期棉花之交易,未为所规定者甚鲜。

在美国仅有定期棉花贸易条例,与棉花交易,关系最切。此条例于一九一四年通过,以后已数经修改。自此条例通过后,每当交易所订定定期棉花交易之契约时,必依照此项条例及交易所之规章。约言之,此条例规定定期交易之标准棉花、政府标定棉花之等次以为定期买卖之交割,及执行交割时标准棉花与其他政府标定棉花之"价值差别"等。中国自民国十年通过物品交易所条例后,政府即根据之以干涉棉花交易所,下列数点为中国物品交易所条例之要点。

一、物品交易所之设立,必呈经农商部核准,由农商部特给营业执照,并拟定章程,呈请农商部核准,其章程有变更时亦同。农

商部认为必要时,得令物品交易所改定章程,或禁止撤销其决议及措置。(以上见物品交易所条例第二、第七及第三十七条)

二、物品交易所之行为,有违背法令或妨害公益或扰乱公安时,农商部得为左列各款之处分:

(一)解散交易所。

(二)停止交易营业。

(三)停止交易所一部分营业。

(四)令职员退职。

(五)停止经纪人之营业或予除名。

(以上见物品交易所条例第三十五条)

三、农商部认为必要时,得派临时视察员检查物品交易所之业务、帐簿、财产,或其他一切物件及经纪人之帐簿。(以上见物品交易所条例第三十六条)

四、物品交易所之营业保证金,为其股本银数三分之一。此项保证金,须于开业以前,按照应缴额数,以商业公债票,由农商部核定,缴存该地方或附在地方经理国库之银行。物品交易所营业执照规费,定为五百元。每次结帐后,应就纯利中提取百分之五,作为交易所税,征解农商部核明之。(以上见物品交易所附则第二、第三条及物品交易所条例第四十五条)

民国十八年十月国民政府新颁交易所法,翌年六月实行。此法与民十所颁物品交易所条例,微有出入。兹将两者不同之点与上述有关者,述之如下:

(一)民十条例规定"物品交易所之营业保证金,为其股本银数三分之一。……营业执照规费,定为五百元。每次结帐后,应就纯利中提取百分之五,作为交易所税,征解农商部核明之。"民十八所颁之交易所法第五章第三十四条，规定"股份有限公司组织之交易所，应缴存营业保证金"。但缴付办法及应缴确数，据附则五十四条所载，系由工商部以部令定之。营业执照规费及交易所税二端，交易所法正文中亦未提及，只于第八章附则第五十三条规定"交易所课税法另定之"。

（二）民十物品交易所条例所谓之交易所，都系股份有限公司组织。民十八交易所法，则于股份有限公司组织之交易所外，尚许有同业会员组织之交易所存在。（第二章第五条）且规定股份有限公司组织之交易所，其为买卖者，以该所经纪人为限。同业会员组织之交易所，其为买卖者，以该所会员为限。（第二章第六条）

中国自有物品交易所条例及新颁之交易所法，使工商部（前农商部）得以干涉交易所之行政，不仅为纽约或利物浦交易所所未有，即如美国定期棉花贸易条例，于上举各权，亦未列载。所载者都专门问题，如定期交易棉花标准之确定等。盖各国政府之政策不一，彼邦政府素取放任主义，而我政府采用干涉主义，以为指导企业之原则。此种政策之不同，其主因有二：

（一）中国物品交易所条例，纯取法于日本。

（二）中国之交易所，与日本之交易所同，纯为一谋利机关，组织之者并非交易所所员，故政府不得不以法律绳之，用以保障并促进交易所所员或经纪人之利益焉。

定期棉花交易所之赋税负担

纽约棉花交易所可谓全世界棉市中之最大者。战前政府不向之征税。欧战时以国用孔亟，国会曾于一九一八年通过国库收入法，向纽约棉花交易所征税，每百包美棉，征美金一元。其始纯为一战时税，故征收之法，即由政府派员，查察交易所会员每日贸易数量之报告，以为税收之标准。其后纽约交易清算所代政府征收此税，改用每月报告，为征收之标准，此制迄今仍沿用之。此种税收之多少，纯为商业上之秘密，多不告诸外人。但据前任交易所所长麦书氏之估计，此项税收，每年平均可得美金四百万元。在英国及印度，棉花定期交易向不征税，印度虽有印花税办法，然每契约一纸仅贴印花四安那（anna）而已。盖因定期契约为商业契约之一，印花税之缴纳，所以给与法律上之效力也。在中国则有物品交易所条例，此中规定，交易所每当年终清结时，须纳利润之百分之五于政府，上文已言及之矣。

棉花交易之定期契约

　　据美国安美尼教授之定义，定期交易云者，为一种契约。认可交货于将来，而不言明货物之批（lot）别。其成立亦有一商业机关，预为订定货物之数量、单位、质量及交货时日等。惟货物之总数及其价格，则纯由买卖两造人自行决之耳。定期棉花交易之契约，即为上言定期货物交易契约之一种。不过对于货物之数量单位、质量及交货时日一层，则仅可因各交易所所处之境地及素来习惯之不同，而异其规定。不但于不同类棉花之定期买卖为然，即在同为一类棉花之定期买卖，亦莫不如是。兹试举一例以明之：美国纽约或纽阿林棉花交易所之定期棉花契约，载明定期交割标准米特林

(basis middling)棉花一百包,其命价即以每磅值若干分为定,每包总共重量为五百磅。其契约之订立,必遵照定期棉花贸易条例第五节之规定,及交易所之法规,不得乖违。至利物浦棉花交易所中之美棉定期交易契约,则与纽约者略有出入,约中载明定期交割标准米特林棉花一百包,命价以每磅若干便士为定,净重四万八千磅,其契约之订立,不为任何政府法律所拘束,仅得与本所惯例无违而已。

印度定期棉花之契约有五类,其中三类为新近置办者,即白洛区(Broach)、阿美拉(Oomra)及彭高(Bengal)棉花是也。每一定期棉花契约,载印棉一百包,总共重量为五十根地(candies)(一根地等于七百八十四磅),命价即以每根地值若干卢比为定。中国国产棉花之定期交易,由华商纱布交易所及证券物品交易所处理之。不过此种交易,由证券物品交易所处理者,较之由华商纱布交易所处理者为少耳。因证券物品交易所贸易之范围甚广,兼及证券及其他物品之交易,非仅限于棉花一端也。华商纱布交易所定期棉花每约交易之单位为一百担,其命价以每斤值若干银两为标准,而证券物品交易所,则每约交易单位,仅五十担。华商纱布交易所,除棉花定期交易外,尚有棉纱之定期交易。每一契约之单位,为五十大包,每大包合四十小包,其命价则以每大包值若干银两为定焉。

棉花之分类

每一定期棉花买卖契约,即为一标准棉花及他种所定之棉花,均可分割。在纽约及纽阿林棉花交易所中，其标准棉花及其他种类，皆为美政府农务部协定。此制度广播全球凡行棉花定期交易者，无不采用之，故名之曰"万国标准"。美政府曾于纽约、纽阿林及休斯敦三地，分设棉花检验局，其工作即为检验在纽约棉花交易所、纽阿林棉花交易所及芝加哥商务局三处执行定期契约交割之棉花，而为之分类，并颁发分类证明书。此种官督分类制度，为由一九一四年之定期棉花贸易条例而来，此法极有效力，迄今仍沿用之。在一九一四年以前，情形大异，纽约棉花交易所中，另成一小机关，专司分类之职，此中人员，多为专家，由交易所特聘。至若纽阿林棉花交易所，其先分类制度，正如现在利物浦或东印度棉花公会之情形，在利物浦棉花公会，每当美国棉花输入后，其定期交易契约到期交割时，必有仲裁之举，以审定棉花之等次。此仲裁委员会，为每年由利物浦棉花公会，就会员中选任，凡每一定期交易契约实行交割时，再由此会推举二人，一人代表买者，一人代表卖者。以仲裁所交割棉花之等次，仲裁结果两方代表人有一共同之判决，若买卖二方同意，则无异议，倘二方不与同意，则必请一公断人，另行判决。每次仲裁之费，为一基尼（即二一先令），买卖二方均需缴纳。设若买卖任何一方对于仲裁者或公断者俱不满意时，则可控于上诉委员会，上诉费为三基尼，由上诉者负担。向使上诉委员会之判决，仍不能遂意时，则买者或卖者，更可上诉于高等上诉委员会，但以必得董事会之同意为条件。此高等上诉委员会，为最后判决之机关，上诉费须十基尼，亦由上诉者担负之。

在华商纱布交易所，关于棉花分类一项，其现行制度，实与纽约一九一四年以前所行者相似。其中棉花视察委员会有十人，率皆富有经验之棉业专门人才，其工作即为分别棉花或棉纱之等第。委员会人员，为交易所重金聘请而来，其决断如何，经纪人唯有遵令照行，殊无异议之余地也。

棉花价值差别之厘定

前言棉花分类之制，为就棉花之质地而言，其如标准棉花之价值与其他种类之价值之订定。在一九一四年以前有二法，一为"确定差别"盛行于纽约，一为"商业差别"盛行于纽阿林。在确定差别制下，其标准棉花之价值及他种类之价值之差别，每年十一月及十二月，各厘定一次。在商业差别制下，其价值之差别，逐日厘定。关于二制之采用，其优劣点之计较，争执甚久，最终美政府通过定期棉花贸易条例，因而产生"平均差别之制"，此制即由商业差别制改造而成。平均差别制，对于价值之差别，仍为逐日订定，一如前状。但标准棉花与其他标定棉花价值之差别，必由农务部指定五处现货交易大市场以上所定者而平均之，非如昔日专取一市如纽阿林棉花交易所者即是也。故此法律之第五节，于一九二七年修改后规定如下：

……当定期交易之棉花到期交割时，其价值高于低于契约价格之差别（此棉花种类与标准种类相较，亦有高下），由收货者结算时，必用平均差别方法，以决定之。决定之法，系采取五处现物交易市场之标准棉花与其标定棉花价值之差，而平均之。此五处现货交易市场，率由农务部长指定之。

确定差别及商业差别二制，在华商纱布交易所及利物浦棉花公会，仍极盛行。华商纱布交易所对于价值差别之确定，率无定时，大旨约每年二次。在利物浦棉花公会，则由定期交易命价委员会厘定之。凡定期交易契约到期，而无实在棉花之交割者，解决之道，莫不取此为本焉。

定期交易之月份

定期棉花交易之月期，各国不同。在美国一年十二月皆可交易，交割时则于贸易成交时所指定之月内，先五日由卖者通告之，例如一卖者欲以其五月份之定期棉花，于五月七日实行交割，则必于五月二日通知买者，一月中第一通知日，大都由交易所委员会规定之。英国贸易月份，可有十二个月十三个月不等，例如一九二九年九月成立之贸易，可延期至一九三〇年九月清交，但无论何月交割，卖者必先期通知买者，买者于十日之内，必须实行交割。印度定期棉花交易之契约有五类，其中白洛区、阿美拉及彭高三类现仍采用，对于三种贸易，其月份亦有限制，大抵白洛区交割月份为四月及五月与七月及八月，阿美拉及彭高为十二月及正月、三月、五月以至于七月。华商纱布交易所棉花及棉纱之定期贸易，其期限不得逾六个月，每月之交割则于其月之第二十五日行之。

证据金及经纪人佣金

定期棉花交易之卖买,必付证据金。但其为数之大小,及行使之松严,则各处市场因时因地而不同。在美国此证据金又分为二类,即本证据金及追加证据金。本证据金现定为每包棉花金洋伍元,纯为交易所向经纪人索取,由纽约棉花交易清算所代为收集,但实际上此数极不一定,每包可由三元至二十一元不等,悉视当时市场情形为转移。本证据金外,尚有追加证据金,在市价变动剧烈时,恒以此为差损之弥补。此二种证据金,每日皆由纽约棉花交易清算所清算之。英国及印度交易所,则全无证据金,凡市价与契约订定之价格,其相差之数,则由棉花公会之清算所为之解决,又非每日必行,大都一星期或二星期一行之。其于利物浦棉花公会,美棉定期交易之契约遇兹事发生时,则每周一解决之。即言每周之末,凡美棉定期契约所定价格,因受市价影响而与原有约价发生差异时,则由棉业银行,(在该所清算所监督之下)于收支往来帐目项下了结之。此种每周解决之举,尚须付偿利息。盖非如此,定期契约即失却法律上之根据也。印度之定期契约,半月解决一次,与英国同。其解决价差之所,为棉业银行,即印度帝国银行,解决时亦须偿付利息。在中国交易所证据金之设,较在外国者为重要,盖华商纱布交易所,为一谋利机关。凡经纪人处置失当,遭蒙巨大损失,皆须交易所负责。该所经纪人之证据金有四,其根本证据金及追加证据金二种,与美国交易所者相同,无庸赘述。在此二种之外,尚有特别证据金及预缴证据金二种,特别证据金在买卖两方之经纪人，皆须缴纳，以防市场之特殊变动，因而有所补偿。预缴证据金在买卖契约尚未订立以前，即须缴纳，以为买卖两方经纪人违约营私及投机蒙损加量之担保。此四类证据金（根本、追加、特别、预缴）均可不必以现款及支票缴付，有价证券亦可代替。此类办法为外国所无，其契约之了结，及保证金之缴纳每日皆由交易所会计部司理之，其制一如美国清算所中之情形也。

华商纱布交易所通行之佣金制，与外国交易所迥然不同，其佣金于交易所及经纪人两方，皆得收受，在外国交易所，则收受佣金者，只为经纪人，交易所无与焉。该所棉花定期交易之佣金，为每包十二两，棉纱每包二十五两，以佣金所得四分之一，归交易所，其于美英及印度之交易所，会员间交易之佣金额，辄当会员与非会员间交易之佣金之半数，在纽约棉花交易所中，会员间交易之佣金，约当契约价值百分之八分之一，即千分之一.二五，而会员与非会员间交易之佣金，须百分之四分之一；在利物浦或东印度棉花公会中之佣金则倍之，会员间交易之佣金，约当契约价值百分之四分之一，会员及非会员间交易之佣金，则为百分之二分之一也。

屯买棉花之事

严格言之，生棉屯买之事甚难。因棉花种植广袤，屯买之事，实非一人或少数人财力所能及。虽然，小规模之屯买及操纵之事仍日有所见，尤以纽约棉花交易所为最，是以防止此种操纵之法亦甚多。下列数种，即其素著成效者：

一、棉花由南方市场交割

此法规定纽约或纽阿林之定期棉花交易，预定南方市场为交割棉花之地。纽约纯为一定期棉花交易之市场,并无现期棉花之买卖,故采行此制。一方面可以扩大纽约定期交易之市场,一方面更可防止因缺乏交割之现货,而致屯买之弊也。此种由南方交割棉花之计划,即由一九二〇年屯贴棉花之役而产生。此法产生后,赞成者与反对者,议论纷纭,至最近始完全成立焉。

二、价格限制

此法规定无论何日遇有市价涨落情绪发生,标准米特林棉花每磅之价格,不得超过或低于前日结算价目二分,更不能超过当日贸易最高价格二分,或低于最低价格二分。

欲知此法来源,必追溯大战时之情景。当一九一七年二月,德国宣告无限制使用潜水艇作战之时,交易所棉价,即由每磅一角七分半,降至一角二分。虽棉商中因此而倒闭者甚少,但大半各蒙亏损。据交易所中老于经纪故事者云,此种损失,极不自然,且可不必有者。观于棉价在一小时内,即行恢复而更显。为稳固将来棉价计,乃创是法。俾与棉花贸易一绝好机会,不待价落即可收缩也。

三、定期贸易量之限制

此法现为清算所法规之一。规定交易所中,每人每月定期棉花贸易之清算,不得超过四十万包云。

一九一四年最足纪念之事件

一九一四年欧战爆发之际,纽约棉花交易所,颇有倒闭之恐慌。此时一切尚未执行交割之契约,为交易所亟待解决之问题。

该所数经讨论,结果责成委员会处置此项因大战而搁浅之棉花。其救济方法即以此搁浅棉花[①]已在南方卖价跌至七分一磅者,每磅由委员会负责津贴二分出售,为弥补亏损计,乃举债金洋二百万元,以所中人员贸易所获几成归公,为此债务之担保,三四年后,此债始得偿清。其他会员在海外亦有棉花贸易,但未得委员会认可为"搁浅棉花"者,所蒙损失尤巨也。

[①] 搁浅棉花(distressed cotton)之真义,可举下例以明之。

某商人于五月中卖出七月份定期棉花若干与某敌国工厂,如云俄国。同时该商人手中并无现货,以备届时交割之用,故复在交易所内购进七月份定期棉花若干。其所以不至七月始购现期棉花以备交割者,诚恐五月至七月之间因棉价暴涨而遭损失也。七月既至,该商人对于买约交割之棉花,既须照例接受。然以战事交通封锁之故,因执行买约所得之棉花,遂不能运往俄国工厂。如是则此项棉花成为搁浅棉花焉。

我国工厂法与纱厂业之关系

一、工厂法之历史

工厂法产生之主要目的,在取缔工厂内工人之工作情形,为近代工业主义发达之副产品。盖自十八世纪中叶以降,产业革命暴发,工厂工业兴起,手艺工业尽被摧毁,手艺工人无以为生,故不得不群入工厂寻觅工作,以求温饱,然工厂主人徒知谋利,对于工人之康健、福利及工作情形概不过问,是故工人工作环境恶劣,处境无异地狱,流弊所至遗害匪浅,社会有识之士起而大声疾呼,政府以职责所在碍难缄默,于是实地调查,颁布法规,改善工人之工作情形,此工厂法之所由产生也。英国工业发达最早,故百余年前(一八〇二)即颁有工厂法规。嗣后影响所及,凡工业占有重要地位之国家无不有工厂法之颁布,即以农业为中心之国家如苏俄、印度,亦各有其工厂法。日本之工厂法,系起草于明治十四年(一八八一),其间经调查、讨论达三十年之久,始于明治四十四年(一九一一)正式颁布,于大正五年(一九一六)施行,大正十二年(一九二三)修正一次,昭和四年(一九二九)复行修正。我国工厂法规,最早者为民国十二年三月二十九日（一九二三）北京政府农商部以部令颁布之《暂行工厂通则》二十八条，该通则虽未经国会通过，仅以部令发表，不得称为国家法律，但实为我国工厂法规之嚆矢。该通则颁布后，以政局变动迄未施行，复以内战频仍，执政者无暇及此，全国劳工立法之工作由是亦音息沉寂。民国十七年北伐告成，国民政府鼎都南京，鉴于劳工问题日形繁杂，乃制定《工厂法》，于民国十八年十二月三十日正式颁布，此法与立法院所颁布之其他法令相同，自起草至颁布，为时不过一年，神速敏捷，开各国工厂法规制定之空前纪录。《工厂法施行条例》，亦于民国十九年十二月十六日颁布，并定于民国二十年二月一日施行，碍于实业界之反对，施行期展缓六个月，改于同年八月一日施行。《工厂检查法》，于民国二十年一月三十一日颁布，并定于同年十月一日施行。政府为养成工厂检查人材起见，特在上海设立工厂检查人员养成所，从事于人材之训练，自六月至八月为第一期，训练人员二十四名，自十月至十二月为第二期，训练人员三十七名，同时并特向日内瓦之国际劳工局聘请专家二人，一名为彭恩先生（C. Pone），一为安德生女士（Dame A. Anderson）来华，逗留三月之久，计划设立检查制度事宜。《工厂登记法》亦于民国二十年十二月十八日公布，虽纷扰一时，准备一切，然对工厂法实施方面毫无所成。民国二十年八月一日，本为规定之实施日，前已言及，惟至时以种种原因施行未果，民国二十年九·一八辽宁事变发生，同年十一月八日津变又起，继之则有民国二十一年一·二八淞沪之战，及本年春季日兵侵扰华北之役，政府当局谋国不暇，无暇顾及工厂法规之实施，是以直至今日，该法规仍堆积案头，迄未施行也。不特此也，在前所规定之实施期（民国二十年八月一日）未至之前，已将该法规第三章第十三条"女工不得在午后十时至翌晨六时之时间内工作"一条准以二年为实施预备时期，然时至今日，实施预备之期已过，而全部法规仍未见诸实施也，更有进者，本年年初，政府自动公布修正的《工厂法》及《工厂法实施条例》，全法共计七十七条，而修正者竟达二十条左右，其主要者则为（一）关于延长工作时间之修正，每月延长工作之总时间由三十六小时增至四十六小时，依民国十八年所颁布之工厂法，则厂主可在此三十六小时内，延长工人之工作时间由八小时至十小时，以至十二小时，然依修正之工厂法，则厂主如须延长工作时间至十二小时时，须取得工会之同意（第十条）。（二）童工不得工作之夜工时间已由十一小时缩为十小时，盖修正工厂法已将童工午后不得工作之时间，由七时改为八时矣（第十二条）。（三）修正法已将原法第三条工厂应备工人名册登记并呈报项内工人之"技能品行"及"工作效率"改为"工人体格"，比较原法似较妥当。（四）第三十七条关于女工分娩前后停止工作八星期，并照给工资一节，原法对女工一律看待，无何限制，修正法则规定，须"入厂工作六个月以上者，假期内工资照给，不足六个月者减半发给"，以上为修正法之重要者，其他则以篇幅有限，恕不一一提及。

二、工厂法与纱厂之关系

按《工厂法》第一条之规定，该法适用于"凡用发动机之工厂，平时雇用工人在三十人以上者"，依据实业部之统计（《国际劳工消息》二卷六期五页），全国工人合乎《工厂法》第一条之规定者只四十万人，按民国二十二年之统计全国纱厂所雇用之工人，合计之约为二十五万八千人，是则适合实施工厂法之工人中，有八分之五系被雇于纱厂，故纱厂业者对于工厂法深加注意，而工厂法之实施，若非得纱厂之合作，恐亦非易易，是则工厂法与纱厂之关系及其施行后之影响，为当前之重大问题。迩来市况不振，商业萧条，纱厂又危机四伏，处于风雨飘摇之中，此问题之探讨，此时尤为重要。

　　工厂法规以适合国情为第一要务，反观我国之工厂法，则大谬不然，以立法论可谓尽善尽美矣，然与我国现在之工业实况毫不相关，立法既不以国内工业之实况为依归，则碍难实施，只可堆积案头，以壮观瞻耳。工厂法内之条例，如对童工女工不作夜工之规定，工作时间八小时之原则，男女工人十六岁以下为童工，及"工人每七日中应有一日之休息作为例假"，并工人以服务年限之长短，每年可有七日至三十日之特别休假，并休假期内照给工资各节，一旦实施，非但使摇摇欲坠之工业增加负担，且足使雇用童工女工之工业（如纱厂丝厂）一部或全部停工。政府制定工厂法时，对于雇有适合该法管理下工人总数八分之五之纱厂业，毫未顾及，无庸讳言。东西情形迥异，立法须因地制宜，欧美纱厂业之工人工作为一班制，昼作夜停，而我国则系两班制，昼夜不息，且在此两般制度之下，女工占数最多，根据民国十九年实业部举办之九省工人生活调查之结果，则可知纱厂工人二〇六，五三二名中，女工占一四三，七六七名，当总数百分之七十，工作为两班制，纱厂工人中以女工为数最多，此二点足可称为我国纱厂业之特征，而制定工厂法时，当局者对此二点概未注意，试一观禁止女工夜工之规定，即可知余言之不误矣。

三、取消女士夜工为工厂法不能实施于纱厂之主因

依修正《工厂法》第八条之规定，"成年工人每日实在工作时间以八小时为原则"，虽因种种情形，得延长工作时间至十小时或十二小时，而所延长之总时间，每月不得超过四十六小时。依第十五条之规定，工人每七日中应有一日之休息，则每月之实在之工作日当为二十六天，以二十六实在工作日除每月延长工作之总时间四十六小时，则每日之延长工作时间不得超过一点三刻，换言之，每日之实在工作时间可由八小时增至九小时三刻。依第十四条"凡工人继续工作五小时至少应有半小时休息"之规定，则工人每日之工作时间名义上当为十又四分之一小时。

纱厂中女工占十分之七，前已言及，故欲实施第十三条"女工不得在午后十时至翌晨六时之时间内工作"之规定，而同时工作仍采每班十小时零一刻之两班制，则非解雇夜班之女工而代以男工不可，纱厂若仍雇用女工，而同时又不与工厂法相抵触，则惟有（一）采取日班制，获得工会之同意，延长工作时间，每日实在工作时间为九小时又三刻，加上半小时之休息，则每日之工作时间，当在十又四分之一小时，或（二）采取日夜班制，每班八小时，除去半小时之休息时间，则实在之工作时间当为七小时又半。东亚各国之纱厂，悉采两班制，而以日本为尤然，故禁止女工夜工之结果，必使采行两班制之中国纱厂尽行解雇夜班之女工而以男工代之，此实一严重问题。政府有鉴于此，乃于民国二十年八月七日，以实业部之命令，准将关于禁止女工夜工一条，以二年为实施预备时期，

换言之,即将《工厂法》第十三条之实施期由民国二十年八月一日起,展缓二年,然至时下止,工厂法何日施行,仍遥遥无期也。

试问今日我国纱厂业,对于修正《工厂法》第十三条之规定,应持何态度。自人道言之,禁止女工夜工为当然之事,不容置喙,西欧工业发达之国早已禁止女工夜工,以英国论,于一八四四年即已禁止女工夜工,然我国之工业尚在幼稚时期,骤行禁止女工夜工未免失之过早,日本工业发展之程度远过吾国,而以纱厂业为尤然,但日本之禁止女工夜工,按步渐进,非禁止于一旦也。日本之工厂法系于明治四十四年(一九一一)颁布,禁止女工夜工一条亦并列入,但规定此条须于十五年后(一九二六)始可实施,十五年期满重行展缓三年,直至昭和四年(一九二九)禁止女工夜工之法令始得正式施行。此次之得以施行,非由政府之强迫,乃环境使然也,盖一九二九年,日本之纱厂业日趋衰落,日本纱厂联合会于是决议全体减工百分之十,依裴尔斯先生(Mr. Pearse)之调查,一九二九年日本纱厂之工作时间如下(见 Pearse, *Cotton Industry of Japan and China* 第一〇三页):

26 日每日工作 20 小时 = 520 小时

减工 10%　　　　　　= 52 小时

每月工作　　　　　　468 小时

自同年七月一日起,全国采用两班制,每班工作八小时又半,则纱厂一月内之工作时间为:

28 日每日工作 17 小时 = 476 小时

若以日本工厂法对于禁止女工夜工实施之速率为标准,则我国《工厂法》第十三条关于禁止女工夜工之实行须先展缓十五年,再行展缓三年,《工厂法》系民国十八年颁布,则禁止女工夜工一条,须延至民国三十六年方可实施矣。姑认为日本因工业发达,已禁止女工夜工,而我国亦有立即仿行之必要,则我国工厂法对于是项之规定,较之日本,且有过之无不及之嫌。依日本工厂法之规定,女工不得在午后十一时至翌晨五时之六小时内工作,而我国修正工厂法则规定女工不得在午后十时至翌晨六时之八小时工作,职是之故,依日本工厂法,纱厂仍可采两班制,每班为九小时,除去半小时之休息(日本工厂法规定,工人继续工作六小时以上须有半小时之休息),则实在工作时间,每班为八小时半。然依我国工厂法采用两班制,每班为八小时,除去半小时之休息,每班实在工作时间为七小时半。二者相较,竟有一小时之差矣。

简言之,若禁止女工一条实施后,则纱厂只有二途,任选其一,一为采取日班制,一为采取日夜两班制。若采取日班制,则纱厂须征得工会之同意,工作定为十小时零一刻,除去休息时间,实在工作时间为九小时零三刻。但东亚各国惯用日夜两班制,故日班制当无考虑之余地。若采取每班十时零一刻之日夜两班制,则纱厂势须召募男工以代替女工,如此则昼班在可能范围内可全用女工,午前六点上工,正午有半小时之休息,午后四点一刻下工。夜班则自午后四点一刻起,至翌晨两点半止,须全用男工。至须解雇女工之多寡,可作约略之估计。纱厂内一部分粗重之工作,女工不克胜任,非男工不可,故无论如何,昼班不能尽用女工。假定纱厂工人五分之一须为女工,则占全国纱厂工人总数百分之三十之女工须以男工代之。盖前已言及,纱厂女工占全国纱厂工人总数百分之七十,昼班改用女工则只能用百分之四十,余下之百分之三十势须以男工代之。若工厂法即行实施,而对于禁止女工夜工一条并无展缓施行之规定,则全国纱厂势须召募纱厂工人总数百分之三十男工参加夜工。根据多数纱厂以往之经验,则可知此事实现为不可能。说者谓年来吾国失业者何止亿兆,女工解雇之空位不难立即填满,此言似是实非,盖失业者虽多,其奈不适于纱厂工作何。有若干纱厂成立之初,即感工人缺乏,广事募集,所费不资。我国之工厂工业尚在幼稚时期,纪律化之工厂生活仍为多数手艺工人所厌弃,故募集工厂工人深感困难。英国工业发达最早,产业革命最盛之时,亦感有同样之困难。姑以为募来之工人甘愿入厂工作,度其纪律化之生活,然机器之运用,工作习惯之养成,技巧及敏捷之训练,又非短时期可以成功。况女工天性伶俐,手臂敏捷,管理棉纺织机器犹远胜于男工耶。总之,政府不欲实施工厂法则已,若果欲实施,则对于"禁止女工自午后十时至翌晨六时之期间工作"一条,须自工厂法实施之日起,展缓五年施行。展缓五年之目的,在使纱厂从容雇佣其所需之男工,以代替其解雇之女工。

四、工厂法实施后为纱厂业所增加之负担

若欲工厂法实施于纱厂内,则除去禁止女工夜工一条外,尚有若干点亦须加以修正,以减轻摇摇欲坠之中国纱厂之负担。据实业部之调查,十六岁下之童工只占全国纱厂工人百分之六,故童工问题对于纱厂本身较为次要,可不深论。工人实在工作时间以八小时为原则,然征得工会之同意或"因天灾事变季节之关系",得将工作时间延长至十小时零一刻,前已提及,此条若"因天灾事变"一句富有伸缩性,若能将"得工会同意"字样照民国十八年十二月三十日所颁布之原法撤消,则对于纱厂业尚无何过甚不便之处。若

能将工作时间规定为每日十小时,即无需引用"因天灾事变季节之关系"之字句,亦无需征得工会之同意(《修正工厂法》第八条)。目下华商纱厂以十二小时为一班,其间工人因疲乏过甚而贪懒,有不少时间上之虚耗。日本纱厂系采两班制,每班之工作时间名义上为九小时,实际工作为八小时半,以日本为借鉴,则我国纱厂依《修正工厂法》,采两班制,每班名义上为十小时零一刻,实际工作为九小时零三刻,自经济方面言之,亦非为不可能。工作时间自十二小时减为十小时零一刻,予工人以相当休息时间,此非但可减少工人缺席次数,且可增加工作效率。而十小时内所得之产量不减于十二时之产量,盖纱厂工人纯依机器而工作,故英人菲南(Vernon)氏根据其在美国纱厂之经验,有言曰:"兹得一结论,即每周工作逾六十小时,其出产之总量,亦未必多于六十小时出产之总合也。"(*Fatigue and Efficiency*,1921,第七一页)

《工厂法》第十五、六、七三条,足使纱厂增加重大负担,该三条规定下列之特别休假、放假及例假期内,厂方须照给工资,每七日中应有一日休息为例假,凡政府法令所规定应放之纪念日均应给假休息,工人按其在厂继续工作年限之长短,每年有七日至三十日之特别休假。每七日中应有一日休息,则每年例假日为五十二天,政府所规定之放假日有八,加上工人七日至三十日之特别休假,则工人一名每年至少可有六十七日之休假,最多者可有九十日之休假,姑以工人每日之工资为国币五角,每厂平均有工人两千人,合而计之,则一厂每年经济上之负担即为由六七,〇〇〇元至九〇,〇〇〇元。按时下纱厂惯例,厂方只对第十六条所规定之放假日照给工资,第十五条所规定之五十二天例假,多数给假而不给工资,第十七条所规定之特别休假日,则向无此例。年来世界经济凋蔽,国内战事频仍,凡业纱厂者之外受舶来品倾销之压迫,内感组织管理之不良,危机四伏,亏累不堪,挣扎于呻咽中而不全部停歇者,盖有其不得已之苦衷在,若《工厂法》第十五及十七二条遽行实施,纱厂之负担更行加重,则纱厂之前途如何,不难臆测。以愚见所及,政府若能顾及当前之事实与困难,则必不遽行实施该二条,或竟将该二条无期展缓也。

其他足以增加厂方之负担者为第六章工作契约之终止、第七章工人福利、第八章工厂安全与卫生设备,及第九章工人津贴及抚恤。关于工作契约之终止,该章规定"凡无定期之契约,如工厂欲终止契约者,应于时前预告工人,其预告之时",依在厂工作期限之长短,由十日至三十日不等(《工厂法》第二十七条)。"工人于接到工作契约终止预告后,为另谋工作,得于工作时请假出外,但每星期不得过二日之工作时间,请假期内,工资照给"(第二十八条)。不特此也,"……预告终止契约者,除给工人以应得工资外,并须给以……预告时间工资之半数,不依第二十七条之规定而即时终止契约者,须照给工人以该条所定预告期间之工资"(第二十九条)。姑以工人每日之工资为五角计,厂方因实行工作契约终止之预告而所受之损失如下列:

预告期	工人请假应付工资日数	最低(元)	最高(元)
10 日	2 6/7 日	1.43	—
30 日	8 4/7 日	—	4.30
10 日	厂方付给预告期工资半数	2.50	—
30 日	厂方付给预告期工资全数	—	13.00
	合计	3.93	17.30

据此可知厂方每终止工人一名之工作契约,其损失最低为

三.九三元,最高为一七.三〇元,平均每一纱厂有二千工人,设其每年解雇之工人占全厂百分之二十,则每年终止工人工作契约之损失至少为一,五七二元,多则可至七,七二〇元。此种损失与第十五及第十七条施行后之损失相较,虽为较少,然若一年之内解雇工人之数目增加,则厂方终止契约而受损失为数亦必可观。但为保护工人、防止工厂任意解雇工人起见,此章实有实施之价值与必要。以愚见所及,鉴于纱厂之当前困难,则此章之实施,亦需有三年至五年之预备期间。

"工人福利"、"工厂安全与卫生设备"及"工人津贴及抚恤"各章,除数点外,对劳资二方皆为公允。关于"工人福利"之规定,其所包括者为:厂方对于童工及学徒应使每星期至少受十小时之补习教育,并负担其费用之全部,对于其他失学工人,亦当酌量补助其教育(第三十六条)。女工分娩前后应停止工作共八星期,其入厂六个月以上者假期内工资照给,不足六个月者减半发给(第三十七条)。厂方协助工人举办工人储蓄及合作社等事宜(第三十八条)。及厂方建筑工人住宅,并提倡工人正当娱乐(第三十九条)等,非但可改善工人之生活,且可增加工厂之产量,盖工人生活改善后,体格强健,精神充足,则工作效率必高;工作效率高,则出产必多,此不待智者而知也。对于惠工事业,在华日商纱厂仿效其本国内纱厂成例,多所建树,远为华商纱厂所不及,其结果,日商纱厂之工人,自效率等方面言之,较优于华厂工人者实多。是故无论为厂方谋利计,或为人道计,华商纱厂对于惠工事业,实有急起直追之必要。

关于"工厂安全"之规定,其所包括者为:工厂应有工人身体上、工厂建筑上、机器装置、及预防火灾水患之安全设备(第四十一条);工厂对于工人应为预防灾变之训练(第四十三条);关于"卫生设备"之规定,其所包括者为工厂应为空气流通、饮料清洁、盥洗所厕所、光线,及防卫生毒质等设备(第四十二条)。无论自经济、自人道立场观之,以上种种皆为工厂内所不可缺少者。故此章宜即施行。然在施行之前,政府宜从速训练工厂检查专门人材,以备辅佐政府实施工厂法也。

关于"工人津贴及抚恤"之规定,第四十五条"……工人因执行职务而致伤病或死亡者,工厂应给与医药补助费及抚恤费……"原则上言之,此条甚为公允,但实际上观之,施行时恐感困难。陈达氏在其"我国工厂法的施行问题"一文内主张将此条暂缓施行(见《国际劳工消息》第二卷第五期),颇为有识之见,盖疾病之染患由于执行职务有时殊难区分。至于因执行职务而致伤及确由执行职务而致工业疾病(industrial disease)并经医生证明者,则医药补助费或残费津贴或死亡抚恤费之给与,宜立即施行,毫无置喙之余地。时下纱厂给与工人因执行职务而致伤以抚恤者,为数亦多。

五、领事裁判权为实施工厂法之最大障碍

立法贵公允,实施须普遍,同在一国之工厂,法之所及须无差别之分,主权完整之国无此问题,然我国即情形迥异。月来甚嚣尘上之上海租界内工厂检查权问题,即为我国工厂法实施之当前难关。此事甚为简单,即上海公共租界之工部局,反对上海市政府社会局检查租界内之工厂,同时自身欲取得租界内之工厂检查权,于是召集纳税西人特别会,修正《洋泾浜章程附则》第三十四条。此

问题既发生于上海公共租界，难免不发生于上海之法租界及其他各工厂城市之租界，难关重重，殊为复杂。若此问题不能圆满解决，则工厂法碍难施行于租界内之华厂，盖同一纱厂以处地之不同而有轩轾之分，殊失公平之道。姑以上海之纱厂论，上海共有华商纱厂二十八厂（民国二十二年《中国纱厂一览表》）。位于租界内者达二十三厂，以锭子论占有上海华商纱厂所有锭子百分之八九强（共有锭子九六八，三八〇），以工人论，占有上海华商纱厂工人数百分之八十二强（共有工人五四，五四一名），若工厂法不能施及租界内之华商纱厂，而只施及于租界外之华商纱厂，则非但失去公允之道，吾人且敢断言工厂法必不能实施。退一步言之，姑以为此次上海公共租界工厂检查权问题得以圆满解决，而其他各租界当局亦皆肯将租界内华厂检查权奉还我政府，而工厂法仍难实施，盖问题之最棘手者，则为享有领事裁判权之外人工厂。彼等工厂有领事裁判权为其护符，可不准中国行政官吏入厂检查，工厂法无从实施。据本年度《中国纱厂一览表》所载，全国共有纱厂一三三厂，其中外商四十四厂（日厂四十一、英厂三），华厂八十九。以锭子论，外商四十四厂共有锭子二，二四六，六四四，占中国纱厂所有锭子百分之四五弱。以工人论，外商四十四厂共有工人七六，八三七名，占中国纱厂所有工人百分之三十弱，工厂法之施行首要问题乃在施行上法律之划一，最低限度亦须有事实上之划一。若外厂不肯就范，则全国无划一之法律，全国工人不能受同等之保护，全国厂主不能受同样之负担，立法公平之原则何在？若外厂不遵我之法令，显然处于优越地位，华厂势难与之相竞争，而劳工待遇亦难期其平等。同处一国之工商业，不能有异样之待遇，工人有同为政府之人民，不能因受雇于外厂而失去法律之保护。故先决问题为领事裁判权之撤消。领事裁判权有条约之根据,要求其全部撤消恐非短时期所能办,故政府不欲实施工厂法则已,若果欲实施,则惟与各关系国进行交涉,务使其对领事裁判权让步,俾促成工厂法施行上之划一也。

国民经济建设之途径

随世界经济之大恐慌，各国无不力图经济之复兴，而复兴之途径，又皆自经济统制入手。经济统制之背景，实可溯至世界大战以前，其时放任经济破绽毕露，已生统制经济之反动。迨大战发生，为适应军事之需要，各国多树立国家经济，于是统制经济得奠初基。当一九三一年以还世界经济恐慌爆发日益深刻，政治上由民治趋独裁，由分权趋集权，统制经济遂更风靡一时，大有席卷世界之势矣！其著者如苏俄在史丹林治下之两次五年计划。德国在希特拉治下之两次四年计划。意大利在墨索里尼治下之以职业为单位组成各种劳方或资方之联合以求劳资合作而促进"联合国家"之实现。美国在罗斯福治下之"新政"。综上所述，莫不以统制经济而谋经济之复兴者也。至展望将来，则以国际间政治经济之矛盾日深，统制经济将更普遍与强化似可断言。

　　我国以积弱之余，处国际竞争日烈之秋，极须图所自树。其道当首推经济建设，至应取之途径，则外审大势，内察国情，仍不能不从统制经济入手。按我国之有系统的经济建设计划，始自孙中山先生之学说及著述。国民党执政以来，因国共分裂，军兴，采取三分军事七分政治之策略，经济建设缘以策进，交通建设尤具成效。民国二十年因东北之沦丧，国人于充实国力已有一致之觉悟，而民二十至二十一年之江淮大水灾损失不赀，于经济建设之刺激尤厉。

民国二十四年之法币政策既为经济统制中之一着,亦所以增加经济统制之便利。近来蒋介石先生于精神建设倡新生活运动,于物质建设倡国民经济建设运动,复成立国民经济建设运动委员会,以为计划策进之基础,今后行见经济建设得踏进大规模之实行阶段,吾人愿于此时略陈一己之见,藉供当局之参考焉!

吾国以经济性质之特殊,矛盾现象几于到处皆然。故于经济建设首重统制,事业进行须别缓急。具体言之,其范围与程序有如左述:

(一)交通 经济事业之首须加统制者,厥为交通。交通为一国之命脉,必交通发展,其他经济事业始能随而活跃。我国交通素极闭塞,即仅有之交通事业中,尚有外资经营者厕杂其间,其余国资经营之一部分,亦缺乏经营之系统与控制。论航运,则多属于外人经营,英日与我国吨位相等,而我国航运机关,复乏效率,航运大权,逐渐旁落。铁路虽多属国营,但经营之无系统实有逾于航运。因我国铁路多系借用外资建筑,借款国别不同,技术管理各异,各省囿于地方观念,亦多各行其政。以路轨言,宽狭有别,轻重不一,平时联运已有阻碍,军事运输更易积运。公路兴修之始,系工厂之副产品,军兴公路修筑顿盛,然亦只为军事上之便利,经济上之价值殊堪怀疑。以上系就三种主要交通工具之本身而言。外此,铁路与公路、铁路与航运、公路与航运间之竞争亦随时随地可以发现。近来当局于交通之建设,颇著成绩,惟如何作整个的调整,则尤为当前之急务也。

(二)农业 农业建设,已有之成绩,消极方面如田赋之整理及水旱灾之防治,积极方面如农作物之改良推广与合作组织之普及等。我国田赋负担之不均及田赋附加之苛重,久为世所诟病。

民二十三全国财政会议决议田赋附加不得超过正税,在正税较轻地域,正税附加合计不得超过地价百分之一,并由财政部通令全国不准巧立名目新征田赋附加,各省已多遵行。至田赋之整理,主要问题在平均负担,治标则举办土地陈报,以铲除有田无粮及有粮无田之积弊;治本则举办土地测量土地登记,以为实施地价税之张本。水旱灾防治之工作,旱灾如筑渠及掘井,前者以西北省区之筑渠工程为著,后者则以晋冀二省为多;水灾防治如疏浚筑堤及造林,前者主管机关有全国经济委员会水利处及南北各水利机关,后者则实业部有林垦署。农作物之改良及推广以选种工作为主,其主持机关如中央农业实验所、全国经济委员会、各大学农学院等,作物种类重要者如棉、麦、稻、高粱、大豆、玉米等等。合作组织本发轫于华洋义赈会之提倡,国民政府成立后,刊为民众运动之一,近复在实业部设合作司专司其事。故合作社进展颇速,迄二十四年底已有社数计二万六千余社,社员百万人。惜品质未能并进,而须加以改善也。

（三）工业　工业统制可分重工业与轻工业二端。前者历次计划甚多,如中山先生之建国方略、孙科之修正计划、民二十年国民大会之六年计划及国联十年计划、孔祥熙之实业计划及陈公博之四年计划。其已见诸实施者,则在中央,机械厂已由京迁沪开工,酒精厂在沪由侨商承办开工,硫酸亚厂由官商合办即将完成,钢铁及造纸二厂亦在筹划中。各省之实业建设则当推广东之三年计划及山西之西北实业公司。次则轻工业之复兴:棉业,则全国经济委员会棉业统制委员会有育殖推广棉种,取缔棉花掺水掺杂及组织棉运合作等之改良原棉产销工作,及促进制造技术之改善等等。丝业,则全国经济委员会蚕丝改良委员会有改良蚕桑及资助江浙丝厂联合产销之工作；各省当局，如苏浙皖粤鲁等省均有蚕丝改良厂之设立，浙粤等省又有蚕丝统制委员会之设立。惟工业统制之大规模的推进则尚有待也。

（四）贸易　我国对外贸易向处不利地位，以贸易差额言，则自一八六四迄今七十余年中其为出超者仅有六年，其余各年皆为入超，且额数与年俱进，近来入超虽减，但系受走私之影响及国民购买力衰退之结果，固不能视为佳象。虽然，若入超内容系机械与生产品之类，则为农业国家步入工业化应有之途径，犹可说也，但一考实际，则入口主要者为消费品，如匹头、粮食、糖、燃料等，而生产品如钢铁、机械等反居其次。输出亦仍以原料品为主。矛盾之象一至于此。此外，进出口贸易之经营多操诸洋行之手，海洋运输工具，亦须借重外人。故贸易之统制，实刻不容缓，已往之成绩，输入方面则自民十八恢复关税自主后，税率已屡经提高。民廿四年十一月新货币政策实行对外汇价贬低，亦有促进出口阻抑进口之效，输出方面，如商品检验局之设立，粮食及白银之禁止出口，出口关税已减低或免除，胥为其重要者。

（五）金融统制　我国金融事业，素称紊乱，以言金融组织，则大部势力操诸外人之手，国人经营者步调不一，势力薄弱，反惟外人之马首是瞻。以言流通货币则钞票发行，并不统一；中心统制，亦不严密，一遇市面缓急，货币流通数额不但不能调剂，反成推波助澜之势。故金融事业之急须统制自不待言，就以往之努力观之，金融组织方面，中央银行之地位日固，外商银行之势力亦因国人金融业者之团结日坚，而渐趋削减。流通货币方面，民国十八年甘末尔币制顾问来华，草成《中国逐渐采行金本位草案》，为民国十九年海关征金之张本，民国二十二年废两改元，民二十三年征收白银出口平衡税,凡此皆为货币改革之阶梯而自征收白银出口平衡税后,我国币制本质且肇转变之机。迨二十四年冬新货币政策实行,停止银洋之运用,而以中中交三行钞票为法币,不啻脱离银本位而入于管理通货制。同时中央银行之地位亦因新货币政策之实行而奠定其为银行之实质的地位,金融统制之机构已大体完成。惟如何谋中央银行之从速改组为中央准备银行,及各省银行钞票与内地私票之取缔,则有待于进一步之努力也。

（六）财政　我国财政制度之不健全,可由数方面证之:如预算制度之未能确立,租税制度之不合理,以及内债种类之多,数额之大,其著者也。国家财政之健否有关政府之行政及人民之负担。就已往整理成绩观之,关于预算制度,民国十九年主计处成立后,预算之编制由主计处独任其责,预算制度可谓已经确立。二十年后有中央统一预算制度之颁行,以谋改善统一各政府机关之预算制度。至于租税制度,则中央主要税收厥为关盐统三税,关税于十八年自主,关员改用华人,税收亦由外商银行改存中央银行,民十九进口税改征海关金单位,民二十二出口税亦改征国币。而沿岸贸易税、通过税,及常关税等亦相继废除。盐税则各省已皆受中央之统制,新盐法亦定分区实行。统税之设,系代替不合理之厘金,出厂征税,一征而后,自由转运,不得再征。此指现有税收之整理,但此胥为间接税,欲求租税之合理化,尚有待于直接税之设立。现所得税已经开征,遗产税亦在进行筹划中矣！内债之整理,第一次在民国二十一年,内容只延本减息以减财政之负担而已,第二次民国二十五年,以五种统一公债换回数额不同期限不同利率不同之三十余种旧公债。利息一率六厘,与旧有公债利率相同,惟偿本期限则延长矣。

以上所述，为我国经济急须统制之要项及已有之建设成绩。虽然，吾人细察国内之经济环境仍甚恶劣，其未受政府统制者姑置勿论，即已受政府统制者，成绩亦少，至全国经济之整个的统制计划，尚付阙如。此概因我国经济统制先决条件之尚未完备也。统制经济之先决条件有三，其一则恃强有力之政府，为统制经济之设计与司令机关，万一设计与司令机关不能呼应，则统制经济之效实微。一则为充分之技术人才，一则为充裕之建设经费，此理固至显，无待赘述，然事实非此先决条件皆已具备，实难求经济统制之奏功。今者，全国统一完成，技术人才之训练，已引起学术机关之注意，且已有为高级人才之训练者。建设经费则客岁有三万四千万元复兴公债之发行及近传中英信用贷款之成立。本年度预算，经费之分配，且特注意重经济之建设。先决条件业已大备，经济统制，似已无问题矣，然政治统一尚不彻底，人才训练亦未普遍，建设经费更嫌不足。此三者既未能彻底解决，则所谓经济建设自难图全功。国难未已之际，国人正高唱国民经济之建设，吾人愿作简截之论曰：经济建设之途径必须由经济统制入手，而欲经济统制之成功，必先彻底具备先决之条件。

工业经济与国货

一

人类经济活动之演进，系由简单而渐趋复杂，由自给而转为交换。当产业革命之初期，生产事业，因技术之跃进与交通之改良，遂能按地理分工之原则，将组织规模，日加扩大，致一地之产品，不仅遍销全国，且能冲破国境，而充斥全球。英国为产业革命发源地，其工业产品因价廉物美，遂渐执世界商场之牛耳。在此期内，西欧各国盛倡自由贸易，不论国货外货，每以价格之高下，为采购之标准。至外货压倒国货后，对于本国经济与政治方面所发生之影响，则初未予计及也。

及至进入十九世纪产业发达之第二期，德美俄日等国均发生产业革命，鉴于英国工业品之畅销，将予本国新兴工业以不利之竞争，遂先后采行保护关税，一方面阻碍外货之进口，一方面促进国货之生产。至是"国货"一词，除经济意义外，又具有政治意义，与战后德意志所提倡之"奥泰基"（Autarchy）运动，以求经济自足自给为目的者，有类似之色彩焉。

我国经济落后，新工业之兴起，虽已九十余年，然以内忧外患之频仍，成绩不甚显著。因之现代工业用品，类多仰给国外，其在国内生产之工业品如棉纺织品，每多为外侨设立之工厂所供给。一九零五年美国禁止华侨进口，引起我国首次抵制外货运动。一九一五年日本乘欧战方酣，向我提出"二十一条"，引起二次抵制外货运动。此后，抵制外货运动——如一九一九年之对日及一九二五年之对英——时有发生。追随抵货运动之后，我国民为谋积极致富图强，遂有"国货"运动之勃兴。此之所谓"国货"，又多一层含义：不仅指提倡我国生产之货品，更进而专指我国生产工业品。良以我国以农立国，农产品尚能自给，进口商品，虽不无农产品等，然究以工业品为大宗，故国货运动，自应以本国工业所生产之货品为提倡之对象也。是故所谓提倡国货，探本溯源，即为提倡我国工业品之制造与推销。而提倡国货之根本要图，即为国家工业经济之稳定的树立。今值《国货与实业》月刊创刊之盛，仅抒关于建设工业经济之意见数端。不谈治标，专言治本，或为热心国货运动前途者所乐观也。

二

工业经济之建树，分资金之筹集，厂基、房屋、机器、原料及服务之获得，成品之制造，及成品之销售四步骤。工业资金分固定资金及流动资金二种，前者如厂基、房屋及机器等，后者如原料及半成品。筹集资金之方法，按上述用途之不同而互异。固定资金，多采用公司股票或公债方式而筹得。而原料之购置与劳工及其他服务如管理与技术人才，水电与保险等之获得，则恒取给于银行贷款及卖主放款。前者为长期放款,属投资银行之范围,后者为短期放款,属商业银行之范围。我国工业落后,从事于工业者,对工商两业恒多不分轩轾,只求近益,不谋远利,故工业金融沦为商业金融之附庸,触目皆是之商业银行,虽有游资充斥之虞,然投资银行,则初未见有成立者。此于工业建设之进展,阻碍实多,诚极宜早日设法予以纠正者也。

厂基、房屋、机器、原料及服务之获得,为工业建设之第二步骤。厂基之经济觅得,亦即工业之地域的合理分布,其先决条件甚多,如交通便利,劳力、原料与水电供给,市场距离,地价高低,租税轻重等皆是。西南资源,素称丰富,但以交通闭塞,致工业发展有限。西南乏棉,故棉纺织业不发达;抗战以来,棉纺织业自东南及华中移向西南,原棉受封锁而不克内输外,当以棉产不足为主因。水电对于工业之重要,不亚于交通与原料。抗战以来,敌人不惜屡次以水电厂为轰炸之目标者,其故不外此。工业生产,必规模宏大,始能获利,故工业建设,恒荟萃于人口稠密及交通便利之区。西南目前之各工业中心,即莫不受惠于上述数因之有利的存在也。

厂基、房屋、机器之获得,取给于固定资金,原料与劳力之获得,则取给于流动资金。固定资金与流动资金之比例,各业不一。此种比例之决定,为从事工业者所不可忽视。如第一次欧战后,我国因欧战而赢利独厚之纱厂,莫不因此种比例措置之不当,固定资金与流动资金成四与一之畸形比例,而竟告失败,可为前车之鉴。

厂基、房屋、机器、原料与服务之获得,应以减低成本至最低限度为原则。如由甲工程师负责设计及修建之工厂,因配置合理,能将生产效率提高至预期标准如百分之百,而由乙工程师负责设计及修建之工厂,因配置之不合理,致其生产效率,仅及百分之八十,则予甲以每年万元之待遇不为高,予乙以每年五千元之待遇不为低。他如机器虽贵而效用大,原料虽昂而品质高,工价虽涨而成绩优,均与经济原则不相背驰,而为从事工业者所必守之原则也。

成品之制造,为工业建设之第三步骤。成品制造问题虽多,要以科学管理原则之合法运用为最要。十九世纪末叶美哲泰楼氏,对于是项原则之阐明,不遗余力,继起者更不乏人,于是凡从事于工业者,莫不奉科学管理为经营工业之圭臬。考科学管理原则,不外厂基、房屋、机器、原料及服务之有效运用及其成本之精密计算,务以最低量成本,制成最高量成品。迩来是学进展甚速,科学管理而外,另倡人事管理一学。前者指物的方面,后者指人的方面。如原料与成品之标准化,属科学管理;雇主与雇工间关系之调整,属人事管理。上述两学,对于工业贡献甚大。就工业进展较速之国家如美国而言,据一九二九年美国商部标准局所发表之统计,各业因未能将原料或成品标准化而遭受之浪费,最高如男子服装业达百分之六十四,最低如五金业达百分之二十九,诚属惊人。我国工业落后,小工业占优势,其因标准不一而遭受之浪费,若与美国比较,自更不言可喻。即以大工业论,标准化运动,方在萌芽,而成本会计制度之设立,亦未加注意,欲求制造成本之减低,更非易事矣。

成品之销售,为工业建设之第四步骤。各业对于成品销售之手续,繁简互异。例如日报日出日发,手续简单。又如汽车种类既多,价值又昂,销售手续繁琐。故汽车一业,必也广告新奇动人,售价分期缴付,则推销始易普遍,大规模生产,方克进行。考销售(广义的)包括广告、仓储、保险、运输及销售(狭义的)等手续,如何而使各手续所应有之费用,减至最低限度,同时,其所得之效用,增至最高限度,实为合理销售(广义的)之鹄的。若就我国情形而论,则销售之不合理，触目皆然。第一，国货次于洋货之心理，深入人心，此就一般情形及我国工业发展落后而言，虽具有相当理由，然亦不乏例外。为我国工业前途计，一方固宜竞谋国货品质之改良，以与外货相颉颃，一方尤须养成民众爱护国货之心理，为民族工业树立广大而可靠之市场，今后广告术之发展，要当着重此点。第二，我国工业组织，规模狭小，制造如此，销售亦莫不然。多数工厂，仅从事于制造，而以销售假手于商号。此种商号，百货兼售，甚少以全副精神，从事于某一商品之销售者。结果，力量薄弱，收效有限。诸如雇主对于商品是否满意，商品价格是否适宜等问题，厂主一概无法探悉而谋适应。制造与销售，既未能密切联系，驯致市场日狭，而成本亦日高，我国工业之一蹶不振，此亦原因之一也。

三

我国经济落后，农业衰落，工业不振，故自海禁开放已还，世界工业国家，群以我国为农工产品——特别工业产品——推销之尾闾。驯致贸易入超，日甚一日，八十余年来，什九以上均为入超，而工业品之进口，为量尤多。抗战已还，因海口被封，外货来源断绝，遂不得不谋自给，以求抗战胜利与民族生存。于是三十余年来所提倡之国货运动，复见抬头。考国货之提倡，应以改良并促进工业品之制造与推销——即工业经济之建树——为主。工业经济之建树，分资金之筹集，厂基、房屋、机器、原料及服务之获得，成品之制造，及成品之销售四步骤。就我国工业现状言，此四步骤均有亟待改进之处。第一，工业金融宜脱离商业金融之束缚而另谋自立之途径。工业或投资银行及工业证券（股票或公债）市场，尤须早日成立。第二，工厂之设立，诸如厂基、房屋、机器、原料及服务之获得，应有统盘之筹划。固定资金与流动资金之分配，应求得一合理之比例。第三，制造方面，应力求合于科学原理，而于人事之调整，成本之计算，则须合于人事管理及成本会计之原则。第四，销售机构与制造机构应求联系，以免两者间之脱节，而提高最后之成本。上述四点，均为当前工业经济建设之要着，若能一一予以实施，则我国工业经济建设与国货运动之前途，其有望乎？

第二编

战时经济与区域经济

THE POST-WAR
INDUSTRIALIZATION
OF CHINA

"Some have spoken of the 'American Century'. I say that the century on which we are entering—the century which will come of this war—can be and must be the century of the common man. Perhaps it will be America's opportunity to suggest the freedoms and duties by which the common man must live. Everywhere the common man must learn to build his own industries with his own hands in a practical fashion. Everywhere the common man must learn to increase his productivity so that he and his children can eventually pay to the world community all that they have received. No nation will have the God-given right to exploit other nations. Older nations will have the privilege to help younger nations get started on the path to industrialization, but there must be neither military nor economic imperialism. The methods of the nineteenth century will not work in the people's century which is now about to begin." — Vice President Wallace, New York, May 8, 1942.

China is one of the United Nations with a tremendous stake in the world of tomorrow. When the invader has been defeated and driven from her lands, China will start afresh on the path to industrialization. Of the desire of the Chinese people to become more productive, there is no doubt. But what have five years of war done to China's industrial beginnings? What industrial progress does China want to make, and by what means, and with whose help?

If America is to play the role suggested by the Vice President, we in this country need to know answers to these questions. The National Planning Association, therefore, asked Dr. H. D. Fong, one of China's leading economists, who has long been interested in China's industrialization, for his views. This compact study throws much light on the road ahead.

CONTENTS

Chapter I. Introduction

Chapter II. China's Resources

    Mineral Resources

    Agricultural Resources

    Human Resources

Chapter III. Fields for China's Post-war Industrialization

    Transport and Public Utilities

    Agriculture

    Industry

Chapter IV. China's Wartime Achievements in Industrialization

    China's Pre-war and Wartime Industrial Areas

    China's Wartime Achievements in Industrialization

        Transport

        Agriculture

        Industry

Chapter V. Japan in China

    Japan in Manchuria since 1931

    Japan in China Proper since 1937

Chapter VI. Capital and Management in China's Post-war Industrialization

    Foreign Capital

        Pre-war Foreign Capital

　　　　　　　　　Wartime Foreign Loans to China
　　　　　　　　　Post-war Foreign Investments in China
　　　　　　　　　　　Purposes of Foreign Investment
　　　　　　　　　　　Forms of Foreign Investment
　　　　　　　　　　　Repayment of Foreign Loans
　　　　　　　Chinese Capital
　　　　　　　　　Public Borrowing
　　　　　　　　　Redirection of Credit
　　　　　　　　　Credit Expansion
　　　　　　　　　Repatriation of Refugee Capital Abroad
　　　　　　　　　Overseas Chinese Remittances
　　　　　　　Management
　　Chapter Ⅶ. Proposals for Organizing the Post-war Industrialization
　　　　　　　in China
　　　　　　　　　Principles
　　　　　　　　　Forms of Organization
　　　　　　　　　The China Reconstruction Finance Corporation
Appendix
Selected Bibliography

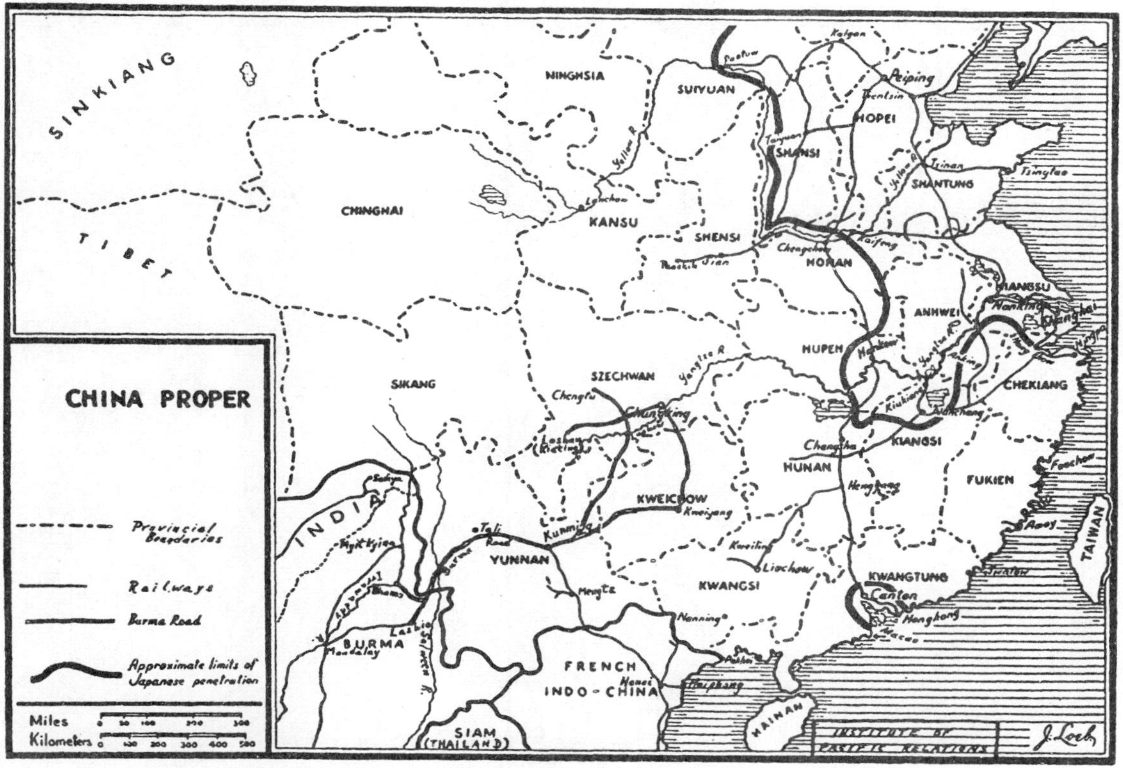
CHINA PROPER
Provincial Boundaries
Railways
Burma Road
Approximate limits of Japanese penetration
Miles
Kilometers
SINKIANG
TIBET
CHINGHAI
NINGHSIA
SUIYUAN
KANSU
SHENSI
SHANSI
HOPEI
SHANTUNG
HONAN
KIANGSU
ANHWEI
HUPEH
SZECHWAN
SIKANG
CHEKIANG
KIANGSI
HUNAN
FUKIEN
KWEICHOW
YUNNAN
KWANGSI
KWANGTUNG
TAIWAN
HAINAN
INDIA
BURMA
FRENCH INDO-CHINA
SIAM (THAILAND)
Peiping
Tientsin
Kalgan
Paotow
Taiyuan
Tsinan
Tsingtao
Lanchow
Sian
Chengchow
Kaifeng
Nanking
Shanghai
Hankow
Chengtu
Chungking
Kweiyang
Kunming
Tali
Mengtze
Changsha
Hengyang
Kweilin
Liuchow
Nanning
Canton
Hongkong
Macao
Amoy
Swatow
Foochow
Hanoi
Haiphong
Lashio
Mandalay
Bhamo
Sadiya
Myitkyina
Yangtze R.
Yellow R.
Salween R.
Burma Road
INSTITUTE OF PACIFIC RELATIONS
J. Loeb

Chapter I. Introduction

Unequal distribution among nations of materials and manpower gives rise to endless difficulties of adjustment in an increasingly interdependent world. Particularly is this so as long as sovereign states exist. The problems created become doubly important if the resources unequally distributed among the different nations have not been evenly developed. China offers a striking example of failure to utilize her existing resources. With one-quarter of the world's population and a fair proportion of the world's natural resources, she possesses only a minute fraction of the world's machinery. Taking the amount of machinery per inhabitant in the industrial countries of northwestern Europe as 100, the corresponding index would be 405 for the United States and only between 0 and 1 for China. [1]

---

[1] Staley, Eugene: *World Economy in Transition*, Council on Foreign Relations, New York, 1939, p. 70. These data are calculated from a table of values of machinery per capita given by Ernst Wagemann, *Struktur und Rhythmus der Weltwirtschaft*, Berlin, Reimar Hobbing, 1931, pp. 406 – 8.

The international repercussions of such a state of affairs are tragically serious. Since the Opium War of 1839 – 42, China has been a victim of international struggle for the expropriation of her vast natural resources as well as for control of markets for trade and invetsment. This struggle has culminated in the present Sino-Japanese War.

Once the war comes to an end, no problem can be of greater concern to the world at large than that of rational redistribution and utilization of the world's resources, which includes especially the economic development of China. If such a development can be effected by carefully considered international action, it may not only improve the economic welfare of one-quarter of the world's population, but may also bring about stability in world social, economic and political relations. With this end in view, the present monograph attempts to show the potentialities for China's postwar industrialization. It indicates her needs for capital and management which, in light of China's present stage of industrial development and the untold destruction wrought by the war, can only be met with through active assistance from the nations now allied to China in the common struggle against the totalitarian powers. Among these the United States, with more capital for export than any other power, will be in a position to play a major role in the international development of postwar China. Dr. Sun Yat-sen, founder of the Chinese Republic, foresaw such a development in 1922. To quote from Dr. Sun, [1]

---

[1] *International Development of China*, New York, 1922, Introduction.

THE POST-WAR INDUSTRIALIZATION OF CHINA

the recent World War has proved to mankind that war is ruinous to both the Conqueror and the Conquered, and worse for the Aggressor. What is true in military warfare is more so in trade warfare. Since President Wilson has proposed a League of Nations to end military war in the future, I desire to propose to end the trade war by cooperation and mutual help in the development of China. This will root out probably the greatest cause of future wars.

The world has been greatly benefited by the development of America as an industrial and a commercial nation. So a developed China with her four hundred millions of population, will be another new world in the economic sense. The nations which will take part in this development will reap immense advantages. Furthermore, international cooperation of this kind cannot but help to strengthen the Brotherhood of Man. Ultimately, I am sure, this will culminate in its being the keystone in the arch of the League of Nations.

Since Dr. Sun's writing, the world has again come to be involved in war, far more extensive in area and far more intensive in destruction than the last. This World War II, begun by Japan on July 7, 1937, has now spread from Asia to Europe, to Africa, to the Western Hemisphere.

According to Peffer,[1] " social reconstruction in China, meaning industrialization and internal reorganization on a principle of economic equality, is a *sine qua* of both equilibrium in China and international

---

[1] Peffer, Nathaniel: *Prerequisites to Peace in the Far East*, Institute of Pacific Relations, 1940, Chapter II.

peace in the Far East. "

China's contribution to world peace after the war must lie in her own rejuvenation as a modern industrialized nation, able to defend herself against foreign aggression and thus to serve as a stabilizing factor in the preservation of freedom and democracy in the Far East.

Chapter II. China's Resources

The reputed wealth of China for many centuries inspired the admiration of the world. In his travels throughout the Far East in 1274 – 95, Marco Polo in his fascinating accounts acquainted the world with the general richness of China. [1]Later travellers confirmed rather than questioned this conclusion, in respect of China's mineral if not agricultural resources. In particular, Baron Ferdinand von Richthofen's description of the iron and coal fields of Shansi in the early seventies of the last century, has often been quoted and probably has had more influence than any other single piece of writing in establishing the widespread belief that China possesses the "untold mineral wealth" in which after-dinner

---

[1] In speaking of the famous Mongol Emperor of China, Kublai Khan, "The Great Lord of Lords", Marco Polo adds, "And of a surety he hath good right to such a title, for all men know for a certain truth that he is the most potent man, as regards forces and lands and treasure, that existeth in the world, or ever hath existed from the time of our First Father Adam until this day. " *The Book of Ser Marco Polo*, 3rd Yule edition, London, 1903, Book II, Part I, Chapter I.

speakers have such firm faith. Indeed, the universal error made by the early observers was to mistake widespread occurrence of minerals for abundance. Unfortunately, more recent investigations have failed to substantiate conclusions drawn from the earlier work. It is still difficult, if not impossible, to make a sound estimate of China's mineral resources since they have not yet been carefully surveyed, yet preliminary researches in the last two decades and a half, tending towards under-rather than over-estimation have provided data which may serve as a starting point for a more adequate understanding of China's mineral resources in the light of needs for industrialization in the postwar world. ①

Mineral Resources

At the present stage of technology, mineral resources seem to play a more important role than agricultural, although recent discoveries by the chemists have tended to stress the potentialities of the agricultural. The leading mineral resources needed for industrialization include coal, iron, oil and copper. Coal, oil and copper are indispensable for the generation and transmission of motive power, while iron supplies the basic mineral for machine civilization. China is deficient in oil and copper, has a reasonable reserve of iron ore, and is fairly rich in coal.

With regard to oil, Bain concludes after extensive summary of the

---

① Bain, H. Foster: *Ores and Industry in the Far East*, revised and enlarged edition, Council on Foreign Relations, New York, 1933, pp. 31 – 32.

earlier explorations that[①]

> nowhere in China do conditions exist which are comparable from a geological standpoint with those existing in the mid-Continent or Pacific oil fields of the United States. Making every allowance for deficiencies in present knowledge of the economic geology of China, its oil reserves are still probably less than one percent of those of the United States.

The two regions where oil reserves may be found are the North Shensi Basin and Szechuen province. The North Shensi Basin, comprising a narrow strip along the western margin, the northern part of Shensi, northeastern Kansu and a part of southern Mongolia, is the most favorable region in North China for petroleum development. The Basin contains an area of over 100,000 square miles. According to recent report, Szechuen and Shensi are estimated to have 1,357 million barrels, or 56,994 million gallons, of petroleum underground — a reserve sufficient to satisfy China's prewar annual requirement of 80 million gallons for over 700 years. In Shensi, one well is said to have a production capacity of 8,000 barrels per day, or one of 100 million gallons per year, but lack of refining facilities renders the crude oil unfit for many essential purposes. In order to meet the urgent requirements during wartime, the Ministry of Economics is establishing a large-scale oil refining plant in Chungking, wartime capital of China; it is developing fuel substitutes by manufactur-

---

① Bain, H. Foster: *Ores and Industry in the Far East*, revised and enlarged edition, Council on Foreign Relations, p. 129.

ing synthetic gasoline from alcohol and vegetable oil. ①

Shale oil is found to a considerable extent in Manchuria. The reserves are estimated at 7,628 million metric tons, of which more than two-thirds, 5,400 million metric tons, are centered in Fushun in southern Manchuria. The oil content varies from three to seven percent. After experiments extending over four years a plant was constructed by the Fushun Collieries—a subsidiary of the South Manchuria Railway Company; it began operation in September,1929. The output of heavy oil,61,000 metric tons in 1931, was reported to have reached 360,000 metric tons in 1939. ② In 1941, the Japanese Cabinet decided to subsidize the SMR's venture to the extent of 100 million yen, with five annual installments of 20 million yen each, beginning with the fiscal year 1941 - 42. From the very outset, the Fushun shale oil had been sold primarily to the Japanese navy at prices which were probably higher than world market prices. Originally, oil-shale was produced in the process of open-cut mining, as the coal was laid bare through removal of oil-shale. In the new expansion plans, however, oil-shale is to be removed, regardless of the progress of coal-mining. This new procedure naturally increases costs.

According to V. K. Ting, China's foremost geologist, deposits of copper ore in China are extremely numerous but few have proved of value due to low ore content (5 percent or lower). The average annual con-

---

① Mitchell, Kate L. : *Industrialization of the Western Pacific*, Institute of Pacific Relations, New York,1942, p. 133.

② *Japan-"Manchukuo" Yearbook,1940*, pp. 766 - 77; *Japan Yearbook, 1914 - 41*; Mitchell, *Op. cit.*, p. 88.

sumption of copper in China is about 7,000 tons, or one-hundredth part of the annual production of 710,000 tons for the United States in 1939; [1] but the production from the mines is much below this amount. Of the two centers of production, Tungchuan in northern Yunnan, where a total of 500 tons is produced every year, has better grade ore, generally near or above 5 percent. Penghsien in northwestern Szechuen, where a smelting plant has been operated with an annual output of over 100 tons, is the second center, with poorer ore but a larger reserve. Copper is also produced in very small amounts from western part of Chinese Turkestan. Crude copper production, according to recent figures, has increased from 400 tons in 1937 to 1,000 tons in 1940. [2]

China is rich in coal. The 1913 International Geological Congress estimated China's coal reserve at 997 billion metric tons. But subsequent survey has considerably scaled down this original and much too optimistic figure. The last one proposed by W. H. Wong of the China Geological Survey at the Fifth Pacific Science Congress at Vancouver, 1933, put the approximate total at 246 billion metric tons, distributed by provinces as shown in Table I of the Appendix. [3] The above reserve is large enough for China, and Wong concludes that at the present scale of production, it

---

[1] *Statistical Yearbook, 1939 − 40*, League of Nations, p. 147.

[2] *Chinese Yearbook, 1935 − 36*, p. 951, article by W. H. Wong, Director of the China Geological Survey. Recent copper production figures, based on official report of the Ministry of Economics in Chinese, can be found in my article on "The prospects of industrialization in China", *Pacific Affairs*, March 1942.

[3] *Ibid*, p. 945.

can last for almost 10,000 years.

China, believed by geologists to contain one of the great coal reserves of the world and much the largest amount known in the Orient, has as yet not fully developed her underground reserves. The great dispersion of coal fields is one factor, and the absence of modern means of rapid and cheap transport is another. The fourteen provinces listed in Table I, each with a reserve of over one billion metric tons, can be roughly classified into four regions, the northern region led by Shansi and Shensi but embracing also Honan, Hopei and Shantung, with a total reserve of 210.4 billion metric tons or 85 percent, the northwestern region including Sinkiang and Kansu with a total reserve of 7.5 billion metric tons or 3.5 percent, the southern region including Szechuen, Hunan, Yunnan and Kweichow with a total reserve of 14.9 billion metric tons or 6 percent, and the northeastern region including Liaoning, Kirin and Heilungkiang with a total reserve of 4 billion metric tons or 1.6 percent.

Coal production in China is distributed among the provinces with relatively small reserve but easy access of market by means of railways and steam navigation. Thus, in 1931, for instance, China had a total coal output of 27.24 million metric tons. As shown by Table II of the Appendix, 56 percent of the output was produced in the two provinces of Liaoning and Hopei, having a combined reserve amounting to only 2 percent of the total but located along the sea coast and connected by railways and steam navigation; while Shansi and Shensi, with 81 percent of the total reserve, produced only 9 percent of the total output. In the south, of the four leading provinces with the largest reserves, only Hunan had an output of as much as 930,000 metric tons, or less than 4 percent of the total output.

In respect of iron ore reserve in China, the most authoritative study is that by Tegengren of the China Geological Survey, made in 1921 - 24. [①] He gave a total of 951.7 million metric tons, with a total metallic content of 368.2 million metric tons, or 38.7 percent of the ore content. This reserve, as Tegengren remarked,

> is by no means much for China and even if continued investigations would—what seems rather improbable—raise these known resources to the double amount, the general situation would not be essentially altered. One thing, therefore, is certain: China can no longer be regarded as a storehouse of inexhaustible future reserves of iron ore, to be drawn upon when the supplies of other countries are beginning to give out. On the contrary, her iron ore resources must be termed very modest, or even scant, when her potentialities of industrial development are taken into consideration, and the strictest economy would be indispensable to guard against future unpleasant contingencies. By way of illustration it may be pointed out that the total quantity of iron ore (both actual and potential) represented by the figures above would be consumed by the iron industry of the United States within less than nine years. And then it has to be noted that the bulk of these resources (740 million tons) consists of the

---

[①] Tegengren, F. R. : *The Iron Ores and Iron Industry of China*, Peiping, China Geological Survey, 1921 - 24.

low grade Manchurian ores (with average metallic content of 34.9%), the exploitability of which is still somewhat problematical, or which at any rate are far below the average standard.

W. H. Wong, in his new estimate based on the work of Tegengren and others of the China Geological Survey, gave in 1935 – 36 a higher estimate of 1,132.6 million metric tons, as shown by provinces in Table III of the Appendix. Wong's estimate of 872.2 million metric tons for Manchuria (concentrated in Liaoning) is undoubtedly too low in light of recent Japanese discoveries. The reserve there is almost doubled according to the *Far Eastern Yearbook* for 1940 – 41, which gives the total at 1,514 million metric tons. Again, new discoveries in China's southwest, especially in Sikang province, will bring Wong's total to a higher figure. In the Luku district of that province, a large reserve of 100 million metric tons, with a metallic content of 65 percent, is recently reported, while elsewhere further prospecting work is bringing new reserves to light. [1]

China Proper during the five-year period 1930 – 34 had an average annual pig iron production of 148,000 metric tons,[2] while Manchuria during 1936, the pre-war year, had one of 647,000 metric tons. Allowing for wartime increase in production in Manchuria, occupied China, and Free China, for which figures are not available, as well as need for increased production during the postwar period in the event of an allied victory when the whole of China including Manchuria will be completely

---

[1] *Chinese Yearbook, 1940 – 41*, p. 570.
[2] *Statistical Yearbook, 1934 – 40*, League of Nations, p. 144.

under Chinese sovereignty, it may not be unreasonable to assume an annual pig iron production of over one million metric tons to meet China's postwar needs for industrialization. In that case, the Chinese iron ore reserve, which is estimated at around 440 million metric tons in terms of metallic content by Wong but can be raised to a higher figure, say 600 – 700 million metric tons, in light of recent discoveries in Manchuria and southwest China, would supply the domestic needs at its present rate of operation for another 600 – 700 years.

Agricultural Resources

China's agricultural resources compare favorably with other nations. In a recent field survey of agricultural China, exclusive of Manchuria, Professor J. L. Buck of the University of Nanking shows that of a total gross area of 1,358,905 square miles in agricultural China, divided into eight regions, the cultivated area reaches 339,644 square miles or 25 percent. This compares favorably with 12 percent for Russia (1928), 17.2 percent for Japan proper, 22.5 percent for Great Britain, and 22.6 percent for the United States, but unfavorably with 43.8 percent for Germany, 44.6 percent for Italy, and 46.3 percent for British India. [1]

A closer examination, however, reveals a quite different state of development in China's disfavor. In the first place, China is a land practi-

---

[1] Buck, J. L.: *Land Utilization in China*, University of Chicago Press, 1937, Vol. I, pp. 33, 172.

cally devoid of pasture farming. Only 4.6 percent of her gross area is devoted to this purpose, as compared with 17.4 percent in Germany, 20.1 percent in Italy, 35.1 percent in the United States, and 56.8 percent in Great Britain. Secondly, China is a land without forestry to speak of. Much of the forested land in earlier times has now disappeared, through neglect, destruction, or otherwise. In the southwest, in Kweichow province for instance, much forestry has been destroyed, burnt down, in order to remove nests for bandit barons. The primary reason, however, is economic. Much of the forest land is converted into land for arable farming; where it is not fit for arable purpose, the forest is removed for use as timber or fuel. The forest area in China today covers only 8.7 percent of the total gross area in Buck's study, as compared with 13.1 percent for British India, 16 percent for Italy, 27.2 percent for Germany, 31.9 percent for the United States, and 56.6 percent for Japan Proper. Thirdly, the proportion of the uncultivated land that is not productive must be considered high in agricultural China. According to Buck's study, only 52.5 percent of the total uncultivated land is productive. Of the total uncultivated land that is productive, the percentage distribution by uses is as follows: forest 22.8, trees and bushes 28.1, grass 23.8, reeds 5.2, pasture 11.9, other 8.2. According to Buck, [1]

> most of this land is unfit for agriculture, but some of it would be better utilized in forests than in grass and bushes.... The rea-

---

[1] Buck, J. L. : *Land Utilization in China*, Vol. I, pp. 180 − 1.

sons for unproductive land in these 172 hsien (surveyed) are several. Such land was reported by 55% of the hsien as too stony, by 14% as being caused by blowing sand, by 9% as caused by the presence of graves, by 8% as too much sand, salt or alkali, and the remainder 14% either for other causes or as unknown.

China's limited agricultural resources are very intensively utilized (in respect of labor) in face of a rapidly growing population which brings a heavy pressure to bear upon the land. The eight agricultural regions referred to above give an average density of 1,485 persons per square mile of crop area, and one of 1,541 persons per square mile of cultivated area. The density varies for the different agricultural regions from 858 persons per square mile of crop area in the Spring Wheat Area, where climate, soil, and topography are unfavorable to agriculture, to 2,636 — a figure which appears rather high — in the Southwestern Rice Area where double cropping, favorable climate, and products from public lands make possible a dense population per square mile of crop area. Consequently, Chinese farms are extremely small, the mean size being 3.76 acres, as compared with 14.28 in the Netherlands, 21.59 in Germany, 39.74 in Denmark, 63.18 in England and Wales, and 156.85 in the United States. This, and other factors such as smaller amount of capital available, result in a smaller per capita production. The number of man-days required to grow one acre of wheat in China is 26 days compared with 1.2 days in the United States; one acre of cotton in China 53 days compared with 14 days in the United States; one acre of corn 23 days in China compared with 2.5 days in the United States. ①

The small farm in China is further handicapped by its fragmentation. There are on the average 5.6 different parcels of land per farm. Two-thirds of the farms have 1 to 5 parcels per farm, and over one-fifth have 6 to 10 parcels per farm. In extreme cases the number of parcels per farm rises as high as 59. These parcels average only 0.94 acre in size. They often contain more than one field per parcel, so that the average number of fields per farm is 11.6 compared with 5.6 parcels. The average distance of all parcels from the farmstead is 0.4 mile. The only way these distances can be reduced would be for the farmers to live on individual farmsteads and to have all their parcels of land in one piece. This fragmentation of land, which reminds one of the strip system in feudal Europe, places many difficulties in the way of agricultural progress and of fuller use of China's limited agricultural resources. In the words of Professor Buck, fragmentation of land②

> limits the size of fields and, therefore, the extent to which improved farm machinery may be used. Scattered fields are difficult to manage, for crops must be protected from stray animals, from pettty thieving and from trespassing. Few fences are found in China because of this fragmentation. Irrigation is extremely difficult, especially from private wells or other private water fields. Some land is largely wasted in strips between the different parcels.

---

① Buck, J. L. : *Land Utilization in China*, Vol. I, pp. 268, 362.
② *Ibid.*, p. 185.

With the great pressure of population on land, resulting in small farms and low productivity, the question of what proportion of the uncultivated land, occupying as it does almost three-fourths of the total gross area in agricultural China, is arable, has become one of great interest. Dr. O. E. Baker, in a stimulating article published in *Foreign Affairs* in 1928, ① gives the estimate that there are 700 million acres of land in the whole of China that are physically fit for agricultural cultivation, of which he considers 180 million acres as being cultivated. This leaves the large total of over 500 million acres that are cultivable but not at present in cultivation. Of this large area, less than 100 million acres is reckoned by Baker to be within Mongolia and Sinkiang. It is argued, therefore, that 400 million acres of potentially cultivable land are at present lying unused within China Proper and Manchuria. Recent detailed studies of Manchuria put the unused land capable of cultivation in that region at 49 million acres. Even if this figure is increased by a considerable percentage, it seems clear that this does not account for the bulk of the estimate quoted. It must be regarded as highly unlikely that such a large area of cultivable land has remained unused within China Proper, even without the mechanical equipment and power which Baker regards as the solution of the problem. ② In his recent study Professor Buck arrives at a figure of

---

① "Agriculture and the future of China", *Foreign Affairs*, April, 1928.
② Condliffe, J. B. : *China Today*; *Economic*, World Peace Foundation, 1932, pp. 26 – 27. Condliffe, quoting Chinese and Japanese estimates of 1929, placed the uncultivated arable land in Manchuria at 24 – 27 million acres, but a Japanese estimate has recently doubled it to 49 million acres. See *Far Eastern Yearbook*, 1940 – 41.

35 million acres of uncultivated land in agricultural China (excluding Manchuria) that is arable, but guards his conclusion with the reservation that[①]

> the limited available data make it impossible to estimate accurately the potentially arable land of China, especially if economical production is to be considered. In any consideration of quantity of additional land which might be brought under cultivation, it must be remembered that land is also continually becoming unfit for cultivation for one reason or another, such as erosion and floods covering good soil with sand.

In light of the above reservation Buck is inclined to place the arable uncultivated land far below the limit of 35 million acres. To him the maximum amount of land that can be made available for further cultivation, including the arable uncultivated land as well as the cultivated land now lying idle or not so intensely exploited, is no more than 25 million acres. [②] This area of arable uncultivated land, though small, would probably suffice for the settlement of 5-7 million families, with 20-30 million people, excluding the arable uncultivated land of Manchuria which may be assumed to suffice for at least as many families and people.

Chinese agricultural production consists largely of crops, which alone use up nine-tenths of farm land (89.6 percent), as compared with 41.9 percent in the United States. The most important Chinese farm

---

① Buck, *Land Utilization in China*, Vol. I, p. 169.
② Buck, J. L. ; *Land Utilization in China*, Vol. I, p. 10.

crops are rice and wheat for food, and cotton for clothing and other textile uses. Other crops characteristic for the country as a whole, occupying 1 percent or more of total crop acreage, in order of importance, are: millet, soybeans, kaoliang, barley, corn, sweet potatoes, rapeseed, broad beans, peanuts, milk-vetch for green manure, green beans, field peas and the opium poppy. The mulberry tree, grown for its leaves for the silkworm, tea, oranges and tobacco are still other crops important in Chinese rural economy. Compared with most Western countries, the production of these crops is more intensive in China because of the absence of hay and other fodder crops required for the livestock industry of such countries. In this respect China is more like Japan, India, and the colonial countries of Monsoon Asia than like the United States or Western Europe.

Among these crops a large portion is reserved for home consumption in the interests of a self-sufficient economy, but cash crops are increasing in view of China's growing industrialization. Such crops include tobacco, opium, peanuts, rapeseed, cotton, cocoons or raw silk, and, to a lesser extent in proportion to the total crop raised (although the proportionate value may be as great), soybeans, wheat, green beans, kaoliang, field peas, sweet potatoes and rice, for both domestic needs and foreign export. Tobacco, cotton, raw silk, tea, soybeans, wheat, kaoliang, millet, and vegetable seeds are used as industrial raw materials, either in China or for export to foreign countries. Among the crops consumed on the farm for industrial purposes, the fibre crops are the most important, over two-thirds of the cotton and over one-half of the hemp being thus used. Bamboo is next with over one-half used industrially on the farm. The other three most important crops used for industrial purposes are small beans, white soybeans and opium seeds. The only other products of which at least from 5 to 10 percent are used for industrial purposes are kaoliang and millet. ①

The dense population in China necessitates the production, within the social and technical limitations of the Chinese agricultural system, of the greatest amount of food possible per unit of land. This is accomplished by growing crops for their seed or tuber products, rather than by devoting the land to pastures and crops for livestock which in turn supply a smaller quantity of food in the form of animal products. For land devoted to grains, or grains and tubers, produces, according to Buck, "six and seven times as much food energy as land raising dairy cows", while the return from poultry farming "is less than one-third of the calories from milk for an acre of crop land". ② The animal industry in China is more highly developed in the frontier regions than elsewhere, and livestock raising is the chief occupation of peoples just west and north of the eight agricultural regions covered in Buck's study. Much of the raw wool for industrial and export purposes is produced in this region.

From the viewpoint of meeting the needs of China's industrialization, the greatest handicap on Chinese agricultural output, aside from the limited supply, is sporadic, unorganized production. Industrial crops, such as raw cotton, wool, and wheat, are not graded or standardized. As a

---

① Buck, J. L. ; *Land Utilization in China*, Vol. I, pp. 10 − 11, 235 − 37.
② *Ibid.*, pp. 257 − 58.

result, any manufacturer in China has to double or triple his purchases before a satisfactory assortment can be made to suit his production needs. It is thus not uncommon for Chinese manufacturers under such handicaps to prefer foreign to Chinese raw materials—for example, to use Australian instead of Honan wheat in Tientsin flour mills. ① The failure to coordinate agricultural and industrial development has its serious repercussions on national production, and it is only recently that attention has been drawn to this aspect of Chinese economic problems. ②The improvement and grading of raw cotton by the cooperative societies in recent years is a hopeful beginning in this direction.

Human Resources

China's tremendous population presents an apparent paradox. On the one hand, we find considerable overpopulation. Within the total area of China some astonishing densities have been calculated, densities higher than those recorded for similarly crowded agricultural regions either in India or in Japan. Walter H. Mallory of the China International Famine Relief Commission quotes an unusually high estimate of 6,880 persons per square mile in a northern famine region. The figure of 2,636 per

---

① See my article on "The industrial organization of China", *Nankai Social and Economic Quarterly*, January, 1937 Vol. IX, pp. 931 – 36; also *Chinese Yearbook*, 1940 – 41, pp. 548 – 49.

② See my article on "The relationship between agriculture and industry", *Southwest Industrial Bulletin* (in Chinese), March issue, 1940.

square mile for the Southwestern Rice Area in Buck's study is sufficiently large to prove the fact of tremendous pressure of population upon resources. This crowded population, meantime, is increasing rapidly. The population survey carried out in the course of Buck's land utilization study indicates that[1]

> there were 38.3 births and 27.1 deaths per 1,000 population, or an annual excess of births over deaths of 11.2 per 1,000 inhabitants. Superficially this rate of natural increase, which would double the population in less than 65 years, suggests that the population of China has increased rapidly.

On the other hand, with this redundant population, there has always been a great scarcity of industrial labor that will meet the urgent requirements of new industrial enterprises of all sorts. Bain, with considerable mining experience in China, observes that[2]

> in planning for new industries in the Far East one must not assume that large or even dense population means abundant available labor. Undoubtedly men and women workers may be had, but recruiting and training them will involve not only direct expense but the further charge due to delay... In the East there is an abundance

---

[1] Buck, J. L.: *Land Utilization in China*, Vol. I, p. 395. This rate of natural increase as computed by Buck is evidently too high, for his figures seem to have been selected from localities not exposed to catastrophic developments like floods, droughts, epidemics, and wars.

[2] Bain, H. Foster: *Ores and Industry in the Far East*, revised and enlarged edition, Council on Foreign Relations, pp. 230, 232.

of labor to be had, but a scarcity upon such terms as are necessary to sustain large-scale industrial undertakings.

Several reasons account for this dilemma. The initial readjustment which every peasant man or woman has to go through in preferring factory to farm work is plain enough. But in China where farming has all along been the traditional means of livelihood and attachment to home has outweighed considerations of mere profit or high wages, the transition and adaptation is not at all an easy one. "America", remarked Bain,[①]

> will not soon forget the widespread economic and social disturbance brought about by the wartime necessity of shifting labor to man the shipyards; and American labor is not only vastly more mobile than is that of the Orient, but in this instance there was no such break with traditions and built-up economic relations making for future security as is involved when a Chinese farmer neglects his planting in order that an American mine may be operated the year around.

Industrial labor requires both skill and discipline. Chinese labor, primarily agricultural, does not possess the necessary skill for the operation of complicated machines and tools imported from abroad. Furthermore, accustomed as Chinese labor has been to the traditions of gild or domestic industries, it lacks the very discipline which is indispensable to successful production under the factory system. The port cities where factory

---

[①] Bain, H. Foster: *Ores and Industry in the Far East*, p. 230.

industry was first introduced, for example Canton and Shanghai, were naturally faced with the problem of industrial labor supply earliest. After decades of development these cities began to build up a reserve of industrial labor to which other centers looked for supply. Thus many of the factory workers in Tienstin and Tsingtao cotton mills, in North China, had to be drawn from these cities in the South, oftentimes resorting to the familiar methods of "pirating" or attracting away workers from one mill to another by lucrative offers for travel, dormitory, and other facilities. Today the war has forced many of the industries to migrate from south and central China to the Great Southwest, and with this migration have also been transferred the industrial workers of Shanghai, Wusih, and even Hankow. These workers now constitute the nucleus through which a new army of industrial labor has to be recruited and trained from the agricultural population in the Southwest. The quantity immediately available for factory employment is inevitably small and insufficient for the purpose of large-scale industrial development, especially in view of wartime need for conscription.

Industrial labor in China as a whole did not amount to two millions even before the present war; what with the destruction of the war and the dispersion and loss of such labor in the course of the war a postwar China must feel more keenly than before the shortage of industrial labor supply. China after the war will have to launch a large-scale program of educational reform with a view to preparing the vast illiterate and agricultural population for industrial development, to be carried out simultaneously with a system of vocational education for the training of mechanics and skilled workers, just as other newly industrialized nations, Japan for example, did many decades ago.

Chapter III. Fields for China's Post-war Industrialization

China is still largely an agricultural nation. The eighty years of industrial development in China, chiefly under foreign initiative and control, have not altered much the fundamental character of her self-sufficient economy. Such development has been confined to a small area accessible to foreign intercourse, mostly along the coast and the Great Yangtze.

Industrial development, as represented by actual industrial plant, differs from the general process of modernization. While the former has been restricted largely to the coastal belt, the latter has parvaded the whole country, with the war contributing to its spread. Modern industrial development is not merely a mechanical process of building industrial plants and herding laborers into the plants. It requires a "modern" mentality, which is equally required for the successful use of "modern" armies. Not China's industrialization, but China's "modernization", has made great strides under the impact of the war of national resistance.

Industrial development in these coastal and Yangtze regions has been greatly retarded by the war. With these regions under her temporary control, Japan has not been slow in carrying out her long-cherished desire of an economic hegemony within which the interests of an agricultural

China will be subjugated to those of an industrial Japan. China, once the war is won, will have to face the urgent task of industrialization in addition to postwar rehabilitation. What, then, will be the fields in which China's postwar industrialization is most likely to take place? Opinions will necessarily differ over a comprehensive program of this character, but certain fundamental trends are clear enough to those familiar with China's economic problems and needs. The fields to be covered in such a program will include transport and public utilities, agriculture, and industry.

Transport and Public Utilities

China must be provided with an economic environment within which a large-scale economy of a modern order can function. She must, in other words, be equipped with a modern system of transport which will not only bring within reach her undeveloped resources of coal, iron and many other essential raw materials for industry, but also serve as a vital factor in the effective establishment and functioning of a unified, central government in charge of a vast program for postwar industrialization. Railway construction for a continental country like China is the first essential need. We may well bear in mind that the whole of China including Manchuria had before the war only 45 kilometers of railways per million population, as compared with 262 for British India, 349 for Japan proper, 511 for Russia, 754 for Great Britain, 884 for Germany, 1,004 for France, and 3,200 for the United States. Dr. Sun, in his *International Development of China* published in 1922, stressed China's great need for modern means of transport by proposing the construction of 100,000 miles of railways, to cost ten billion yuan (roughly three billion U.S. dollars at that time) by his son, Dr. Sun Fo, in 1928. [1]

Transportation and communication in America have made possible, relatively speaking, an economic distribution of the country's population; whereas because of China's backwardness in these essentials, about six-sevenths of her population is congested in one-third of her area. Railway freight rates in the United States average slightly more than 1 cent per ton-mile, contrasted with transportation costs in China via beasts of burden, human carriers, carts or wheelbarrows of about ten times this amount. Improvement in transportation will not only reduce costs of freight, but will also release for industrial employment considerable manpower now engaged in transport. The statement that 20 percent of the population of China is engaged in transportation is, no doubt, an exaggeration; but it is not wholly unrealistic.

Another major item of transport will be steam navigation. With a sea coast of 2,150 miles (5,000 miles including indentations), and two of the world's foremost rivers—2,500 miles of the Yellow River and 3,200 miles of the Yangtze River, China's steamship tonnage, 553,000 registered tons in China Proper and 353,000 tons in Manchuria, must be considered inadequate, as compared with 14,632,000 registered tons for the

---

[1] See my monograph *Toward Economic Control in China*, China Institute of Pacific Relations, 1936, pp. 16 – 17, 19.

United States — the former being only one-sixteenth of the latter. ① After the war, there will undoubtedly be greater need for shipping facilities in China because of wartime destruction as well as postwar needs of industrial and commercial expansion. Any postwar excess tonnage in foreign countries might be diverted to fill a part of China's most urgent needs; provided proper arrangements for its investment and operation on the China Seas during the postwar period could be satisfactorily made. Other items, such as highways, canals, inland waterways, and air transport, together with port and terminal facilities, as well as public utilities, such as electric light and power, waterworks, gas plants, and street railways, will also be embodied in any program for the development of China's modern transport system, as has been outlined by Dr. Sun in his program for the international development of China.

Agriculture

Before China plunges into a program of industrial development, she must first improve her agriculture. It will be setting the cart before the horse if industry is to develop without simultaneous improvement in agriculture. Four-fifths of China's population depend upon agriculture for a

---

① Figures for shipping tonnage in China Proper refer to the year ending June 30, 1936, and are taken from *The Statistical Abstract of the Republic of China, 1940* (in Chinese), Chungking, p. 190; those for Manchuria are from the *Far Eastern Yearbook, 1940 - 41*, p. 797; and those for the United States are from the *Statistical Abstract of the United States, 1940*, p. 464.

livelihood. If the mass of her agricultural population remains on the verge of minimum subsistence, and constantly in danger of starvation and destruction from the recurrence of wars, famines, pestilence and other forms of Malthusian checks to population growth, industrial development cannot proceed very far. There will not be forthcoming industrial raw materials from the farms, nor will there be a prosperous farming population essential to the development of a large domestic market to support the modern industries of China.

Agricultural policy in China must have as its chief objectives the following: (1) the stabilization of agricultural production through reduction of risks and uncertainty arising from recurrent famines due to flood or drought, (2) the increase of agricultural production through better use of the cultivated land and fuller use of the arable uncultivated land, and (3) the standardization of agricultural production to meet the growing needs of largescale manufacturing and export. ① Farming has all along been a risky business in China, but more so in recent years on account of the neglect to maintain public works designed to assure normal agricultural production. Soil erosion, deforestation, neglect of river conservancy and irrigation—all these tend to increase the frequency of famines arising

---

① Lack of space forbids a detailed discussion of the vitally important problem of land tenure in China. Reforms in land tenure, as proposed by Dr. Sun Yat-sen and embodied in the avowed policy of the Kuomingtang Party, are indispensable to social and economic progress in China. Whether such reforms are carried out by giving tenants' rights of perpetual lease to the surface and protecting such rights, or by more radical reforms as advocated by the Chinese communists, they are necessary for agricultural progress.

from recurrent floods and droughts. Large-scale projects for reforestation, soil and river conservation, extensive construction of irrigation dams and wells will be the first steps towards postwar reconstruction in order to stabilize agricultural production. Creditable work was done on some of these before the war by the National Economic Council, the National Reconstruction Commission, and the China International Famine Relief Commission, and during the war by the various provincial and central governmental agencies in China's southwest and northwest.

Agricultural production may be increased in two ways: by better use of the cultivated land, and by fuller use of the arable uncultivated land. Under better use may be included many methods of scientific farming. These methods have already been tried out in China with a fair degree of success under the leadership of the National Agricultural Research Bureau, the various provincial agricultural institutes, and the two missionary universities — Nanking and Lingnan. Improvement in seed has given increases in yield of 30 percent or more for raw cotton. Insect and disease control has prevented huge losses at small cost, losses often amounting to 10-20 percent of the crop yield. Use of commercial fertilizers will increase production. The problem here is one of obtaining a cheaper supply of fertilizer, of extending credit at reasonable rates for its purchase, decreasing the cost of transporting fertilizer by more modern methods of transportation and discovering a sanitary method of using human manure — chief source of fertilizer for Chinese farmers at present — without diminishing its fertilizing value. Finally, the consolidation of holdings, which will eliminate the boundary lines and thus save the much needed land for further cultivation, will facilitate the introduction of farm machinery, reduce the difficulties of irrigation, and result in a general increase of production. The fuller use of arable uncultivated land, through reclamation, introduction of new crops in regions where dry farming is possible, and other methods, will also increase production; provided that the limiting factors, including availability of water, capital, fertilizer and erosion control, can be removed.

The standardization of agricultural production is a pre-requisite to the use of farm crops for large-scale manufacturing as well as export. The small scale, decentralized, and disorganized production of farm crops fails to meet the requirements of modern industry for raw materials of a uniform grade that can be obtained in sufficient quantities to meet the needs of continuous operations, whether for domestic consumption by industries in China or for export to foreign manufacturers. The task rests not with the government alone, but also with the peasants themselves. The Chinese government, through its national and provincial agricultural institutes, has demonstrated the superiority of improved seeds of a uniform grade. The peasants, by organizing themselves into cooperative societies responsible for the distribution of these seeds, can enforce their cultivation among the members. These rural cooperatives can go a long way in standardizing Chinese agricultural production and in obtaining for it facilities of purchase, credit and marketing that may tend to reduce the cost of agricultural production on the one hand, and to raise farm income on the other.

The stabilization, increase and standardization of agricultural production will call for considerable capital outlay on the part of the government for the provision of those services to agriculture which the state, with its resources and political authority, is able to undertake. Next to transport, it is a field which must be given a prominent place in any program of China's postwar industrialization.

Industry

Four main types of industry will have to be developed, although a clear-cut demarcation as to the order of development is difficult to make at the outset, and will have to be worked out as occasion may call for. The first is the consumers' goods industries, such as clothing (mainly textiles — cotton, silk, woolen, ramie — but also boots and shoes, etc.), food (flour milling, rice cleaning, oil pressing, food canning, wine distilling, tobacco rolling, etc.), and other necessary articles of daily use (paper, soap, matches, salt, glass, enamelware, stationery and printing, etc.). Much of China's industrial development during the last half century has taken place in these branches of industry, and a hopeful beginning already made may serve as a good starting point for postwar industrialization.

The consumers' goods industries command several advantages that the other three types do not seem to possess completely. The first advantage is that they can be operated on a large or small scale. Cotton spinning is, of course, a large industry; while cotton weaving has been operated on a large scale, in power plants, or on a small scale, in weaving sheds in suburban districts or villages all over China. The small units represent by far the most typical form of Chinese industrial organization. They operate under the craftsman and merchant employer systems well known to the West in the pre-industrial age. Large plants will continue to flourish under private initiative and enterprise; while small units have been, or will be during the war, reorganized into industrial cooperatives, thus reaping the full benefit of large-scale economy in the purchase of raw materials, standardization of design, application for credit, and organization for marketing.

A second advantage of the consumers' goods industry is that it will cater largely to domestic instead of foreign needs. In a world where competition for markets among the industrially advanced nations has brought into existence innumerable tariff barriers, import quotas, bilateral trade arrangements and many other devices of a similar sort, and has even provoked wars for the control of markets, China, as an industrial newcomer, will have a slight chance in finding foreign markets for the absorption of her industrial products. The market will for some time to come be largely, if not wholly, domestic; although more favorable developments towards freer trade after the war are now evolving gradually. The Atlantic Charter of August 14, 1941, for instance, declares in the fourth and fifth sections of the Eight-Point Program, that the allies

> will endeavor to open equally to all nations — victor and vanquished — world trade and raw materials needed for their economic prosperity, and will desire to bring about the fullest collaboration be-

tween all nations with the object of improving labor standards, economic adjustment, and social security.

A third advantage of the consumers' goods industries lies in their small requirements of capital, their large use of labor, and their main dependence upon raw materials locally available — all of which fit in well with Chinese economic conditions. China is poor in capital, due to low margin of production over consumption. Chinese production cannot be increased unless accompanied by mechanical improvements that will have to come through industrialization. The low standard of living in China, now being reduced on account of wartime inflation, cannot be expected to sustain further encroachments after the war. Thus consumption cannot be reduced through lowering the standard of living. China, however, has a redundant population suffering from permanent under-employment. This excess population, given skill and discipline, can serve as a potential reserve of industrial labor. Much of the raw materials for the consumers' goods industries can be supplied at home — cotton, silk, wool, ramie, soybeans, wheat, rice, tobacco, bamboo, salt, etc. Even if China is deficient in some of these materials at the initial stage, production can be increased in a short time. A case in point is that of raw cotton. China, after the rapid development of her nascent cotton industry during the World War I, was faced with a serious shortage of raw cotton, and had to rely upon India and the United States for her supply. But within a decade or so cotton production increased rapidly and China became almost self-sufficient. The average annual production for the five-year period,

1925 – 29, was only 4.46 million quintals, which was doubled in the year before the war, 1936 – 37, when it reached 8.66 million quintals. ① The raw cotton import, on the other hand, declined from the 1931 peak of 2.8 million quintals to 0.5 million quintals in 1935. ②

A second category of industries to be developed in China after the war will be for defense purpose. These military industries, covering iron and steel, other metals, chemicals, ammunition, airplanes, trucks, and shipbuilding, require heavy capital outlay in which China is deficient. China before the war did possess several iron mines, smelting plants, steel works, machine shops and foundries, arsenals engaged in the production of light armaments, a new ammonia sulphate plant, and several dockyards. In Manchuria, military industries had been making rapid headway under Japanese domination. After the war broke out, many of the defense plants in China Proper were either abandoned or removed to Free China, especially those in the Central China provinces of Hupeh, Hunan and Kiangsi started by the National Resources Commission in 1936. Today in Free China, in addition to the iron and steel works and government arsenals, assembling plants for imported American planes and trucks are being built under extreme difficulties of wartime transportation and air-raids. Once the war is over, these industries, so vital to the maintenance of China's minimum defense needs, will certainly be expanded

---

① *Statistical Yearbook, 1939 – 40*, League of Nations, p. 122.
② Ting, Leonard G. : *Recent Developments in China's Cotton Industry*, China Institute of Pacific Relations, 1936, p. 13.

THE POST-WAR INDUSTRIALIZATION OF CHINA

under state ownership and operation. Capital equipment and probably also a part of the necessary personnel① may have to be supplied by the Allied Nations, notably the United States. The American program of wartime defense production, aiming at 125,000 planes, 75,000 tanks, 35,000 anti-aircraft guns, and 10,000,000 deadweight tons of shipping for 1943, will entail a highly difficult task of postwar readjustment to peacetime needs. The task can be lightened if a part of the productive equipment devoted to wartime defense production in the United States, together with the key technical and managerial personnel, can be transplanted to Chinese soil at the conclusion of the present war, under some workable arrangement which will prove to be satisfactory to both countries.

The third type of industries will be primarily for export. China in her postwar industrialization will have to depend largely upon foreign investments for the supply of capital. The flow of capital into China will give rise to the difficult problem of servicing the foreign debts, which will be especially serious during the first five or ten years. Production will increase in the course of time, but not so rapidly as to afford a surplus that will help to balance her unfavorable balance of payments arising from the servicing of new foreign loans. But foreign debt servicing cannot be post-

---

① China before and during the war has already built up an efficient technical personnel for undertaking construction of heavy industries and arsenal production by the National Resources Commission of the Ministry of Economics and the Arsenal Administration under the Ministry of War, both being manned by native staff. But postwar development in these branches will necessarily call for an expanded personnel to be partly supplied by friendly nations.

poned indefinitely, and after a period of say five to ten years, China must find her own way of facing the long-term problem of payments. The need for developing export industries thus arises, and must be considered from the very beginning. In the light of her available resources and manpower, four groups of export industries may be developed. The first is the mining and smelting of certain minerals of which China possesses a major portion of the world's supply, e. g. tungsten, antimony, and to a lesser extent, tin. China in 1937 supplied 58 percent of the world production of tungsten, 37 percent of antimony, and 5 percent of tin. Once the war is over, the demand for these minerals may decrease. Both tungsten and antimony are strategic war materials; their production in Bolivia is being increased as a wartime necessity due to increasing difficulty of transportation between China and America. The present substitution of molybdenum, produced chiefly in the United States, for tungsten, may increase. Tin production for the world may have to depend upon the policies of the International Tin Cartel; while competition from Nigeria, Belgian Congo and Bolivia may increase. The prospect for mineral exports from China is therefore not so hopeful after the return of peace.

A second group of export industries relates to the processing of staple agricultural exports such as soya beans, wood oil, vegetable oils, tea, silk, bristles, furs, hides and skins, wool, sausage casings, eggs and egg products. Before the war many refining or processing plants for these products could be found in leading ports such as Shanghai, Dairen, Tientsin, Canton, and Hankow. Except for those at Dairen, much destruction has been wrought upon these industries by the present war, but a postwar revival under more scientific management and closer government supervision will help in increasing the quality as well as quantity of these exports. The pressing of vegetable seeds for the production of oil fats, which is increasing in wartime China, will increase after the war, as demand for vegetable fats in Europe is likely to increase owing to the wartime destruction of livestock. On the other hand, the substitution of dehydrated castor oil for wood oil, and of nylon for silk and bristles, may tend to reduce the prospect for China's exports of these raw materials.

A third group of export industries — the handicrafts, in which China has advantage of production on account of her abundant but skillful labor, promise to fill a genuine need of western consumers for variety and taste in an age of mass standardization. Under cooperative arrangements, these craftsmen can unite to supply the world market for handicraft products with better designs, greater output, and higher returns. During the war Madame Chiang Kai-shek has taken a keen interest in the production of handicraft articles such as embroidery, lacework, and table linens by refugee women and girls for the growing American market. Many articles on sale at the five-and-ten stores in the United States — toys, trays, cigarette boxes, vanity boxes, table linens, hairnets, etc. — which used to be supplied by the Japanese, would have been replaced during the present war by similar wares from China were China in a position to provide them in large and dependable quantities. ①

A fourth group of export industry will be the tourist industry. China, with her four thousand years of history, has always held the imagination of people all over the world through her historical monuments, folkways, folklores, and countless variety of handicrafts, not to speak of the bewildering agglomeration of human tribes, wild animals, plants and flowers. For over a decade the China Travel Service has provided the facilities required by modern travel. It has developed the tourist industry in regions formerly accessible only to the wealthy few. With a renewed interest in China after the war, this "cradle of civilization" in the Orient will undoubtedly attract an increasing number of American and European tourists—whether scholars in pursuit of archaeological, geological, or sociological information, or adventurers in search of new pleasures of life or business opportunities. This is even more likely if a new age of air commerce is to evolve after the war.

Finally, as China proceeds with her task of industrialization, her production will gradually shift from purely consumers' goods to include a larger proportion of capital goods. During the last eighty years of China's industrial development, lack of foresight and planning on the part of government and industry has placed her in a position of permanent dependence upon foreign industrialized nations for the supply of capital goods like machinery and machine tools. Such a course of development may be

---

① Moser, Charles K. : *Where China Buys and Sells*, Trade Information Bulletin No. 827, U. S. Bureau of Foreign and Domestic Commerce, Washington, 1935.

typical of any country embarking upon a course of industrialization, especially when it is not given a free hand to pursue a policy inimical to foreign imperialistic interests. For this lack of foresight and subjugation to foreign imperialistic interests China has paid dearly. Before the war Chinese industries were conspicuous by the heterogenous variety of machines and equipment which their plants and factories installed. In the cotton industry, the leading factory industry in pre-war China, each mill had a set of spindles and looms manufactured by a different manufacturer in a different country—Britain or America. Often, as the mill underwent an expansion, a new source of supply for the spindles and looms was resorted to, resulting in a medley of capital equipments mutually non-interchangeable. There were cases where certain mills using American machinery were unable to secure parts for replacement because of frequent changes in American models and designs, and as a result, were forced to tear down a complete machine — ginning, carding, roving, or spinning — in order to use the parts for replacement. Just before the war a beginning was made in supplying machine parts for the cotton industry, and here and there small-scale foundries and machine works began to appear. But on the whole, capital goods producing industries were still in their infancy. The present war, including the Japanese blockade and the wartime scarcity of shipping facilities, has impressed Chinese industrialists more than ever with the importance and urgent need of introducing capital goods industries.

Chapter IV. China's Wartime Achievements in Industrialization

An indication of China's prospects for postwar industrialization can be found in the record of her wartime economic development. This has taken place largely in China's Southwest and Northwest, that is, in those regions of Free China relatively removed from the arena of war operations. ①

China's Pre-war and Wartime Industrial Areas

Before describing China's wartime economic development in the Southwest and Northwest, a word of introduction about the significance of these two areas in the Chinese national economy is in order. China before the war confined its industrial development largely to six areas which were relatively accessible to foreign intercourse, trade and investment; namely, (1) Southern Manchuria with the iron and steel mills of Anshan and Penghsihu; the Fushun coal mine — the largest in China; the largest railway shops, shipyard, and cement factory; and chemical and other light industries; (2) the Yangtze Delta within the triangle of Shanghai, Nan-

---

① This chapter has drawn heavily on a memorandum on the wartime economic development of China privately prepared for the International Secretariat of the Institute of Pacific Relations.

king and Hangchow, with two-thirds of China's textile industry (cotton and silk), large power houses and flour mills, cigarette factories, import and export concerns, and many other large and small industries; (3) Northeastern Hopei along the Peiping-Mukden Railway from Peiping to Chinwangtao, with the Kailan Coal Mine, China's second largest, and the three industrial centers of North China; Tangshan with its large cement factory; Chinwangtao, the coal exporting center, with the largest glass factory in China; and Tientsin, the chief port as well as cotton textile center in North China, with many factories for the preparation for export of materials such as raw cotton, wool, furs, hides and skins, eggs and egg products, and a salt refinery and a soda manufacturing plant in Tangku — gateway to Tientsin; (4) Eastern Shantung along the Tsinan-Kiaochow Railway, with Tsingtao as the chief port and with coal-mining and iron industries, cotton textile mills, and vegetable oil plants; (5) Hunan and Hupeh in the triangle between Hankow, Pinghsiang and Changsha, with the Hanyehping Coal and Iron Company, the largest iron and steel works in China Proper, and several textile mills and industries for the preparation of export products such as eggs, tea, cotton, tung oil, vegetable oils in Hankow, Hanyang, and Wuchang; textile factories, flour mills, and refineries for non-ferrous metals in Changsha; (6) Pearl River Delta along the Canton-Kowloon Railway, with silk filatures and other light industries in Canton and the neighborhood.

All these six areas, with the exception of Changsha in the fifth area, are temporarily lost to the Japanese; and in their place new industrial centers have arisen in China's Southwest and Northwest, such as

Chungking, Chengtu, Kiating, Kunming, Kweiyang, Kweilin, Sian and Lanchow. These two areas, the Southwest and the Northwest, which by no means comprise the whole of Free China, are chosen for wartime economic development because they are fairly rich in agricultural and mineral resources, and easily within reach of Chungking, China's wartime capital located in the heart of the Southwestern Area. The two regions, with five provinces in each, have a combined area of 4,885,000 square kilometers or 44 percent of China's total area of 11,103,000 square kilometres, and a combined population of 100,583,000 or 22 percent of China's total population of 450,000,000. ①

In food resources, the Southwest and the Northwest are barely self-sufficient, having a surplus of rice and other food crops except wheat — i. e. oats, barley, beans, peas, kaoliang, millet, maize, potatoes, etc. The distribution among the provinces is uneven. Among the three most important provinces—Szechuen and Yunnan in the Southwest and Shensi in the Northwest—Szechuen has a surplus of rice and other food crops but is short of wheat, while Yunnan and Shensi are short of rice and wheat. In other food crops Yunnan has a surplus but Shensi has a deficit. When the war is over and transport is restored to its normal condition, the food situation in China's Southwest and Northwest will be less critical, and can be alleviated by surplus crops from the neighboring provinces of Hunan and others. Szechuen, with one half of the total population for the whole of China's Southwest and Northwest, is self-sufficient, and even has some

---

① See Appendix, Table Ⅳ.

surplus food. It is within this province that wartime economic development in Free China has made the most rapid strides.

In raw materials the Southwestern and Northwestern provinces are practically self-sufficient, except in raw cotton, in which the combined production claims only four percent of China's total. But the National Government has made vigorous efforts to increase cotton production during wartime. Szechuen, in particular, is rich in many agricultural products of which a great number, e. g. tung or wood oil, silk, tea, furs and skins, and bristles, together with wool from the Northwest, are being exported to the United States and Soviet Russia to pay for China's wartime foreign loans from these countries. Extensive forest reserves in Sikang, Chinghai, Ninghsia, and western Szechuen, sufficient to feed many pulp and paper factories of the first magnitude, have been discovered by the Ministry of Economics.

In mineral resources, the ten provinces in the Southwest and Northwest possess sufficient reserves for a moderate degree of industrialization for many years to come. The coal reserves reach 92.5 billion metric tons, out of a total of 246 billion metric tons for the whole of China, or 37.6 percent. Shensi leads with 71.9 billion tons or 29.2 percent, followed by Szechuen with 9.9 billion tons or 4.0 percent, Sinkiang with 6 billion tons or 2.4 percent, Yunnan and Kweichow each with 1.6 billion tons or 0.6 percent, and Kansu with 1.5 billion tons or 0.6 percent. The ten provinces are poorly supplied with iron ore. But recent geological survey has resulted in important discoveries, especially in Sikang province. The Luku deposit in this province is said to possess a high grade iron ore of 100 million tons, with 65 percent metallic content as compared with 35 percent for the low grade Manchurian ore—China's largest known reserve. Northern Shensi Basin and western Szechuen are the only regions in China possessing petroleum reserves. In non-ferrous metals, gold in Szechuen, Sikang and Chinghai, tin in Yunnan and Kwangsi, copper in Yunnan and Szechuen, mercury in Kweichow, are all well known; while other metals, such as tungsten, antimony, lead, zinc, manganese and alunite, can also be found in Yunnan, Szechuen, and other provinces.

In the Southwest and Northwest, four industrial centers exist with potential possibilities for development, of which two in the province of Szechuen are already on the road to industrialization under government encouragement. The Southwestern Szechuen Industrial Area, with Chungking as its center, is based on two coal fields, one in the valley of the Kialing River flowing southward into the Yangtze River in Chungking, the other in Nanchuan county south of Chungking; and on the Chikiang iron deposits in southeastern Szechuen. The Kialing River coalfield, with a reserve of 491 million tons, is situated in the five counties around Chungking, and has a pre-war annual production of half a million tons which is now being increased through government efforts. The Nanchuan coalfield is situated closer to the Chikiang iron deposits which, estimated at 15 million tons, possess a high metallic content of around 54 percent. The availability of coal and iron in adjacent districts is making this area the principal center of heavy industry for wartime China, for Chikiang pig iron now is the main source of supply for the iron and steel plants as well as the arsenals in Chungking.

The second industrial area, the Southwestern Szechuen Area, is located in the fourteen counties around Kiating or Loshan, south of Chengtu city. This is the center for many industries such as sugar, salt, paper, silk, matches, pottery, and cotton. The power resources of this region consist of bituminous coal and hydraulic power. The coal reserve reaches 2.4 billion tons, and is widely distributed. But the annual production of half a million tons is not sufficient to meet the growing demand from salt refining and other industries. Especially since the loss of China's coastal salt-producing area, much of the salt consumed in Free China today has been supplied by the salt wells in this region. The total water power resources of the province reach 4.6 million horse power, almost one-fifth of the country's total; the largest power site in the province, perhaps the largest in the whole of China, is the Tatuho site, situated on the western fringe of this area, with an estimated power resource of three million horse power. The potential power of this site is indicated by the fact that over a distance of some five miles the water drops about eighty feet. A power plant, the Minkiang Electric Power House, with a planned maximum capacity of 10,000 K. W., is now in operation to supply the power requirements of the many factories that have been moved into this region since the beginning of the war. The whole area, however, lacks iron ore deposits of any importance in its immediate vicinity. The large Luku deposit in Sikang is now inaccessible; but if a railroad branching from the proposed Yunnan-Szechuen Railway can be built along the course of the Tatuho River to connect the Luku deposit with Wutungchiao or Suifu, not only the Luku deposit but many other resources of this extremely rich territory can be opened up.

The two other areas in China's Southwest and Northwest still await development. The Yunnan Industrial Area, around Kunming, produces tin and copper and is abundantly provided with coal. It is poor in iron ore, but can draw upon the Luku deposit in Sikang if a branch line of the proposed Yunnan-Szechuen Railway, linking Kunming with the county of Mienning in Sikang province, can be constructed. The Northwestern Industrial Area, with Sian and Lanchow as possible centers, has reserves of coal and petroleum, and production in raw cotton and wool. Given proper development of modern transport, especially railways, it has also a hopeful future in industrial development. This area, because of its proximity to the scenes of war operations in North China, especially Shansi, has not received so much attention for development from the government as the other three areas.

When China, with the other United Nations, emerges victorious from this war, she will regain sovereignty over Manchuria as well as over the whole of occupied China. In that case, there will be at least three bases for heavy industries, of which South Manchuria in Northeastern China will, in order of importance, take the first place, followed by the Central China area with Hankow as its center, and the Southeastern Szechuen Area with Chungking as its center. In addition, the Japanese are developing a new center for heavy industry in North China, using ore from the Lungyen mines and coking coal from the Tatung area. The other areas, led by the Yangtze Delta with Shanghai as its center, northeastern Hopei with Tientsin, eastern Shantung with Tsingtao, Pearl River Delta with

Canton, the Yunnan area with Kunming, and the Northwest area extending from Sian westward to Lanchow, will probably continue to flourish as the nuclei for light industries. Most of these developments presuppose, of course, China's ability to defend the long East China coast with a minimum naval and air force still to be built, and a coordinated system of railways and steam navigation along the Yangtze and from coast to coast — a program of naval and economic reconstruction calling for a mobilization and utilization of resources unprecedented in the history of modern China. It seems imperative that Formosa, lost to Japan in the Sino-Japanese War of 1894 – 95, be restored to China; since Formosa, by its strategic location southeast of Fukien province, constitutes an ideal base for naval and air invasion of China by Japan.

China's Wartime Achievements in Industrialization

With the above summary of the southwest and northwest regions and resources, and their relative position among the pre-war industrial areas of China, we may now proceed to describe in brief the wartime economic development in transport, agriculture, and industry, in Free China, mainly in these two regions, and largely through governmental efforts.

Transport. In the field of transport, the outstanding wartime achievements lie in highway construction, with some beginning in railways. Not only has there been a complete blockade of the China coast, and the loss of leading ports including Tientsin and Tsingtao in North China, Shanghai in Southeastern China, and Canton in South China, but also the Great Yangtze River, along with the Pearl River, has been closed to traffic, as far as Ichang, between Free China and occupied China and the outside world. The construction of railways requires materials and equipment which a blockaded China can neither produce nor import from abroad; so highway building becomes the main feature in wartime transport. A network of highways has been set up in the course of the war, in China's Southwest and Northwest, of which the best known is the Burma Road.

The southwest network embraces: (1) the Szechuen-Yunnan system; (2) the Yunnan-Burma Highway and Railway; (3) the Yunnan-Indo-China Railway; (4) the Hunan-Kwangsi-Kweichow system; and (5) other lines. The Szechuen-Yunnan system embraces several routes, chiefly highways, but also contemplated railways and waterways. The two highways that have been completed cross the province of Kweichow. The first, 531 kilometres from Chungking to Kweiyang and 662 kilometres from Kweiyang to Kunming, is longer and less direct than the second from Luhsien on the Upper Yangtze to Kunming. A railway is planned to follow a large part of this second highway, starting from Suifu, the Yangtze port, to Kunming, and covering a distance of 773 kilometres. Work began in September 1938 after the fall of Hankow. By July 1939 about 15 percent of the construction work had been finished. Due to lack of materials, equipment and personnel, the completion of the railway is still a remote possibility. In addition, one more route can be developed between Szechuen and Yunnan. This is the water route, 1,340 kilometres long, between Chungking and Kunming, by way of Suifu, the westernmost terminal on the Yangtze for steamship navigation, and Fuming, a town not far from north of Kunming on the Putu River, an estuary of the Yangtze River. Between Chungking and Kweichow, there are two water routes deserving consideration, the one by way of Wukiang and the other traversing the Chikiang and Sunkang Rivers. Much conservancy work, however, has to be carried out before navigation is possible.

The second basic system in the southwestern network is the link between Kunming and Burma, consisting of the Yunnan-Burma Highway and the projected Yunnan-Burma Railway. The Yunnan-Burma Highway is divided into several sections. From Kunming to Wanting on the border is a distance of 974 kilometres, after which there are two branches, one bearing northwest for 176 kilometres to Bhamo on the Irrawaddy River, and the other continuing south for 185 kilometres to Lashio on the Burma Railway. The total distance from Kunming to Lashio is 1,159 kilometres, and from Chungking to Rangoon via Kunming, 3,360 kilometres. The highway between Kunming and Wanting consists of two sections—the first section of 421 kilometres from Kunming to Siakwan built by the Yunnan Provincial Government in 1935, and the second of 552 kilometres from Siakwan to Wanting built between August 1937 and May 1939. The building of the second section represents a human feat achieved by over 150,000 conscript laborers, for even the road-rollers were cut out of solid rock by hand. It "is above all things a monument to the real hero of China, the patient, smiling, tireless coolie", said Richard Watts, the first western traveller on the road.

The Burma Road used to be the lifeline of China, through which she poured forth her best troops to reinforce the allied defense of Burma, while the United States sent ammunition and necessary war equipment on the return truckloads into Free China for operations against the Japanese. The fall of Rangoon in early March has, however, made it necessary to seek for another supply line to China, the new India Road in process of construction which will traverse the even more mountainous terrain of Sikang province in Western China and Assam in Northeastern India.

The third basic system in the southwest network is the Yunnan-Indo-China Railway, which suspended operations when the Japanese occupied French Indo-China in the summer of 1940. This Railway, however, had proved its usefulness to wartime China between the fall of Canton and the Japanese occupation of French Indo-China, for a period of two years. Formally inaugurated in 1910, it runs 469 kilometres southward from Kunming to the border town of Hokow and then veers southeastward to Hanoi and Haiphong, the port city. Traversing some of the largest mountains in southern Yunnan, it crosses 47 bridges over 20 meters long and passes through 147 tunnels, totalling 15 kilometres in length. Nearly 45,000 Chinese laborers from Kwangsi, Kwangtung, Tientsin, Foochow, and Ningpo, participated in the construction work, under conditions of unbelievable hardship.

The fourth basic system in the southwest network consists of the completed section of 530 kilometres of the Hunan-Kwangsi Railway from Hengyang on the Canton-Hankow Railway to Kweilin and Liuchow in Kwangsi province, thence by highway to Chennankwan on the French Indo-China border via Nanning. From Liuchow where the Railway ends

THE POST-WAR INDUSTRIALIZATION OF CHINA

a highway goes north-westward to Kweiyang, thence northward to Chungking, thus linking together the four provinces of Hunan, Kwangsi, Kweichow and Szechuen. It was along this route, which is reputedly in better condition and less dangerous than the route through Kunming to Kweiyang, that most of the goods from the outside world were transported to Chungking before the Japanese occupation of French Indo-China.

In addition to the main railway connections mentioned above, there are two trunk lines in the southwestern network on which construction had already begun before the war but had to be temporarily suspended because, in comparison with the Hunan-Kwangsi, the Szechuen-Yunnan, and the Yunnan-Burma systems, they were considered less urgent from a military standpoint. One is a railway, 980 kilometres long, connecting Chuchow, a station in Hunan on the Canton-Hankow Railway, with Kweiyang. The section between Chuchow and Lantienlo, about 230 kilometres long, has already been opened to traffic. The other is the line connecting Chengtu with Chungking, 523 kilometres in length, which has been suspended because of the difficulty of bringing in materials purchased through credit arrangements with French interests.

In the Northwest, the backbone of the internal transport system and the only avenue of international contact is the Chinese-Soviet Highway, with a distance of 3,451 kilometres—one of the longest highways in the world—divided into five sections with termini at Sian, capital of Shensi province; Lanchow, capital of Kansu province; Sinsinchia on the Kansu-Sinkiang border; Urumchi, capital of Sinkiang province; Tachen on the Sinkiang-Soviet border, where the Highway connects with a Soviet highway running to Sergiopol on the Turk-Sib Railway. From Sian, newly finished highways spread out in five directions: northwestward to Kansu and Sinkiang; northeastward to Shansi; northward through Yenan and Suiteh to Yulin; eastward to Loyang, to Nanyang, and along the Han River via Paochi and Hanchung; and southwestward through Paochi and Hanchung to Chengtu. The Sian-Hanchung-Chengtu road is especially important. Before the old dirt road was converted into a modern highway, it was for two thousand years regarded as one of the chief strategic lines of transport and communication in China. It was completed before the war, and constitutes today the main link, apart from air service, between the Northwest and the Southwest. In addition to this route, the Government is constructing two other important connections between the Northwest and the Southwest. One line lies far west of Sian and Hanchung and will join Lintao in Kansu with Kwangyuan in Szechuen; the other runs from Chungking northward to Kwangyuan.

All in all, in the middle of 1941, there were in Free China 2,800 kilometres of railways, 40,000 kilometres of motor highways, and 9,000 kilometres of inland waterways; as compared with 9,600 kilometres of railways, 110,000 kilometres of motor highways, and 18,000 kilometres of inland waterways in pre-war China (exclusive of Manchuria). Because of scarcity of motor vehicles, gasoline supplies, and steam vessels, a system of stage transportation, using mainly rubber-tired carts pulled by horses, mules, camels and sometimes coolie labor, has been introduced since September 1940. The 40 main and branch lines cover 28,340 kilometres in 13 provinces. Eight national stage transportation lines have been opened, totalling 9,048 kilometres; branches under provincial administration measure 19,292 kilometres. The goods handled during the year September 1940 to August 1941 amounted to 99,334,428 ton-kilometres, distributed as follows: commercial goods 47.9 percent, government goods 32.2 percent, military supplies 14.3 percent, foodstuffs 1.5 percent, postal matter 1.2 percent, others 2.9 percent. It is estimated that a rubber-tired cart, pulled by two or three horses in the northwestern provinces, is capable of travelling with a cargo of 1.2-1.5 tons 20 kilometres a day. In 1941, 7,165 such vehicles were in use, in addition to other means of transport pulled by beast or human labor.

Much of the wartime efforts in highway and railway building is conditioned by the progress of the war and China's needs for mobilization of troops and resources and maintenance of contact with the Allied nations. When the war is over, peacetime conditions may require re-examination of the value of the efforts made during the wartime chiefly with military ends in view. With the re-opening of the Yangtze, and the restoration of the Yunnan-Indo-China Railway, it remains a problem for careful study as to what extent the proposed Yunnan-Burma Railway or the completed Yunnan-Burma Highway, may function economically. The Yunnan-Burma Railway, if completed, will compete not only with the Yunnan-Indo-China Railway, but also with the Shanghai-Yangtze shipping system. Moreover, the Canton-Hankow Railway, which at Hengyang is connected with the partly completed Hunan-Kwangsi-Kweichow Railway, may become a potential competitor even to the Yunnan-Indo-China Railway, especially if it is to be extended to the neighboring provinces of Szechuen and Yunnan.

Agriculture. In agriculture, wartime development in China is less spectacular than that in transport or industry; for agriculture, being a widespread industry in a vast country devoid of modern transport, is less subject to government control. However, the wartime needs for feeding the civilian and military population, for the supply of the raw material requirements of the growing number of industrial plants, and for the maintenance of the continuous stream of staple exports to pay for American and Soviet commercial loans, call for increasing agricultural production in Free China which continues to shrink in area as further retreat to the interior becomes imperative, especially during the early stage of the war. The results already achieved in these directions, although relatively small, are still impressive enough, considering the immense difficulties China has to overcome in respect of agricultural reconstruction. The more important include the erection of irrigation works, the reclamation of new land, the substitution of cereal for opium crops, the improvement of seeds, the control of insects and pests, and the extension of cooperative form of organization. The leading governmental agencies engaged in this field include the Agricultural Credit Administration of the Ministry of Economics, a quasi-public corporation which maintains a network of cooperative banks and warehouses all over the great Southwest and Northwest regions; the Farmers' Bank of China which since the spring of 1941 has taken over the cooperative banks from the Agricultural Credit Administration; the National Agricultural Research Bureau of the Ministry of Agriculture and Forestry, which, together with the newly established provincial agricultural institutes in Szechuen, Kweichow, Kwangsi and other provinces, is in charge of agricultural improvement in its technical and scientific aspects; and the Agricultural Production Promotion Commission of the Executive Yuan, in charge of agricultural extension work in Free China. The Ministry of Food, inaugurated in the fall of 1941, is exerting its efforts in increasing food production and improving food distribution through establishment of government granaries throughout Free China, especially in the province of Szechuen.

The erection of irrigation works not only helps to increase agricultural production, but also prevents recurrent floods. Irrigation works have been maintained for centuries as public enterprises, while their neglect has often given rise to floods and famines. [1] It is therefore not surprising that, despite the war, the Government has continued work on its irrigation projects and is making plans for further expansion, extending to a cultivated area of over 400,000 acres. In July 1938, despite the fact that the war had been raging for a year, the Ministry of Economics was able to report the completion of two large irrigation projects in the Northwest—the Mei Huei Canal in Shensi irrigating 30,000 acres of land and the Tao Huei Canal in Kansu irrigating over 5,000 acres. In addition, several new projects are still under way in various provinces—the Lo Huei Canal irrigating 100,000 acres, the Hei Huei Canal irrigating 16,000 acres, and the Chien Huei Canal irrigating 25,000 acres, all in Shensi; so are plans for the irrigation of 60,000 acres in Szechuen, 1,800 acres in Kweichow,

---

[1] Chi, Chao-ting: *Key Economic Areas in Chinese History*, Allen & Unwin, 1936.

20,000 acres in Hunan, 60,000 acres in Kwangsi, and 100,000 acres in Yunnan. The technical staffs on the various river conservancy commissions, notably the Yellow River, the Yangtze River, and the Hwai River, are concentrating their resources on the irrigation works in the Southwest and Northwest, now that the river valleys have been temporarily lost to the Japanese. Extensive loans for financing these works are being granted by the Agricultural Credit Administration through the provincial governments of the Chengtu Headquarters of the Generalissimo. By the end of September 1939, the total costs of projects completed, under construction, or shortly to be started, amounted to eight million yuan, with loans totalling six million yuan.[①] The total area to be irrigated by these projects was 150,000 acres, in seven provinces, mainly in Shensi and Szechuen. Other projects under survey were three in Yunnan, for the improvement of 40,000 acres of land at a cost of two million yuan, and one in Kiangsi, costing 1.2 million yuan.

For the purpose of increasing production new lands have been reclaimed for cultivation or made available through the suppression of opium culture; while better methods of farming have been introduced. Extensive study carried on by the Ministry of Economics in cooperation with

---

① *Chinese Yearbook, 1940 – 41*, pp. 601 – 606. In view of rapid wartime inflation, the value of Chinese yuan has depreciated. The exchange ratio, in terms of US cents per Chinese yuan, is as follows for the period 1934 – 41:

1934	34.094	1937	29.606	1940	6.000
1935	36.571	1938	21.360	1941	5.313
1936	29.751	1939	11.879		

Source: *Federal Reserve Bulletin*, February, 1942, p. 189.

the National Relief Commission for a period of seven months since the autumn of 1938 has brought to light a vast tract of waste but cultivable land, capable of supporting over half a million refugee settlers, in the Northwest and Southwest, and in Kiangsi and Fukien. The three reclamation areas in Shensi — Huang Lung Shan in the east central part of the province north of the Wei River, Li Ping area in the Lower Han River Valley on the border of Szechuen, Yen Shan region on the north bank of the Upper Wei River — have a reclamation area of over 160,000 acres, able to accommodate 120,000 settlers. By the autumn of 1938, 5,000 persons had already been settled in the first of the three areas. Other areas include over 200,000 acres in Sikang, 100,000 acres in northern Szechuen, 30,000 acres in Kansu, and 800,000 acres in Yunnan. As for Kwangsi, half of its cultivable land is not yet cultivated, and the potentialities for reclamation are reported to be great. In the early part of the war, the Government was also active in reclamation work in Hunan, Kiangsi, and Fukien; but as the war progresses, efforts in this direction are most likely to be concentrated on the further development of the projects in the northwestern and southwestern provinces.

According to a study made by the Anti-Opium Society, if all the land growing opium were converted into grain fields, China's grain production would increase by about 25 million piculs, which is the average amount of foreign rice imported annually before the war (1 picul being equivalent to 133 1/3 pounds). Before the war an Anti-Opium Conference held in Chungking adopted a program of gradual suppression of opium culture in a period of six years 1935 - 40, which was vigorously carried out under the personal supervision of the Generalissimo. In 1938, the National Agricultural Research Bureau attributed the increase in the production of crops largely to the sharp curtailment of opium cultivation in Szechuen, Yunnan, and Kweichow, which had dropped sixty percent in comparison with the previous year.

Better methods along the line of scientific farming are being introduced all over Free China through the efforts of the National Agricultural Research Bureau established in 1932 and removed to Chungking in 1938, with the five main stations in the five provinces of Szechuen, Kweichow, Hunan, Kwangsi and Yunnan, and a staff of more than 200 graduates of agricultural colleges in China or abroad. Other development agencies have been the provincial agricultural institutes, notably the Szechuen Provincial Agricultural Institute organized early in 1938 with a staff of 300 workers; and the College of Agriculture and Forestry of the University of Nanking founded in 1913 by the late Joseph Bailie, American missionary. Since its establishment the College has graduated 1,500 students, or more than one-third of the graduates of all agricultural colleges in China; it operates over 30 agricultural experimental stations all over China. Through improvement of old and introduction of new seeds, use of better fertilizers, control over insects and pests, application of farm machinery and principles of farm management, veterinary medicine, etc., these agencies, together with the Agricultural Production Promotion Commission of the Executive Yuan, and under the guidance of the Ministry of Agriculture and Forestry, have succeeded in increasing China's wartime agricultural production.

The extension of cooperative organizations among Chinese peasants has been very rapid during the war. From before the war to the end of 1940 the cooperative societies trebled in number. At the latter date, the 146,297 rural societies registered with the central authorities, including the 103,444 full-fledged cooperatives and others in a less advanced stage of development, had a total membership of 7,582,107. [1] There were in the Municipality of Chungking and sixteen provinces — including the eight southwest and northwest provinces (Chinghai and Sinkiang excepted) 89,999 credit societies in existence, or 87 percent of the 103,444 cooperatives. Other cooperative units include 9,085 producers', 2,027 transportation and selling, 1,461 consumers', 473 supply, 349 public utilities, 6 insurance and 44 unclassified. 24,146 societies, or 18 percent were to be found in the province of Szechuen alone. The general rural credit outstanding at the end of 1940, 209 million yuan, was largely granted through the cooperatives, the loans of which amounted to 156 million yuan.

Industry. In industry, the main achievements during wartime include the removal of several hundred factories from Shanghai to Hankow during the first year of war and thence to the Southwest and Northwest; the establishment of a dozen industrial bases for both heavy and light industries in Free China; and the rapid growth of the industrial cooperative movement among the small handicraftsmen. All these developments are

---

[1] *China after Four Years of War*, China Information Committee, Chungking, 1941, pp. 90-91.

increasing China's wartime industrial production in an undeveloped, blockaded hinterland.

In addition to the Arsenal Administration of the Ministry of War, three organizations—two governmental and one semi-public—are mainly responsible for the rapid advances in China's industrial production during the war. These are: the National Resources Commission of the Ministry of Economics in the building up of heavy industries under government ownership and operation, the Industrial and Mining Adjustment Administration of the Ministry of Economics in assisting privately owned industries, mostly light, to remove from the war-ridden areas for re-establishment and expansion in the vast hinterland of Free China, and the Chinese Industrial Cooperatives in mobilizing the refugee craftsmen and organizing them into cooperative units in guerilla areas of occupied China as well as in Free China.

The National Resources Commission was established in 1932 in response to the urgent public demand for a strong national defense policy, and engaged itself exclusively in research and planning during the ensuing three years. On the conclusion of the preliminary research and planning in March 1935, the Commission decided to start the construction of heavy industries in July 1936, with the help of as much foreign capital and technical assistance as possible. The program of action for the first three years, calling for an investment of 230 million yuan, of which 72 million was to come from Central Government appropriations and the rest to be secured through foreign borrowing, consisted of the following projects. ①

(1) Government control of the production of tungsten and antimony and the construction of a tungsten refining plant with a yearly capacity of 2,000 tons;

(2) Construction of a steel works in Hsiangtan and Maanshan with a yearly capacity of 300,000 tons, half of China's domestic needs;

(3) Exploitation of the iron mines in Linhsiang and Kialing with a yearly production of 300,000 tons;

(4) Exploitation of the copper mines in Tayeh, Yanghsin, and Penghsien, and construction of a copper smelting plant with a yearly capacity of 3,600 tons, half of China's domestic needs;

(5) Exploitation of the lead and zinc mines in Shuikoushan and Kweihsien with a yearly production of 5,000 tons, all of China's domestic needs;

(6) Exploitation of the coal mines in Kaokang, Tienlo, Tanchiashan, and Yuhsien, with a yearly production of 1.5 million tons, sufficient to make up for the shortage of coal in Central and South China;

(7) Construction of a plant for extracting oil from coal, and ex-

---

① Chien, Chang-chao: "Experiences and Reflections after two and a half Years' Struggle in the Creation of a Heavy Industry", *New Economist* (in Chinese), Chungking, May 16, 1939.

ploitation of the oil resources in Yenchang, Pahsien, and Tahsien, bringing the total yearly production of oil up to 25 million gallons, half of China's domestic needs;

(8) Construction of a nitrogen plant with a yearly production of 50,000 tons of sulphurous acid; and manufacture of sulphuric acid for use in the munitions industries;

(9) Construction of a machine factory, including a plant for making airplane motors, a plant for making other motors, and a plant for making tools;

(10) Construction of a plant for manufacturing electrical supplies, including an electric-wire factory, a radio-tube factory, a telephone apparatus factory, and an electric-motor factory, with a yearly production sufficient to meet domestic needs.

The plan, as outlined above, was centered in the central China provinces of Kiangsi, Hupeh and Hunan in view of the Japanese occupation of Manchuria and its consequent threat to North China. It represents the first concrete program for the development of China's heavy industry, and, if carried out, will supply a large part of China's pre-war needs of strategic industrial products. For the fiscal year 1936 (July 1936 to June 1937), the first year of the plan, the Central Government appropriated 10 million yuan for the construction of enterprises. This sum, together with a considerable amount of credit obtained from foreign interests, was used by the Commission to start work on most of the projects; and the only works that were planned but not started were the Hsiangtan steel works, the airplane motor factory, the coal liquefication factory, the nitrogen plant, and the lead and zinc mines in Kweihsien. The result of the first year of the program was so successful that the Government doubled its appropriations for the second year, the fiscal year 1937.

With the outbreak of war, a drastic change in the plan was called for. Since the projects in the process of development were mainly located in the provinces of Hunan, Hupeh and Kiangsi, which within a year after the beginning of the war were menaced by the enemy, many of them had to be stopped or abandoned, and some removed to the interior. By 1941 the Commission had succeeded in establishing more than 70 units in interior China, including 29 industrial, 22 mining, and 20 electrical engineering units. Special emphasis is given to the development of mechanical, chemical, smelting and electric appliance industries, while in the field of mining, priority is given to mines having a bearing on national defense such as coal, iron, petroleum, copper and on China's barter trade with foreign countries such as antimony, tin, mercury, and tungsten.

The Industrial and Mining Adjustment Administration, organized at the beginning of the war as a part of the National Military Council, was transferred to the Ministry of Economics at its organization in January 1938. Ever since its establishment the Administration has been mainly responsible for the removal of private factories from the war areas and their re-establishment and expansion in Free China, through financial, technical, and other aids. Up to the end of 1940, factories removed from Shanghai, Hankow and Ichang to Free China through the encouragement and assistance of the Administration numbered 450, while the total weight of their equipment shipped was given at 116,375 tons, of which one-half belonged to the Hanyehping Iron and Steel Works in Hanyang—the largest in prewar China outside of Manchuria. The equipment removed, although not large, represented the most indispensable part of a basic industrial set-up for wartime production, selected only after deliberate consideration of needs and priorities. These factories, manufacturing a large variety of products for both military and civilian requirements, are now scattered over the various industrial centers in Free China, especially in the three industrial areas in the Southwest around Chungking, Loshan and Kunming. Along with the removal of machinery and equipment, the Administration has also paid for or subsidized the travelling expenses of 12,000 skilled workers to the interior. This does not include the 30,000 other workers moved inland with assistance from other sources. According to a report made at the end of 1940, there were in Free China 1,354 factories operated by mechanical motive power each with a capital of more than 10,000 yuan and a labor force of over 30, distributed by groups as follows: mechanical 312, mining and metallurgical 93, electrical 47, chemical 361, textile 282, miscellaneous 259. These factories had a total combined output of 4.7 billion yuan (approximately 265 million U. S. dollars at that time), with 1.8 billion for textile, 1.4 billion for chemical, and 1.5 billion for others. ①

---

① *China After Four Years of War*, pp. 59, 64 − 65. The exchange ratio in December 1940 was 5.69 cents of US currency for every Chinese yuan.

The Chinese Industrial Cooperatives, otherwise known as the CIC or Indusco, was sponsored, before the fall of Hankow in the autumn of 1938, by Dr. H. H. Kung, then President of the Executive Yuan and concurrently Minister of Finance, with an initial government grant of five million yuan. Rewi Alley from New Zealand, founder and moving spirit of the movement, and a group of American trained Chinese engineers who acquired practical experience at the Ford plants in Detroit through the efforts of Joseph Bailie, and were thus known popularly as the "Bailie boys", constitute now the nucleus of the movement. The Indusco has a staff of 900 persons, including those at the central headquarters and at the 70 depots in 16 provinces, most of whom are college graduates. The plan of the movement was to construct throughout China chains of small industries using local materials to supply the manufactured goods necessary to the life of the people, under a cooperative form of industry which helps to give the workman the best chance to develop initiative, responsibility and security, and to lay the foundation for a sound industrial life, valuable both to the community and to the individual. [1] Since its founding in the fall of 1938 the movement has made rapid strides. On December 31, 1939, there were 1,284 cooperatives under the Indusco with 15,610 members, but on March 31, 1941, the number of societies had reached 1,664, with a membership of 21,199. The great variety of indus-

---

[1] The present writer urged the adoption of a cooperative system for small industries in a monograph entitled *Rural Weaving and the Merchant Employers in a North China District*, Nankai Institute of Economics, Tientsin, 1935.

trial products manufactured by the CIC, estimated at a yearly value of five million U. S. dollars, is reflected in the distribution of 1,664 cooperatives by industries as follows: textile 547, chemical 303, sewing and clothing 196, mining and metallurgy 173, building construction 117, food 105, machinery 53, culture and stationery 50, transport 14, and miscellaneous 106. These societies produced in 1940 no less than 114 kinds of goods. Today the one-million-blankets-for-the-army movement has given new impetus to the wool spinning and weaving industry of the CIC. Among the plans for the future is the important program of standardization and betterment of means of production. Simple standardized tools and machines, thoroughly adapted to local conditions, will be devised, experimented with, and perfected for use by the cooperatives. ①

Chapter V. Japan in China

The preceding chapter sketched the progress of industrialization in Free China during the war. In the present chapter the course of industrialization in Manchuria since 1931, as well as in occupied China since 1937, under the domination of Japan, will be given in order to give a complete picture of industrialization in the whole of wartime China.

---

① *China after Four Years of War*, chapter on "Indusco's Rapid Growth". See also Nym Wales, *China Builds for Democracy: A Story of Cooperative Industry*, Modern Age, New York, 1942; Edgar Snow, *The Battle for Asia*, 1941; *Far Eastern Survey*, September 22, 1941.

Japan in Manchuria since 1931

Manchuria, comprising the Four Northeastern provinces of Liaoning, Kirin, Heilungkiang, and Jehol, has an area of 1,247,000 square kilometres, or 11.2 percent of China's total area, with a population of 39,454,000, or less than one-eleventh of China's total population. 37,581,000, or 95 percent of the total Manchurian population, are Chinese, the rest being Chosenese, Japanese and others. The increase of Japanese population from 116,600 to 642,300 during 1932 – 39 is not wholly a result of civilian settlement, but attributable to the influx of military, diplomatic and political personnel.

The arable land in Manchuria was estimated in 1935 at 316,979 square kilometres, or 25.4 percent of the total area. The area of arable land that is still uncultivated is estimated at 200,000 square kilometres or 49 million acres, which is larger than the arable uncultivated land area in agricultural China excepting Manchuria, 35 million acres. The importance of Manchuria as an outlet for China's surplus and over-crowded population cannot therefore be over-estimated. [1]

As is commonly known, the primary crops of Manchuria are soya beans, kaoliang, millet, corn, and wheat. The total land area used for the raising of these products is estimated at 80 percent. The remaining crops are paddy rice, upland rice, beans, green peas, buckwheat, cane, barn-

---

[1] *Japan Yearbook*, 1940 – 41, Tokyo. See section on "Manchukuo".

yard grass, rye, barley, cotton, tobacco, hemp, flax, etc. Together with cabbage, hops, fruits and lucerne, the entire agricultural products of Manchuria number some 40 or 50 species. Soya beans is the mainstay of Manchurian export in the form of bean oil and bean cake, chiefly to Germany; while wheat is ground locally in flour mills for export to other port cities in China, especially Shanghai.

The total forest area in Manchuria is estimated at 358,684 square kilometres, which is equal to 28.8 percent of the entire area of the country. The volume of standing timber is estimated at 150 billion cubic feet, but due to deforestation may have been reduced to 90 billion cubic feet. The lumber industry is carried on in the districts of Antung, Kirin and Harbin, but that in Antung district is best known. Total lumber production in 1938 was estimated at 3.6 million cubic meters. The pulp industry also flourishes in Eastern Manchuria, the production of which has risen from 13,737 metric tons in 1934 to 37,672 metric tons in 1938. [1]

Manchuria is rich in mineral resources, especially iron and oil shale. The *Far Eastern Yearbook* for 1940−41 gives the following figures for Manchurian mineral reserves:

Mineral reserves of Manchuria (in million metric tons)

| Coal | 17,417 | Fire clay | 100 |
| Iron ore | 1,514 | Aluminum shale | 25 |

---

[1] *Japan Yearbook*, 1940−41, p. 960.

			continued
Oil shale	7,628	Gold ore (kgs)	6
Magnesite	5,000		

Since the occupation of Manchuria by the Japanese in 1931 mineral production has shown some rise, but not to the extent originally expected by the Japanese militarists. In Table V of the Appendix are given the annual figures on the mineral production of Manchuria for the period 1929 - 37, as compared with those for the five-year plan during 1937 - 41. Although little is known about the volume of production in Manchuria in recent years, production in 1937 was showing a considerable increase, but the actual volume was still small and was only a fraction of the result hoped for under the Five-Year Plan. The production of gold, coke, magnesite, fire clay rose by more than 100 percent between 1933 and 1937; the figures for iron ore and electricity generated by nearly 100 percent, pig iron by approximately 65 percent and coal by more than 35 percent.

Side by side with the development of heavy industries, chiefly in the form of mineral and power production for military purposes, Manchuria witnessed during the ten years of Japanese occupation a rapid increase in transport development — mainly railways and highways. When the new state of "Manchukuo" was proclaimed in 1932 it took over the Chinese owned railways (2,939 kilometres) and made them a part of the state system, but left the Chinese Eastern Railway (1,732 kilometres) and the South Manchurian Railway (1,124 kilometres) in the hands of the Russian and Japanese companies. In February 1933 the government entrusted the entire management of the "Manchukuo" State Railways to the South Manchuria Railway Company. The latter was to operate the existing lines and build new ones according to a ten-year program which would bring the total network up to 10,000 kilometres. Later in the same year the administration of the North Korea Railway, which connected the eastern regions of Manchuria with these ports, was turned over to the Company. In 1935, after two years of negotiation, the Chinese Eastern Railway (now the North Manchuria Railway) became a part of the state system when the Soviet Government sold its interest, thus marking the end of the forty year struggle between Japan and Russia to dominate and develop Manchuria.

The ten-year goal for railway expansion was actually attained in less than seven years by the end of 1939, when Manchuria was in possession of 10,000 kilometres of railways distributed in three categories as follows: 8,365 kilometres of state lines, 1,291 kilometres of South Manchuria Railway lines, and 344 kilometres of North Chosen lines. [1] As to highways, the total length at the end of 1937 was reported to be 50,468 kilometres, classified under four categories as follows: usable year-round 10,772 kilometres or 20 percent; unusable after rains 18,267 kilometres or 36 percent; unusable in rainy reason 15,723 kilometres or 32 percent; and usable in winter only 5,706 kilometres or 12 percent. [2]

---

[1] *Far Eastern Yearbook, 1940 - 41*, p. 673.
[2] *Ibid.*, p. 789.

Total Japanese investments in Manchuria were estimated at over ¥4,500 million at the end of 1939. Investments prior to the Manchurian Incident amounted to ¥1,617 million, of which ¥742 million, or 48 percent, represented outlays by the South Manchuria Railway Company. Additional investments in the four-year period, 1932-35, were estimated at ¥899 million and in the four-year period, 1936-39, ¥2,154 million. Shares in Manchurian corporations and bonds of the South Manchuria Railway Company and of the Manchurian government and its agencies were acquired by industrial and semi-official companies and by individuals in Japan. Manchuria was expending large sums for labor, materials and equipment in the process of expanding her transportation facilities and in developing mines and industries. The Japanese investment was received in the form of imports of materials and machinery for mines and factories and of textile materials, flour and sugar for the labor employed. The export from Japan of both capital goods and consumption goods was stimulated by the Japanese investment in Manchuria and these investments were further stimulated by high prices in Manchuria.

From 1912 to 1932, Manchuria had an active balance of trade with exports consistently and considerably in excess of imports. In 1933, Manchuria became a capital importing country and the excess of exports was replaced by an excess of imports. [1] This great influx of Japanese capital and equipment for the development of military industries and strategic transport lines has had but one end in view, complete conquest.

---

[1] See Appendix, Table VI.

Japan in China Proper since 1937

China has a total area of 11,103,000 square kilometres. China Proper, excluding Manchuria, Mongolia, Sinkiang and Tibet, has a total area of 3,970,000 square kilometres or 35.7 percent. Manchuria, with an area of 1,247,000 kilometres, claims 11.2 percent.

From the occupation of Manchuria on September 18, 1931, to the outbreak of the Sino-Japanese War in China Proper on July 7, 1937, is an interval of barely six years. The one is but a prelude to the other, yet both differ in at least one vital respect. Japanese occupation of Manchuria is complete; while strictly speaking after almost five years of war between China and Japan there is hardly any Japanese-occupied "area" in China Proper. There are only Japanese-penetrated "lines" and "points". The Japanese have captured a number of industrial and commercial centers — points along the coast, the Great Yangtze, and the main railway lines that are vulnerable to attacks of modern warfare; nowhere does Japanese control extend beyond the reach of the machine gun. The term "Occupied China", when contrasted with "Free China", must be understood in this sense of "points" and "lines". According to one estimate in July 1941 no more than 10 – 12 percent of China Proper falls within the zone of Japanese occupation. Of the 1,500 counties in China Proper, only 50 counties or 3.3 percent are under Japanese administration. In these counties, only 37 – 42 million Chinese, about 10 percent of the total population of 400 million in China Proper, are living under moderately effective Japanese control. ①

"Occupied China", excluding Manchuria but embracing within it all of the four industrial areas in China Proper of prewar days, and a part of the fifth, is now being exploited by the Japanese military with the same methods as they used in Manchuria and with the same objectives. But the exploitation is not as effective because of the shorter duration of occupation, greater Chinese resistance, and smaller influx of Japanese capital. In order to exploit the natural resources of China Proper, with a view to the establishment of Japan's economic supremacy in the Far East, the Japanese government has carefully mapped out and organized a series of commercial and industrial development schemes in North and Central China, based on its findings and experiences in Manchuria. These schemes are engineered and directed by the China Affairs Board in Tokyo, set up on December 16, 1938, by the Japanese Cabinet. Created in connection with and existing for the duration of the China Affair, the new Board is presided over by the Prime Minister. Exclusive of purely diplomatic affairs its business comprises:

1. Political, economic and cultural problems relating to the China Affair;
2. The study and investigation of governmental policies to be

---

① "Four years of the Chinese-Japanese War", *Contemporary China*, July 10, 1941. Hudson, G. F., Rajchman, Marthe, and Taylor, George E.: *An Atlas of Far Eastern Politics*, New York, 1942, p. 173, show a larger area for occupied China than is conceded by the official figure here quoted.

adopted in regard to the matters coming under the above category;

3. Supervision of the operations of the companies established under special laws for the purpose of doing business in China as well as the control of the business transactions in China by persons who are so engaged; and

4. The maintenance of unity in the administrative affairs of the different government offices relating to China.

Under this Board, two big holding companies—the North China Development Company and the Central China Development Company — were formed on November 7, 1938, to push Japanese trade and industrial activities in the occupied territories. The two development companies are intended to branch out into all the strategic lines of economic activity in China, and to become virtual monopolies in their respective fields.

The North China Development Company, entrusted with the function of developing the natural wealth and trade enterprises in North China, is organized under the laws of Japan, with a proposed capital of ￥350 million, half of which is reported to be provided by the Japanese government and the other half by public subscription, preference being given to families of soldiers. Of the share to be borne by the Japanese government, only ￥55.6 million have been paid up, while the private shareholders have paid in only ￥43.8 million. The manifold and large-scale activities which the Company proposes to undertake may be easily seen from the following summary of trade and industrial monopolies it is now trying to establish directly and indirectly in North China: ①

1. North China Raw Cotton Company, organized in March, 1938, with a capital of ￥3,000,000 to control cotton production in North China where prior to the present hostilities, the output reached 36 percent of the total production for all China.

2. North China Industrial Development Company, organized in 1938 with a capital of ￥100,000,000 to develop mineral resources and heavy industries, such as:

    a. Coal. —Japanese plans for coal in North China include the urgent development of the Tatung coalfields, estimated to contain a coal reserve of 12 billion tons, to the extent of 700,000 tons a year in order to assure an adequate supply of boiler coal for Japan, the doubling of transport capacity for coal on the Peiping-Suiyuan Railway, the development of mines in East Hopei for coking coal, a 20 - 40 percent increase in output in the coal mines along the Peiping-Hankow Railway such as Lincheng and Liuhokow, and the rehabilitation of coal mines in Shantung province.

    b. Iron. —Japanese plans for iron in North China include the development of the iron resources in Chahar, Hopei,

---

① Lowe, Chuan-hua: *Japan's Economic Offensive in China*, London, 1939, Chapter III. See also "Railways in North China", *Far Eastern Survey*, Jan. 29, 1942.

Shansi, and Shantung, the restoration of the Lungyen mine and the improvement of the Shihchingshan Iron Works near Peiping, which is to be managed by the Japan Iron Manufacturing Company. Iron ore reserves in Lungyen are estimated at 100 million tons, and the ores are being smelted in Shihchingshan, aiming at an output of 80,000 metric tons a year.

3. North China Telephone and Telegraph Company, organized in Peiping in 1938 with a capital of ￥35,000,000, of which ￥13,000,000 are controlled by the North China Development Company. The new company is to "take over" and operate all tele-communication facilities in North China.

4. North China Salt Company, organized with a capital of ￥30,000,000 as a subsidiary of the North China Development Company, to control and develop the famous Changlu salt fields, which will then provide an adequate supply for soda, rayon and glass industries in Japan. Japanese firms participating in the new salt enterprise include the Oriental Development Company, the Dai Nippon Salt Industry, etc. For the first period of the new development program, an annual output of one million metric tons of salt is aimed at.

5. North China Transport and Communications Company, set up in April 1939, at a capitalization of ￥300,000,000, is to "take over" and operate all former Chinese government railways in North China, totaling 5,530 kilometres before

the end of 1940. The South Manchuria Railway Company, subscribing to ¥120,000,000, is playing a leading role in this new enterprise.

6. North China Metallurgical Development Company, capitalized at ¥10,000,000, to develop and monopolize the mining of nickel and other light ores in North China.

7. North China Petroleum Syndicate, organized with a capital of ¥20,000,000, to enjoy the sole right of importing and selling petrol and petroleum products in North China and Inner Mongolia.

8. North China Wool Manufacturers' Association, formed in Kalgan with a capital of ¥8,000,000 by eight Japanese controlling companies. This association is charged with the exclusive purchase of wool, camel hair, etc., in the "autonomous Mongolian area", as well as with the management of former Chinese government woolen mills in Peiping and Suiyuan. Under Japanese supervision, the association will also push wool production in Mongolia and establish new plants in Tientsin.

9. North China power monopoly. Japanese power and light enterprises in North China are chiefly in the hands of the Hsing Chung Kung Ssu ("Reviving China Company"), which controls and operates the power and light plants in Peiping, Tientsin, and Tungchow. A new company is to be created soon to "take over" and operate the plants in Kal-

gan, Tatung, Kweihua and Paotow.

10. Shantung Flour Company, organized to "take over" and operate all former Chinese-owned mills in Tsingtao, Tsinan, and other cities in Shantung.

The Central China Development Company is reported to have a capital of ￥100,000,000, which is to be shared equally by the Japanese government and private interests. Actually, the 14 subsidiary companies now under its control received an investment from the parent company of ￥34,000,000 by the end of 1939, and ￥51,000,000 by the end of 1940.

The Central China Development Company is obviously aiming to secure control of all the leading economic activities in Central China, just as the sister organization is aiming to do in North China. As instruments for enforcing this policy of economic control and domination, the Central China Development Company has invested in the 14 subsidiary companies, 13 of which are briefly described below:[1]

1. Central China Iron Mining Company, formed on April 8, 1938, with a capital of ￥20,000,000 fully paid up, as a joint undertaking of the Hsing Chung Kung Ssu (affiliated with the South Manchuria Railway Company), Japan Steel Tube Company and the Asano Iron Works. The Com-

---

[1] Smith, David S.; "The Central China Development Company", *Far Eastern Review*, March 1941; Lowe, *op. Cit.*, pp. 60 – 63.

pany operates the mines at Maanshan, Fenghuangshan and Tungkwanshan in Anhwei and Kiangsu provinces, and is doing much prospecting work also. It plans to "take over" the famous Tayeh Iron Works in Hupeh, aiming at an annual production of one million tons of iron ore. In May 1940 the Company spent ¥300,000 to organize a special laboratory in the suburbs of Shanghai to analyze the contents of mineral ores.

2. Hwainan Coal Mining Company, established on June 15, 1939, with a capital of ¥15,000,000, has a paid-up capital of ¥9,676,000. In the early days of its operation, the company turned out 1,000 tons of coal every month, but since May 1940 the monthly production was increased under the Five-Year Production Plan.

3. Central China Salt Company, established on August 21, 1939, with a capital of ¥5,000,000, has a paid-up capital of ¥1,250,000. The company sustained heavy losses in 1939 as some of its important salt fields were washed out by high water. From November 1, 1939, to October 31, 1940, business condition improved and no less than 180,000 tons of salt were supplied to different companies and provinces.

4. Central China Electricity and Waterworks Company, organized in June 1938 with an authorized capital of ¥25,000,000, has a paid-up capital of ¥20,000,000. In November 1940 the

company operated 16 power plants and nine waterworks in different cities of Central China formerly belonging to private Chinese interests, supplying electric light to 95,551 households and electric power to 4,471 industrial establishments, as well as 5,512,281 cubic meters of water.

5. Central China Tele-Communication Company, established on July 31,1938, with an authorized capital of ￥15,000,000, has a paid-up capital of ￥10,000,000. It controls and operates all the Chinese telegraph and telephone companies in the occupied areas of Central China, and expects to inaugurate a radio service between Shanghai and Japan.

6. Shanghai Inland Water Navigation Company, organized on July 28,1938, with a capital of ￥2,000,000, has a paid-up capital of ￥1,074,075. It has control of all the shipping lines between Shanghai and the interior cities of occupied Kiangsu, Chekiang and Anhwei provinces.

7. Central China Railway Company, organized in April 1939 with a nominal capital of ￥50,000,000, of which 40 percent will be theoretically allotted to the Nanking puppet regime as counter-value of the 770 kilometres of railways in the hinterland of Shanghai, another 40 percent to the Central China Development Company, and the remaining 20 percent to Japanese railway concerns, has a paid-up capital of ￥35,000,000. It now operates the Nanking-Shanghai, Shanghai-Hangchow-Ningpo, Hwainan, southern section of

the Tientsin-Pukow and the railways of the Kiangnan Railway Company at Wuhu. In May 1939 the company operated 700 kilometres of railways, but in January 1941 it operated 1,100 kilometres of railways.

8. Central China Bus Company, organized on April 30, 1938, with a capital of ¥3,000,000, has a paid-up capital of ¥2,277,500.

9. China Shipping Company, organized in February 1940 with a capital of ¥30,000,000, has a paid-up capital of ¥24,500,000; it operates the shipping lines in Chinese waters formerly undertaken by the Toa Shipping Company.

10. Greater Shanghai Gas Company, organized in December 1938 with a capital of ¥3,000,000, has a paid-up capital of ¥900,000. It was reported to have completed the construction work of the gas plant in 1940.

11. Shanghai Real Estate Company, organized in September 1938 for the purpose of developing the Kiangwan and Woosung area with a capital of ¥20,000,000, has a paid-up capital of ¥15,000,000.

12. Central China Sericultural Company, organized in August 1938 for the purpose of controlling the production and marketing of silk cocoons in Kiangsu and Chekiang provinces, and "taking over" and operating former Chinese-owned silk filatures in Wusih, Changchow, Hangchow and Shanghai, has an authorized capital of ¥10,000,000, and

a paid-up capital of ￥6,500,000.

13. Central China Marine Products Company, organized on November 6, 1938, to control the fishing business along the East China Coast and to operate the fish market at Woosung, has an authorized capital of ￥5,000,000 and a paid-up capital of ￥3,165,000.

Thus, through the two developmental companies in North and Central China, with a third one for South China still in process of organization, Japan is exploiting the vast resources of China Proper in the five fields of transport, communication, public utilities, minerals and industry, mainly in the "points" and along the "lines" that constituted the industrial and commercial areas of pre-war China. The above subsidiary units of the two developmental companies in North and Central China may be classified by fields as follows:

1. Transportation—railways, highways, and waterways:
    a. North China Transport and Communications Company—railways.
    b. Central China Railway Company.
    c. China Shipping Company.
    d. Shanghai Inland Water Navigation Company.
    e. Central China Bus Company.
2. Communications—telephone, telegraph, and wireless:
    f. North China Telephone and Telegraph Company.
    g. Central China Tele-Communications Company.

3. Public utilities—electricity, water, and gas:

   h. North China Power Monopoly—Hsing Chung Kung Ssu.

   i. Central China Electricity and Waterworks Company.

   j. Greater Shanghai Gas Company.

4. Light industries—cotton, silk, wool, flour, and marine products:

   k. North China Industrial Development Company—coal, iron.

   l. Central China Iron Mining Company.

   m. Hwainan Coal Mining Company.

   n. North China Metallurgical Development Company—nickel and other light ores.

   o. North China Salt Company.

   p. Central China Salt Company.

   q. North China Petroleum Syndicate—monopoly over import and sale of petroleum.

5. Light industries—cotton, silk, wool, flour and marine products:

   r. North China Raw Cotton Company.

   s. Central China Sericultural Company.

   t. North China Wool Manufacturers' Association.

   u. Shantung Flour Company.

   v. Central China Marine Products Company—control over East China Coast fisheries and Woosung Fish Market in Shanghai.

6. Other—real estate and housing:

   w. Shanghai Real Estate Company—development of Kiangwan and Woosung area in Greater Shanghai.

   x. Central China Housing Company.

Because of earlier occupation, Japanese exploitation of Chinese resources has made greater headway in North than in Central China, in transport and industry, than in agriculture. The five leading exports to Japan, coal, iron ore, salt, raw cotton, and wool, have come largely from North China during the period of the war. In these Japan has been more successful with the three minerals—more so with coal and salt than with iron ore, as iron ore used to be mined in Central rather than in North China; while over the two agricultural exports, raw cotton and wool, Japan has met with bitter disappointments.① The vast rural population, even in North China where Japan's military and political control appears to be more effectively established because of its closer situation to Manchuria, Korea and Japan Proper, as well as longer occupation, has put up a policy of non-cooperation and sabotage in agricultural production. Cash crops, such as raw cotton and wool highly desired by the Japanese exporters and manufacturers, are replaced wherever possible by subsistence crops, thus freeing the Chinese peasant farmers from the necessity of having to sell the cash crops to the Japanese traders at a deplorably low price and to

---

① See Appendix, Table Ⅶ.

buy from them foodstuffs at an exorbitantly high price. ①

Despite the large number of corporations Japan has established for the exploitation of the resources in occupied China, stressing mainly transport for military control and minerals for export to Japan, the achievements are insignificant when placed side by side with what she succeeded doing in Manchuria, where the results obtained fell short of expectations. Japan has confiscated, or seized outright, almost every industrial, commercial, and transport facility in China, whether public or private, in addition to the industries in the Shanghai area which she destroyed during the first half year of war, and which were estimated to have a value of 300,000,000 yuan (or US $85,000,000 at that time). The properties thus seized probably account for a large part, if not all, of the so-called paid-up capital of the two development companies — 99.4 million yen for the North China Development Company in 1939 and 51 million yen for the Central China Development Company in 1940, a total "paid-up" capital of 150.4 million yen out of an authorized capital of 450 million yen. Compared with the capital export of three billion yen

---

① George E. Taylor, author of *Japan in North China* (Institute of Pacific Relations, New York, 1940), recently summarized Japan's failure in North China in following terms: "There is no evidence whatsoever that the economic chaos in North China has given place to a reasonably ordered economy. The development companies are frustrated in their attempts at exploitation by the Japanese Army, which acts independently, by labor difficulties and by lack of capital. . . . Briefly speaking, economic development in North China by the Japanese means, to date, that everything which could be seized has been taken, that nearly all public utilities are run by the Japanese, and that no Chinese is permitted to engage in any business which can hope to make a profit." (*Far Eastern Review*, Oct. 10, 1941, p. 236.)

during the eight year period 1932－39 from Japan to Manchuria, Japanese capital investment in occupied China, 150.4 million yen, represents only a small fraction—five percent! Counting all other Japanese investments in China that have not gone through the channels of the two development companies and allowing for subsequent additions by the two companies, the total during the period of war certainly cannot have been doubled or trebled. Even so, the grand total represents only 10－15 percent of what was invested in Manchuria during the eight year period 1932－39.

The reasons are not far to seek. A war of several weeks has been prolonged *ad infinitum*, now into the end of the fifth year. The strain which the war places upon Japan's national economy must be tremendous. According to a recent study, at the end of 1940, after three and a half years of war with China Japan had spent approximately 17 billion yen as the direct cost of war operations, a sum slightly above her national income in 1936 — the pre-war year! The indirect cost of the war, of course, is much more than this. For example, expansion in war-essential industries, necessitated by the war exigency, has meant earmarking a large portion of national income for net investment. Consumers' outlay therefore suffered *double* encroachment, and shrank steadily from 62.7 percent of "available national income" in 1936 to 35.0 percent in 1940. In terms of real consumption goods and services, this meant a decline of 11.3 percent in the first year, 14.0 percent in the second, and 28.0 percent in the third year of the war. This is roughly a decline of one half during the three years. For a people a majority of whom were on a semi-colonial standard of living prior to the war, this has meant no small degree of privation and sacrifice. ①

The above summary of Japan in China points clearly to Japan's foremost objectives in her undeclared war against China—complete economic conquest of China couched in the none too realistic slogan of "New Order in East Asia". The treacherous attack on Pearl Harbor has, of course, made the true meaning of the "New Order in East Asia" doubly clear. It resounds the echoes of the Tanaka Memorial back in 1927: ②

> In order to conquer China we must conquer first Manchuria and Mongolia. In order to conquer the world we must first conquer China. If we succeed in conquering China, the rest of the Asiatic countries and the South Sea countries will fear us and surrender to us. Then the world will realize that Eastern Asia is ours and will not dare to violate our rights.

Chapter VI. Capital and Management in China's Post-war Industrialization

A brief outline of China's wartime achievements in industrialization is convincing proof that China has succeeded, under enormous difficulties, in making reasonably good use of the available resources for wartime

---

① Hu, T. Y. : *Japan's Economy under War Strain*, Washington, 1941, p. 62.
② Vinacke, Harold M. , "The Roosevelt White Paper and the Tanaka Memorial", *Amerasia*, January, 1942, p. 475.

development. Such development in the three fields of transport, agriculture, and industry would have been more rapid, and the consequent achievements would have been more impressive, were China not so cut off from the outside world. When the war comes to an end, with victory assured to the United Nations, China will naturally turn to her Allies for capital and technical assistance in order to speed up the process of her postwar industrialization. To what extent is China deficient in capital and management? By what means can further supply be increased both within China and from abroad? If foreign capital and management are to flow into China at the end of war, in what manner can they be provided so that the arrangement will be mutually advantageous, and will not repeat the bitter experiences of the past century? An attempt is made here to offer a tentative answer; necessarily unsatisfactory to all, it is designed merely to provide a starting point for more mature consideration.

Foreign Capital

One of the pre-requisites to industrialization is the possession of capital. In the West the accumulation of capital had taken place for many centuries before industrialization set in during the second half of the eighteenth century. In England, the birthplace of industrialism, the expansion of foreign trade from the fourteenth century onward resulted in an accumulation of capital which provided the basis for industrial development. In China, capital accumulation is insignificant for many reasons. There foreign trade is negligible when compared with her enormous population. The predominance of agriculture over industry and trade ties up whatever meagre capital China may have accumulated in the form of investment in land which is immobile. The time-old family system calling for equal division of property among the descendants is a deterrent to large-scale accumulation of wealth, which probably accounts for the necessary provision of capital by the Manchu government when the first factories were started in the early sixties of the last century. After a period of eighty years, modern industrial capital in China before the war amounted only to 3.8 billion yuan (pre-war value, approximately equivalent to 1.2 billion US dollars), which estimated on the basis of a population of 450 million gave a per capita share of less than nine yuan (or US $2.70). [1] It must also be noted that small as the total industrial capital in China was, the share for domestic capital reached only 0.98 billion yuan or 26 percent, the other 2.82 billion yuan or 74 percent being foreign capital invested in China.

The problem of capital looms large when it is remembered that a part of modern industrial capital in pre-war China has been destroyed in the course of the war. Much of such capital is located in areas now occupied by the Japanese; while in Free China, mainly in the southwestern and northwestern regions, modern industrial capital is only a recent development. Before the war southwestern and northwestern China did not

---

[1] Estimate by a Chinese economist, Koh Tsung-fei, in an unpublished article on Chinese industrial capital. Evidently, it fails to include the influx of Japanese capital into Manchuria since 1931, and refers to the industrial capital in a narrow sense, covering only capital in modern industries.

possess, at the best, more than one-tenth of the modern industrial capital of China. Although modern industrial capital in Free China today has increased over that in pre-war days, in aggregate it cannot have reached, as a rough approximation, two-tenths of the modern industrial capital in pre-war China.

After allowance for wartime destruction and subsequent additions by the Chinese in Free China and by the Japanese in occupied China, modern industrial capital may, in amount, remain unchanged if not reduced. Even so, the sum of 1.2 billion US dollars is altogether inadequate to serve as a basis for China's postwar industrialization on a moderate scale, and naturally gives rise to the question of the sources of capital supply once the present war is over and the all-embracing blockade is lifted. In the following paragraphs, the sources of capital supply, both foreign and Chinese, will be outlined. In respect to foreign capital, its early history, war time development, and postwar possibilities and problems, will be briefly discussed.

Pre-war Foreign Capital. Foreign capital came to China in increasing magnitude after the conclusion of the Opium War of 1839 - 42. Remer, defining foreign investment in China as "a source of income owned by a 'foreigner' who may live in China or outside of China", placed its total at US $787.9 million of 1902, US $1,610.3 million in 1914, and US $3,242.5 million in 1931.[①] The last sum was larger than

---

[①] Remer, C. F., *Foreign Investments in China*, Macmillan, 1933, Chapter V. See Appendix, Tables VIIIa to VIIId.

foreign investment of US $2,000 - 3,500 million in India, and much larger than foreign investment of US $1,275 in Japan. Remer concludes:

> Taking foreign investments in China to mean the value of all sources of business income within the country owned by foreigners and foreign holdings of government obligations, we find these investments to have doubled between 1902 and 1914 and doubled again between 1914 and 1931, and to be worth today about US $3,300 million. Business investments we find to be of predominant importance and to have been so since the foreign business man first made a place for himself on the coast of China. Nearly 80 percent of the foreign investment in China is direct business investment. This is probably a greater percentage than in any other country in the world. The investments have gone, first of all, into the provision of transportation facilities. Shanghai and Manchuria account for about three-fifths of the investments and the relative importance of Shanghai has increased, especially since 1914. Great Britain has always been the chief creditor country, with Russia not far behind in 1902 and Japan not far behind in 1931.

Since Remer completed his study in 1932 significant changes have occurred not only in the total of foreign investments in China, but also in the percentage distribution of the shares of the main creditor countries. Though their magnitude cannot yet be even approximately stated, the nature of the changes may be briefly indicated. (1) Since the Japanese occupation of Manchuria in 1931, Japan's investments in Manchuria have expanded steadily from ￥1,617 million in 1931 to ￥4,500 million at the end of 1939. (2) Russia's investments have become very small after the sale of the Chinese Eastern Railway to Japan for ￥170,000,000 in 1935. (3) Great Britain, Germany, France and Belgium have participated actively in the construction of railways in China, with Czechoslovakia and the United States playing a minor part and Japan practically out of the picture. (4) There have also been some developments of significance in the field of commercial aviation in which both the United States and Germany have figured prominently. ①

Taking into account some of these changes and excluding Manchuria from the totals, the American Economic Mission to the Far East, of which Professor Remer was also a member, placed the investments of the principal creditor countries in China at the beginning of 1935 at US \$1,000 million for Great Britain, US \$500 million for Japan, and US \$200 million for the United States. "The outstanding difference", according to the Mission, ②

> is the decline in the importance of Japanese investments, when Manchuria is excluded. The new investments include those of the British in railways, Japanese in cotton mills, and American in aviation. These estimates take account of the decline of land values in

---

① Lin, W. Y., "The Future of Foreign Investment in China", in *Problems of the Pacific*, 1939, p. 213.

② *Report of the American Economic Mission to the Far East*, National Foreign Trade Council, New York, 1935, p. 26.

Shanghai. New loans to the Chinese Government have been few. They include the wheat and cotton loan from the United States.

The latest estimates for the British, American and French investments in China may also be indicated, because it is largely the interests of these three Powers that have been seriously threatened by Japan's policy and activities in China. Recent estimates place British investments in China at £ 300,000,000 or US $1,400,000,000,[1] American investments at US $242,000,000,[2] and French investments at Frs. 5,800,000,000 or US $165,000,000.[3] These figures, however, are not strictly comparable with the earlier estimates of Remer's. They are given here merely to show the general order of magnitude of the economic interests of the principal Western Powers in China.

Wartime Foreign Loans to China. Since the war in 1937 new foreign loans, chiefly from the United States, Great Britain, and Soviet Russia, have flowed into Free China in continuous streams, to the extent of about US $1,250 million, if the Lease-Lend Aid to China from the United States be excluded. Of these loans, more than one half are still outstanding, and cannot be effectively translated into war materials and equipments on account of the interruption of transportation and the lack of

---

[1] E. A. Ch. -Walden, "The Sino-Japanese War and the Open Door", *International Affairs*, Vol. XVII, No. 5, September-October, 1938, p. 631.

[2] Tyler Dennet, "Alternative American Policies in the Far East", *Foreign Affairs*, Vol. XVI, No. 3, April, 1938, p. 390.

[3] Norman D. Hanwell, "France Takes Inventory in China", *Far Eastern Survey*, Vol. VII, No. 19, September 28, 1938, p. 222.

shipping facilities.

Among the leading Powers, the United States has been the source of the largest loans to China during wartime. The first of these was the Export-Import Bank loan of US $25,000,000. This loan, announced in December 1938 with a view to bolstering China's morale after the fall of Canton and Hankow, is limited to the purchase of United States products of a non-military nature through the Universal Trading Corporation — a Chinese government enterprise organized under New York State corporation laws. It is to be repaid by the sale of tung oil from China in the United States. The second Export-Import Bank loan of US $20,000,000, announced in March 1940, also covers the purchase of non-military supplies and is to be repaid by the sale in the United States of Yunnan tin. The third loan, announced in September 1940 — in the dark days of the Japanese occupation of Haiphong and the suspension of the Yunnan-Indo-China Railway, consists of an Export-Import Bank loan of US $25,000,000 granted for the purpose of meeting China's purchases of supplies from the United States, repayable through the sale of tungsten. ①

---

① China has been repaying these loans from the Export-Import Bank of Washington on schedule. Of the first Export-Import Bank loan, China has borrowed US $22,000,000 and up to April 1942 has repaid the entire sum in tung oil. On March 24, 1942, Jesse Jones, Secretary of Commerce, made the following remark on China's record as a debtor nation: "The deliveries of wood oil in quantities more than sufficient to repay the loan have been made by the Chinese people under the most trying and difficult circumstances. Their splendid efforts indicate not only China's determination to meet her financial obligations, but are also an evidence of the courage and resourcefulness of her people in face of tremendous hardships. " See article on "The American and British Loans to China", *Contemporary China*, April 6, 1942.

The intensification of the European war greatly weakened isolationist sentiment in the United States. After the election of November 1940 it became much easier for China to secure additional financial assistance from the United States. In December 1940 a loan of US $100,000,000 was announced. This loan was divided into two parts. One half was granted by the Export-Import Bank for the purchase of supplies, while the other half was contributed by the United States Stabilization Fund "for the purpose of monetary protection and management between American and Chinese currencies", as the United States Treasury statement phrased it. This stabilizatiön agreement was signed on April 25, 1941. Under the terms of the Lease-Lend Act, passed in March 1941, the United States Government pledged increased aid to China. Although, in a sense, assistance under this Act is also a form of credit, it is frankly political in character; and the means of liquidating this special type of credit need not necessarily be financial.

Only recently, another loan, the largest so far, has been granted to China. This loan, amounting to half a billion US dollars, was requested by President Roosevelt on February 2, 1942, two weeks before the fall of Singapore, to be authorized by the Congress as a means of strengthening China's position "as regards both her internal economy and her capacity in general to function with great military effectiveness in our common effort". It was voted by the Congress with "unusual speed and unanimity" on February 6, 1942. The loan, to quote from President Roosevelt's message to Generalissimo Chiang Kai-shek on February 7, 1942, will contribute substantially toward facilitating the efforts of the Chinese Government and people to meet the economic and financial burdens which have been thrust upon them by an armed invasion and toward solution of problems of production and procurement which are essential for the success of their armed resistance to what are now our common enemies.

The first wartime loan to China from Great Britain followed closely upon the first American loan from the Export-Import Bank in December 1938. The British Government, through the Export Credits Guarantee Department, granted to China a loan of £500,000 for the development of trade and communications between China and Burma. This credit to China was later raised to £3,500,000 upon the authorization of an increase of £10,000,000 placed at the disposal of the Department, in June 1939. Earlier in March of the same year British assistance took the form of a loan, with guarantee against eventual loss by the British Treasury, by the two senior British banks in China — the Hongkong and Shanghai Banking Corporation and the Chartered Bank of India, Australia, and China — of £5,000,000. In December 1940, simultaneously with the announcement of the American loan of US $100,000,000, a £10,000,000 loan to China was announced by the British. Half of this sum is to be used for purchasing general supplies, and half for the purpose of currency stabilization. With the grant of the half billion dollar loan from the United States in February 1942, Great Britain extended a similar loan to China of £50,000,000 or US $200,000,000.

From Soviet Russia came a series of four loans based on barter agreements, beginning in October 1938, right after the fall of Canton and Hankow. Under these arrangements, China is enabled to purchase general supplies on credit from Soviet Russia, particularly mechanical equipment and other war materials, and to liquidate the credits by means of shipment of agricultural products, chiefly tea and wool. The first loan of US $50,000,000 was followed by credits of US $50,000,000 in February 1939, US $150,000,000 in August 1939, and US $50,000,000 in December 1940—a total of US $300,000,000.

The other loans negotiated included a credit of Frs. 150,000,000 advanced by France in April 1938 for the construction of the Annam-Chennankwan Railway, which in December 1938 was augmented by an additional credit of Frs. 480,000,000 to aid in financing the construction of the Suifu-Kunming Railway connecting Szechuen with Yunnan province.

Post-war Foreign Investments in China. When Dr. Sun Yat-sen advocated in 1922 foreign investments for Chinese industrial development, the world was confronted with the problem of excess industrial capacity left over from the First World War. The Second World War now in full swing is far more extensive in area, as well as intensive in both capital development and capital destruction. When it comes to an end, it remains a problem whether the excess industrial capacity left over in the more fortunate countries will be diverted entirely to rehabilitation at home by the respective foreign governments or in part to foreign investment. It seems certain that the United States, as the world's leading nation in possession of exportable capital, will, despite the economic and financial drain which she may have had to sustain on account of the war against Germany, Japan and Italy, have sufficient capital available for foreign investment after the war is over. In that case, investments in China appear likely for more than one reason. An industrialized China will be a more powerful ally for the United States in the Pacific. China has already proved by valiant resistance against Japanese aggression her usefulness in hampering the totalitarian onslaught against world democracy; may she not be entitled to play an even more important role in this respect after the war? The *New York Times*, in its December 30, 1941 editorial, has well remarked in this respect:

> An Asia dominated by the Prussian mind of the Japanese militarists could be a threat to the world's peace for centuries to come. An Asia in which a new and revitalized and democratized China plays a role in proportion to its size and wealth can be a mighty force for peace and progress.

The reason for foreign investment in China's postwar industrialization is clear. It remains to consider the purposes for which foreign capital may be best used, the forms in which foreign capital may be best invested, and the ways and means by which foreign capital may be satisfactorily repaid.

Purposes of Foreign Investment. Fundamentally, the approach to the whole problem of China's postwar foreign borrowing should be reoriented from the prewar emphasis upon China's capacity to pay to the more

The intensification of the European war greatly weakened isolationist sentiment in the United States. After the election of November 1940 it became much easier for China to secure additional financial assistance from the United States. In December 1940 a loan of US $100,000,000 was announced. This loan was divided into two parts. One half was granted by the Export-Import Bank for the purchase of supplies, while the other half was contributed by the United States Stabilization Fund "for the purpose of monetary protection and management between American and Chinese currencies", as the United States Treasury statement phrased it. This stabilizatiön agreement was signed on April 25, 1941. Under the terms of the Lease-Lend Act, passed in March 1941, the United States Government pledged increased aid to China. Although, in a sense, assistance under this Act is also a form of credit, it is frankly political in character; and the means of liquidating this special type of credit need not necessarily be financial.

Only recently, another loan, the largest so far, has been granted to China. This loan, amounting to half a billion US dollars, was requested by President Roosevelt on February 2, 1942, two weeks before the fall of Singapore, to be authorized by the Congress as a means of strengthening China's position "as regards both her internal economy and her capacity in general to function with great military effectiveness in our common effort". It was voted by the Congress with "unusual speed and unanimity" on February 6, 1942. The loan, to quote from President Roosevelt's message to Generalissimo Chiang Kai-shek on February 7, 1942, will contribute substantially toward facilitating the efforts of the Chinese Government and people to meet the economic and financial burdens which have been thrust upon them by an armed invasion and toward solution of problems of production and procurement which are essential for the success of their armed resistance to what are now our common enemies.

The first wartime loan to China from Great Britain followed closely upon the first American loan from the Export-Import Bank in December 1938. The British Government, through the Export Credits Guarantee Department, granted to China a loan of £500,000 for the development of trade and communications between China and Burma. This credit to China was later raised to £3,500,000 upon the authorization of an increase of £10,000,000 placed at the disposal of the Department, in June 1939. Earlier in March of the same year British assistance took the form of a loan, with guarantee against eventual loss by the British Treasury, by the two senior British banks in China — the Hongkong and Shanghai Banking Corporation and the Chartered Bank of India, Australia, and China — of £5,000,000. In December 1940, simultaneously with the announcement of the American loan of US $100,000,000, a £10,000,000 loan to China was announced by the British. Half of this sum is to be used for purchasing general supplies, and half for the purpose of currency stabilization. With the grant of the half billion dollar loan from the United States in February 1942, Great Britain extended a similar loan to China of £50,000,000 or US $200,000,000.

important, but largely overlooked, conception of China's capacity to borrow. In the past, all loan negotiations have centered almost invariably upon the discussion of the provision of securities and guarantees and the hypothecation of specific revenues, to the neglect of how the proceeds should be employed to improve the borrower's capacity to service these obligations. During the postwar period, foreign capital should be employed for productive purposes and, through increased productivity, provide the necessary service charges. Any attempt to bring in foreign capital without at the same time taking steps better to equip the productive capacity of the country will sooner or later involve the borrower in serious financial difficulties. The moral of unhappy consequences of China's foreign borrowing in the past is particularly instructive. Early public loans, and even those under the defunct Peking Government, were made to meet either indemnity payments or general administrative expenses. Excepting the construction of railways, the proper use of foreign capital was quite beyond the comprehension or the administrative capacity of the governments then in power. True, foreign loans increased, but China's fiscal and economic capacity to meet the stipulated service failed to show a corresponding improvement. When these loans were diverted, intentionally or otherwise, from the productive purposes to which they should have been devoted, to financing civil wars and political intrigues, the ensuing defaults and arrears became as inevitable as they were disastrous. ①

Foreign capital placed in China during the postwar period, to stimu-

---

① Lin, W. Y., "The Future of Foreign Investment in Chine", pp. 245 − 46.

late productive enterprise in the three fields of transport and public utilities, agriculture and transport as outlined in a previous chapter, will preferably be long-term in character. For the successful execution of developmental projects in these fields, China will be particularly in need of long-term foreign capital rather than short-term foreign funds, important and useful as the latter may be in tiding over temporary deficits in the balance of international payments. It has unfortunately become a disturbing feature of international finance that long-term capital, because of the fears of war or currency depreciation, has very largely been held in the shape of short-term funds which move capriciously from one financial center to another and often against the short-term interest differentials. This shortage of long-term foreign capital, in the face of her pressing needs, lays China open to the danger of a substitution of short-term money for long-term in her industrial development. To apply short-term funds to capital development purposes is fundamentally unsound and dangerous. If they are recalled on short notice or repaid in a few years, it will be certain to arrest capital development requiring a considerable time to complete, and to cause undue disturbances to the financial structure. Though in dire need of foreign capital, China should be cautious and resolute enough to refuse to commit herself to this mistaken policy.

In the course of her postwar industrialization, China will attempt to be self-sufficient in necessary raw materials, labor power, buildings and sites; but for industrial machinery and equipment, she must look to foreign nations for assistance and acquire them by means of the foreign capital to be lent to China. These long-term foreign loans, in the form of machinery and equipment, as well as raw materials in which China is for the time being deficient, e. g. steel, must be accompanied by foreign technical and managerial personnel in the initial stage of China's postwar industrialization; so that they can be properly and rapidly set up and utilized. China will have to guarantee these foreign experts legal security in order to secure their willing co-operation and service. She will welcome them not as advisers, whether from the respective foreign nations or from an international organization like the League of Nations, but as responsible executive officers with power to enforce decisions and complete tasks assigned to them. ① Chinese experience with advisers in the past has been a disappointment to both sides. The advisers were disappointed to realize only after painful experience that their recommendations had been shelved; while the Chinese Government regretted its lack of means— political, financial, or technical — to carry out their recommendations once the advisers had to leave China upon completion of their respective missions, which in certain cases did not even extend to a few months.

Forms of Foreign Investment. There are several forms in which foreign capital, both public and private, may be made available to China during the postwar period. It may come in through: (1) direct government borrowing from another government, as in the case of the commer-

---

① Professor J. B. Condliffe, a former League staff member, wrote in his recent work on *The Reconstruction of World Trade* (Norton, 1940, p. 388) on this point as follows: "Only when the experts (from the League) were themselves responsible officials prepared to execute the decisions agreed upon in consultation —usually in politically minor, but not unimportant, matters— have effective results followed."

cial loans from the Export-Import Bank of Washington to China since 1938; (2) government borrowing from private sources under the guarantee of the government of the lending country, such as the recent currency stabilization credits from the British banks and the credits obtained under the Export Credits Guarantee System; (3) public issues in the leading financial centers of the world, as in the case of prewar Chinese government and railway obligations; (4) direct investments by foreigners — the predominant type of foreign investment in prewar China; (5) indirect investments by foreigners, i. e. borrowing by Chinese industrial and commercial interests from abroad; and finally, (6) foreign investments in partnership with Chinese capital, notably in the two commercial aviation corporations — the Sino-American China National Aviation Corporation and the Sino-German Eurasia Aviation Corporation.

In China indirect investments by foreigners have been negligible. For under a regime of extraterritoriality foreign investors are more inclined to place their funds in corporations subject to their own management and control. The abolition of extraterritoriality after the war, already promised by the governments of the United States and Great Britain, will bring an end to the prewar predominance of direct investments by foreigners. In that case, foreign indirect investments will grow in proportion to the growth of Chinese corporate enterprises which in the past has been hampered by slow adaptation to modern methods of industrial management, cost accounting, and corporate financing, as well as by absence of an organized securities market. A more promising form, however, will be for foreign investors to participate in Sino-foreign joint enterprises. Sir

Arthur Salter, after several months' first-hand observation of Chinese economic conditions, has come to the same conclusion. According to him,[1]

> the best basis, from both the foreign and internal point of view, will probably prove in future to be the association on equal conditions (but not necessarily in equal proportions) of foreign and domestic investment. More and more it is probable that the foreigner will come to regard his best security as consisting in a close association with Chinese investors, whose fortunes are linked with his, and who will bear the controlling share of responsibility, and in the credit of the persons undertaking the enterprise and its intrinsic prospects.

Sino-foreign joint investment appears to offer certain definite advantages over other forms in which foreign capital may be or has been employed. It will be governed more by economic considerations, such as the prospects of business earnings, than by political intrigues. It will render unnecessary the assignment of specific revenues as security or the granting of special privileges or protection which had been enjoyed by purely foreign enterprises in China. And, as a method of corporate financing, profit-sharing equities, as contrasted with fixed interest-bearing obligations, are distinctly better because they secure to a large degree the automatic adjustments to the varying fortunes of good times and bad. It is particularly important, from the standpoint of the balance of international payments, to remember that while dividend payments vary with the gen-

---

[1] *China and the Depression*, Nanking, 1934, p. 46.

eral business conditions, fixed interest charges become an intolerable strain in times of depression. ①

Whereas the Chinese Company Law of 1929 does not prohibit a foreign controlling interest in a Sino-foreign enterprise, certain conditions have, however, been laid down in a resolution of the Central Executive Committee, passed at the 179th meeting of the Central Political Council and communicated to the Legislative Yuan on March 13, 1930, requiring that (1) Chinese shares shall be over 51 percent of the total capital; (2) a majority of the directors of the company shall be Chinese; and (3) the chairman of the board of directors and the general manager of the company shall be Chinese. Notable examples of joint Chinese and foreign investments organized along these lines are the two aviation corporations (China National Aviation and Eurasia) engaged in the operation of domestic mail and passenger services. The underlying principles of joint investment and joint enterprise may be further extended to apply to partnerships not only between foreign commercial interests and the Chinese Government but preferably between private commercial and financial interests at home and abroad.

In recent years there has been an increasing tendency for governments to enter the field of international investment. The Export-Import Bank of Washington offers a striking example. Organized in February 1934, the Bank had by the end of 1941 approved commitments aggregating US $837,705,261, of which US $327,313,604 had been actual-

① Lin, W. Y., "The Future of Foreign Investment in China", p. 247.

ly disbursed. Although its operations have largely been confined to the countries of the Western Hemisphere, the Bank has extended four successive loans amounting to a total commitment of US $120,000,000 to wartime China. Its activities have gone through several phases, from the government financing of exports, to government loans for liquidation of blocked balances, exchange stabilization and the control of capital movements, and the financing of development projects in the Latin American Republics. [1] There seem, in light of these developments, to be hopeful possibilities for the Chinese Government to borrow directly from another government through an official institution such as the Export-Import Bank of Washington, or from private sources with the guarantee of a government organization such as the British Export Credits Guarantee Department.

Finally, public issues, if properly managed and adequately safeguarded, would appear to be a type most suitable for the development of large scale public projects such as the construction of railways, power plants, irrigation works and dams. But, in view of the prevailing restrictions on public issues in the United States arising from the bitter experience of the Depression in Europe and Latin America, the prospects in this direction after the present war cannot be very bright. On the other hand, such prospects might be entirely reversed, despite past bad experience, if an integrated developmental program, intergovernmentally sponsored by a supra-national development authority, such as an International

---

[1] *Preparing for Postwar International Investment*, National Planning Association, Washington, unpublished manuscript.

Reconstruction Finance Corporation, could be instituted after the war. Professor Hansen of Harvard University thus suggested, as part of the postwar policies to be adopted by the United States Government, "international collaboration to pursue internal policies designed to promote active employment; to explore developmental projects in backward countries; and to implement ways and means to open outlets for foreign investment, promote world trade and the effective worldwide use of productive resources."①

Others, like Professor Corbett of McGill University, proposed to set up in the reorganized League of Nations — the Assembly of the World Commonwealth — a Governing Body on international economic and financial matters composed, like the International Labor Organization, partly of government delegates and partly of persons representing associated employers and workers. The Governing Body, responsible to the Assembly, will be composed of the specific agencies related to trade, banking, development, migration and settlement. International investments might be made to pass through a Development Commission, which will have at its disposal substantial funds for financing public works and industrial installation with the double object of raising standards of living in undeveloped areas and furnishing new outlets for the productive capacity of existing industrial countries. The Commission will have supervision over the purpose, terms, and securities for such investments; and states might be

---

① *After the War — Full Employment*, National Resources Planning Board, Washington, 1942, p. 19.

forbidden to prevent or encourage cross-boundary capital movements save with its consent. ①

Repayment of Foreign Loans. The repayment of foreign loans by China may be difficult if prewar trends towards a passive balance of payments should continue. The loans from foreign countries during the postwar period will preferably be as small as possible; these loans will preferably be on an equity basis, thus relieving China from the repayment of principal in the early years. Non-essential imports, mainly luxury articles of consumption for the wealthy, will be reduced under a system of government import control which has already achieved success during the war period; while other imports, for which Chinese substitutes can be found, will be discouraged. Again, with the progress in China's postwar industrialization she may find it possible to develop her trade in exports that will find a market of their own in foreign countries. These industries, including (1) mining and smelting of minerals such as tungsten, antimony and tin; (2) processing of staple agricultural exports such as soya beans, wood oil, vegetable oil, tea, silk, bristles, furs, hides and skins, wool, sausage casings, eggs and egg products; (3) handicraft products such as toys, trays, cigarette boxes, vanity boxes, table linens, hairnets, embroidery, laces, stitchwork, porcelain, fans, slippers, cushions, artificial

---

① Corbett, P. E. : *Postwar Worlds*, Institute of Pacific Relations, 1942, pp. 133 – 34. See also Eugene Staley, "The Economic Organization of Peace", in *International Conciliation*, No. 369, Carnegie Endowment for International Peace, April, 1941; as well as his *World Economy in Transition*, Council on Foreign Relations, New York, 1939, pp. 165, 179 – 87, 198.

flowers, straw plaits, carpets, cloisonné, etc. ; and (4) tourist industry, have been discussed in a previous chapter.

As China proceeds with her postwar industrialization, through foreign financial and technical assistance, there will be a fuller use made of Chinese resources, both human and natural. Such fuller use will in itself create additional income and raise the purchasing power of the Chinese masses. There will inevitably be a rise in the Chinese standard of living sooner or later, although industrialization in its early stages may lead to an increase in population, largely through a reduction in death rate arising from improvement in public health and sanitation, and in turn tend to lower the standard of living. Once this transitional stage is bridged over, the additional wealth that Chinese industrialization may help to create ultimately will go towards the repayment of foreign debts, as has been the experience of many other nations having undergone similar transformations.

The servicing of foreign loans along orthodox and traditional lines requires the creation of an export surplus, either through the development of export industries or through the accumulation of new wealth by the very process of industrialization. Many modern economists, under the leadership of John Maynard Keynes, lay stress on the expansionist tendencies of full employment and maintenance of a high level of living, and challenge the traditional views on saving and investment. According to them, if foreign investment be assigned a new role of helping to develop the resources of capital-deficient countries after the war, and thus to remove one of the most potent causes for future wars, the servicing of foreign loans may not become such an immediate matter of concern. Long-term financing may then be possible, and the responsibility for debt servicing may not arise until the borrowing nation, with the assistance of foreign loans, has developed sufficiently so that fuller use of resources and higher level of income will in turn provide the necessary means for the repayment of these loans. ① Even this remote arrangement for eventual repayment may be dispensed with, if the fifth point in the Atlantic Charter declaring the "desire to bring about the fullest collaboration between all nations in the economic field with the object of securing, for all, improved labor standards, economic adjustment and social security" — the famous "freedom from want" of President Roosevelt's — be strictly interpreted.

Chinese Capital

The postwar sources of capital supply from the Chinese themselves are twofold, namely, from the Chinese at home and from the Chinese overseas. The former embraces four categories—public borrowing, credit redirection, credit creation, and repatriation of refugee capital abroad; while the latter refers to the overseas Chinese remittance.

Public Borrowing. China's prewar public debt amounted to 4,500 million yuan, or US $1,350 million. Of this, the internal debt reached 2,709 million yuan £ 4.2 million, and US $2 million — a total of US

---

① *Guides for Postwar Planning*, National Planning Association, 1941; Hansen, Alvin H. : *Fiscal Policy and Business Cycles*, Norton, 1941.

$832 million, leaving the external debt at US $518 million. ① Since the war, because of rapid monetary inflation, the pre-war internal debt, converted at the *present* ratio of one US dollar to 20 Chinese yuan, instead of the *prewar* ratio of one Chinese yuan to 0.30 US dollar, has been reduced to US $154 million. The total prewar public debt of China thus stands at US $672 million.

Since the war, ten internal loans have been issued by the Chinese Government, amounting to 3,430 million yuan, 100 million customs gold units, 20 million pounds sterling, and 300 million US dollars, giving a total of US $592 million. ②

Adding the wartime external debt of US $1,250 million to the wartime internal debt of US $592 million, the total wartime public debt of China reaches US $1,842 million, in addition to the total prewar public debt of US $672 million. Deducting from the wartime public debt the two loans that have just been issued and not yet tapped — the internal loan of US $200 million in the form of allied victory bonds and savings certificates, and the joint American and British loan of US $700 million — the total public debt burden of China today is US $1,614 million; US $546 million for the internal debt and US $1,068 million for the external debt.

The internal debt burden of US $546 million is not large, and leaves

---

① Young, Arthur N. : China's financial progress, in *Foreign Policy Reports*, April 15, 1938, p. 33; *Chinese Yearbook*, *1940 – 41*, Chapter on "Public finance".

② See Appendix, Table IX.

ample margin for further increase. In the first place, it is equivalent to the total internal loans issued by the National Government during the ten prewar years 1928-37, namely, US $ 504 million. ① Secondly, it is equivalent to 7.7 percent of the average annual income of a Chinese, although the total debt burden, both internal and external, is equivalent to 22.8 percent. ② Finally, as the Institute of Pacific Relations' memorandum notes: ③

> the capacity of the Chinese public to absorb more loans has by no means been exhausted, but the extent of that capacity depends on the methods by which the new loans are floated: From the point of view of the lending capacity of the money market, the outlook is definitely favorable. As a result of refugee movements, bank deposits in the interior have increased enormously. Large amounts of accumulated capital have found no better employment than speculation in

---

① According to the *Chinese Yearbook*, *1940 - 41*, these internal loans amounted to 1,616 million yuan, £4.2 million, and US $2 million. The conversion ratios used are as follows: 1 yuan for 30 US cents, 1 pound sterling for 4 US dollars.

② Buck's figure of 52.19 yuan as annual per capita earnings for Chinese farm population during the years 1921-25 is the only comprehensive average now available, covering 2,866 farms in 17 localities of seven provinces in China. (*Chinese Farm Economy*, University of Chicago, 1930, p. 85) Since four-fifths of Chinese poulation depend upon farming for livelihood, farm earnings may be roughly taken to indicate average earnings for the Chinese population as a whole. Calculating on the basis of a population of 450 million for the whole of China, a total public debt burden of US $1,613 million gives a per capita debt burden of US $3.58 — US $1.21 for the internal debt burden and US $2.37 for the external. Buck's figure of 52.17 yuan or US $15.65 is here used as a base of 100 percent, from which the present percentages are derived.

③ See *Supra*, P. 158 note①.

commodities and real estate, and interest rates are by no means high. There is every reason, therefore, to believe that the maximum limit of the lending capacity of the Chinese money market is far from being reached; with proper stimulation, public loans of very large dimensions can still be raised.

It is important to remember, however, that the money market in China, as compared with that in countries with a more developed money economy, is a far less accurate index of the capacity of the public to contribute toward the emergency needs of the country. The bulk of China's wealth has not yet assumed the form of money, and a considerable proportion of the wealth that has already been converted into money is hoarded and has not yet been placed at the disposal of the money market. Thus the capacity of the people to absorb state loans, in the sense of contributions of their resources to national defense, is limited only by the resources available for mobilization. For if public bonds are given to those who lend money to the State, there is no reason why public bonds could not be issued to those who lend commodities or labor power to the State. The fact that suggestions of this kind have already appeared in isolated articles in the Chinese press indicates that the idea of a broad conception of public loans comes quite naturally to economists in a country where money economy has not yet become dominant. On the basis of this broad conception of public loans, which regards them merely as one of the means of mobilizing resources, it is conceivable that a broad national plan could be mapped out under which money, commodities, and labor power, would be borrowed or conscripted.

Redirection of Credit. Before the war China's banking and credit structure was dispersed over three distinct markets — the modern Chinese banks, the modern foreign banks, and the native banks. During the ten years before the war, the first group was advancing rapidly under increasing government leadership and control; the second receded in importance as foreign banks lost their control over costless or cheap resources such as customs and salt revenue, foreign loan funds, and foreign remittances, which amounted to fairly large sums and were employable at high profit. During 1936 and 1937 the Chinese government banks directed their efforts to absorbing commercial paper arising from foreign trade; with the nationalization of silver stocks in 1935 and the accumulation of foreign balances in their hands, they took away from foreign banks the traditional privilege of being the money bags and exchange brokers of the country. The third group was being liquidated with the advance of modern Chinese banks, and catered only to providing the credit needs of small traders and craftsmen. All three groups, especially the modern Chinese banks, were alike in their concentration on short-term financing of a commercial and speculative character. Speculation in government bonds, bullion, commodities, real estates, and to some extent industrial bonds and stocks, as well as short-term financing of domestic and foreign trade, constituted the principal activities of these banks.

The redirection of credit, therefore, becomes one of the main postwar banking problems in China. The shift from short-term commercial to long-term investment banking is one means by which more capital may be made available to take care of China's needs for postwar industrialization. The investment banking situation in Shanghai, China's prewar financial center, described in the following quotation from Dr. Tamagna, was decidedly unsound, and should be corrected: ①

  Dealings in the stock market were limited to a small group of bonds and shares. Aside from debentures of local public utilities and real estate companies registered under foreign laws, the attention of the operators was chiefly directed toward rubber shares (traded in Shanghai), Philippines gold mine shares (traded in Hongkong), and bonds of the National Government. Buying and selling were essentially speculative in character, as indicated by the fact that cash prices for actual delivery were quoted only occasionally. The market activity was limited to a restricted group of speculators, without important participation of the general public. New issues were not, as a rule, disposed of directly in the market; government bonds were usually delivered to the banks as security for loans, and private shares became saleable only when large dividends were distributed. The establishment of the China Development Finance Corporation represented an important step toward bringing available funds and investing institutions into the capital market, and its early operations were a significant success. The creation of an investment market re-

---

① Quoted from the manuscript of his forthcoming book on *Chinese Banking and Finance* to be published by the Institute of Pacific Relations.

mained, however, in an experimental stage.

Credit Expansion. Another method of raising capital will be credit expansion other than by means of public borrowing, including the creation of a commercial bill market and the registration of land deeds for the issue of land mortgage credit. The most significant weakness of the Chinese credit structure before the war was the lack of commercial paper and the absence of a bill market. The reasons are not far to seek. As pointed out by Dr. Tamagna: ①

> as long as the credit rating of native banks was high, their cashier's orders represented an important paper, freely accepted and circulated. The introduction into the market of drafts issued by modern banks did not compensate for the decline in importance of this native document. The traditional practice of granting credit on passbook (overdrafts) made borrowers generally reluctant to abide by new methods which appeared cumbersome in their procedure and rather tricky in their legal provisions. Moreover, the lack of reliable credit information discouraged most banks from engaging extensively in open market discount operations. As for rediscount facilities, although provisions were made in the Central Bank Law and in the Shanghai Bankers' Acceptance House Covenant, no actual practice of rediscounting was developed. This was due to lack of commercial

---

① Quoted from the manuscript of his forthcoming book on *Chinese Banking and Finance* to be published by the Institute of Pacific Relations.

paper and to the reluctance of the merchants to have their notes circulated.

The registration of land deeds will open the way towards the acceptance of these deeds as securities for long-term financing of agricultural development. Thus far, these deeds have seldom been used for such purpose because they are in most cases based on land surveys carried out over two centuries ago, in 1713. Subsequent ownership and other changes have never been properly registered with the public authorities, and consequently their legal status has always been most costly to establish and insecure. Cadastral survey offers the basic solution. It was attempted under the Peking Government in certain parts of Kiangsu, Chekiang, and Heilungkiang provinces. Since the establishment of the National Government in Nanking in 1927, these surveys have been carried out, partly or wholly, in Kiangsu, Chekiang, Kwangtung, Yunnan, Kiangsi, Anhwei, Hunan, Hupeh, Honan, Ninghsia, and other provinces, as well as municipalities such as Shanghai and Nanking. But because of the diversity of methods employed and of the haphazard manner in which these surveys were made, the results achieved were incomparable with the efforts spent. One notable exception to this is the aerial survey in Nanchang, Kiangsi province, which has been found to be both time-saving and economical, and which the Land Department of the Ministry of Interior contemplated extending to other parts of China before the outbreak of the present war.

A quicker and less expensive process than the cadastral survey is the reporting of land titles by the owners themselves — a sort of semi-cadastral survey. After much experiment in Chekiang, Kiangsu and Anhwei provinces before the war, a workable procedure, first perfected in Tangtu Hsien of Anhwei province, has been found by which land titles properly registered may serve not only as a security for mortgage loans, but also as an adequate basis for land value taxation advocated by Dr. Sun Yat-sen and already carried out in some of the Chinese municipalities. During the war, further attempts in this direction have been made in interior provinces. These will undoubtedly be extended in view of the land tax reform in 1941 to provide for much needed revenue for the national treasury, now that the main sources of national tax revenue from customs duty, salt gabelle, and excise tax, which before the war contributed as much as eighty percent of China's total revenue, have been largely lost through Japanese occupation of the fertile and coastal provinces.

Repatriation of Refugee Capital Abroad. A fourth source of capital supply for China's postwar industrialization is the repatriation of Chinese capital abroad, largely in the United States, during the war. Capital flight from China was greatest after the summer of 1937, immediately after the outbreak of war; it did not subside until the end of 1938. During the years 1937 and 1938 the total inpayments in China's balance of international payments amounted to about US $330 million; apparently all of this was absorbed by the private demand for foreign exchange, and thus for capital flight. The opening of hostilities in Europe in the summer of 1939 had the effect of reversing the trend, for as soon as foreign exchange control was introduced in the British Dominions and colonies, Shanghai again became a relatively safe port for Chinese refugee capital, and the Chinese national yuan again became a relatively desirable currency, free from any restrictions. Today, various estimates place the total Chinese capital in flight, chiefly in the United States, at around US $300 million. Much of this capital will return to China after the war when the country is ready for large-scale economic development and can offer sufficiently attractive returns to investors.

Overseas Chinese Remittances. Overseas remittance from the ten million Chinese abroad, mainly in the "South Seas" embracing the Malaya Peninsula, Singapore, Netherlands East Indies, Java, Thailand, Burma, French Indo-China, the Philippines, and Hongkong, has for years contributed an annual sum of 300 - 400 million yuan (pre-war value), equivalent to over US $100 million—an important item in correcting China's unfavorable balance of payments for many decades. In recent years the volume of remittances from abroad has in no way diminished; on the contrary, there are indications that it has increased substantially since 1936. Reliable estimates show these remittances, in terms of million US dollars, at 110 in 1936, 150 in 1937, 135 in 1938, 225 in 1939, and 150 in 1940. [1] Remittances in 1939 and 1940 are especially large, as they include repatriation of Chinese capital in flight remitted from Hongkong, French Indo-China, and Thailand, as a consequence of the

---

[1] Figures for 1936 are given by the Bank of China, those for 1939 by the leading Chinese paper *Ta Kung Pao* (L'Impartial), and those for 1937, 1938 and 1940 by reliable sources.

Japanese pressure in these zones. Just what the future may bring in respect of overseas remittances is, however, less optimistic. The spread of world war to the Pacific and to the peninulas and islands where most of the overseas Chinese reside, is bringing destruction to economic capital in these areas, including that owned by the overseas Chinese. Even before the Pacific War, the imposition of restrictions on capital export by most of the governments to which overseas Chinese are subject, especially since 1940, and the narrowing of opportunities for profit-making and capital accumulation by the overseas Chinese in recent years, had tended to reduce the prospect for capital investment by overseas Chinese in China's post-war industrialization.

Management

Scarcity of management will be no less urgent than the lack of capital. In the early days of China's industrialization, management was partly supplied by the capital-exporting nations. In the state owned factories of the early sixties of the last century, the engineer might be a foreigner from the capital-exporting nations; while the managerial staff was made up of responsible or petty bureaucrats as the case demanded. In the course of time these bureaucrats began to leave these factories and managed to raise funds among friends, relatives, or colleagues for financing new enterprises of their own. Meantime, factories financed by foreign capital and staffed by foreign managers and engineers usually employed Chinese assistants on account of language difficulties. These assistants, commonly known as "compradores", began to operate as middlemen and learned the secrets of the trade from their foreign superiors. It is from these three classes, namely, foreigners, bureaucrats, and compradores, that managers and entrepreneurs for Chinese industrial enterprises were recruited.

Gradually, other sources of supply were added. Overseas Chinese, having made a fortune from business enterprises abroad, returned to China to establish new undertakings in various fields of industry, and usually became managers as well as proprietors. As the need for trained personnel became more keenly felt, the Chinese Government, at first at its own expense but since 1908 through the Boxer Indemnity Funds returned first by the United States, then by Great Britain and other nations, began to send students abroad, first to Japan, later on to Europe and America, for advanced study in various branches of pure and applied science. Upon completion of their study abroad, some of these students came back to assume managerial and technical posts in industrial enterprises. Very few students now remain in Japan or Europe on account of the war, while those sent to Great Britain by the Boxer Indemnity Fund have been transferred to Canada or the United States. In the last two countries, mostly in the United States, there are, not counting the 700 overseas Chinese students, altogether about 1,000 students from China studying with government or private support in American universities and colleges. In addition, the Chinese Government, with the cooperation of the American Government, has been sending pilots and engineering staff for further training in this country, numbering over a hundred. These persons upon their return will naturally participate in some part of the postwar industrialization program.

Just before the war, through cooperation with the League of Nations, the National Government of China used the services of various technical experts in the state plants engaged in the production of minerals, iron and steel, machinery and electrical apparatus.

The most important source, however, remains that of graduates from the Chinese colleges and universities. Here a large number of recruits are being drawn year by year into active industrial service. It is difficult to estimate the number of graduates annually available, but judging from the number of graduates for the prewar year of 1936 – 37 from universities, colleges and technical schools, namely, 4,330, the recruits entering industrial fields could not have been too large in view of the rapid spread of industrialization in China. For this reason, the five years before the war witnessed an unusual supply of opportunities for college graduates. Whereas previously they had experienced great difficulty in securing jobs upon graduation, each of them then had three or four positions open for choice.

China, when the war is over, will undoubtedly face a serious shortage of technical and managerial personnel to carry out her postwar program of industrialization. The increase of student enrollment in universities, colleges and technical schools is an encouraging sign in this respect, although the quality of training, due to lack of facilities, has deteriorated since the outbreak of war. ①Despite the increase in enrollment, the number being trained still falls far below the actual need. To satisfy the pressing demand for technical and managerial personnel in China's postwar industrialization program, large number of technicians and managers from foreign countries especially the United States, some of whom are already in active service in China, will be indispensable if foreign capital is to be profitably and effectively invested in China. More and more the importance of technical cooperation, in addition to economic, is being realized in the sphere of international reconstruction. As has been pointed out in a recent manuscript on postwar international investment, "finance is likely to be auxiliary to the work of the engineers and technicians who can visualize the possibilities of civilized growth in the latent wealth of every region." ②

Chapter VII. Proposals for Organizing the Post-war Industrialization in China

The above survey has brought to light several basic conclusions upon

---

① Latest reports show that such enrollment has increased from 31,188 in 1937 to 44,422 in 1940. More students are being matriculated in the field of science instead of arts — an indication that engineering will be a preferred field. In 1940, 3,771 out of 7,024 students who passed the national matriculation tests took engineering, science, agriculture, or medicine as major courses, while 2,443 specialized in arts, law and commerce and 810 others were to be trained as teachers.

② See *supra*, P. 223 note①.

which to postulate the principles and the forms of organization for China's postwar industrialization. China's resources for industrial development, although not so rich as those of the United States, are sufficient to support a moderate degree of industrialization for many years to come. Her labor power, given sufficient training in skill and discipline, is unlimited. China, however, lacks capital and technical and managerial personnel which she will have to import from the advanced industrial nations, especially the United States. Her capacity to industrialize, even under the extremely difficult conditions of wartime blockade and lack of modern means of transport and industrial equipment, has been reasonably proved by her wartime achievements in Free China, in the three essential fields of transport, agriculture, and industry.

Principles

The principles that must guide us in the postwar industrialization of a new, united, independent and victorious China, with international financial and technical cooperation, may be tentatively suggested as follows: In the first place, the two world wars have proved to us, if nothing else, the futility of isolation for any nation in an age which, thanks to science and the shortening of distance, has brought all nations closer together than ever before. An undeveloped China with its rich agricultural and mineral resources, and unlimited manpower, would forever be a cause for possible international conflict over her control. That this is so has been amply proved by the imperialistic rivalry and struggle in the Far East, especially in China, during the last hundred years. China herself cannot rest satisfied with the lot assigned by her aggressive neighbor Japan, and for that matter by any other nation with similar intentions, namely, "Co-prosperity of Greater East Asia" under which an agricultural China will constantly be at the mercy of an industrial Japan. In modern warfare, an agricultural land must inevitably surrender to an industrial land just as a handicraft culture must inevitably stoop before a machine culture.

Secondly, international cooperation must take the place of international rivalry in the development of China's resources along industrial lines. Chinese industrialization must not add to the dis-equilibrium in postwar economy, but must be so worked out as to mitigate any maladjustments in international economic development that have contributed to the outbreak of the two world wars. Economic organization in the world of today has advanced ahead of political organization. After World War II a better adjustment between the world's political and economic organization should be the prime aim of every statesman. China after the war must find her proper place in the world's economy, especially in the economy of Southeastern Asia. China, Japan, India and some new federation or "Indonesian Union" comprising French Indo-China, British Malaya, Thailand (or Siam), Burma, the Netherlands East Indies, and the Philippines, must be brought within the orbit of this Southeastern Asiatic economy. ①

---

① This proposal by Mr. W. L. Holland of the Institute of Pacific Relations is summarized in a chapter on "Peace in the Pacific" by P. E. Corbett, *Postwar Worlds, op. cit.* An alternative scheme for a "South China Sea Area" has recently been described in an Institute memorandum by Dr. Kurt Bloch.

Thirdly, given assurance of peace and order under a unified government, foreign investments will be welcome in China's postwar industrialization on the basis of equal treatment and with no infringement of Chinese sovereignty. Foreign investments, as a powerful means towards achieving the postwar objective of freedom from want and fear in general, and of rebuilding a strong and free China as a stabilizing factor in Far Eastern peace and prosperity, must come in accord with the new precepts of postwar international finance: (1) Foreign investments should be used for the purchase of capital equipment and materials in which China is deficient, as well as for the employment of foreign technical and managerial personnel which China lacks during the initial stage of postwar industrialization. They should no longer be used for political, non-productive purposes. (2) They should carry low interest, say three to five percent, for a long term, say a minimum of ten years, in order to facilitate and assure their repayment. (3) They should be accompanied, wherever necessary and advisable, by trade agreements which would provide for repayment in terms of goods in the production of which China enjoys distinct advantages.

Fourthly, thorough-going survey of Chinese resources must precede scientific planning of large-scale developmental projects for a postwar China. Despite the information already available, a great deal remains to be done if rational and effective use of China's undeveloped resources, in accordance with the best principles of industrial location as well as considerations of national security, is to be the primary concern. A beginning in this direction has been made in China since the organization in the spring of 1941 of the Central Planning Bureau, whose first contribution lies in the drafting of a Three-Year Program for Wartime Reconstruction for the period 1942 - 44.[1] But an international resources survey, conducted by a joint group of Chinese and foreign experts, would go a long way in securing the fundamental facts of Chinese resources that may serve as a concrete basis for the planning of large-scale developmental projects to be launched in postwar China. The comprehensive and thorough-going plans laid out by the National Resources Commission for a three-year program of development in heavy industries during 1936 - 37 to 1938 - 39 will serve as a model for similar plans in other fields such as transport and agriculture; nevertheless, the Commission's program will have to be reconsidered in the light of a free and independent China including the outlying territories of Manchuria, Mongolia and Tibet.[2]

Forms of Organization

No single form of economic organization — socialism, capitalism, or cooperation — will adequately meet the needs of China in her postwar industrialization. Different sectors of China's postwar economy will require a different form of economic organization. Thus, the heavy industries

---

[1] Chen, P. T. : "China's Three-year Plan for Wartime Reconstruction", *China Quarterly*, Spring, 1941.

[2] The Commission's program, drawn up with the aid of German experts, concentrated the development of heavy industries in Central China, chiefly because Manchuria in China's Northeast was then occupied by Japan while North China was under constant threat of attack by the same nation. A five-year plan for the postwar industrial development of China is being drafted by the Commission.

which China must establish in order to satisfy her minimum defense needs as a modern nation must be owned and operated by the state for several reasons. These industries require a large capital outlay which private enterprise, still in its infancy in China, is not in a position to furnish. They are usually risky and not profitable; they are too vital to the needs of national defense to be left to develop in an uncontrolled manner by private enterprise and free competition. In heavy industries, as well as in large-scale public works and public utilities, state ownership and operation seems to offer the best solution.

Light industries, which supply the daily necessities of modern economic life, may well be developed by private capital, both foreign and Chinese. These industries, which alone flourished to a reasonable extent in pre-war China, will continue to grow under private capitalism, but with state regulation in respect of working conditions and other matters affecting public welfare. In this connection, it must be stressed that despite its rapid wartime growth, government enterprise is officially viewed as a means of supplementing private enterprise and by no means as a method of gradually eliminating private enterprise and socializing the economic system. Indeed, the *regulation* of private capitalistic enterprise, not its elimination, constitutes one of the two principal features of the Kuomintang policy of achieving the Principle of People's Livelihood as taught by its founder, Dr. Sun Yat-sen. [1]

---

[1] The other feature is agrarian reform, through equalization of the rights of land ownership. See Sun Yat-sen, *San Min Chu I, or The Three Principles of the People*, tr. by Frank W. Price, China Committee of the Institute of Pacific Relations, Shanghai, 1927.

The largest sector of China's postwar economy will have to be organized on the basis of cooperation, whether agricultural or industrial. Four-fifths of the Chinese population depend upon farming as the principal source of livelihood. Four-fifths of Chinese industrial production are derived from small-scale industries carried on either by the peasant families during off seasons or by the urban craftsmen in homes or workshops. Both agriculture and industry in China are, in other words, predominantly decentralized and small-scale in character; they depend more upon manual labor than upon capital equipment. For this form of decentralized, small-scale, and handicraft production cooperation seems to offer the best hope for improvement. It affords to peasants and craftsmen alike the advantages of large-scale economy in purchasing, financing, and marketing, without affecting the mode of production except in designs and other technical details related to standardization and improvement in the quality of product. It is for this reason that both agricultural and industrial cooperatives have made such rapid strides in wartime China. In Free China today there are 146,300 agricultural cooperatives and 1,660 industrial cooperatives, with a membership of 7,582,000 and 21,200 respectively. Reckoning roughly on a population of 300 million in Free China, with an average family of five persons, the 7,603,200 cooperative membership affects a population of 38 million. In other words, one out of every eight Chinese in Free China is affiliated with the cooperative form of organization. Cooperation, affecting industry and agriculture alike, therefore seems to offer the most prevalent form of economic organization in postwar China. ①

The China Reconstruction Finance Corporation

With the above principles in mind, let us visualize a government program of moderate industrialization for postwar China during a period of five years, with a total capital outlay of one billion US dollars, of which one half would be raised in China and the other half abroad. The total investment might be distributed on an increasing scale over the five years tentatively as follows: 100 million during the first, 150 million during the second, 200 million during the third, 250 million during the fourth, and 300 million during the fifth year.

The capital needed for China's postwar industrialization should be entrusted to a government organization for developmental purposes, under the name of China Reconstruction Finance Corporation (CRFC). This corporation could have as its main function the financing of China's postwar industrialization in the three fields of transport and public utilities, agriculture, and industry, by furnishing all or a part of the necessary capital for various projects. These might be undertaken by private enterprise with or without participation of foreign capital and management, or by the

---

① Strickland, C. F. : *Rural Finance and Cooperation*, Chunghwa Book Company, Shanghai; Tayler, J. B. : *Farm and Factory in China*, Student Christian Movement, London, 1928; Fong, H. D. : *Rural Industries in China*, China Institute of Pacific Relations, Shanghai, 1933; Fong, H. D. : *The Cooperative Movement in China*, Nankai Institute, Tientsin, 1934. See also *supra*, P. 184 note①.

state when the projects in view are vital to national defense and national well-being, call for huge outlay which private capital cannot well afford to furnish, or require long-range planning and development that does not promise immediate pecuniary return. Command over capital would enable the corporation to fulfill many allied functions, including:

(1) Scientific surveying of resources to serve as a basis for planning the various developmental projects,

(2) Purchasing from abroad necessary raw materials and capital equipment in which China is deficient,

(3) Training in China and abroad of technical and managerial personnel of all grades for developmental projects,

(4) Procurement of high-grade technical and managerial ability for responsible advisory or executive tasks from foreign countries, and

(5) Provision of transportation facilities for raw materials, equipment, laborers and staff members from China or foreign countries to the various localities where the projects are to be developed.

One principle—that of decentralization of execution of the projects, but centralization of planning, financing, and procurement of materials, equipment, and personnel—should be observed throughout. A number of governmental or quasi-governmental corporations should be organized under the various ministries, commissions and departments of the Chinese Government, some national but others provincial or county-wide in scope, whose function would be to carry out the respective projects initiated by the CRFC. The capital stock of these subsidiary corporations should be partly or wholly subscribed to by the CRFC, and if need arose, their short-term financing would also fall upon its shoulders. Simultaneously, the needs of these subsidiary corporations for raw materials, equipment, workers, technical and managerial personnel should be taken care of by the CRFC under a coordinated plan.

Precedents that may serve as a pattern for the proposed CRFC are not lacking. The China Development Finance Corporation, established in June 1934, has as its main object "to study the worth of any business proposition, and, if it is found suitable, to arrange for the subscription of capital, Chinese and foreign, both singly and jointly, and later to follow through the development of the particular enterprise on behalf of those financially interested." The capital of the corporation was fixed at 10 million yuan, and was subscribed by seventeen leading banks, including three of the Four Government Banks (Bank of China, Central Bank, and Bank of Communications). The assets of the corporation, amounting to 14.8 million yuan, jumped a year later to 115 million yuan (approximately US $35 million). In effect, the corporation, with its ten million yuan capital, could not by itself develop any extensive investment policy. Its role, therefore, was more of an intermediary agent between the banks and the investment market. The largest part of the loans made by the corporation on behalf of the Chinese Banking Syndicate (composed mainly of the seventeen banks referred to above) has been for railway purposes. The corporation arranges such loans to the Ministry of Railways, or for direct building purposes, or in the form of security granted by the Syndicated Banks on credit opened for purchase of railway materials by foreign firms (German, Czechoslovakian, British, Belgian, French). This intervention on the part of the Chinese banks revived the flow of foreign capital during the years immediately preceding the outbreak of the war on strictly business principles. The Government either issues to the banks through the corporation, or delivers to the corporation or to its trustees (generally the Bank of China) bonds as security for loans. The same intermediary policy has been followed to finance public works in charge of the Ministry of Communications and municipal public utilities developments. In both instances the corporation arranged loans from Chinese or foreign sources, in the form of long-term loans or medium-term credit, for the purchase of materials. ①

The China Development Finance Corporation may serve as a pattern upon which to model the financing activity of the proposed CRFC. In the handling of raw materials, equipment, and technical personnel from abroad, the National Resources Commission, engaged since 1936 in the establishment of heavy industries for China, is another model. A start in planning has been made by the Central Planning Bureau organized since the spring of 1941. Abroad, there are already two organizations that have functioned during the war for the procurement of materials and equipment to meet China's wartime economic and military needs — the China De-

---

① *Finance and Commerce*, June 6, 1934 and June 17, 1936; The China Development Finance Corporation, *Semi-Annual Report*, June 30, 1936, Shanghai.

fense Supplies established in May, 1941, and the Universal Trading Corporation established in December, 1938. The former handles Lend-Lease Aid to China in Washington of trucks, gasoline, spare parts, aeroplanes, and ordnance. It has six technical committees on aviation, ordnance, engineering, transport, signals, and general supplies. Each committee is headed by a Chinese technician, working side by side with an American colleague on the detailed specifications before applying for procurement to the United States Government Defense Aid Division and other governmental departments in accordance with the usual procedure. ① With Dr. T. V. Soong as Chairman of the Board of Trustees, the CDS has David Cochran as its President, with over one hundred staff members, largely Chinese, at work. *Fortune* says of the CDS, ②

> China Defense Supplies, however, is not a one-man show. The young Chinese assisting T. V. on technical and other matters are men of exceptional ability. They form a compact, hard-driving group that has made an excellent impression everywhere in Washington. Especially do they appeal to the young men of the New Deal, and the New Deal has taken China Defense Supplies to its bosom.

The Universal Trading Corporation in New York City was established in December, 1938, under the New York State law. The Corporation, with Archie Lochhead, formerly Technical Assistant to the United

---

① A detailed description of the whole procedure is given in an article in *Fortune*, 1941, pp. 150-51.

② *Ibid.*, p. 150.

States Secretary of Treasury Morgenthau, as President, and S. D. Ren, an experienced financier and industrialist from interior China, as Executive Vice-President, has performed a notable service in maintaining trade relations between wartime China and the United States. In December 1940, more than a year ago, it was reported that:①

> since its formation in October (December?), 1938, Universal has sold 41,000,000 pounds of tung oil — it expects to deliver 60 percent of US requirements this year — and a miscellaneous amount of tin, bristles, silk, and skins. In the same time its US-educated Chinese engineers have purchased some $32,000,000 worth of highly specialized machinery and goods in this country.

The Corporation, in other words, is a purchasing agent for the Chinese Government on the one hand, and on the other, a distributing center for Chinese exports to the United States in repayment of the loans from the Export-Import Bank. The exports include tung oil, tin, antimony, and tungsten; while the imports into China include trucks, motorcycles, mobile repair and machine shops, tires, gasoline, kerosene, fuel oils and lubricants, telephones, radios, iron and steel shapes and specialties, aluminum, copper, brass and other metals in the non-ferrous group, khaki cloth, cotton blankets, and a wide variety of chemicals, drugs, and surgical instruments, road machinery and construction materials, etc.

---

① *Fortune*, December, 1940, p. 134. See also S. D. Ren, "China and Tung Oil", a speech presented before the 52nd Annual Convention of the National Paint, Varnish and Lacquer Association, Washington, D. C., on October 31, 1940.

By the end of November, 1941, the loans outstanding amounted to US $74,000,000, the rest being still available as commitments. The job of collecting and exporting tung oil, tin, tungsten, and antimony has been carried on by two organizations in China—the Foo Shing Trading Corporation, a subsidiary of the Foreign Trade Commission of the Ministry of Finance, for tung oil, and the National Resources Commission of the Ministry of Economics for minerals. The procedure for procurement in the United States works somewhat as follows: [1]

> The Chinese Government uses Universal as its US purchasing agent. The departments (in China) do not work directly with Mr. Lochhead's Corporation but send their orders through the Minister of Finance, Dr. H. H. Kung, for clearance. Dr. Kung gives Ren and his engineers a green light in the form of a duly authorized memorandum with a supporting requisition worked out in Chungking.... Appropriations are also made through Dr. Kung, who knows the exact amount of Universal's commitments and the extent of China's other dollar balances. Thus, when Ren gets an order he passes it on to one of seven general purchasing sections for study and specification.... Invitations to bid are sent to a list of approved manufacturers together with complete specifications, terms of purchase, and instructions. Bids must be returned sealed and they are opened at a specified hour with formality by Universal's only other

---

[1] *Fortune*, December, 1940, p. 134.

American executive, Captain James A. Bull, U. S. Navy supply officer with experience on procurement. They are then carefully inspected by the engineer in charge to see that all specifications have been met, and the award is made to the lowest conforming bidder. Universal prides itself on buying at rock-bottom prices.

In short, organizations already exist in wartime China today which have functioned well in meeting China's wartime needs for resistance and reconstruction. Adapted, coordinated, and reorganized, the CRFC will have already a working structure, with reasonably adequate personnel and facilities to rely on. In China the CRFC's respective functions can be taken care of by the existing organizations in a reorganized form — financial functions by the China Development Finance Corporation, technical by the National Resources Commission, and planning by the Central Planning Bureau; while abroad, in the United States for instance, the procurementment of raw materials, equipment, and technical personnel can be shared jointly between the China Defense Supplies and the Universal — the former for heavy industries, transport and public utilities, the latter for light industries and agriculture. A good deal of shifting and adaptation, as well as expansion in order to meet the greater needs for China's postwar industrialization, still remain to be undertaken, but the outline laid out in the preceding paragraphs, it is hoped, may serve as a useful suggestion for the kind of development that is to take place when China emerges victorious with the United Nations in this war. China as a cooperating member of the United Nations can then play her role in erecting the new world of freedom of speech and religion, of freedom from want and fear.

Acknowledgement

I wish to acknowledge my indebtedness to many friends who have kindly read over the manuscript or made useful suggestions, although I alone am to be held responsible for the views expressed in this paper. In particular I want to thank Professor Alvin H. Hansen of Harvard University, Professor Eugene Staley of the Fletcher School of Law and Diplomacy, Professor Nathaniel Peffer of Columbia University, Mr. W. L. Holland and Dr. Kurt Bloch of the Institute of Pacific Relations, Dr. C. F. Remer of the Far Eastern Section of the Office of the Coordinator of Information, Mr. E. J. Coil of the National Planning Association, Dr. Kan Lee of the Chinese Embassy, and Dr. A. Manuel Fox of the Chinese Currency Stabilization Board. Above all, I wish to express my gratitude to the Rockefeller Foundation for having given me an opportunity to make use of the facilities in the United States for the completion of this paper as a part of my program of research.

H. D. FONG.

May 12, 1942.
Cambridge, Mass.

Appendix

Table I. —Coal Reserves of China Distributed by Provinces, 1933 (In billion metric tons)

	Anthracite	Bituminous	Lignite	Total
Shansi	36.5	88.0	2.7	127.2
Shenai	0.7	71.2	–	71.9
Szechuen	0.1	9.8	–	9.9
Honan	4.6	2.0	–	6.6
Sinkiang	–	–	–	6.0
Hopei	1.0	2.1	–	3.1
Liaoning	0.2	1.6	–	1.8
Hunan	0.5	1.3	–	1.8
Shantung	–	1.6	–	1.6
Yunnan	–	1.5	0.1	1.6
Kweichow	0.8	0.8	–	1.6
Kansu	–	–	–	1.5
Kirin	–	1.0	0.2	1.2
Heilungkiang	–	0.6	0.4	1.0
Other[a]	1.0	3.7	...	9.3
Total	45.4	185.2	3.4	246.1

(a) Includes provinces with a reserve of less than one billion metric tons each. The estimate for Manchuria, covering the four northeastern provinces of Liaoning, Kirin, Heilungkiang and Jehol, is too low, being 4.6 billion metric tons. The *Far Eastern Yearbook*, 1940 −41, iasued in Tokyo, places the total coal reserve of Manchuria at 17.4 billion metric tons; while the *Japan Yearbook*, 1940 −41 considers the minimum reserve to be 20 billion metric tones. Meantime, in the southwestern provinces, notably Szechuen, new coal reserves have recently been discovered. Wong's estimate, therefore, must be taken as a minimum.

Source: *Chinese Yearbook*, 1935 −36, p. 945.

Table II. — Coal Production of China Distributed by Provinces, 1931 (In million metric tons)

Liaoning	7.70	Anhwei	0.28
Hopei	7.66	Hupeh	0.28
Shansi	2.27	Heilungkiang	0.24
Honan	1.84	Shensi	0.23
Hunan	0.93	Chekiang	0.23
Jehol	0.70	Kwangtung	0.22
Szechuen	0.66	Other[a]	2.96
Kirin	0.58		
Kiangsi	0.46	Total	27.24

(a) Including ten provinces with an output of less than 200,000 metric tons each. The total output for the four Manchurian provinces of Liaoning, Kirin, Heilungkiang and Jehol is given here as 9.22 million metric tons in 1931, but has increased to 12.54 million metric tons in 1937.

Source: *General Statement on the Mining Industry*, 1929 − 31, Geological Survey of China, Peiping, 1932, Table 25. Water as a source of motive power may be mentioned here. Estimates on the potential water power resources in China are incomplete and conflicting, ranging from 20 − 40 million H. P. According to the World Power Conference, the potential total for China reaches 20 million H. P., or five percent of the world's total (i. e. 444,574.000 H. P.). (*Power Resources of the World*, World Power Conference, London, 1929, Table XX) Julean Arnold, American Commercial Attache in China for many years, places the potential total at 25 million H. P., while a German estimate raises it to 31 − 40 million H. P. (Arnold, Julean: *China Through the American Window*, Shanghai, 1932, p. 25; for German estimate see *Chinese Yearbook*, 1935 − 36, pp. 997 − 8).

Table III. — Iron Ore Reserve of China Distributed by Provinces, 1935 − 36 (In million metric tons)

Liaoning	872.2	
Hopei	123.7	Luanhsien 32, Hsuanhua-Lungkwan 91.7

continued

Hupeh	39.6	Itu 4.0, Tayeh, Ocheng, etc. 35.6
Hunan	21.0	Ninghsien, Chaling, and Hsinhua
Anhwei	19.8	Tungkuanshan and Chikuanshan 8.9, Tangtu and Changlingshan 10.9
Chekiang, Fukien, Kwangtung	19.4	
Shantung, Honan, Kiangsu	17.4	Chinlingchen, Hungshan, Likuoyi
Kiangsi	15.2	Pinghsiang and Yungsin 8.9, Chengmenshan 6.3
Kiangsu	4.4	
Total	1,132.6	

Source: *Chinese Yearbook*, 1935−36, p. 946.

Table Ⅳ. —Estimated Area and Population of the Northwest and Southwest China

	Area(1,000 sq. km.)		Population(1,000)	
Northwestern provinces:				
Shensi	187		10,112	
Kansu	378		6,081	
Ninghsia	275		667	
Chinghai	697		1,195	
Sinkiang	1,828		2,453	
		3,365		20,508
Southwestern provinces:				
Szechuen	431		46,824	
Sikang	372		1,048	
Yunnan	320		11,795	
Kweichow	179		7,023	
Kwangsi	218		13,885	

continued

	Area(1,000 sq. km.)	Population(1,000)
Total	1,520	80,075
Grand total	4,885	100,583

Source: For area see *The Quarterly Journal of Statistics* (in Chinese), Ministry of Interior. January, 1937; for population see *The Chinese Yearbook*, 1938 − 39, pp. 32 − 35.

Table V. — Mineral Production of Manchuria, 1929 − 37 (In 1,000 metric tons)

	1929	1933	1934	1935	1936	1937	Annual output goal Five-year Plan Original	Revised†
Iron ore	986	1,177	1,133	1,478	1,795	2,257	6,600	12,000
Pig iron	294	434	476	608	647	739	2,400	4,860
Steel ingots	−	−	−	137	344	427	2,500	3,500
Steel rolled	−	−	−	−	−	−	−	2,000
Gold (kgs)	−	−	464	1,887	3,959	−	Y200m.*	Y300m.*
Coal	10,024	9,063	10,619	11,187	12.082	12,540	27,000	38,000
Coke	388	476	521	667	712	1,114	−	−
Oil shale	−	2,683	2,106	3,228	3,648	−	−	−
Crude oil	−	87	58	120	123	−	−	−
Liquid fuel	−	−	−	−	−	−	1,356	2,500
Coal liquefaction	−	−	−	−	−	−	500	1,700
Shale oil	−	−	−	−	−	−	800	650
Alcohol	−	−	−	−	−	−	56	150
Cement	−	−	331	371	650	797	−	−
Sulphate of ammonia	−	−	26	156	181	182	−	−
Magnesite	32	71	100	225	192	350	−	−
Fire clay	69	112	79	138	148	266	−	−
Salt	520	607	405	901	891	834	875	1,000

continued

	1929	1933	1934	1935	1936	1937	Annual output goal Five-year Plan Original	Revised†
Electricity generated (1,000,000 KWH)	–	–	782	949	1,248	1,481	–	–
Electric power (1,000 KW)	–	–	–	–	–	420	1,445	2,600
Hydraulic	–	–	–	–	–	–	575	1,260
Coal	–	–	–	–	–	–	870	1,340

* Over five years. †Revised in 1938.

Source: Schumpeter, Elizabeth B. and Others: *The Industrialization of Japan and "Manchukuo"*, 1930 – 40, Macmillan, 1940, p. 388; Mitchell, Kate L.: *Industrialization of the Western Pacific*, Institute of Pacific Relations, 1942, pp. 84, 86.

Table VI. —Foreign Trade and Investments in Manchuria, 1932 – 39, Foreign Trade of Manchuria
(In million yuan)

Year	Imports	Exports	Balance	Imports of construction materials	Japanese investments in Manchuria (million yen)	Japanese Empire export surplus with Manchuria and Kwantung (million yen)
1932	337.7	618.2	+280.5	–	97.2	–
1933	515.8	448.5	-67.4	–	151.2	–
1934	593.6	448.4	-145.1	154.3	271.7	–
1935	604.1	421.1	-183.1	157.8	378.6	–
1936	691.8	602.8	-89.1	151.9	263.0	225
1937	887.4	645.3	-242.1	224.3	348.3	322
1938	1,274.7	725.5	-549.3	410.6	439.5	519
1939	1,783.4	826.2	-957.2	555.0	1,103.7	959

Source: Schumpeter, *op. cit.*, pp. 398 – 99. In November, 1935, the yuan in Manchuria was stabilized at parity with the Japanese yen by agreement between the two governments. So yen and yuan became interchangeable after that date.

Table VII. — China's Export of Mineral and Agricultural Products to Japan, 1933 - 40
(In 1,000 quintals)

Year	Iron ore	Coal (1,000 metric tons)	Salt[a]	Cotton. Raw	Wool, Camels'. Goats' & Sheep's
1933	5,926	392	2,369	332	7
1934	8,558	569	2,115	167	7
1935	13,152	616	2,149	215	637
1936	13,014	1,000	3,124	258	960
1937	5,865	1,275	4,330	234	158
1938	785	1,611	5,924	964	952
1939	1,017	2,369	3,501	48	142
1940	2,304[b]	3,785	6,794	32	298

(a) Including salt exported to Korea. (b) Including 842,000 quintals exported to the Kwantung Leased Territory.

Source: China Inspectorate General of Customs. *Trade of China*, Vol. III: *Foreign Trade Analysis of Exports*, 1933 - 40. The data in the Customs trade reports do not include Manchuria since 1933 — the year when the new puppet state of "Manchukuo" became formally established.

Table VIIIa. — Distribution of Foreign Investment in China by Types, 1902 - 31 (Amount in million U. S. dollars)

	Business investment		Government obligations	
Year	Amount	Percent of total	Amount	Percent of total
1902	503. 2	63. 9	284. 7	36. 1
1914	1,084. 5	67. 3	525. 8	32. 7
1931	2,531. 9	78. 1	710. 6	21. 9

Table VIIIb. —Distribution of Foreign Investment in China by Purpose or Nature of the Business, 1914 and 1931

(Amount in million U. S. dollars)

Purpose	1914 Amount	%	1931 Amount	%
General purposes of the Chinese government	330.3	20.5	427.7	13.2
Transportation	531.1	33.0	846.8	26.1
Communications and public utilities	26.6	1.7	128.7	4.0
Mining	59.1	3.7	128.9	4.0
Manufacturing	110.6	6.9	376.8	11.6
Banking and finance	6.3	0.4	214.7	6.6
Real estate	105.5	6.5	339.2	10.5
Imports and exports	142.6	8.8	483.7	14.9
Miscellaneous (undistributed)	298.2	18.5	282.8	8.7
Obligations of foreign municipalities	–	–	14.2	0.4
Total	1,610.3	100.0	3,242.5	100.0

Table VIIIc. —Geographical Distribution of Foreign Investment in China, 1902 - 31

(Amount in million U. S. dollars)

	1902 Amount	%	1914 Amount	%	1931 Amount	%
Shanghai	110.0	14.0	291.0	18.1	1,112.2	34.3
Manchuria	216.0	27.4	361.6	22.4	880.0	27.1
Rest of China	177.2	22.5	433.1	26.9	607.8	18.8
Undistributed	284.7	36.1	524.6	32.6	642.5	19.8
Total	787.9	100.0	1,610.3	100.0	3,242.5	100.0

Table VIIId. — Distribution of Foreign Investment in China by Creditor Countries, 1902-31
(Amount in million U. S. dollars)

	1902 Amount	%	1914 Amount	%	1931 Amount	%
Great Britain	260.3	33.0	607.5	37.7	1,189.2	36.7
Japan	1.0	0.1	219.6	13.6	1,136.9	35.1
Russia	246.5	31.8	269.3	16.7	273.2	8.4
United States	19.7	2.5	49.3	3.1	196.8	6.1
France	91.1	11.6	171.4	10.7	192.4	5.9
Germany	164.3	20.9	263.6	16.4	87.0	2.7
Belgium	4.4	0.6	22.9	1.4	89.0	2.7
Netherlands	–	–	–	–	28.7	0.9
Italy	–	–	–	–	46.4	1.4
Scandinavian countries	–	–	–	–	2.9	0.1
Others	0.6	0.0	6.7	0.4	–	–
Total	787.9	100.0	1,610.3	100.0	3,242.5	100.0

Source: Remer, C. F., *Foreign Investments in China*, Macmillan, 1933, Ch. V.

Table IX. — China's Wartime Internal Loan Issues, 1937-42

		Amount of Loan (in millions)			
Name of Loan	Date of Issue	Yuan	CGU	£	U.S. $
26th Year Liberty Loan	Sept., 1937	500	–	–	–
27th Year Defense Loan	May, 1938	500	–	–	–
27th Year Gold Loan	May, 1938	–	100	10	50

continued

Name of Loan	Date of Issue	Amount of Loan (in millions)			
		Yuan	CGU	£	U. S. $
27th Year Relief Loan	July, 1938	30	–	–	–
28th Year Reconstruction Loan	Aug., 1939	600	–	–	–
28th Year War Supplies Loan	Oct., 1939	600	–	–	–
29th Year Reconstruction Loan	May & Oct., 1940	–	–	10	50
29th Year War Supplies Loan	March & Sept., 1940	1,200	–	–	–
31st Year Allied Victory Bond	March, 1942	–	–	–	100
31st Year Savings Certificate	March, 1942	–	–	–	100
Total		3,430	100	20	300

Source: *Chinese Yearbook*, 1940 – 41; *Contemporary China*, April 6, 1942; *Chinese Nationalist Daily* (in Chinese), March 26, 1942, New York City. The conversion ratios are as follows: £ to U. S. $4, CGU1 to U. S. $0.40, and U. S. $1 to Yuan 20.

Selected Bibliography

American Economic Mission to the Far East, *Report*, National Foreign Trade Council, New York, 1935.

Bain, H. Foster: *Ores and Industry in the Far East*, revised and enlarged edition, Council on Foreign Relations, New York, 1933.

Barnett, Robert W.: *Economic Shanghai: Hostage to Politics, 1937 – 41*, Institute of Pacific Relations, New York, 1941.

Buck, J. L. : *Land Utilization in China*, University of Chicago Press, 3 vols. ,1937.
Chen, Han-seng: *Industrial Capital and Chinese Peasants*, Kelly & Walsh, Shanghai, 1939.
China after Four Years of War, China Information Committee, Chungking, 1941.
Condliffe, J. B. : *China Today: Economic*, World Peace Foundation, Boston, 1932.
Corbett, P. E. : *Postwar Worlds*, Institute of Pacific Relations, New York, 1942.
Cressy, George B. : *China's Geographic Foundations*, McGraw-Hill, 1934.
Fong, H. D. :
    China's Industrialization, China Institute of Pacific Relations, Shanghai, 1931.
    Industrial Capital in China, Nankai Institute of Economics, Tientsin, 1936.
    Industrial Organization in China, Nankai Institute of Economics, Tientsin, 1937.
    Rural Industries in China, China Institute of Pacific Relations, Shanghai, 1933.
    Toward Economic Control in China, China Institute of Pacific Relations, Shanghai, 1936.
Great Britain. Economic Mission to the Far East: *Report*, H. M. Stationery Office, London, 1931.
Hansen, Alvin H. : *After the War — Full Employment*, National Resources Planning Board, Washington, 1942.
Hu, T. Y. : *Japan's Economy under War Strain*, Chinese Council for Economic Research, Washington, 1941.
Hubbard, G. E. : *Eastern Industrialization and its Effects on the West*, Oxford University Press, London and New York, 1935.
Hudson, G. F. , Rajchman, Marthe, and Taylor, George E. : *An Atlas of Far Eastern Politics*, John Day, New York, 1942.
Lin, W. Y. : *The Future of Foreign Business and Foreign Investments in China*, China Institute of Pacific Relations, Hongkong, 1939.
Lowe, Chuan-hua: *Japan's Economic Offensive in China*, Allen & Unwin, London. 1939.
Mitchell, Kate L. : *Industrialization in the Western Pacific*, Institute of Pacific Relations, New York, 1942.

Mitchell, Kate L. and Holland, W. L. (ed.): *Problems of the Pacific*, 1939, Institute of Pacific Relations, New York, 1940.

Moser, Charles K.: *Where China Buys and Sells*, Trade Information Bulletin No. 827, U. S. Bureau of Foreign and Domestic Commerce, Washington, 1935.

Peffer, Nathaniel: *Prerequisites to Peace in the Far East*, Institute of Pacific Relations, New York, 1940.

Remer, C. F.: *Foreign Investments in China*, Macmillan, New York, 1933.

Salter, Sir Arthur: *China and Silver*, Economic Forum, New York, 1934.

Schumpeter, Elizabeth B. and others: *The Industrialization of Japan and " Manchukuo", 1930 – 40*, Macmillan, New York, 1940.

Staley, Eugene: *World Economy in Transition*, Council on Foreign Relations, New York, 1939.

Sun, Yat-sen

 San Min Chu I, or The Three Principles of the People, tr. by Frank W. Price, China Committee of the Institute of Pacific Relations, Shanghai, 1927.

 The International Development of China, New York, 1922.

Tayler, J. B.: *Farm and Factory in China*, Student Christian Movement, London, 1928.

Tawney, R. H.: *Land and Labor in China*, Allen & Unwin, London, 1931.

Wales, Nym: *China Builds for Democracy: A Story of Cooperative Industry*, Modern Age, New York, 1942.

THE JAPANESE DEVELOPMENT COMPANIES IN OCCUPIED CHINA

TABLE OF CONTENTS

Prefatory Note

Chapters

Ⅰ. Summary

    A. Place of Development Companies in Japanese Economic Control over Occupied China

        1. Relation of Development Companies to Other Agencies of Economic Control

        2. Nature and Characteristcs of Development Companies

    B. Nature and Extent of Control Exercised by the Two Companies over Economic of Occupied China

        1. Nature of Control

        2. Extent of Control by Fields

            a. Transportation

            b. Communication

            c. Mining

            d. Power and Other Utilities

            e. Cotton and Silk

    C. Significance of the Development Companies

Ⅱ. The Pre-War Developmnet Company: Kochukoshi — China Development Company

    A. Organization

    B. Activities

C. Dissolution

Ⅲ. The North China Development Company

   A. History

   B. Organization and Government Control

   C. Finance

   D. Fileds of Development — Plans and Results

      1. Transportation

      2. Communication

      3. Electric Power

      4. Coal

      5. Iron and Iron Ore

      6. Salt

      7. Cotton

Ⅳ. The Central China Promotion Company

   A. History and Organization

   B. Finance

   C. Programs of Development — Plans and Results

      1. Transportation

      2. Communications

      3. Power and Other Utilities

      4. Iron and Iron Ore

      5. Coal

      6. Salt

      7. Raw Silk

      8. Marine Products

Appendices

Ⅰ. North China Development and Affiliated Companies, March 31, 1941 (In 1,000 yen)

Ⅱ. Central China Promotion Company and Subsidiaries, March 31, 1941 (In 1,000 yen)

Ⅲ. Fundamental Principles Government the Development of North China Adopted by the North China Policy Committee…December 24, 1937

Ⅳ. Organic Law of the North China Development Company Law No. 81 (Japan, 1938) Promulgated April 30, 1938

Ⅴ. Summary of the Diet Bill for the Central China Promotion Company Submitted to the Lower House on March 18, 1938

List of Tables

1. Paid-up Capital of the Subsidiary Enterprises of the Two Development Companies, March 31, 1941 (In 1,000,000 yen)

2. Estimated Iron Ore Available to Japan from Occupied China, 1942 (In metric tons)

3. Authorized Capitalization of NCDC's Subsidiary Enterprises, 1938 (In 1,000,000 yen)

4. Chinese Investments in NCDC's Subsidiary Enterprises, 1938 (In yen)

5. Proposed Debentures to be Floated by NCDC's Subsidiary Enterprises in Five Years (In 1,000 yen)

6. NCDC's Investments Classified by Enterprises, March 31, 1941 (In

1,000,000 yen)

7. Investments in North China Ore Mining Offices Established Under the Association System, March 31, 1941 (In 1,000 yen)

8. Business Results of the NCDC, 1939 – 40 (In 1,000 yen)

9. Authorized Capital and Proposed Debentures of NCDC's Subsidiary Enterprises, March 31, 1941 (In 1,000 yen)

10. Proposed and Actual Capital and Debentures of NCDC's Subsidiary Enterprises Compared, March 31, 1941 (In 1,000 yen)

11. Railways in North China under Control of the North China Transportation Company, 1942 (In kilometers)

12. Operation Statistics of North China Railways, 1937 – 39

13. Coal Reserves in North China (In billion metric tons)

14. Subsidiary Companies and Mining Offices in the Coal, Industry Financed by the NCDC, March 31, 1941

15. Iron Ore Reserve in North China (In 1,000 metric tons)

16. Salt Production Expansion Plan of the North China Salt Company in Hopei Province, 1939

17. Japanese Planned Expansion of Changlu Salt Fields, 1938 – 48 (In metric tons)

18. Cotton Production and Export to Japan in Occupied China, 1937 – 38 to 1941 – 42 (In metric tons)

19. Proposed Capital of CCPC's Subsidiary Enterprises, 1938 (In 1,000,000 yen)

20. Capitalization of CCPC's 13 Subsidiary Companies, December 31, 1940

21. Authorized and Paid-up Capital of CCPC's 13 Subsidiary Compa-

nies, December 31, 1940 (In 1,000 yen)
22. Railways in Central China under Control of the Central China Railway Company, 1942 (In kilometers)
23. Iron Ore Reserves in Central China (In 1,000 metric tons)
24. Iron Ore Production in China Excluding Manchuria, 1934 (In tons)
25. Coal Reserves in Central China (In 1,000,000 metric tons)
26. Salt Production in Central China, 1937 (In metric tons)
27. Production Program of the Central China Raw Silk Company

Prefatory Note

In the preparation of the present report on the Japanese development companies in Occupied China, the writer has been given access to the personal files of Mrs. Dorothy J. Orchard and other materials available at the Board and elsewhere.

Information on major strategic industries controlled by the two companies, such as transportation, communication, mining and power, are fuller than those for minor branches such as cotton and silk, especially for the period after the Pearl Harbor Incident on December 7, 1941. Taken as a whole, the materials here assembled, though fragmentary, give nevertheless a comprehensive picture of the nature and extent of control exercised over the economy of Occupied China by the Japanese military through the medium of the two development companies and their subsidiary enterprises.

H. D. Fong: ms
February 1, 1943

I . Summary

A. Place of Development Companies in Japanese Economic Control over Occupied China

1. Relation of Development Companies to Other Agencies of Economic Control. The overall super-structure for the economic exploitation of Occupied China by Japan is the Asia Development Board formally inaugurated on December 15, 1938. This Board, presided over by the premier and with the four ministers of Foreign Affairs, Finance, Army, and Navy as deputy-governors, is in charge of a secretary-general with the rank of a minister in Tokyo, with its four departments — political, economic, cultural, and technical — and a China committee largely of a consultative character. In addition, the Central Liaison Department of the Board has control over the local liaison offices, which incorporate the Special Service section of the Japanese army and navy. Thus far, there

have been set up two liaison offices in Occupied China—the North China Liaison Office in Peiping headed by an army man and the Central China Liaison Office in Shanghai headed by a navy man.

The liaison offices are the all powerful organs for political, economic, and cultural control over occupied areas. They set up the respective puppet regimes in North China, Inner Mongolia and Central China, which in turn establish the various ministries of agriculture, industry, commerce and finance, and governmental agencies for control over trade, tariff, exchange, and finance, such as the Chinese Maritime Customs Administration, the Federal Reserve Bank of North China, the Central Reserve Bank of China, and the Inner Mongolia Bank. They also supervise the super-holding companies — the North China Development Company and the Central China Promotion Company — charged with the functions of economic exploitation in the key fields of transportation, communications, mining, and power. Internal trade is regulated under the military permit system, while manufacturing is left largely in the hands of big Japanese business interests in China. Control over agriculture is exercised through requisitioning of crops at prices fixed by the Japanese military, usually the Liaison Offices; but the results achieved in this field have been the poorest as compared with those realised in other fields.

The establishment of the Greater East Asia Ministry on the first of November 1942, resulted in the absorption and reorganization of the overall Asia Development Board. The Ministry, next only to the Army and Navy Ministries in importance, is composed of a Board of six Councillors and four Bureaus — General Affairs, Manchurian Affairs, China

Affairs and Southern Affairs. The China Affairs Bureau, which replaces the Asia Development Board, is composed of three departments — North China, Central China, and Mongolia. Details on the reorganization are still lacking up to the present writing. So far as the North China Development Company and the Central China Promotion Company are concerned, their supervision and control seem to have been transferred to the ministers at Peking and Nanking, who are in turn subordinate to the Japanese Ambassador to the "National Government at Nanking" (see Chart I). The transfer of supervision and control of the two development companies from the Japanese military to the apparently diplomatic authorities under the GEA Ministry remains to be clarified by further developments, as recent dispatches from Tokyo are silent as to the role which the Japanese military in Occupied China may play in respect to economic exploitation. The present situation can be explained only in terms of identification of the GEA Ministry with or its subordination to the Japanese military clique. As has been remarked by the Federal Communications Commission[1], the creation of the GEA Ministry,

> "supplies machinery for greater control by the military clique. It introduces into positions of power undistinguished bureaucrats who will be amenable to the demands of the military."

2. Nature and Characteristics of Development Companies. The two development companies were formally inaugurated on the seventh of

---

[1] *Radio Report on the Far East*, No. 7, November 10, 1942, A2-3.

November 1938 — eight months after bills for their establishment were passed by the Japanese Diet. Both companies follow closely the pattern set by the South Manchuria Railway Company organized in 1906, and possess special characteristics not found in ordinary commercial companies. They are created by special legislation of the Japanese Diet as special Japan companies with monopolistic powers over the development in newly conquered areas. Although jointly financed on the basis of equal subscription by the Japanese government on the one hand, and the Japanese people on the other, these companies serve as media to implement important national policies of Japan, and thus need not conform to commercial principles of profitability in their operations. The Japanese government exercises strict supervision and control over these companies, in respect to organization, personnel, finance, and operation. Decisions in regard to changes in the articles of organization, amalgamation or dissolution shall not be effective unless approved by the government. The governor and the deputy-governors of the company shall be appointed by the Japanese government with the approval of the Emperor. The government exercises control over the making of budgets, issue of debentures, payment of dividends, and disposal of profits. It issues orders in regard to the supervision of the company's business enterprises, or the coordination and adjustment of the company's enterprises in their relation to Japan's national defense and the economic development of the areas in which the company operates.

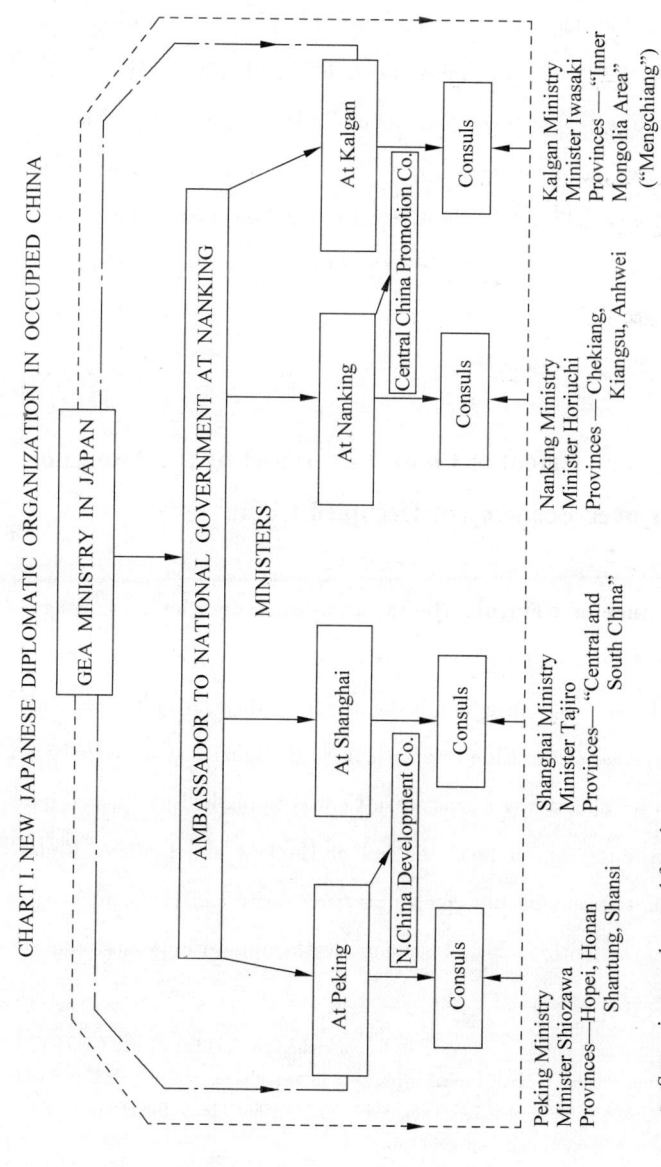

CHART I. NEW JAPANESE DIPLOMATIC ORGANIZATION IN OCCUPIED CHINA

```
                    ┌─────────────────────────┐
                    │  GEA MINISTRY IN JAPAN  │
                    └───────────┬─────────────┘
                                │
                                ▼
        AMBASSADOR TO NATIONAL GOVERNMENT AT NANKING

                              MINISTERS

   ┌──────────┐    ┌────────────┐    ┌──────────┐    ┌──────────┐
   │ At Peking│    │ At Shanghai│    │ At Nanking│   │ At Kalgan│
   └────┬─────┘    └─────┬──────┘    └─────┬────┘    └────┬─────┘
        │                │                 │              │
  ┌─────┴──────────┐     │      ┌──────────┴──────────┐   │
  │N.China         │     │      │Central China        │   │
  │Development Co. │     │      │Promotion Co.        │   │
  └─────┬──────────┘     │      └──────────┬──────────┘   │
        ▼                ▼                 ▼              ▼
   ┌──────────┐    ┌──────────┐      ┌──────────┐   ┌──────────┐
   │  Consuls │    │  Consuls │      │  Consuls │   │  Consuls │
   └──────────┘    └──────────┘      └──────────┘   └──────────┘
```

Peking Ministry
Minister Shiozawa
Provinces—Hopei, Honan
Shantung, Shansi

Shanghai Ministry
Minister Tajiro
Provinces— "Central and
South China"

Nanking Ministry
Minister Horiuchi
Provinces — Chekiang,
Kiangsu, Anhwei

Kalgan Ministry
Minister Iwasaki
Provinces — "Inner
Mongolia Area"
("Mengchiang")

⟶ Supervisory and control functions

---- "The GEA Ministry will have direct control over specific business concerning 'the Federated autonomous governments of Mengchiang' and North China Political Council (Domei; Dec. 16)"

--- "The Minister for GEA affairs will directly guide and supervise all consulates—generals (in regard) to legal affairs pertaining to (agricultural judicial matters)."

Both companies are in the nature of holding companies. The North China Development Company had an original capitalisation of ¥350,000,000, which was raised to ¥443,000,000 in April 1942. On its fourth anniversary on November 7, 1942, Tokyo broadcast by Domei reported the Company's direct investment in its subsidiary enterprises at ¥434,837,000. The Central China Promotion Company had an original capitalisation of ¥100,000,000, but by the end of 1942 it was reported that its investments in the subsidiary enterprises had reached ¥221,000,000. ①

B. Nature and Extent of Control Exercised by the Two Companies over Economy of Occupied China

1. Nature of Control. The two companies were formally inaugurated sixteen months after the outbreak of the Sino-Japanese War, on November 7, 1938. They came into being at a time when Japan had concluded the first stage of the China war, when North China had been in Japanese hands for almost a year, and when Central China had just passed into Japanese military control upon the fall of Hankow and Canton. Under these circumstances, the two companies necessarily had to comfine their activities to certain branches of economy in Occupied China most vital to

---

① *Radio Report on the Far Fast*, No. 8, November 24, 1942, C2. By the end of March 1941, the Company's total capital investment in subsidiaries reached ¥226,040,000, while its loans to the subsidiaries amounted to ¥368,000,000. "Direct investment" quoted in the text refers to share subscriptions.

the successful prosecution of her war effort. These branches include, in order of importance, transportation and communication; mining of coal, iron ore and salt; public utilities including power; and industrial raw matarials embracing cotton and silk. Transportation is essential to the movement of troops and supplies; so is communication to the transmission of military intelligence. Coal, iron ore, and salt are exported to Japan for transformation into war supplies. Cotton and silk constitute a different category, but serve the purpose of acquiring the foreign exchange that Japan needs badly to pay for her military imports, up to the Pearl Harbor Incident on December 7, 1941. Public utilities, especially power and light, have to be maintained in important industrial and commercial centres so that these centres may serve as strategic bases for the purpose of Japanese war operations. Table 1 giving the distribution of investments of the two companies by fields, gives a rough approximation of the relative importance of these fields:

Table 1. Paid-up Capital of the Sursidiary Enterprises of the Two Development Companies, March 31,1941 (In 1,000,000 yen)

	NCDC's subsidiaries		CCPC's subsidiaries		Total	
	Amount	%	Amount	%	Amount	%
Transportation	247.7	53.3	55.2	35.4	302.9	48.8
Communication	20.5	4.4	15.0	9.6	35.5	5.7
Mining	95.1	20.5	30.9	19.8	126.0	20.3
Power & light	79.0	17.1	29.4	19.0	108.4	17.4
Other	22.8	4.7	25.6	16.2	48.4	7.8
Total	465.1	100.0	156.1	100.0	621.2	100.0

2. Extent of Control by Fields

a. Transportation. The two companies' activities in the field of transportation extend to railways, steam navigation, canal and harbor construction, highway building and bus service. Railway rehabilitation and construction proceeded more rapidly in North than in Central China. New constructions of 901 kilometers all took place in North China, aiming largely at connecting the various trunk lines passing through the strategic centres like Peking, Tatung, and Shihmen (or Shihchiachuang). Lunghai is linked to Peking-Hankow by Kaifeng-Sinsiang branch, while Peking-Hankow is linked to Tientsin-Pukow by Shihmen-Tehchow branch. On the Tatung-Puchow line the narrow gauge is reconstructed on the standard gauge basis up to Ningwu, and from Taiku to Yutse. Among the pre-war railways of 10,638 kilometers including main lines and branches, the companies are now operating 7,185 kilometers including 15 completely operating lines and 4 partially operating lines. The kilometrage here given does not include second tracks, although in some cases, such as the Peking-Shanhaikwan line, second tracks added during the period of war reach 465 kilometers, as compared with 478 kilometers for the main and branch lines. (For kilometrage of respective railways being constructed and operated by the Japanese, see Tables 11 and 22.)

In other fields of transportation, control by the two companies is not so complete as in railway transportation. In steam navigation, it is restricted to the Lower Yangtze River and the vicinity of Shanghai. Coastal and other interior shipping is still in the hands of private Japanese interests such as the Nippon Yusan Kaisha and the Osaka Yusan Kaisha. Some harbor improvement work has been carried out in Taku and Tsingtao. The companies are reported to be in control of 3,800 kilometers of rivers and canals in North China, of which the most significant is the Tientsin-Shihmen Canal now under construction. In North China, 13,000 kilometers of highways are in their hands, the most important of which is the new highway connecting Peking with Tsinan. In Central China, about 1,000 kilometers of bus service is maintained, with another 300 kilometers for the six cities along the Shanghai-Nanking and Shanghai-Hangchow railways, namely, Shanghai, Nanking, Soochow, Hangchow, Wusih, and Chinkiang.

b. Communication. The companies' control over communication is more complete than that over railway transportation. Pre-war communication enterprise, largely under Chinese government control, has been taken over by the two development companies. Telephones, telegraphs, cables, wireless, and telephoto services combine to supply a fast and efficient intelligence system, for military rather than economic purpose. The international broadcasting and receiving station in the suburb of Shanghai maintains service with America (up to December 7, 1941), Europe, and nearly all places in East Asia, including Japan, Manchuria (Dairen), Hongkong, the Philippines (Manila), Thailand (Bangkok), and Occupied China (Tientsin, Tsintao, Nanking, Soochow, Hangchow, Hankow), as well as Japanese ships. Telephoto service is maintained between Shanghai and Tokyo, and direct radio telephone service between Shanghai, Japan and "Manchoukuo", as well as between Tokyo and Tientsin. A network of long distance telephones has been established, while all of the telegraph and cable offices in Occupied China have been placed under the control of the two companies.

c. Mining. Iron ore mining in pre-war China used to be concentrated in the Central China provinces of Hupeh and Anhwei, which jointly accounted for 98 percent of the total production of 950,000 tons of iron ore from the principal mines. Iron ore production from native mines — 409,580 tons — came from Shansi (180,000 tons) in North China and the southwestern provinces in Free China.

The companies' policy in the exploitation of iron ore resources in Occupied China consists largely in the rehabilitation or erection of modern mines in Hupeh, Anhwei, Chahar, and Shantung. In 1936, the pre-war year, China's export of iron ore to Japan and the Kwantung Leased Territory amounted to 1,303,000 metric tons, which declined to 587,000 tons in 1937, 79,000 tons in 1938, but rose again to 102,000 tons in 1939, 230,000 tons in 1940, and 391,000 tons in 1941. The Customs statistics here quoted cover only exports from North China from 1938 onward, and do not include those from Central China, i. e., output from Tayeh and Wuhu mines. They are thus under-estimated. The latest estimate for 1942, as shown in Table 2, is 2,427,000 tons, which is almost twice the pre-war total of 1,303,000 tons for 1936.

Table 2. Estimated Iron Ore Available to Japan from Occupied China, 1942 (In metric tons)

Lungyen mines, Chahar*	500,000
Consumption by Shihchingshan blast furnace, Hopei	100,000

	continued
Tayeh(Hupeh)& Wuhu mines **	1,805,000
Shansi mines ***	20,000
Chinlingchen mine, Shantung	2,000
Total	2,427,000

* Based on export from Chinese ports in 1941; since Yangtze Valley ore exports, although known to have been made, were not recorded.

** Includes 1,080,000 tons from Tayeh mines, and 725,000 tons from Wuhu mines.

*** Covers production by one large company.

Coal reserves in China (excluding Manchuria) are estimated by the Chinese Geological Survey at 241.5 million metric tons, of which 210.4 million or 87 percent are in the five North China provinces of Shansi, Shensi, Honan, Hopei, and Shantung. A recent Domei dispatch dated November 7, 1942, claimed that

> "of the total coal deposits in North China estimated at 240,000,000 tons, the North China Development Corporation controls 70 percent, while the amount of production of bituminous coal is now exceeding the quantity for export to Japan."

Of the pre-war coal output in China (excluding Manchuria) of 22,250,000 tons in 1936, 16,897,000 tons or 76 percent were produced in the five above-mentioned provinces in North China. Coal export to Japan amounted to only 1,000,000 metric tons in 1936, but increased to 1,275,000 tons in 1938, 1,611,000 tons in 1939, 3,785,000 tons in 1940, and 4,000,000 tons in 1941. If the output of bituminous coal by the North China Development Corporation "is now exceeding the quantity for export to Japan", which in 1941 reached 4,000,000 tons, such output represents about one-fourth of the total pre-war coal output from North China. Coal output by the largest coal mine in North China — the Kailan Mining Administration, is reported to have increased, according to Japanese plan, from 5,500,000 tons to 6,500,000 tons; and the export of coal from Occupied China to Japan has been estimated at 6,000,000 tons for 1942 and 1943, out of a total output of 20,000,000 tons for Occupied China.

The Central China Promotion Company is working the Hwainan mines in Anhwei through one of its subsidiaries, the Hwainan Coal Mining Company. It is said to be producing 1,000 tons per day.

In salt the two companies are in control of the five principal districts of production, which jointly accounted for 33,391,000 shih piculs (1,669,550 metric tons) or 55 percent of the total production of 60,621,000 shih piculs (3,031,050 metric tons) in 1936 — the pre-war year. These districts are: Lianghwai 10,290,000 shih piculs (of 110 pounds), Sungkiang 1,435,000 shih piculs, and Liangche 4,532,000 shin piculs, in Central China; Changlu 8,244,000 shih piculs, and Shantung 8,890,000 shih piculs, in North China.

Salt export to Japan and Korea during the period of war has shown a steady increase except in 1939, due to weather conditions. Such export, handled through the two companies, inereased from 312,000 metric tons in 1936 — the pre-war year, to 433,000 metric tons in 1937, 592,000 metric tons in 1938, 679,000 metric tons in 1940, and 704,000 metric tons in 1941. The export for 1939 was, however, reduced to 350,000 metric tons.

d. Power and Other Utilities. The larger electric power and light plants in North and Central China have been taken over by the two companies, including those in Tientsin, Tsintao, Tsinan, Chefoo, and Inner Mongolia in North China, and those in the fifteen cities in Eastern Central China, especially Shanghai. The generating capacity of the plants under the two companies' control reaches 326,270, k. w. in North China and 108,492 k. w. in East Central China. In East Central China, the one outstanding exception is the Shanghai Power Company, with a generating capacity of 198,500 k. w. , Taking all together, the total generating capacity reaches 633,262 k. w. , as compared with the pre-war total for China estimated at 631,165 k. w. [1]

Other public utilities under the control of the Central China Promotion Company include water and gas supply. Eight waterworks are reported to be furnishing 5.5 million cubic meters of water per month in East Central China, chiefly Shanghai. In Shanghai, the Company started the construction of a gas plant in February 1940, which began production in 1941 with a daily capacity of 7,000 cubic meters and an annual capacity of 25,000 Imperial gallons of coal tar by-products.

e. Cotton and Silk. In the Pacific areas occupied by the Japanese military since 1937, China is the main producer and supplier of raw cotton. For the year 1942, Occupied China is expected to supply 435,000

---

[1] *Statistical Abstract of the Republic of China. 1940*, Directorate of Statistics, Chungking, p. 84.

bales of raw cotton (of 500 lbs. net) to Japan, as compared with 155,000 bales from other sources in Southeast Asia. ① The North China Development Company has been given the monopoly of cotton purchase in North China for the purpose of export to Japan, while in Central China cotton export to Japan, being limited in quantity, is left in the hands of Japanese cotton marchants under direct supervision of the Japanese military.

Silk export from China to foreign countries, especially the United States, was taken over by the Central China Promotion Company, so that the foreign exchange obtained might revert to the Japanese Treasury for war purposes. At one time, attempt was made to reduce silk export from China in favor of Japanese silk exporters' interest. Upon the loss of American market since December 7, 1941, the Companys' efforts in respect of Chinese silk have been directed towards the replacement of mulberry by cotton farms, with a view to increasing cotton production for meeting Japan's taxtile needs.

C. Significance of the Development Companies

The two Japanese development companies in Occupied China, formally inaugurated sixteen months after the outbreak of the Sino-Japanese War, have thus far been "economic mobilization" agencies, not development agancies *per se*. The enterprises which they have taken over are primarily

---

① See my report on *A Preliminary Survey of the Cotton Textile Industry in Occupied China*, BEW, December 1, 1942.

strategic, secondarily economic. Four years after the establishment of the two companies, the strategic enterprises under their control have not yet been fully restored to the pre-war level, although those that they have succeeded in controlling have been more highly regimented than ever before, for the purpose of war. Those companies, through the organization of subsidiaries and active participation of private Japanese business interests in these subsidiaries, have been able to mobilize the Chinese transportation system for the movement of troops and supplies, as well as the Chinese communication system for the transmission of military intelligence. Production of strategic minerals including iron ore, coal and salt, has been restored or has exceeded the pre-war level, while by means of military control exercised through these two companies and their subsidiaries, increasing quantity has been exported to meet the needs of Japan's war industries. Similarly, control over the supply of electric power has been sufficient to enable the Japanese authorities in Occupied China to acquire a key position over the operation of Chinese industries, and to subjugate the interests of the Chinese industrialists to those of the Japanese.

The duration and outcome of the war may determine whether the development companied in Occupied China may in the end become "development agencies" *per se*, instead of agencies for wartime economic mobilisation. The degree of success which the two companies have already achieved points to a future not all too comforting to the United Nations. If the war be unduly prolonged beyond, say, another three years in favor of the Axis Nations, these companies may likely be able to make a start in the exploitation of Chinese resources for **long-term** development, instead of their mobilization for war purpose. These companies will then play a role in Occupied China similar to that performed by "the South Manchuria Railway Company" since 1906, or more recently by "the Manchuria Industrial Development Company" since 1937.

On the other hand, there is also the possibility that in case of an Allied victory, the groundwork already laid out by the two companies may afford to Free China a basis in her program for post-war industrialisation. The various strategic enterprises which Japan has striven to restore, and even to expand, during the period of war will than be rightfully taken over by the Free China Government, as a just indemnification of the tremendous losses in life and property she has suffered at the hands of the Japanese military in the course of war.

II. The Pre-war Development Company: Kochukoshi — China Development Company

A. Organization. Kochukoshi, a subsidiary of the South Manchuria Railway Company (SMR) known in Chinese as the Hsing-Chung Kungesu and in English as the China Development Company, was organized in Dairen in 1935, with an authorised capital of Yen 10,000,000, all owned by the SMR. Up to the outbreak of the China Incident in July 1937, Kochukoshi, with the political, financial and technical backing of the SMR, had attempted to push through an energetic program of economic development in North China altogether incomparable to the size of its capital resources,[1] In his proposal to the Japanese authorities concerned, including the military circles and the SMR Company, Mr. Shinji Sogo, President of the Kochukoshi, outlined the following program of development for Kochukoshi at the end of September 1937. [2]

1. The Kochukoshi should be reorganized into a pure holding company with a view to making investigations necessary for exploitation of resources and to undertaking, if possible, new enterprises in order to improve transport facilities and develop heavy, chemical and farming industries.
2. Salt, electric and some other industries already launched upon should be operated by existing companies respectively.
3. Necessary funds should be supplied from Japanese financiers, such as Mitsui, Mitsubishi, Sumitomo, Okura, Yasuda, the SMR and the Oriental Development Company, only through the medium of the Kochukoshi.
4. Investors may send their respective representatives to the Kochukoshi to take part in the latter's businese.

Further, it was reported that Mr. Sogo intended to increase the

---

[1] Prof. N. Skene Smith of the University of Commerce, Tokyo, reported in an article on "Japan's Economic Purpose in China" for March 1938 issue of *Trade and Engineering* an increase of the Company's capital to Yen 50,000,000, not elsewhere confirmed.

[2] "SMR and Kochukoshi to play major roles in North China plan", translated from the *Economist* issued November 21, 1937.

capital of his company ten times to ¥100,000,000, and that his plan included, as immediate projects, the development of the Lungyen iron mine and the Chinghsing colliery, iron manufacture, harbor construction at Tangku, cotton growing, and railway building.

B. Activities. The enterprises which Kochukoshi actually undertook included electric power, coal, iron ore, salt, and cotton, some of which were subsidiaries of the Company. In the field of electric power Kochukoshi founded the Tientsin Electric Power Company, capitalized at ¥8,000,000, through cooperation with the Electric Power Association of Japan and Chinese interests. The 160,000 shares were equally divided between the "Big Five" in the Japanese Electric Power Association — the Tokyo Electric Light Company, the Teho Electric Power Company, the Showa Electric Power Company, the Nippon Electric Power Company, and the Ujigawa Electric Company; and the Tientsin Municipal Government, with 1/4 of the aurthorized capital being paid up. In addition, Kochukoshi advanced a loan of ¥1,000,000 to the Tientsin Electric Power Company, whose plans included the erection of a 20,000 kilowatt steam-operated power plant to serve the First Special Area of the Tientsin Municipality (formerly German Concession returned to China upon conclusion of the First World War). The Company was inaugurated on August 20, 1936, and hailed by the Japanese in North China as marking the first step in the much-heralded Sino-Japanese program for the economic development of North China. It was, however, considered illegal on three grounds by the Reconstruction and Legislative Commissions of the Hopei and Chahar Political Council on September 12, 1936, as follows[1]:

1. The National Government of China in Nanking has banned electric power enterprises jointly financed by Chinese and aliens.

2. The contract was signed, without the approval of the Reconstruction Commission, between Mayor Chang Tzu-chung of Tientsin and President Shinji Sogo of Kochukoshi.

3. The contract was concluded without being previously submitted to the Legislative Commission.

Irrespective of the Commission's rulings, the Company proceeded to build two steam power generating stations with a combined capacity of 18,000 kilowatts, in addition to supplying light and power in Tientsin with the plant originally built by the Germans in 1908.

In iron production, Kochukoshi was placed in charge of the Shihchingshan Iron Works, located at a distance of 19 kilometers west of Peking. The Works, capitalized at 5,000,000 yuan, was founded in 1919 for the purpose of smelting iron ore from Lungyen in Chahar Province. Due to political disturbances and slump of iron price after the First World War, the Iron Works has not been operated after its establishment. In 1924, it was planned in vain to start the smelting work. On January 20, 1938, the Works was turned over to Kochukoshi for operation under the

---

[1] *North China Herald*, Shanghai, September 16, 1936.

supervision of Japanese army. The supplementary work of construction was resumed on April 20 of the year by Kochukoshi with cooperation of the Japan Iron Manufacturing Company. The 250-ton blast furnace was blown in on November 20, and produced 150 tons of pig iron daily. The iron production of Shihchingshan will supply the local demand, but Japan has the first priority of getting the supply whenever she needs it.

The iron ore for the Shihchingshan foundry came from the Lungyen iron mine under Kochukoshi's management. According to *Trans-Pacific* of February 2, 1939, "although the Japanese authorition in North China are hoping for an eventual annual output of 500,000 tons of ore, actual production in the immediate future is not expected to exceed 150,000 tons. Lack of adequate transportation facilities for the mine is proving the principal obstacle. This year (1939) out of the estimated output of 150,000 tons, 100,000 will be shipped to the Yawata foundry of the Japan Iron Manufacturing Company and the remainder will be supplied to the Shihchingshan Iron foundry in Peiping."

In coal mining, Kochukoshi, at the request of the military authorities, has managed most of the 20 representative coal mines taken over by the Army since July 1937. In Shantung Province, Lincheng and other less important coal mines were reported by *Trans-Pacific* on March 10, 1938, to be under Kochukoshi's control and turning out coal steadily. In Hopei Province, Kochukoshi succeeded in buying up German shares of the Sino-German Chinghsing Coal Mining Administration for 1,450,000 yuan, in October 1937. The mine, with an investment of 3,375,000 yuan from the Hopei Provincial Government at Paoting which collapsed soon after the China Incident and a German investment of 1,125,000 yuan, had an annual production capacity of 1,500,000 tons, but was then turning out only 700,000 to 800,000 tons good for coking purpose. The first shipment of Chinghsing coal, amounting to 8,450 tons, was sent from Tangku by way of Peiping to Kawasaki on March 18, 1938, for the Japan Steel Tubing Company to which Kochukoshi had sold 10,000 tons. ① Besides, Kochukoshi has been collaborating with the Sino-British Kailan Mining Administration with the object of exploiting coal and alumina (bauxite) deposits. ② It was also in charge of the transportation and export of Tatung coal to Japan.

Salt production and export is another field of activity for Kochukoshi. The creation in November 1935 of a puppet regime in East Hopei under the name "East Hopei Communist Prevention Autonomous Council" paved the way for Japanese control over the Changlu Salt Field in that region. On September 19, 1936, a contract was signed by the authorities of the Changlu Salt Inspectorate with Kochukoshi for the sale and shipment to Japan of 70,000 metric tons of industrial salt, the contract to be valid for one year only. On March 10, 1937, a second contract was signed by the same parties for the sale and shipment of 230,000

---

① *Trans-Pacific*, March 10, 1938 and September 28, 1938; "Japan concentrates on development of continental coal mines"; extract translated from the *Economist*, September 2, 1940.

② "SMR and Kochukoshi to play major roles in North China Plan", translated from the *Economist*, November 21, 1937.

tons. Meantime, the Japanese were developing plans for the annual manufacture of 50,000 tons of salt in East Hopei by Kochukoshi. The outbreak of the Sino-Japanese War in July 1937 resulted in the prompt Japanese military occupation of the Changlu salt field and the "taking over" of the Tientsin head office of the Inspectorate in August 1937. By the end of that month Kochukoshi had "taken over" the exportation of salt to Japan, and the management of the Chiu Ta Salt Refinery and the Yungli Chemical Works at Tangku, important factors in the North China salt and soda-products industries. A large-scale program to boost the output of Changlu salt to 1,000,000 tons a year, of which 700,000 tons were to be exported to Japan, was meantime reportedly worked out by Kochukoshi in cooperation with the SMR Company. [1].

In the field of cotton growing, Kochukoshi assumed the leadership in establishing the North China Raw Cotton Company with the ultimate object of producing 20,000,000 piculs a year (121,212 metric tons). The Company is capitalized at ￥3,000,000 of which ￥1,000,000 is invested by Kochukoshi, ￥1,500,000 by the Cotton Spinners' Association of Japan and the Association of Japanese Cotton Spinners in China, and ￥500,000 by the Cotton Traders' Association of Japan. According to the *Economist* issued November 21, 1937,

"in order to give economic relief to Chinese farmers and to supply as much raw cotton as possible to this country (Japan), the

---

[1] "SMR and Kochukoshi to play major roles in North China Plan", translated from the *Economist*, November 21, 1937.

firm will encourage cotton cultivation and improve the breed of cotton plants at least to the strict middling grade. As measures for promoting exports of this material, standard qualities will be adopted, warehouses and packing plants will be established, and export facilities will be enlarged."

The fields of activity covered by Kochukoshi appeared thus large and diversified. By September 1938, it was reported that Kochukoshi had become interested in more than 60 enterprises, large and small, with a total investment estimated at ￥27,000,000. [1]

C. Dissolution. Kochukoshi's large-scale program of development for North China, as originally contemplated by President Sogo of the Company and Mr. Matsuoka, President of Kochukoshi's parent company (SMR), was frustrated by the Hopei-Chahar Political Council before the China Incident, and by the Japanese army in North China after it. The illegal rulings against the Tientsin Electric Power Company by the Legislative and Reconstruction Commissions of the Council illustrates the conflict between Kochukoshi and the Hopei-Chahar Council. [2] Usually the objections raised by the Council were ignored. But the outbreak of hostilities between China and Japan since the Loukouchiao Incident decided the fate of Kochukoshi. The rapid developments that followed placed the Japanese army in control of North China developments vis-a-vis the SMR

---

[1]　*Trans-Pacific*, September 8, 1938.
[2]　For other negotiations that failed, see *Trans-Pacific*, September 8, 1938.

and its subsidiary, Kochukoshi. The passage of Diet bill for the establishment of the North China Development Company in March 1938, made it necessary for Kochukoshi to retrench, and eventually to be absorbed as one of its subsidiary companies. The dissolution, however, was not effected without attempts to combat it on the part of the SMR and Kochukoshi. Both Matsuoka and Sogo argued in early part of May 1938 that matters involving commercial relations with foreign interests in Central and South China could best be handled by Kochukoshi. But during latter part of the mouth, Matsuoka, upon return from Toyko to Dairen on May 18, declared that Kochukoshi would be dissolved. At the third meeting of the establishment committtee of the North China Development Company in September 1938, a decision was passed to dissolve Kochukoshi on October 30. The Company's paid-up capital of ￥10,000,000, almost wholly invested by SMR, would be shifted to the North China Development Company as SMR's investment in the new concern. In the meantime, the iron, coal mining, electric power and salt manufacturing enterprises, hitherto undertaken by the Kochu interests, would be assigned to the subsidiary concerns established by the NCDC. Three free industries, so far developed by the Kochu interests, would be transferred to other companies. All shares held by the Kochu interests in the North China Raw Cotton Company would be transferred to the Japan Cotton Spinners' Association, their shares in the East Hopei Gold Mining Company to the Sumitomo interests, and their shares in the Fukudai Trading Company to "the Formo-

sa Development Company" ①. Subsequent negotiation between the NCDC and the SMR, Kochu's parent company, resulted in the retenting of Kochu as a subsidiary company of NCDC, together with its original capital of ￥10,000,000. ② Mr. Omura, new president of SMR succeeding Mr. Matsuoka on April 27, 1939, announced, in referring to Kochu, that "Tatung coal sales, Changlu salt and other North China enterprises, including electric power transmission, must be carried out by it." ③

III. The North China Development Company (Kita-shina Kathatsu Kabushiki Kaisha)

A. History. Positive action by the Japanese government to develop North China resources began with the organization of the Kochukoshi or China Development Company as a subsidiary concern of the South Manchuria Railway Company (SMR), with a paid-up capital of ￥10,000,000 contributed largely by the SMR. Kochukoshi was to develop North China resources — power, coal, iron, salt, and cotton; while SMR was to engage in large-scale transportation enterprises, especially railways, in North China. With the ascendency of the Japanese army in North China after the China Incident in July 1937, Kochukoshi had to retrench its am-

---

① *Trans-Pacific*, September 29, 1942.
② *Ibid.*, December 1, 1938.
③ *Ibid.*, May 4, 1939.

bitious program, and was formally absorbed by the North China Development Company (NCDC) as a subsidiary concern in October 1938. SMR, meantime, participated actively in railway rehabilitation and construction in North China through the organization of the North China Transportation Company, a subsidiary of the NCDC with a capitalization six-seventh as large as that for the NCDC.

Simultaneously with the establishment of the Peking Provisional Government on December 14, 1937, the North China Policy Committee consisting of the officials of the Planning Board of the Japanese Cabinet (most powerful administrative organ in Japan), the Army and Navy, the Finance and Foreign Ministries and the Manchurian Affairs Bureau of the Japanese Cabinet, adopted the fundamental principles governing all economic development in North China. The Committee recommended the establishment of a special national policy corporation for the development and control of all essential industries in North China, including railways, harbor and port construction, highway construction, general transportation facilities, telegraph and telephone systems, the electric power industry, and the mining industry (including coal and iron). Enterprises in the cotton spinning industry, cotton growing and all other similar industries were to be free to private concerns. Regarding railway business in China, the proposed special corporation would obtain a franchise from the Peking Provisional Government; and, if necessary, a subsidiary railway company might be established in which the SMR might be allowed to participate. The authorities would arrange for the SMR to offer technical and other assistance to the corporation, although the SMR would not be allowed directly to operate any lines. In regard to Kochukoshi or China Development Company, its investments in the electric industry and development works in North China would be taken over by the special corporation. The company would have to be dissolved and all its employees transferred to the special control corporation. ①.

On the basis of the fundamental principles, two important bills calling for the establishment of a North China Development Company and a Central China Promotion Company were presented to the Lower House on March 18, 1938, and passed at the 73rd session of the Japanese Diet. An Organic Law, to be described later, was promulgated on April 30, with seven chapters and 34 articles. On May 12 the committee entrusted

---

① Tokyo dispatch by Reuter of December 20, 1937, published in the *North China Herald*, Shanghai, January 5, 1938. Mr. Matusoka, President of the SMR, made a clearout statement to the newspapermen aboard the train by which he left Tokyo on route to Dairen around the tenth of February 1938, in regard to the proposed North China Development Company, as follows:

"I have nothing to say against the proposed company, now that the matter has been decided by the Government, but I have great doubt over its prospects. It is regrettable that Japan will lose at least four or five years...

"Strong control measures will make the future of the proposed company gloomy. Free activity is the best policy for Japan's economic development in North China. As regards this, I perfectly agree with the opinions of Osaka financiers...

"How active the Kochukoshi will be in North China in the future is unknown but there is an ample field for it. Too much activity, however, is not advisable, if it interferes with the expansion of private industrial companies. I emphasized this point with Mr. Shinji Sogo, its president.

"Kochu is, so to speak, an intermediary between North China enterprises and Japanese financiers. When it finds a promising industry, the matter should be introduced to Japanese financiers and industrialists."

(Quoted in *Trans-Pacific*, February 17, 1938.)

with preparations for the establishment of the two China companies held its first meeting; it approved the rules that would govern its work, heard reports on conditions in China, and decided to have two subcommittees, the one to arrange for the North China Development Company headed by Baron Seinosuke Goh, and the other to handle details of the Central China Promotion Company headed by Mr. Seihin Ikeda. At the meeting where nearly 70 members of the Committee, together with the government members including the Premier, the Foreign, Finance, and Commerce and Industry ministers, President of the Planning Board, were present, Premier Konoye gave the following address:[①]

"Since the outbreak of the China Incident, the Government has stinted no sacrifice in moving closer to its goal, stabilization, of East Asia and co-existence and co-prosperity among "Manchoukuo", China and Japan. To attain this goal and achieve real results, not only must the anti-Japanese forces be crushed but economic rehabilitation and development must be effected in the areas of North and Central China occupied by the Japanese army. The capital and technique of China and Japan must be pooled in order to bring about mutual prosperity.

"In accordance with this aim, the Government has decided to invest in or finance various important enterprises in North and Central China to help economic rehabilitation and development from the

---

[①] *Trans-Pacific*, May 19,1938.

standpoint of national policy. In the 73rd session of the Diet, it obtained approval for establishment of the North China Development Company and the Central China Promotion Company, the laws for which were promulgated recently.

"Economic rehabilitation and development in North and Central China are just now the most important and most urgent enterprises. They are of such a nature that little success can be hoped if they are not backed with solid cooperation, the Government and the people acting in perfect accord.

"I desire earnestly that you endeavor ardently to bring this matter to a successful issue, contributing thereby to rapid achievement of the final goal in the current hostilities."

The establishment subcommittee for the NCDC was busily engaged in outlying plans of development, drawing up the charter and the prospectus for the company, allotting capital investment to Japan's "Big Three" business houses and life and accident insurance groups, and recommending personnel for approval by the Cabinet after its organization on May 12. On November 7, 1938, the subcommittee held its final meeting, and inaugurated the establishment of the NCDC. The officials of the Company were announced to consist of the following:

President: Mr. Sonyu Otani;

Vice-Presidents: Mr. Tsuneo Yamanishi, Mr. Tsunetaka Komuchi;

Directors: Mr. Teiji Okubo, Mr. Hiroshi Yoshida, Mr. Shigeji

Moriguchi, Mr. Katsujiro Mikumo, Mr. Kiyomatsu Kamemiya;

Auditors: Mr. O. Nakamura, Mr. Masuzo, Nomura, Mr. Masatsune Ogura.

Mr. Sonyu Otani, a former Overseas Minister of the Konoye Cabinet in 1937, died of pneumonia on the first of August 1939; he was succeeded by former Finance Minister Okinori Kaya.

B. Organization and Government Control. The North China Development Company is, according to the Organic Law of the Company promulgated on April 30, 1938, a limited company established for the purpose of accelerating, controlling, and coordinating the economic development of North China,① with its head office in Toyko. As it is a special company of Japan organized for the execution of important national policies of Japan in North China, with the participation of Japanese government capital, Japanese government control over the company permeates everywhere in organization, personnel, finance, and operation.

Organization. Decisions in regard to changes in the articles of organization, amalgamation or dissolution shall not be effcetive unless approved by the Japanese government.

Personnel. The governor and the deputy-governors shall be appointed by the Japanese government with the approval of the Emperor. The Japanese government shall appoint a government inspector to oversee the

---

① The law is reproduced in *The Chinese Yearbook*, *1938 - 39*, Council of International Affairs, Chungking, 1939, pp, 244 - 247.

business of the company, who: (1) shall have right to inspect the treasury and books, documents, and other articles of the company; (2) may order the company to submit reports and figures regarding the business condition of the company should he deem it necessary; and (3) has the right to attend shareholders' meetings and other conferences and to present his opinion. The government may invalidate the decisions of the company or discharge its staff members in case the decisions or actions should be found to have contravened the law or other measures or regulations based on the law.

Finance. The Japanese government exercises control over the making of budgets, issue of debentures payment of dividends, and disposal of profits. The company shall: (1) compile budgets for investments and loans for every fiscal year and submit them one month before the beginning of the fiscal year to the government for approval; (2) apply for government approval before issuing any debentures; (3) pay no dividend on government shares in case the profits of the company for any fiscal year should be insufficient to pay a dividend of 6 percent on private shares; and (4) have the amount of difference made up by the government for the first five years in case the profits of the company for any of the five years fall below 6 percent, but in the distribution of profits if the dividend for the commercial shares should exceed 6 percent, have the excess used for the purpose of refunding the government for the money advanced in the above connection.

Operation. The government may issue necessary orders in regard to the supervision of the company's business enterprises, or the coordination and adjustment of the company's enterprises in their relation to Japan's national defense and the economic development of North China. However, when orders necessary in point of national defense are proclaimed by the government, such losses as the company may sustain shall be compensated by the government, to the extent of not exceeding the limit set by the Imperial Diet.

Immediately after the formal inauguration of the NCDC and the CCPC on November 7, 1938, a China Affairs Board (or Kao-In), later known as the Asia Development Board, was set up in Toyko on December 16, 1938, by the Japanese Cabinet, with the Prime Minister as President of the Board, and the Ministers for Finance, Foreign Affairs, Army and Navy as the four Vice-Presidents. Created in connection with and existing for the duration of the China Affair, the new Board is presided over by the Prime Minister. Exclusive of purely diplomatic affairs its business comprises:

1. Political, economic and cultural problems relating to the China Affair;
2. The study and investigation of governmental policies to be adopted in regard to the matters coming under the above category;
3. Supervision of the operations of the companies established under special laws for the purpose of doing business in China as well as the control of the business transactions in China by persons who are so engaged; and

4. The maintenances of unity in the administrative affairs of the different government offices relating to China.

In accordance with item 3 above, the NCDC was placed under the supervision of the Asia Development Board, whose first chief, Lt. - Gen. Yanagawa, was promoted a Tokyo Cabinet Minister in Prince Konoye's government reshuffle in late 1940. Under the Board are the Peiping and Nanking Liaison Offices, with an army officer directing the former and a navy officer the latter. These two officers, in turn, supervise the two companies under the chairmanship of the two former bankers, O. Kaya for the NCDC and K. Kodama for the CCPC.

C. Finance. According to the Organic Law of the North China Development Company, the capital of the Company shall be ¥350,000,000, which may be increased at any time with the approval of the Japanese government. The Japanese government shall invest ¥175,000,000, or one-half of the total authorised capital, which may be in kind. The capital may be increased even before the original shares have been paid up.

The private investment of ¥175,000,000 was apportioned among the leading Japanese firms and the Japanese public before the Company was formally established on November 7, 1938. Premier Konoye on July 5, 1938, invited more than 200 leading economic and financial figures to his official residence and asked for their unanimous support of the two development companies in North China and Central China. On the composition of the private investment of ¥175,000,000 for the NCDC, the *Trans-Pacific* reported on July 14, 1938 as follows:

"the four groups, namely, the Mitsui, Mitsubishi, Sumitomo and Insurance, will invest ￥15,750,000 each, an aggregate of ￥63,000,000. Shares totalling ￥17,500,000 will be offered for public subscription. The remaining ￥94,500,000 will be subscribed by the Soda Industry Guild Federation, Japan Sugar Association, Japan Cotton Spinners' Association, Japan Coal Association and many other industrial and economic bodies."

One of the features for public subscription is that applications from bereaved families of soldiers and sailors, and families whose members are summoned for military operations on the Asiatic continent, will be given preference. Their applications must be made with certificates from village headmen, town and city mayors, and chairmen of retired soldiers' associations. ①

While the North China Development Company is financed jointly by the Japanese government and the Japanese people, the subsidiary companies to which the NCDC subscribes shares or advances loans, invite capital participation by the puppet Chinese government and the Chinese people. As to the authorised capitalization of the subsidiary companies, investments by the NCDC, and the Japanese and Chinese investors, amounted respectively to ￥341,000,000 and ￥347,000,000 — a total of ￥688,000,000, according to *Trans-Pacific* of June 23, 1938.

---

① *Trans-Pacific*, August 4, 1938.

Table 3. Authorised Capitalization of NCDC's Subsidiary Enterprises, 1938 (In 1,000,000 yen)

Enterprise	Authorised Capital of Subsidiary Companies	Invested by NCDC	Public Investments
Railways, harbors	300	175	125
Automobile	16	8	8
Communications	30	15	15
Iron and steel	50	25	25
Coal mining	60	20	40
Coal liquefaction	150	75	75
Telegraphy	70	20	50
Salt industry	12	3	9
Total	688	341	347

In principle, these subsidiary concerns are to be established on the basis of Sino-Japanese joint management, Chinese investments taking the form of property. But Chinese capital participation is extremely limited. According to the *Trans-Pacific* dated November 3, 1938, investment by China amounted to only ￥73,000,000, or one-eleventh of the total proposed investment of ￥688,000,000. The Chinses investment was distributed by enterprises as follows:

Table 4. Chinese Investments in NCDC's Subsidiary Enterprises, 1938 (In Yen)

Railway and harbor	￥15,000,000
Automobile	6,000,000

	continued
Communications	3,000,000
Iron and steel	5,000,000
Coal mining	20,000,000
Electricity	20,000,000
Salt	4,000,000
Total	￥73,000,000

The Chinese investment of ￥73,000,000 represented largely the assessed value of Chinese government property forcibly taken over by the Japanese military, not liquid funds invested by the Chinses public. Such assessed value was necessarily arbitrary, and considerably underestimated.

According to a digest of the Company's charter and prospectus published in the *Trans-Pacific* of July 7, 1938, its investments for the five years 1938–42 will be distributed annually as follows: ￥94,050,000 in 1938, ￥284,710,000 in 1939, ￥181,720,000 in 1940, ￥198,540,000 in 1941, ￥120,500,000 in 1942 — a total of ￥879,520,000 during 1938–42.

During the five years, subsidiary companies to the NCDC are scheduled to float ￥940,696,000 worth of debentures, consisting of ￥189,441,000 for the second year, ￥272,890,000 for the third year, ￥297,610,000 for the fourth year, and ￥180,755,000 for the fifth year. These debentures are distributed by enterprises below.

Table 5. Proposed Debentures to be Floated by NCDC's Subsidiary Enterprises in Five Years
(In 1,000 Yen)

Enterprise	2nd Year	3rd Year	4th Year	5th Year	Total
Railway, ports	68,555	80,640	55,750	17,000	221,945
Automobile	–	2,650	3,000	3,000	8,650
Communications	5,800	6,600	3,500	3,300	19,200
Iron and steel	20,500	61,500	24,600	2,000	108,600
Coal mining	15,750	25,000	25,000	26,000	91,750
Coal liquefaction	31,500	62,500	162,500	105,000	361,500
Electricity	30,836	30,000	20,260	21,455	102,551
Salt	16,500	4,000	3,000	3,000	26,500
Total	189,441	272,890	297,610	180,755	940,696

At the end of March 1941 the NCDC's affiliated enterprises totalled 21 companies, 8 associations, and one independent bureau of the SMR Company. (See Appendix I). Affiliated companies in which the NCDC made investments numbered 18, the other three receiving loans only. The total authorised capital of the 18 affiliated companies subscribed by the Company was ¥272,250,000, of which ¥226,040,000 was paid up; loans to all the subsidiary enterprises totalled ¥368,000,000. When the ¥18,360,000 loans made to the eight associations were added, the total amount invested and loaned by the parent company reached ¥612,400,000 at the end of March 1941, which was secured by its paid-up capital of ¥218,000,000, development debentures of ¥385,000,000, and loans reaching ¥23,000,000 — a total of

¥626,000,000.① The total investment of ¥612,400,000 by the parent company in the subsidiary enterprises at the end of March 1941 was distributed by fields as follows:

Table 6　NCDC's Investments Classified by Enterprises, March 31, 1941 (In 1,000,000 yen)

Enterprise	Share Investment	Loans	Total	Percentage
Transportation	153.3	295.0	448.3	73.2
Communications	6.5	23.1	29.6	4.8
Electricity	15.1	21.9	37.0	6.0
Ore mining	33.8	21.4	55.2	9.0
Salt manufacture	12.2	1.3	13.5	2.2
Others	23.4	5.4	28.8	4.7
Total	244.3	368.0	612.4	100.0

Note: Includes investments in associations.

The associations, not yet organized into companies, were under military control for the time being as a transitional measure. By the end of March 1941, these enterprises in the ore mining field numbered eight, as follows:

---

① According to Mr. Shinrokuro Hidaka, Chief of the Economic Department of the Asia Development Board, the total investments in and loans to subsidiaries by the NCDC amounted to ¥30,000,000 in 1938 and ¥226,000,000 in 1939. He added "Though it is impossible to make any definite statements about what these subsidiaries are accomplishing, they seem to be able to declare 4 percent dividends with the help of government subsidies." (*Trans-Pacific*, March 21, 1940.)

Table 7 Investments in North China Ore Mining Offices Established Under the Association System, March 31, 1941 (In 1,000 yen)

	Total Investment	Investment by NCDC
Chunghsing Mining Office	3,620	1,810
Tawenkou Mining Office	2,500	1,250
Shansi Mining Office	2,460	1,460
Tzuhsien Mining Office	2,100	1,050
Tsiaotsa Mining Office	2,092	2,092
Liuyuang Mining Office	900	900
Shihchingshan Iron Mining Office	7,059	6,059
Shansi Iron Mining Office	4,479	3,679
Total	25,210	18,300

According to *Peking Chronicle*, April 25, 1942 the NCDC was expected to increase its capitalization from the present 350 million yen to 443 million yen as the permission of the central authorities in this connection had been duly obtained on the basis of the revised NCDC law passed by the 79th session of the Japanese Diet. An earlier dispatch published in the *Japan Times and Advertiser*, dated February 20, 1942, stated the increase to be 500 million yen. It further added that,

> "the allotment of new shares thus to be issued will be decided at the extraordinary general meeting of shareholders to be held in April, but the greater part of it is expected to be taken up by the Government. The Government will not pay its subscriptions in cash but transfer the North China Development Corporation railway facilities which have been lent to the North China Transportation Company (a

subsidiary of the NCDC). The value of these facilities will be estimated at an Assessment Committee to be organized in a month or so."

On the fourth anniversary of the establishment of the NCDC, the total amount of direct investment made by the NCDC to the subsidiary companies was reported to have reached 434,837,000 yen, while total capital of these subsidiary companies was similarly reported to have reached 645,404,000 yen, both together "representing 1,080,000,000 yen employed in the development of the natural resources in North China." ① The dispatch further added that,

"a total of 26 concerns financed by the NCDC include four communications companies, four (news) agencies, five electric companies, seven collieries, and three salt companies."

The four communications companies referred more correctly to the transport companies, while the four (news) agencies referred to communications companies including telephone and telegraph.

On December 23,1942, Domei from Tokyo reported that the Industrial Bank of Japan had announced the terms and conditions of the 30th Debenture Loan of the North China Development Company aggregating 50,000,000 yen, of which 5,000,000 yen would be sold on the market. It was proposed that the debenture be redeemable within 12 years and carry an annual interest rate of 4.5 percent, and 100-yen par value debentures would be sold on the market at 99.50 yen.

---

① P62255 Tokyo Domei in English at 8:04 p.m. to the world, November 7,1942.

THE JAPANESE DEVELOPMENT COMPANIES IN OCCUPIED CHINA

An Osaka dispatch dated January 14, 1943, quoted an interview with Juicmi Tsushima, President of the North China Development Company on the proceeding day, as follows: ①

"He disclosed that the (North China) Development Company at present has under control more than 30 subsidiaries connected with all-important industries such as iron, transportation, telephone and telegraph.

"He said that to raise working funds for these affiliates, the North China Development Company during the 1941-42 fiscal year floated 280,000,000 yen worth of debentures, and will issue 360,000,000 yen worth during the 1942-43 fiscal year. Inclusive of profits of those subsidiaries, the working capital of those affiliates is expected to total 1,400,000,000 yen."

Investments in and fund supplied to the affiliated companies are the sources of revenue of the NCDC, but the revenue from investments at the end of March 1941 was not yet so satisfactory as that from loans; as out of the affiliated companies, five were paying dividends as low as 5 or 6 percent. Affiliated companies were urged to plow back their profits and utilise them as much as possible in developing their respective enterprises. Therefore, though the number of companies paying dividends on investment may increase, it is difficult to expect 6 percent dividend

---

① Foreign Broadcast Intelligence Service, Federal Communications Commission, *Daily Report — Foreign Radio Broadcasts*, January 15, 1943, F13.

usually paid by private companies, based on their own earnings.

In view of the mission and nature of the NCDC, the business results of the NCDC, therefore, cannot be compared with those of general business companies.

Table 8　Business Results of the NCDC, 1939－40(In 1,000 yen)

	1940(January to March)	1940 fiscal year (April 1940 to March 1941)	1939 fiscal year
Revenue			
Investment revenue	820	980	–
Fund supply revenue	4,112	10,143	2,818
Interests received	46	160	367
Miscellaneous revenue	4	131	831
Government subsidy	1,367	6,199	2,133
Subsidy for investigations	868	691	–
Total	7,218	18,303	6,150
Expenditure			
Operating expense	1,543	4,882	2,551
Interests paid	3,900	9,219	1,346
Various redemption	170	565	64
Investigation expenses	868	691	–
Total	6,480	15,356	3,961
Balance			
Profit	737	2,947	2,189
Dividend rate	6%	6%	4.5%

Recent figures are not available to show the extent of Chinese "capital" participation in the NCDC and its affiliated enterprises, but the comment by the *Oriental Economist* on the Company's financial position at the end of March 1941 is significant. ①

> "The immediate problem confronting the company is the acquisition of capital within North China. The policy of raising funds jointly by Japan and China has been adopted but the cooperation from China in the existing enterprises has only been extended by Government. To effect real Sino-Japanese cooperation, popular support of Chinese capital is necessary. The Company is said to be considering the issue of debentures with a high interest rate of 7 percent or 8 percent or the issue of lottery tickets for securing the local fund. Yet as money interest is high in North China, it is quite doubtful whether debentures bearing 7 percent or 8 percent will be welcomed there. Though the burden of the Company for operating enterprises with such high interest capital must not be overlooked, it is important for the company to secure local capital to solidify its foundation in North China, even at the risk of various disadvantages."

Before the outbreak of the Pacific War on December 7, 1941, Chinese capital failed to participate in the North China Development Company not because of the low interest of the Company's debentures, but due chiefly to the fear for political and economic control by the Japanese authorities. This applied also to foreign businessmen in North China, even

---

① *Oriental Economist*, August 1941, p. 409, in article on "North China Development Company".

though to a much less extent than the Chinese. Mr. Okinori Kaya, president of the NCDC, and Finance Minister in the Konoye Cabinet, in a luncheon on May 27, 1940, with British and American businessmen and newspapermen, reiterated his desire for the cooperation of foreign capital in the development of North China. Businessmen at the meeting pointed out that while foreign capitalists wanted to cooperate, that cooperation would be more than difficult if exchange control restrictions in North China made it impossible for them to send a reasonable amount of their profits out of the country. It was pointed out that in one specific instance, at least, the authorities concerned had been unwilling to guarantee permission to export what the foreign businessmen considered a reasonable percentage of profit. To this President Kaya replied that exports of 20 to 30 percent of the capitalization in the form of dividends and annual liquidation of investment could not be considered reasonable. Even 10 percent would be an overly large figure. It might be that in particular cases the Japanese would suggest that the sending of dividends (or at least of sizable dividends) out of the country might be postponed for a year or several years after the investment was made. The reason for this difficulty about the export of dividends, he pointed out, was the necessity of controlling foreign exchange so long as the incident lasted (and probably after). ①

D. Fields of Development—Plans and Results. According to the Organic Law of the Company promulgated on April 30, 1938, the NCDC shall invest or advance money towards the following enterprises and shall

---

① *Trans-Pacific*, June 6, 1940.

also control and coordinate their functions:

(a) Enterprises relative to communications, transportation, and harbor establishments.

(b) Telephone and telegraph enterprises.

(c) Electric power enterprises.

(d) Mining enterprises.

(e) Salt and relative enterprises.

(f) Other enterprises contributive to the economic development of North China which require special control and coordination.

The Company's fields of development and their relative emphasis can be approximately gauged by an analysis of its proposal for the financial set-up of the subsidiary companies.

Table 9 Authorized Capital and Proposed Debentures of NCDC's Subsidiary Enterprises, March 31, 1941 (In 1,000 yen)

Enterprises	Authorized capital	Proposed Issue of Debentures	
		End of third fiscal year (March 31, 1941)	End of fifth fiscal year (March 31, 1943)
Transportation			
Railways, harbors	300,000	149,195	221,945
Automobile	16,000	2,650	8,650
Communications			
Communications	30,000	12,400	19,200
Telegraphy	70,000		

continued

Enterprises	Authorized capital	Proposed Issue of Debentures	
		End of third fiscal year (March 31,1941)	End of fifth fiscal year (March 31,1943)
Electricity		60,836	102,551
Mining			
Iron and steel	50,000	82,000	108,600
Coal	60,000	40,750	91,750
Coal liquefaction	150,000	94,000	361,500
Salt industry	12,000	20,500	26,500
Total	688,000	462,331	940,696

A comparison between the authorized capital and debenture issues as proposed by the NCDC for the subsidiary companies, and their paid-in capital and loans from the NCDC, shows approximately the extent to which the NCDC's program of development has actually been carried out up to the end of the third fiscal year ending March 31, 1941 — the latest date for which comparable data can be obtained.

Table 10 Proposed and Actual Capital and Debentures of NCDC's Subsidiary Enterprises Compared, March 31,1941 (In 1,000 yen)

Enterprise	Proposed			Actual			% of Proposed
	Capital	Debentures	Total	Capital	Loans	Total	
Transportation	316,000	151,845	467,845	247,700	295,000	542,700	116
Communication	100,000	12,400	112,400	20,500	23,000	43,500	39
Electricity	–	60,836	60,836	78,950	21,900	100,850	166

continued

Enterprise	Proposed			Actual			% of Proposed
	Capital	Debentures	Total	Capital	Loans	Total	
Mining	110,000	122,750	232,750	78,883	21,400	100,283	43
Coal liquefaction	150,000	94,000	244,000	–	–	–	–
Salt	12,000	20,500	32,500	16,250	1,300	17,550	54
Other	–	–	–	22,800	5,400	28,200	–
Total	688,000	462,331	1,150,331	465,083	368,000	833,083	79

The following quotation from a Domei dispatch on the fourth anniversary of the establishment of the NCDC, on November 7, 1942, shows the extent to which the various fields of economic activity in Occupied North China have been placed under the control of the NCDC, [1] or have supplied the needs of Japanese economy.

"Of the total **coal** deposits in North China estimated at 240,000,000,000 tons, the Corporation (NCDC) controls 70 percent, while the amount of production of bituminous coal is now exceeding the quantity for export to Japan.

"The **iron** industry under the management of the Corporation promises a great future with the total amount of iron ore deposits in North China estimated at 300,000,000 tons which have an iron content of 50 percent. The export of pig iron from North China exceeds 'Manchoukuo'.

"**Salt** production covers requirements of Japan and still leaves a surplus for developing soda dye and other chemical industries.

---

[1] P62255 Tokyo Domei in English at 8:04 p. m. to the world, November 7, 1942.

"Production of **cotton** is being spurred in North China.

"Capital invested by the North China Development Corporation in **communications** (i. e. **transportation**) enterprise amounts to 69.5 percent of its total investments, while capital loaned to subsidiary companies put together operates railway lines covering a distance of 6,000 kilometers, bus lines extending 13,000 kilometers and inland waterways of 3,800 kilometers."

1. Transportation. One of the foremost objectives of the development companies in North and Central China is the rapid exploitation of Chinese resources to meet the immediate needs of Japan's plan for the establishment of an "East Asia Co-existence and Co-Prosperity Sphere". Control over transportation, together with the development of strategic industries, is imperative to any program of economic exploitation, as it assures Japan of the basic framework with which economic exploitation can be successfully carried out. Before the establishment of the NCDC, SMR had been active in the occupation and operation of North China railways; after its establishment, the new "manmouth" concern has gradually liquidated SMR's control over transportation in North China, especially railways.

For the purpose of rehabilitating and developing transportation in North China, three subsidiary companies have been organized and financed by the North China Development Company, as follows:

Name	Type of organization	Date of establishment	Authorised capital
North China Transportation Co.	China special corporation	April 1939	￥300,000,000

continued

Name	Type of organization	Date of establishment	Authorised capital
Taku Transportation Company	Japan ordinary corporation	February 1937	¥6,000,000
Tsingtao Wharf Company	Ditto	September 1938	¥2,000,000

Of the three companies, the most important is the North China Transportation Company, also known as the North China Railway Company, North China Communications Company, or North China Traffic Company. The capitalization of the Company, ¥300,000,000, represents 43.6 percent of the total capitalization proposed for the subsidiary companies under the NCDC. Ninety percent of it was provided by the NCDC and the SMR — 50 percent by the former and 40 percent by the latter, the remaining 10 percent being contributed by the puppet North China regime — the Provisional Government of Peking, in kind.

The manmouth concern was placed in charge of construction and improvement of railways, motor bus service, and inland river transportation. Of these, the construction and improvement of railways is the most important, and claims the largest share of the Company's investments.

Prior to the outbreak of the Sino-Japanese War in July 1937, railways in North China (including the Lunghai Line) had an aggregate distance of 6,753 kilometers (Table 11). The 6,753 kilometers of railways represented two-thirds of the total kilometrage of railways in China excluding Manchuria. The damages they sustained after the start of hostilities were reported to have totalled about ￥1,000,000,000 by the Japanese. Immediately following the outbreak of the war, the South Manchuria Railway Company set up a North China Bureau with a view to reconstructing as soon as possible the damaged railways, rolling stock and other facilities. But when the North China Transportation Company was incorporated in April 1939, the SMR Bureau was abolished, transferring all its railways, bus, river navigation projects in North China and Inner Mongolia to the newly established company. Three months after the esatablishment of the new Company, great floods swept over the entire provinces, dealing more serious damage to railways than actual fighting. Thus, the Japanese forces and the railway authorities had to redouble their efforts in order to rehabilitate and develop the strategic lines for military purpose. The railway reconstruction program undertaken by the Company included rehabilitation of existing lines, double tracking of important lines such as the Peking-Shanhaikwan, standardisation of gauges on the Chengting-Taiyuan and Tatung-Puchow lines, and construction of new strategic lines notably the Shihmen-Tehchow line, the Tatung-Ningwu line, the Peking-Kupeikow line, and the Kaifeng-Sinsiang line. As a result, the railway length in North China today has been restored to 5,992 kilometers which is close to the pre-war level of 6,753 kilometers.

The most important line now under construction is that from Tatung to Tangku, covering 488 kilometers at an estimated cost of ￥198,000,000. The line, which is expected to transport 10,000,000 tons of Tatung coal for export to Japan by way of Tangku, will be divided into ten sections, to be completed in four years. The first section to be constructed is that from Sachen on the Peking-Paotow line to Fengtai on the Peking-Shanhaikwan line, which will be parallel to the Peking-Paotow line, and cover a distance of over 100 kilometers at an estimated cost of Yuan 37,000,000. Proposals to build the new line came up in late 1939 and early 1940, but difficulties of heavy drain on the already depleted rail and rolling stock production of Japan prevented early execution of the project. Alternative plan to double-track the Peking-Tangku section of the Peking-Shanhaikwan line in the spring of 1940, and the Tangku-Tangshan section later, was considered, although definite information as to its actual progress has not been available. ① It is likely that the section from Tientsin to Tangku may have been double-tracked and that surveying work on the Sachen-Fengtai section may have been carried out up to the present moment of writing. ②

Table 11. Railways in North China under Control of the North China Transportation Company, 1942 (In kilometers)

	Main Line		Branch Line		Date Completed or Opened to Traffic
	Operating	Total	Operating	Total	
New construction*			901	901	

① The Tangshan-Shanhaikwan section was double-tracked at early stage of the Sino-Japanese War.
② For details on the proposed construction of the Tatung-Tangku line, see *Peking Chronicle*, October 22, 1939; December 10, 1939; January 26, 1940.

continued

	Main Line		Branch Line		Date Completed or Opened to Traffic
	Operating	Total	Operating	Total	
Peking-Kupeikow (Peking-Paotow)			145		1938 April
Tatung-Ningwu (Tatung-Puchow)			200		1938 December
Yutse-Taiku (Tatung-Puchow)			35		1939 December
Kaifeng-Sinsiang (Peking-Hankow)			103		1940 May
Paotow-Wangpoyaotze (Peking-Paotow)			14		1940 July
Hsitao-Mataochen (Peking-Hankow)			21		1940 November
Shihmen-Tehchow (Tientsin-Pukow)			181		1941 February
Tungkuan-Luan (Tatung-Puchow)			152		1941 March
Shouyang-Huangchai (Chengting-Taiyuan)			50		1942 March
Partially operating lines**	1,115	2,487		290	
Peking-Hankow (Peking-Sinsiang)	614	1,215	–	257	1938 April
Lunghai (Kaifeng-Lienyun)	501	1,272	–	33	1939 December
Operating lines	3,694	3,694	282	282	
Peking-Shanhaikwan	436		49		1937 July
Peking-Paotow	816		43		1937 December
Kiaochow-Tainan	393		58		1938 March
Tientsin-Pukow***	1,152		96		1939 April

	Main Line		Branch Line		Date Completed or Opened to Traffic
	Operating	Total	Operating	Total	
Chengting-Taiyuan	240		36		1939 October
Tatung-Puchow****	657				1939 December
Total in operation	4,809		1,183		
Total length		6,181		1,473	

continued

* Names in brackets refer to the main lines to which the branch lines newly constructed belong.

** Names in brackets refer to the operating section of the line.

*** From Tientsin to Pengpu. The section between Pengpu and Pukow, 313 kilometers, is controlled by the Central China Promotion Company.

**** From Fenglingtukow south of Puchow to Ningwu only. The section from Ningwu to Tatung is listed under "new construction".

Railway leadings have increased considerably along with the progress of the reconstruction program. Passenger transportation, as well as railway revenues from passengers, freight, and other sources, have increased since the war, as shown below:

Table 12. Operation Statistics of North China Railways, 1937 – 39

		No. of Passengers (in 1,000)	Revenues (¥1,000)			
			Passengers	Freights	Others	Total
1935		14,756	23,310			
1937	2nd half	5,935	9,868	15	5,935	15,818
1938	1st half	10,724	17,953	405	10,724	29,082
	2nd half	17,518	28,891	627	17,518	47,036
1939	1st half	19,875	32,499	569	19,875	52,943

In an English-language broadcast (October 30, 1942, 11:00 p. m. EWT) to the world, Domei from Tokyo cites a Peiping report made by the North China Development Company during the fourth day's session of the Hsin Min Society Conference which disclosed that 55 percent of the Company's investments on June 30, 1942, was in communications enterprises, including railway, bus and inland water navigation, as well as electrical communication. According to the report,①

> "the total length of railway under management of the Company now exceeds 6,000 kilometers, accounting for 50 percent of the entire railway system in China. New railway lines have been constructed since the outbreak of the China Affair and the volume of goods handled increased by 56 percent over figures prior to the outbreak of the China Affair. The number of passengers carried by the Company's lines during the last year (ending June 30, 1942) reached 40,000,000, showing an increase of 115 percent as compared with figures for the year preceding the China Affair."

Intensive use of the available rolling stock and other equipment accounts for the increase in passenger and freight traffic on the North China railways under Japanese management and operation, but such increase indicates growing utilization for military rather than economic purpose. Thus, for the operating year ending March 31, 1940, freight traffic over

---

① *Daily Report*: *Foreign Radio Broadcasts*, Foreign Broadcast Intelligence Service, Ferderal Communications Commission, Oct. 31, 1942, F4.

the North China railways was reported at 30.5 million tons — an increase of 50 percent over the previous year, and equivalent to the pre-war tonnage for the same lines. However, of the 1940 traffic 42 percent was official or military and 39 percent was in mineral products, mostly coal.

The shortage of rolling stock has been keenly appreciated by the Japanese military. It springs from the fact that the Chinese armies in retreating from North China took most of the removable railway equipment with them. Large amount of rolling stock was brought in from "Manchuria" and Japan during early years of war, but not enough to fill the needs of the North China railways. Furthermore, because of the demands of war economy, there is now a shortage of rolling stock in "Manchuria" and Japan. The North China Rolling Stock Car Manufacturing Company, capitalized at ¥30,000,000, was therefore established on June 1, 1940, when it took over the old railway workshops to Tsingtao. To this new subsidiary company the NCDC agreed to contribute $8,500,000 in kind. The erection of a plant in the East Suburb of the Peking Industrial Zone was under way in June 1940, while proposal to erect another one at Shanhaikwan at an estimated cost of $30,000,000 was scheduled for June 1941. The latter was expected to manufacture 1,000 freight cars within the next three years and to build locomotive engines and passenger coaches. ①

Employees of the North China Transportation Company were reported to total more than 90,000 by the middle of 1941, or around 90 percent of

---

① *Peking Chronicle*, May 31, 1940.

the total railway workers in North China before the outbreak of war. Of this total, it is significant to note that Japanese staff accounted for over 20,000, and Chinese staff 70,000. Naturally, all the important posts were occupied by the Japanese, leaving the Chinese in subordinate positions under their control.

In automotive transport, the North China Transportation Company purchased the North China Motorbus Company, an affiliate of the SMR, and is presently engaged in absorbing Chinese bus lines. It now operates 13,000 kilometers of motor roads, of which the most important is the highway from Peking to Tsinan. The first part from Peking to Pahsien was completed in 1941. The preparation for building new macadam road on the second and the longest part from Pahsien in Hopei to Tehhsien in Shantung, about 213 kilometers in length, passing through Hsinchen, Chongchowchen, Jenchiu, Hochien, Hsienhsien, Duchen and Chinghsien, was started in April 1942. A number of bridges were also to be constructed spanning the Tzeyao, the Nanyunho, and the Tachingho rivers. This road, when completed, will be of immense communicational, economic and strategic value as it will be the first longitudinal highway connecting Eastern and Central Hopei with Shantung. ①

The waterways, embracing canals and inland rivers, on which shipping service is maintained by the North China Transportation Company, totalled 3,800 kilometers by November 1942. A project under contemplation by the North China authorities, if realised, will enable Tientsin to

---

① *Peking Chronicle*, April 14,1942; also March 29,1941.

have access to an uninterrupted canal traffic as far as Shihmen (formerly Shihchiachuang). Under the present plan of the Reconstruction Board a number of rivers on the Hopei plain will be connected by new canals, thus covering a distance of 320 kilometers from Shihmen to Tientsin. As the first step in the project work will be started at Liusinchuang on the Peking-Hankow Railway near Shihmen for the construction of a canal. The entire project will require five years, at an estimated cost of FR $40,000,000. The Projected canal traffic, if opened, is expected to make annual transit of some 2,000,000 tons of commodities between Tientsin and Shihmen and will greatly contribute to trade. The ceremony, officially marking the commencement of work in the construction of the canal, took place on April 19, 1942, in the presence of Director-General Yin Tung of the Construction Board of the North China Political Affairs Commission and many high Japanese and Chinese officials. ①

The North China Transport Company had a total paid-up capital of ￥239,700,000 by March 31, 1941, of which NCDC contributed ￥67,200,000. In 1939, it issued a debenture of ￥250,000,000 through a syndicate of 14 banks including the Industrial Bank of Japan, which was guaranteed by the Japanese Government. The revenus for the fiscal year ending March 31,1941, amounted to ￥220,414,000, and the expenses amounted to ￥220,223,000, thus leaving a meagre profit of ￥191,000 for the year, with no payment of dividend.

In the field of harbor construction, the North China, New Ports Tem-

---

① *Peking Chronicle*, March 29, 1942, April 23, 1942.

porary Construction Office, an independent bureau of the SMR, is rushing the expansion of the Taku harbor; while new harbor facilities at Taku were completed by the NCDC in May 1941 for use solely in handling iron and coal shipments to Japan. The Taku Transportation Company, to which the NCDC furnished ¥2,700,000 of its total authorized capital of ¥6,000,000, was founded as a subsidiary concern of Kochukoshi which itself has now been absorbed by the NCDC as a subsidiary concern under the Chinese name Hsingchung Company. The Company during the fiscal year ending March 31, 1941, had a revenue of ¥2,070,000 and an expense of ¥1,863,000, leaving a profit of ¥207,000 and paying dividend at 6 percent to its shareholders.

Improvement of the harbor at Tsingtao is in the hands of the Tsingtao Wharf Company, which during the fiscal year ending March 31, 1941, had a total revenue of ¥2,612,000 and a total expense of ¥2,136,000, leaving a profit of ¥474,000 and paying a dividend of 6 percent to its shareholders. In 1941, a radio compass on Chalien Tao Island, about 36 miles east of Tsingtao harbor, was installed and another radio beacon at Tuan Tao completed.

2. Communication. The operation of communication enterprises is now monopolized by the North China Telephone and Telegraph Company established in July 1938, as a special China corporation, with an authorized capital of ¥35,000,000,000 subscribed by the following:

North China Development Company	¥13,000,000
Peking Provisional Government	

¥6,000,000 in kind	
¥4,000,000 in cash	¥10,000,000
International Electric Communication Company of Japan	¥4,000,000
Manchurian Telegraph and Telephone Co.	¥4,000,000
Telephone & Telegraph Company	¥4,000,000

The Company "took over" all former Chinese-owned commercial telegraph, cables, telephones and wireless facilities in North China. It now operates exclusively in the provinces of Hopei, Shansi, and Shantung. Services in Suiyuan, Chahar and "Meng-Chiang" have been put under the unified operation of the "Meng-Chiang" Telephone and Telegraph Company (also known as Inner Mongolia Electric Communication Equipment Company), a joint Japanese-Mongolian enterprise with a capital of ¥12,000,000 from the "Meng-Chiang Government" and the Japanese Telephone amd Telegraph Company, with which the NCDC has at present no financial relation. Primarily with military rather than economic considerations in view, the North China Telephone and Telegraph Company has since 1938 steadily advanced under a "Seven Year Plan" towards the unification and development of telecommunications in its region. It has converted many manual telephones to automatic exchanges; and has perfected long distance and radiophone networks linking North China with Central China, "Manchuria", Korea, and Japan Proper. Telephoto service has been established between Tientsin and Tokyo.

On October 31, 1940, there were 121 telegraph offices and 156 telephone exchanges; in June 1941, negotiations were in progress to take over some 60 telephone and telegraph offices in East Hopei which had been held by the Manchurian Telephone and Telegraph Company. In 1941, it claimed 329 telegraph offices to be operating. More than 200 telephone offices were under its control and the long distance telephone services embraced, besides many shorter and interport circuits, one circuit with Japan, seven circuits with "Manchoukuo", and two with "Meng-Chiang". ① Approximately 20,500 automatic telephones were in service in 1941 in Tsingtao, Peiping and Tientsin, with an additional 8,000 scheduled for installation. Total telephone lines reach 47,179, distributed as follows: Peking 16,307; Tientsin 19,811; Tsinan 2,827; Tsingtao 6,062; Chefoo 947; Taiyuan 576; Tangshan 649.

Messages handled by the Company during the three years are as follows:

Year ending	Telegraph	Long distance calls	Telephone calls
October 31, 1939	7,162,927		
October 31, 1940	11,780,369	2,615,269	
October 31, 1941			80,000,000

The Company's paid-up capital reached ￥20,500,000 by March 31,1941, of which ￥3,250,000 was provided by the NCDC. For the fiscal year ending March 31,1941, the Company had a total revenue of ￥16,364,000 and a total expense of ￥14,463,000, leaving a profit of

---

① *Peking Chronicle*, December 4, 1941.

¥1,901,000 and paying a dividend of 6 percent.

3. Electric Power. Electric power enterprises are now in the hands of five subsidiary companies of the NCDC, four in North China and one in Inner Mongolia. The North China Electric Company, the largest, was established as a special China corporation in November 1939 with an authorized capital of ¥100,000,000 and a paid-in capital of ¥49,750,000. Of the total authorized capital, one-half was assigned to the Chinese, while the other half, being Japanese, was jointly shared by the NCDC (30 percent) and the Japanese electric combine (20 percent). The two subsidiary enterprises of the Kochukoshi, the Tientsin Electric Company and the East Hopei Electric Company, have been absorbed by this company. The other three subsidiary companies in North China are all ordinary China corporations located in the province of Shantung, namely, Chiaokiao Electric Company in Tsingtao established in May 1937 with an authorized capital of ¥8,000,000 (all paid-up), the Tsinan Electric Company in Tsinan established in February 1939 with an authorized capital of ¥4,00,000 (half paid-up, of which ¥500,000 is from NCDC), and the Chefoo Electric Company in Chefoo established in March 1939 with an authorized capital of ¥2,000,000 (¥1,200,000 paid-up, of which ¥300,000 is from the NCDC). The NCDC does not own shares in the Chiaokiao Electric Company, but supplies funds to it.

The Inner Mongolia Electric Company is, like the North China Electric Company, a special corporation, but organized in Inner Mongolia. It was established at Changchiakow (Kalgan) in May 1938 with an authorized capital of ¥18,000,000, all paid-up, of which the NCDC subscribed ￥2,750,000.

In Hopei, Shantung, Shansi and Honan provinces and the "Mengchiang" area, there are reported to be 79 electric plants (53 public and 26 private), with a total generating capacity of 326,270 k. w. [①] Electrification in North China and Inner Mongolia is, however, still not fully developed because of the small demand for electric power, non-integrated control of numerous small steam power houses, diversity of standards and poor equipment. These were all unified by the North China and Inner Mongolia Electric Companies with a view to standardization, expansion of steam power houses and establishment of transmission systems. At present the generating facilities in North China are entirely based on steam. In consideration of future demand for electric power due to industrial progress, large-scale hydraulic generation at Luanho and Yungtingho rivers and the Yellow River are now being made. The Yungtingho project calls for a dam near Hwailai on the Peking-Paotow Railway, to be 100 meters high, to create a reservoir with a surface area of 15 square ri (1 square ri equals 5.955505 square miles), and a storage capacity of 1 billion cubic meters of water, with a generating capacity of 150,000 k. w. [②]

---

① See *World Electrical Markets, China*, by American Consul A. Viola Smith, dated September 19,1940, pp. 92 - 96 for details on plants.
② *Peking Chronicle*, December 4,1941.

Meantime, attempt has been made to shift small steam power plants from Japan Proper to North China and Inner Mongolia. According to Hochi, sooner or later all of Japan's small steam power generation plants will shift to the two regions. This movement, encouraged by the North China Electric Company and other Japanese and Chinese electric power generation and transmission companies on the continent, is a result of the over increasing demand for electric power in North China and Inner Mongolia, a shortage made more serious because of the inability to ship sufficient materials to the continent to make possible a normal electric power expansion program. Recently, continued the Hochi, the Toho Electric Power Company, one of the largest concerns in Japan, removed two of its 5,000-kilowatt dynamos to Inner Mongolia, placed than under the supervision of the Inner Mongolia Electric Power Company. The Tokyo Electric Light Company transferred one 2,000-kilowatt dynamo from the company's Shizuoka plant to Shihchiachuang in Hopei Province, North China. [1]

4. Coal. The principal resources of North China which Japan desires for immediate utilization and in which she is deficient embrace coal, iron, salt, cotton, and wool. From military viewpoint coal is especially important, as it supplies the very fuel and motive power to the transport system in Japan and controlled areas, as well as to the heavy industries engaged in the production of armamonts. Next to the development of transportation and communication for military purpose, mining of coal, iron and salt becomes the primary concern of the Japanese development

---

[1] *Trans-Pacific*, May 16, 1940.

companies in Occupied China.

Estimated coal deposits in the five North China provinces of Shansi, Shensi, Honan, Hopei and Shantung amount to 210.4 billion metric tons, or 87 percent, of a total reserve of 246.1 billion for the whole of China including Manchuria, distributed as follows:

Table 13. Coal Reserves in North China

(In billion metric tons)

Province	Bituminous	Anthracite	Lignite	Total
Shansi	88.0	36.5	2.7	127.2
Shensi	71.2	0.7	–	71.9
Honan	2.0	4.6	–	6.6
Hopei	2.1	1.0	–	3.1
Shantung	1.6	–	–	1.6
Total North China	164.9	42.8	2.7	210.4
Total China	185.2	45.4	3.4	246.1

North China, meantime, is the largest coal producing region in China. Of the pre-war coal output in China (excluding Manchuria) of 22,250,000 metric tons in 1936, 16,897,000 tons or 76 percent were produced in the five above-mentioned provinces in North China.

In view of the concentration of coal reserve and production in North China, it has been Japan's primary concern to develop the coal resources there in order to meet her pressing industrial requirements. For this purpose, five subsidiary companies and six offices under the association system have been organized or financed by the NCDC as follows:

Table 14. Subsidiary Companies and Mining Offices in the Coal Industry Financed by the NCDC, March 31, 1941

Subsidiary Companies Capital (In ¥1,000)

Company	Date estab'd	Authorized	Paid-up	Revenue	Expense	Profit	Dividend
Tatung Coal Co.	January 1940	¥40,000	¥33,750	¥6,152	¥9,691	−¥3,540	—
Chinghsing Colliery Co.	July 1930	30,000	20,000				
Shantung Mining Co.	May 1937	5,000	2,250	1,270	650	620	6%
North China Coal Sales Co.	October 1940	20,000	10,000				
Inner Mongolia Mineral Sales Co.	July 1939	2,000	500				

Offices Under Association System (In ¥1,000)

Office	Province	Total Investment	Investment by NCDC
Chunghsing Mining Office	Shantung	3,620	1,810
Tawenkou Mining Office	Shantung	2,500	1,250
Shansi Mining Office	Shansi	2,460	1,460
Tzuhsien Mining Office	Hopei	2,100	1,050
Tsiaotsa Mining Office	Honan	2,092	2,092
Liuyuang Mining Office	Honan	900	900

Three of the five subsidiary companies are engaged in coal mining, along with the six mining offices, while the other two subsidiary companies deal with coal distribution primarily for export to Japan. In coal mining in North China and Inner Mongolia, the NCDC invests in all of the three companies and six offices, but capital participation from private Japanese interests is also an important factor. The following is a list of the principal mines in North China and their financiers, including the NCDC, Japanese business interests, and the puppet Chinese Government. [1]

Mine	Financiers (Government and corporations)
Tatung	"Meng Chiang Government", NCDC, and SMR
Chinghsing, Chengfeng and Liuhokow	Puppet Chinese Government, NCDC, & Kaishima Colliery
Shansi	Puppet Chinese Government, NCDC, & Okura Oumi
Tsuhsien	Puppet Chinese Government, NCDC, & Meiji Mining
Chunghsing	Puppet Chinese Government, NCDC, & Mitsui
Tawenkow	Puppet Chinese Government, NCDC, & Mitsubishi
Shantung	NCDC, SMR
Tsiaotsa	NCDC
Liuyuang	NCDC

Besides, there are several coal mines outside the control of the NCDC. Of these, the most important is the Kailan Mining Administration under Sino-British management. With a view to controlling the distribu-

---

[1] Article on "Japan concentrates on development of continental coal mines", extract translated from the *Economist*, Sept. 2, 1940.

tion of coal supplied by this mine, the Kailan Coal Sales Company was established in April 1938, through cooperation of the Japan Iron Manufacturing Company and five other firms requiring this coal. A contract was signed to deliver 1,700,000 tons of coal for shipment to Japan during the year, which was increased to 2,500,000 tons during the following year 1939. For the purpose of making the increase possible, Major E. J. Nathan, Chief Manager of the KMA, made a trip to London to raise more capital for the expansion of production from 5,500,000 tons to 6,500,000 tons, which has now been achieved.

In addition to the KMA, other mines not under the control of the NCDC include: collieries in Shantung Province under management of Lu Tah and Company (Japanese-owned); Hsintai, Liukiang, Changcheng, and a number of collieries in the northwestern part of Hopei Province including Pangshan, Mentowkow, Fangli, Tataishan, etc.

In the areas under construction, the Tatung district seems to be the most promising from viewpoint of reserves and production. This district is reputed to have a deposit of 12 billion tons, but a new engineering survey completed under the direction of the Ministry of Industry in the Federated "Meng Chiang Autonomous Government" has raised it to 40 billion tons. The coal deposits are reported to be of far better quality than had been expected, the calory content (when burned) being high, an essential in the production of steel. The coal is also held to be particulary easy to liquify, a quality desirable at the present time because of Japan's need for synthetic oil. ①

In early May 1938, it was reported by Nikkan Kogyo that an annual output of 12,500,000 metric tons of coal beginning in 1943 would be the objective of a plan calling for the development of the Tatung coal mine. The first step to be taken in connection with the plan would be the construction of railway to facilitate shipments. This increase in production is necessary in view of the growing shortage of coal in Japan Proper. The total demand for coal in Japan for 1938 was estimated at about 50,000,000 metric tons as a result of phenomenal strides by heavy industry. An increase of demand by 5,000,000 tons annually was estimated, calling for 70,000,000 tons in 1942. Against this, the present coal output in Japan Proper was about 40,000,000 metric tons — 10,000,000 tons below present requirements. Since it would be difficult for Japan to increase output in a brief period, her determination to rely on coal in its colonial and newly conquered territories, Manchuria and North China,

---

① *Trans-Pacific*, of February 9, 1939 reported that preparations were being made by the North China Development Company in cooperation with the Teikoku Fuel Development Company for the establishment of a large coal-liquefaction company with a capitalization of ¥150,000,000, according to the Nikkan Kogyo. Tatung coal in North China will be used as material for liquefaction and the projected concern will be named the North China Coal Liquefaction Company. If possible, this company will be established some time this year and the years 1940 and 1941 will be set aside as the period for building a factory. The company's yearly production of liquefied coal is to be one million tons. Three methods of low carbonization, gas synthesis and dircet liquefaction will be used by the company. The 1,000,000 tons include gasoline for automobiles and airplanes, heavy oil, ammonium sulphate and other chemical by-products. According to Dec. 1938 issue of the *Mitsubishi Monthly Circular* (p. 25), as a part of Japan's development program of major industries in North China, 1,000,000 tons of heavy oil will be produced annually by the end of 1942.

THE JAPANESE DEVELOPMENT COMPANIES IN OCCUPIED CHINA

has gained strength. The plan estimated that of 12,500,000 tons, one-fifth would be consumed in North China and the rest sent to Japan. ① The cost of the mine development is estimated at about ￥152,000,000. But actually, the Tatung mine in June 1939 was reported to be capable of producing only 1,500 tons a day at Putsin, while at Petungtsun an increase of 500 tons daily was expected when the railway line between Petungtsun and Yungtingchwang was completed. The daily output of the Tatung coal mine including Putsin and Petungtsun would than be expected to exceed 5,000 tons a day. ②

In Shantung and Hopei the mines were heavily damaged in the course hostilities between the Chinese and Japanese troops. The Chunghsing coal mines in Yihsien, Shantung, with an annual output of over 1,300,000 tons in 1934, were completely blown up by the Chinese troops about the middle of January 1938, on orders from Generalissimo Chiang Kai-shek. All the company's equipment, offices, and buildings were completely destroyed, the Chinese reportedly fearing that the mine would fall into the hands of the Japanese. Poshan and Tzechwan mines in Shantung, along Tsinan-Kiaochow Railway, were destroyed beyone repair by the Chinese troops in the famous battle of Taierchwang in the early spring of 1938. The Chinese owned Chinghsing coal mine, with a production of about 800,000 tons in 1934, was also completely destroyed by the Chinese Eighth Route Army in the fall of 1940. The pits were all flooded and

---

① *Trans-Pacific*, May 5,1938.
② *Trans-Pacific*, June 1,1939.

the stocks extracted set on fire. ①

The total production of coal in North China, which was about 15 million tons in 1936, declined during the two succeeding years, but the Japanese in the summer of 1941 asserted that production at the principal North China collieries during 1939 had exceeded the 1936 total, and that a further increase was registered in 1940. Fourteen anthracite mines, 20 coking coal mines and 9 non-coking coal mines were being worked. According to Japanese statistics, during the year ended March 1941, the North China railways carried 16,000,000 tons of coal; an increase of 33 percent over the previous year. Coal traffic represented 75 percent of the total civil freight carried by the railways and a large proportion went over the Peking-Tientsin lines. During Januany-November 1940, coal shipments from North China ports totalled 4,300,000 tons, the bulk of which went to Japan. This represented a large increase over the pre-1937 figure, although it remained small in relation to Japan's total needs. To a considerable degree the increase in coal exports to Japan was secured at the expense of North China's own consumption and also at that of exports to Shanghai, which had to turn to India and Indo-Chinese markets. ②

According to the coal production plan, the Japanese authorities in North China intend to produce 22,000,000 tons of coal a year after

---

① Trans-Pacific, February 3, 1938; North China Herald, Sept. 16, 1940.
② Series C, No. 118, January 8, 1942, DSS 5944.11B, Review of the Foreign Press, Foreign Research and Press Service (Royal Institute of International Affairs), Balloil College, Oxford.

1940. This estimate consists of 6,000,000 tons of coal for shipment to Japan, including Kailan coal, and 16,000,000 tons for local consumption. The sum of ¥160,000,000 is required for the North China coal development plan. ① Thus far, the goal seems to have been realized. According to recent estimate, coal production in Occupied China during 1942 may have reached 20,000,000 tons, of which 6,000,000 tons are available for export to Japan. ② The part which the NCDC plays in North China coal production may be gauged from the statement issued by the NCDC upon its fourth anniversary, on November 7, 1942, as follows: ③

"Of the total coal deposits in North China estimated at 240,000,000 tons, the North China Development Corporation controls 70 percent, while the amount of production of bituminous coal

---

① *Trans-Pacific*, September 15, 1938.

② Production of coal in 1942 in the Japanese controlled areas, and the amount available to industry in Japan Proper, is estimated as follows:

	Production	Available in Japan
	(Million Tons)	
Japan Proper	53	53
Karafuto	6.5	5.5
Manchuria	20	1
Korea	6	2
Formosa	2.5	0.5
Occupied China	20	6
Indo-China	2.5	1
Sumatra	0.25	–
Total	110.75	69.0

③ P62255 Tokyo Domei in English at 8:04 p.m. to the world, November 7, 1942.

is now exceeding the quantity for export to Japan."

5. Iron and Iron Ore. Next to coal, iron ore is the second important mineral Japan expects to develop in North China. According to Nichi Nichi, the first five-year plan drawn by Godo called for a combined production of 10,000,000 tons of steel in 1940, — 7,000,000 tons from Japan and 3,000,000 tons from "Manchoukuo", in order to meet the demand for 9,000,000 tons in Japan and 1,000,000 tons in "Manchoukuo". As a result of the China Incident, a new five-year iron and steel production plan was prepared early in 1938 by the Ministry of Commerce and Industry, the "Cabinet Manchurian Affairs Bureau" and the "Cabinet Planning Board". Under the new plan, the steel production will be increased to 11,000,000 tons, for which 12,500,000 tons of pig iron must be obtained in the three regions of Japan, "Manchoukuo" and North China. "Manchoukuo", Korea and North China are able to get ores from their own sources, but Japan Proper must import at least 12,000,000 tons of iron ore for satisfactiory operation. Japan imported during 1937 5,500,000 tons of iron ore — 1,500,000 tons from Korea and 4,000,000 tons from abroad. The import will have to be more than doubled to 12,000,000 tons by 1940. By the prospective development of the Mozan mine in North Korea, Japan will be able to get 2,500,000 tons, but as to the remaining 9,500,000 tons of iron ore, she must import from the South Seas, British India, and Central China. The occupation of North China, especially of the rich Lungyen mines in Chahar, gives rise to a new source of supply, which has not been tapped by the

Chinese ever since the drastic fall of iron and steel prices after the 1918 Armistice. The development of Lungyen ores thus constitutes the most urgent concern of the Japanese authorities in North China. ①

The iron ore reserve in China is estimated by the Chinese Geological Survey at 1,206,437,000 tons, of which 883,521,000 tons or 73 percent are located in Manchuria. Of the 322,916,000 tons of iron ore in China Proper, North China claims 174,604,000 tons or 54 percent, as shown below: ②

Table 15. Iron Ore Reserve in North China
(In 1,000 metric tons)

Province	Reserve	
Chahar		91,645
Hsuanhua, Lungkuan	91,645	
Hopei		42,179
Luanhsien	32,424	
Yihsien	1,500	
Chinghsing	7,755	
Kailan Basin	150	
Linyu, Funing	350	
Shantung		14,340
Chinlingchen	13,700	
Mihsien	640	
Honan		2,740
Hungshan	740	

① *Trans-Pacific*, December 2, 1937; March 24, 1938.
② *General statement of the mining industry*, fifth issue, 1932 – 34, China Geological Survey, Nanking, pp. 175 – 179.

continued

Province	Reserve	
Hingyang	2,000	
Kiangsu		3,000
Likuoyi	3,000	
Suiyuan		700
Kungyiming	700	
Suiyuan, Honan, Shensi, Kansu	20,000	20,000
Total		174,604

Although the largest iron ore reserve in North China, 91,645,000 tons or 53 percent, is located in Chahar Province, it has not been tapped for years until the Japanese occupation of North China. In 1934, the iron ore production in China Proper reached 1,359,580 tons, of which North China contributed only 205,180 tons or 15 percent, including 198,000 tons from Shansi, 25,000 tons from Honan, and 180 tons from Shensi.

The occupation of North China by the Japanese was immediately followed by the exploitation of the rich iron ore reserves in Chahar province, located in the famous Lungyen district. The task of exploitation, at first entrusted to the Kocku Koshi, a subsidiary of the South Manchuria Railway Company, was transferred to the Lungyen Iron Mining Company, established in July 1939 as a special corporation under the Inner Mongolia Government, with an authorized capital of ¥20,000,000. The paid-up capital by March 31, 1941 amounted to ¥14,983,000, of which ¥4,525,000 represented the shares from the NCDC. The Company expected to produce 1,100,000 tons of iron ore in 1940, to be increased further to 2,000,000 tons in 1941, and 2,500,000 tons in 1942.

The Lungyen mines, with an iron content of 54 - 60 percent, include four different lots, with a total estimated deposit of 124,000,000 tons according to the Japanese survey, instead of 92,000,000 tons estimated earlier in 1934 by the Chinese Geological Survey, distributed as follows:

Lungchiapao	65,000,000 metric tons
Sinyao & Sanchakou	30,000,000 metric tons
Cholu	15,000,000 metric tons
Yentungshan	14,000,000 metric tons

On June 7, 1939, the ground-breaking ceremony for the railway siding between Hsuanhwa on the Peking-Paotow railway and Lungchiapao, site of richest ore deposits, took place. This new line, covering a distance of 43 kilometers, was expected to be completed within the year. The Lungchiapao mines, never exploited before, were expected to yield 200,000 tons of iron ore in 1939, 600,000 tons in 1940, 900,000 tons in 1941, and 1,200,000 tons in 1942. Following operations at the Cholu mine in 1941 together with the annual output of about 500,000 tons from the Yentungshan mines, the total output of the Lungyen iron mines should reach 2,500,000 tons by 1942, an mentioned above. ① Meantime proposal was also made to complete another railway line leading to the Sinyao lot, by 1940. ②

---

① *Trans-Pacific*, June 15, 1939, *Manchuria*, Dairen, June 15, 1939.
② *East Asia Economic News*, October 1939.

Actually, the production in Lungyen mines fell below Japanese expectations. The production for 1940 was estimated at 700,000 tons of iron ore, as compared with original goal of 1,100,000 tons.

Elsewhere, mining operations on a smaller scale were carried out in Shansi, Hopei and Shantung, by the NCDC and private Japanese interests. Necessary preparations for resuming operation at the Chinlingchen Iron Mine in Shantung Province, started in September 1941 by the Japan Steel Pipe Manufacturing Company, will be completed by the end of June 1942, and the actual mining on a large scale will be started in July. ① Various iron mines in Shansi Province, in Taiyuan and Yangchuan, were entrusted to the joint operation of the NCDC and the Okura Mining Company. Two mining offices under the association system — the Shihchingshan Iron Mining Office and the Shansi Iron Mining Office — respectively had a total investment of ￥7,059,000 (￥6,059,000 from the NCDC) and ￥4,479,000 (￥3,679,000 from the NCDC) for the fiscal year ending March 31, 1941.

In pig iron production the only plant under the NCDC's control is the Shihchingshan Iron Works, operated by the Kochu Koshi, a subsidiary of the NCDC. The Works has a 250-ton blast furnace, producting at first 250 tons daily but later reduced to 150 tons daily; it plans, however, to increase its production to 300,000 tons per year by 1941. ②

In view of the increasing importance of the iron industry in the eco-

---

① *Peking Chronicle*, February 26, 1942.
② *East Asia Economic News*, January 1940.

nomic reconstruction of East Asia, the Japanese government in early 1942 decided to establish a ￥100,000,000 iron manufacturing company in North China. The proposed concern, which will be created as a Japanese juridical person, will jointly be financed by the Japanese Iron Manufacturing Company and the NCDC. According to the present plans, the proposed company immediately upon its establishment, will erect a giant iron-mill equipped with 700-ton blast furnaces in the Peking-Tientsin area. It is understood that the company will confine its activities to the production of pig iron and coke by-products in the initial stage, using iron ore from Lungyen and coal from Chinghsing, Liuhoukow and Tzehsien. ①

6. Salt. The growing demand for salt in Japanese chemical industry in years immediately preceding the war impelled Japan to seek for sources of increased supply abroad. Total salt consumption in Japan, of which two-thirds are for industrial uses and one-third for food requirements, has been estimated in the neighborhood of two and one-half million tons a year recently, although the original plan calls for 4,000,000 tons. Of the 2.5 million tons consumption requirement, Japan produces 600,000 tons and "Formosa" 200,000 tons, the rest being imported. Up to the end of 1940 Japan imported annually 700,000 tons from sources not now available to her, chiefly Africa. After the Pacific War in December 1941, Japan has planned to increase import from adjacent areas now under her control to 1,800,000 tons, distributed as follows:

---

① *Peking Chronicle*, April 24, 1942.

Occupied China 900,000 tons, Manchuria 500,000 tons, N. E. I. 200,000 tons, Thailand 100,000 tons, and French Indo-China 100,000 tons. In other words, Occupied China is expected to supply one-half of the total imports of salt into Japan.

Salt export from Occupied China to Japan and Korea reached 433,000 tons in 1937, 592,000 tons in 1938, 350,000 tons in 1939, 679,000 tons in 1940, and 704,000 tons in 1941. Such export comes chiefly from the Changlu field in North China, whose export to Japan was planned to increase to 900,000 tons in 1942 and 1,000,000 tons in 1943.

Salt production and export to Japan in North China was before the war entrusted to the Kochu Koshi. With the establishment of the North China Development Company in November 1938, a systematic production augmentation plan was drawn up for North China, to be executed by two companies under Japanese control, one in Hopei and another in Shantung. In Hopei the North China Salt Company, a subsidiary of the NCDC, was established on August 20, 1939 with a capitalization of ¥25,000,000, to take over the operations formerly carried out by the Kochu Koshi. The Company, a China ordinary corporation, is entrusted with the improvement of the Changlu salt fields — one of the two salt fields in North China. More specifically, its functions are: (1) manufacturing, refining, reproduction and sale of salt; (2) financing Chinese salt producers; (3) manufacturing and sale of soda, etc.; and (4) handling other businesses affiliated with the salt industry. The Company's plan for the increased production of salt in Hopei Province is as follows: ①

Table 16. Salt Production Expansion Plan of the North China Salt Company in Hopei Province, 1939

	Area (in chobu)	Date of Completion	Productive Capacity (in M. T.)	Investment (in Yen)
Improvement of old salt fields	6,283	1939	314,000	850,000 (Advances)
New Taku salt fields	10,000	End of 1940	500,000	4,000,000 (Construction expenses)
New Tatsing-ho salt fields	6,000	End of 1941	300,000	2,400,000 (Construction expenses)
Total	22,283		1,114,000	7,250,000

Note: 1 chobu is equivalent to 2.4507 acres.

Upon the completion of the plan, the Company is expected to ship to Japan approximately 450,000 metric tons in 1939, 600,000 metric tons in 1940, 750,000 metric tons in 1941, 900,000 metric tons in 1942, and 1,000,000 metric tons in 1943, as shown in Table 17:

Table 17. Japanese Planned Expansion of Changlu Salt Fields, 1938 - 48 (In metric tons)

	Changlu fields		Shantung	Total
Year	Production	Exports to Japan	Production	Production
1938	650,000	400,000	330,000	980,000
1939	840,000	450,000	340,000	1,180,000
1940	980,000	600,000	350,000	1,330,000

---

① *Far Eastern Yearbook*, 1941, pp. 972 - 974.

continued

Year	Changlu fields Production	Exports to Japan	Shantung Production	Total Production
1941	1,200,000	750,000	400,000	1,600,000
1942	1,500,000	900,000	440,000	1,940,000
1943	1,800,000	1,000,000	520,000	2,320,000
1944	1,850,000	*	560,000	2,410,000
1945	1,950,000	*	620,000	2,570,000
1946	2,050,000	*	620,000	2,670,000
1947	2,150,000	*	620,000	2,770,000
1948	2,200,000	*	620,000	2,820,000

* Not estimated.

The program of salt production for Hopei Province contemplated a total production of 840,000 metric tons in 1939. However, the typhoon in 1939 washed away approximately 100,000 metric tons of salt on the fields and damaged the banks and ditches of the new Taku salt field under construction and many of the old salt fields, frustrating all hopes of attaining the goal. The increase of salt export from Occupied China, chiefly North China, to Japan, from 350,000 tons in 1939 to 679,000 tons in 1940 and 704,000 tons in 1941 might be interpreted either as increase in production or increase in production coupled with Japanese pressure to drain Chinese consumption quota. With the increasing difficulties of shipping which Japan has been faced since the Pacific War, even if increased production be possible, transportation for a bulky commodity like salt remains a bottleneck in Japan's designs to secure larger salt export from Occupied North China. A recent dispatch from Domei stated to the effect that. ①

"decline in Japanese salt production is to be compensated by increased salt production in North China. In view of magnitude of salt deposits in North China, Japanese requirements can be met if shipping allocation plan is carried out."

According to Japanese plans, the following four producers of refined salt will be required is participate in the North China Salt Company, namely, (1) Chiu Ta Salt Refining Company in Tangku capitalized at $2.1 million, (2) T'ung Yi Salt Refining Company in Chefoo capitalized at $420,000, (3) T'ung Ta Salt Refining Company in T'angfang capitalized at $500,000, and (4) Yung Fu Salt Manufacturing Company in Tsingtao capitalized at $3.2 million. By the cooperation of these four firms, the North China Salt Company hopes to double refined salt output in this region within two or three years.

The salt refining plant at Hanku, completed in August 1939, commenced operation with an annual capacity of 120,000 metric tons. The Chiuta Refining Plant was rehabilitated in February 1938, producing 35,000 metric tons of refined salt in 1939.

According to the *Far Eastern Yearbook, 1941*, the Tanku Soda Factory of the Yungli Chemical Industry Corporation will probably be merged into the North China Salt Company. The factory, capitalized at 5,500,000

---

① London, November 25, 1942, based on broadcast issued by the *DNB Economic Service* during the period November 12 to 18, 1942.

yuan, reopened its soda ash plant in July 1938 and its caustic soda plant in February 1939. The two plants regained half of their former capacity with a daily output of 85 metric tons of soda ash and 10 metric tons of caustic soda, respectively.

The other company, the Shantung Salt Company, was organized in April 1937, with a paid-up capital of ￥1,000,000, to monopolize the business of purchasing and shipping salt produced in Shantung Province. Although the salt manufacturing industry was to be controlled by the North China Development Company, the operations of the Shantung Salt Company have been and still are in the Company's own hands in view of its vested rights, according to the *Far Eastern Yearbook, 1941*. In 1938, the Company's capital was increased to ￥10,000,000, of which ￥3,250,000 was paid up, in order to cope with the demand for increased production under the new plan. The output from the Shantung salt fields under the new plan was to increase from 330,000 tons in 1938 to 340,000 tons in 1939, 350,000 tons in 1940, 400,000 tons in 1941, 440,000 tons in 1942, 520,000 tons in 1943, 560,000 tons in 1944, and 620,000 tons in 1945 up through 1948. Details of the new plan are as follows: (1) to increase the productive capacity of one chobu from the present 45 metric tons to 65 metric tons by improving the old salt fields extending over 6,000 chobu; (2) to revive 300 chobu of waste salt fields, and (3) to create by the end of 1941 new salt fields of 700 chobu adjacent to the waste salt fields.

In 1939 attempts were made to increase the producing capacity of the existing salt fields in Shantung Province by laying out a 500 chobu salt field at Tsingtao Bay. But as in Hopei, salt fields in this province were damaged by the August typhoon which caused a two million yen loss in equipment and 200,000 metric tons in salt. Thus, the output for the fiscal year 1939 - 40, according to the *Far Eastern Yearbook, 1941*, " is estimated at only 450,000 metric tons, and it is reported that the allotment for Japan was reduced from 290,000 metric tons to 150,000 metric tons. "

To what extent the North China Development Company has succeeded in exploiting the salt resources of North China to most Japan's salt needs cannot be ascertained statistically in view of lack of information. On the fourth anniversary of the establishment of the Company, a report was broadcast to the effect that[1]

> "production covers requirements of Japan and still leaves a surplus for developing soda dye and other chemical industries. "

7. Cotton. Japan, although one of the world's leading cotton manufacturers, does not produce raw cotton. Practically all of her annual cotton requirements estimated at 775,000 metric tons for the four pre-war years 1933 - 36, were imported, with the United States and British India (including Burma) supplying 85 percent and China 5 percent.[2] The war with China since 1937 has necessitated a drastic reduction in Japan's cotton import from abroad, meantime compelling her to look for supplies

---

[1] P62255 Tokyo Domei in English at 8:04 p. m. to the world, November 7, 1942.

[2] *The economic vulnerability of Japan in raw cotton*, prepared for the Office of the Administrator of Export Control by the Interdepartmental Committee on Raw Textile Fibres, First Draft, April 5, 1941, p. 10.

from those areas closely linked with the yen bloc or occupied by her in the course of war.

Among those areas from which Japan may look for sources of cotton supply, China is the most important. In the pre-war year of 1936-37,— the peak year in Chinese cotton production — China produced 866,000 metric tons of raw cotton, or 13 percent of the world's cotton production,① (ranking second) only to the United States and British India. The war with Japan reversed, however, the trend of expanding production. Occupied China, from which three-quarters of Chinese cotton production was derived in per-war years, contributed declining shares in the ensuing years. Cotton production in Occupied China decreased from 561,000 metric tons in 1937-38 to 285,000 metric tons in 1938-39, and 166,000 metric tons in 1939-40. Many factors were responsible for this decline, but the most important was the Japanese policy of requisitioning raw cotton from Chinese producers at an artificially depressed price which at times was only one-half to one-third of the price on the free market. Under such circumstances, it was only natural for the Chinese farmers to substitute food crops for cotton production. To Japan the decline in cotton production in Occupied China was especially serious, in view of her increasing dependence on Chinese imports for which payment involved on loss in the foreign exchange, but called only for great production from her printing press. Cotton export from Occupied China to Japan thus decreased from 104,000 metric tons in 1937-38 to 60,000 metric tons in

---

① *League of Nations Statistical Yearbook*, 1939-40, p. 122.

1938-39, and 57,000 metric tons in 1939-40. In terms of total cotton production in Occupied China, such export claimed, however, an increasing share, rising from 19 percent in 1937-38 to 29 percent in 1938-39 and 34 percent in 1939-40. ①

Table 18. Cotton Production and Export to Japan in Occupied China 1937-38 to 1941-42 (In metric tons)

Year (Oct.-Sept.)	Production	Export to Japan	% of Export (in Production)
1937-38	561,000	104,000	19
1938-39	285,000	80,000	29
1939-40	166,000	57,000	34
1940-41	227,000	68,000	30
1941-42	259,000	99,000	39

After three years of bitter experience Japan had to change her policy in order to encourage cotton production by the farmers in Occupied China. Prices paid for the cotton requisitioned from the farmers were raised in approximate agreement with those prevailing on the free market. Production of cotton in Occupied China was increased, from 166,000 metric tons in 1939-40 — the poorest year, to 227,000 metric tons in 1940-41, and 259,000 metirc tons in 1941-42. Similarly, cotton export from Occupied China to Japan increased from 57,000 metric tons or 34 percent of the total cotton production in Occupied China in 1939-40

---

① See my report on "A Preliminary Survey of the Cotton Textile Industry in Occupied China", Board of Economic Warfare, December 1, 1942.

to 68,000 metric tons or 30 percent in 1940 – 41, and 99,000 metric tons or 39 percent in 1941 – 42. For 1942 – 43 cotton production in Occupied China may increase to 295,000 metric tons, of which 115,000 metric tons or 39 percent will probably be exported to Japan.

Total cotton import into Japan has been on the decline since the war in 1937. It decreased from an annual average of 773,000 metric tons for the five years 1934 – 38 to 509,000 metric tons in 1939 – 40 and 347,000 metric tons in 1940 – 41. For the year 1942 it dropped drastically to 133,070 metric tons. This decline in total import of raw cotton into Japan from major sources of supply including the United States, Brazil, British India and Egypt, would have dealt a most serious blow to the Japanese cotton textile industry but for the increasing quantity of cotton being exported to Japan from Occupied China. Whereas during the five years 1934 – 38 China supplied only 4.8 percent of Japan's total cotton import, her share increased to 6.6 percent in 1939 – 40, 12.5 percent in 1940 – 41, and 74.0 percent in 1942.

Cotton export from Occupied China to Japan comes largely from North China. In 1941 – 42 the cotton production in Occupied China is estimated at 1,138,000 bales of 500 lbs. each, of which 717,000 bales come from North China. [1] Cotton export from North China is handled by the North China Raw Cotton Company, formerly a subsidiary of the Kochu Koshi. Since the eatablishment of the North China Development Company in November 1938 the North China Raw Cotton Company has become a subsid-

---

[1] From a wire to the Department of State dated November 17,1941.

iary of the NCDC, no longer of the Kochu Koshi which itself is a subsidiary of the NCDC. The Company has an authorised capital of ￥3,000,000, of which ￥1,500,000 is paid-up (￥500,000 from the NCDC).

IV. Central China Promotion Company[①]
(Chu-Shina Shinko Kabushiki Kaisha)

A. History and Organization

The Central China Promotion Company was inaugurated on the same day as the North China Development Company, on November 7, 1938, along the same principles as those adopted for the latter on December 14, 1937. The bill for the establishment of the CCPC was presented to the Lower House on March 18, 1938, passed by the 73rd session of the Japanese Diet, and approved by the Japanese Cabinet on March 15. On May 12 the subcommittee entrusted with preparations for the establishment of the CCPC was appointed with Mr. Seihin Ikeda as the head,

---

[①] For literature on the company in genenal, see *Oriental Economist*. October 1941; *Far Eastern Review*, March 1941; A. Viola Smith, *Industrial Capacity in Occupied Areas of China and Hongkong Now Available for Use by the Japanese*, Far Eastern Unit, Bureau of Foreign and Domestic Commerce, Washington, May 11, 1942 (typewritten for confidential use).

which held its final meeting on November 7, 1938 and inaugurated on the same day the formal establishment of the CCPC. The officials of the Company were announced to consist of the following:

> President: Mr. Kenji Kodama
> Vice-President: Mr. Ganame Hirasawa.
> Directors: Mr. Kiyoshi Kanai, Mr. Saburo Sonoda, and Mr. Kyoichi Yutani.

As compared with the NCDC having one president, two vice-presidents, five directors, and three auditors, the CCPC has one president, one vice-president, and three directors.

The CCPC is a special juridical person organized in Japan for the purpose of promoting the economic rehabilitation and development of Central China. This is in contrast with the NCDC whose chief objectives are to exploit the natural resources and to establish industries in North China. The difference between the purposes of the two companies is partly due to the variations in degrees of the economic development of the two regions, and partly to the extent of destruction wrought in the course of the war and the consequent need for "economic rehabilitation" in Central China.

The CCPC, like the NCDC, is a special, national policy, holding corporation organized in Japan, with its main office in Shanghai. Like other special corporations, half of its ¥100,000,000 capital is subscribed by the Japanese government. It is similarly subject to government control and supervision as the NCDC, in respect of organization, personnel, finance, and operation.

The role that is to be played by the CCPC has become more and more important upon the conclusion of the Sino-Japanese basic treaty in November 1940, and the Japanese loan to the puppet Nanking regime following Wang Ching-wei's visit to Japan in 1941. Placing particular importance on the reconstruction of industries and public welfare facilities which were destroyed by the war, the Company has carried on its business in accordance with the three-year reconstruction plan of the Nanking puppet government. Many enterprises in different branches have been rehabilitated by 1941, and some of them are now being expanded.

B. Finance

Besides being a special juridical person, the CCPC is the central holding company controlling all the reconstruction and development enterprises. Of its authorised capital of ¥100,000,000, ¥50,000,000 is subscribed by the Japanese government, part of which may be invested in kind; and the other half by private Japanese interests. The Company may increase its capital on approval by the government. It may raise debentures, subject to official sanction, to the value of five times the paid-up capital. The government may guarantee the payment of interest and principal of the debentures issued by the Company.

Proposed enterprises of the Company were announced in November 1938 to consist of the following, with a total capital investment of ¥175,000,000, of which ¥95,450,000 was to be invested by Japan, and ¥79,550,000 by China. ①

---

① *Trans-Pacific*, November 3, 1938.

Table 19. Proposed Capital of CCPC's Subsidiary Enterprises, 1938 (In 1,000,000 Yen)

Enterprises	Capital	Invested by Japan	Invested by China ①
Communications	15	10.00	5.00
Railways	100	50.00	50.00
Electricity	25	10.00	15.00
Bus and trolley	5	3.00	2.00
Gas	10	7.00	3.00
Marine products	10	6.00	4.00
Iron ores	10	9.45	0.55
Total	175	95.45	79.55

The CCPC had by the end of 1940 ¥45,048,000 in paid-up capital, as compared with the authorized capital of ¥100,000,000. Since its establishment it floated debentures twice to the combined total of ¥40,000,000, bearing an annual interest of 4.5 percent. ② In addition, it borrowed ¥14,000,000 of funds in advance from the syndicate bankers on its projected debenture issue, up to the business year ending December 31, 1940.

---

① *Oriental Economist*, May 1940, p. 293, in referring to the Chinese share of the capital for the Central China Promotion Company, commented, "As most of the Chinese investments were by the Reformed Government (of Nanking) which furnished in kind, they could hardly be called undertakings with the collaboration of native Chinese capitalists. In this respect, the North China Development Company is in the same situation, and actual economic cooperation of Japanese and Chinese peoples is still to be seen in the future."

② The first issue of debentures by the Company was on April 20, 1940. Of this amount ¥7,500,000 were taken up by the Japanese government, ¥5,000,000 by the syndicate bankers, and ¥7,500,000 by the Japanese public. Maturity of the bonds is 12 years; interest is paid at the rate of 4.5 percent per annum. Issue price is ¥99.50. After two years, amortization at the rate of ¥300,000 or more will take place semi-annually.

By the end of 1940 the Company had 13 subsidiaries, with a combined capitalization of ¥221,000,000 derived from following sources:

Table 20. Capitalization of CCPC's 13 Subsidiary Companies, December 31, 1940

		Amount		Percent
Japanese interests		¥136,230,000		61.6
CCPC	¥83,379,000		37.7	
Other	¥52,851,000		23.9	
Chinese interests		¥84,770,000		38.4
Total		¥221,000,000		100.0

The capital investment of the CCPC in the 13 subsidiary companies and housing associations reached ¥51,526,000 by the end of 1940, while its loans to the various enterprises amounted to ¥47,140,000. The total investments and loans thus reached a sum of ¥98,666,000, which showed a steady increase from ¥13,740,000 in 1938, and ¥42,710,000 in 1939.

The authorized and paid-up capital of the 13 subsidiary companies may be tabulated by enterprises as follows:

Table 21. Authorized and Paid-up Capital of CCPC's 13 Subsidiary Companies, December 31, 1940 (In 1,000 yen)

Enterprise	No. of Companies	Authorized Capital	%	Paid-in Capital	%
Transportation		85,000	38.4	55,173	35.4
Railway	1	50,000		33,815	
Steamship	2	32,000		19,094	
Bus	1	3,000		2,264	

continued

Enterprise	No. of Companies	Authorized Capital	%	Paid-iń Capital	%
Communication	1	15,000	6.8	15,000	9.6
Public utilities		66,000	29.9	45,290	29.0
Electricity	1	43,000		29,390	
Gas	1	3,000		900	
Real Estate	1	20,000		15,000	
Mining		40,000	18.1	30,925	19.8
Iron	1	20,000		20,000	
Coal	1	15,000		9,675	
Salt	1	5,000		1,250	
Agriculture & Fishery		15,000	6.8	9,665	6.2
Silk	1	10,000		6,500	
Fishery	1	5,000		3,165	
Total	13	221,000	100.0	156,053	100.0

For 1938 three out of six subsidiary companies of the CCPC declared dividends at the rates of 5 percent, 6 percent and 8 percent, respectively. For 1939, seven out of 12 companies declared dividends, one at 4 percent, four at 6 percent, one at 8 percent and another at 10 percent. For 1940, nine out of 13 companies declared dividends, four at 6 percent, two at 8 percent and three at 10 percent. As for the term which closed at the end of March 1941, three out of four companies which had hitherto passed dividends were expected to distribute profits at the rate of 4 percent to 5 percent.

Owing to this increase in the payment of dividends by the subsidiary companies the earning position of the CCPC seemed to have been apparently improved. The net profit of the company, ￥35,000 in 1938, rose to ￥659,000 in 1939, and ￥936,000 in 1940. In these figures were included, however, the Japanese government's subsidy of ¥11,000 for 1938, ¥371,000 for 1939, and ¥734,000 for 1940. Of the Company's gross income of ¥3,419,000 for the business year 1940, receipts from dividends represented ¥1,022,000 (30 percent), receipts from interest ¥1,513,000 (44 percent), and government subsidy ¥734,000 (21 percent). The ratio of government subsidy to gross income showed a decline from 24 percent for the previous business year, while its ratio to net profit rose from 56 percent in 1939 to 78 percent in 1940. "These latter percentage figures", commented the *Oriental Economist* (October 1941, pp. 519-520), "undeniably demonstrate that the Company depends excessively on government subsidy in distributing its profits among the shareholders. The question thus remains to be solved later as to how to enable the Company to emerge from its present position of depending on government help."

Due to the apparent improvement in the financial position of the subsidiary companies through increase in government subsidy, the profits of the CCPC increased from 4.5 percent on private-owned shares for the 1939 business year to 6 percent for 1940. For the extra business term during the first three months of the 1941 calender year,[1] the Company maintained the dividend rate unaltered at 6 percent. During this extra business term of three months the Company's investment totalled ¥290,000,000, which went to the Central China Mining Company, the Central China

---

[1] This resulted from the adoption of the new business year, April 1 to March 31 of the following year, instead of the former business year of January to December.

Railways Company, and the Shanghai Inland River Steam Navigation Company on a priority basis. Meanwhile, loans advanced by the Company to the different enterprises aggregated ￥13,524,000 during the extra term. According to the *Oriental Economist*, October 1941.

"Under its positive business policy hinging on investments and loans in accordance with the priority principle, the Company is expected to display more vigorous activity in perfecting and expanding the enterprises with which it is concerned and which have now emerged from the stage of reconstruction to that of expansion. New investments and loans projected by the Company for the new business term beginning from April 1 of the current year are roughly estimated to be between ￥40 and ￥50 million. " (p. 527)

According to recent report, the CCPC's total investments in its subsidiaries reached 221 million yen by the end of the fourth fiscal year ending November 7, 1942. Of this total, the greatest part — approximately 105 million yen, has been invested in the Central China Railway Company. The sum of 52.3 million has been earmarked for the Central China Mining Company. [①]

Recent developments after the outbreak of the Pacific War in December 1941 point to a greater participation of the Chinese capital in the CCPC's enterprises, and greater readiness on the part of the CCPC authorities to accept Chinese investments directly in the CCPC shares,

---

① D. N. B. dispatch, Shanghai, December 4, 1942.

instead of indirectly through its subsidiary enterprises. A Domei dispatch from Shanghai dated October 14, 1942 reported that the enormous amount of idle capital in Shanghai, estimated at seven billion yuan, was gradually finding its way into banks and industries. No less than 545,000,000 yuan was reported to have been invested in new banks established for the respective trades such as coal, salt, silk, fishery, cotton, medicine, and cloth; with additional 1,450,000,000 yuan in stocks and shares, and 1,200,000,000 yuan in government bonds. Saburo Sonoda, Director of the CCPC, thus urged Chinese to invset in the economic development of Central China. Hitherto the exploiting of the resources of Central China depended upon Japanese capital and material, with the exception of contributions in kind from the puppet Chinese government representing the assessed value of industrial propertion taken over by the subsidiary enterprises of CCPC; but the present situation, according to Domei, " calls for the intensification of such exploiting with Chinese funds. " With this end in view, Kenji Kodama, new President of the CCPC, upon arrival in Shanghai on January 15, 1943, from a trip to Japan, was expected to conduct concrete discussions on the reorganization of various subsidiaries of the CCPC. According to Domei, [1]

> "The reorganization of government-subsidized concerns is expected to take the form of unification of all shareholders and incorporation of all investers in these firms on a joint Sino-Japanese basis into the Central China Promotion Company, the holding company

---

[1] Foreign Broadcasts Intelligence Service, Federal Communications Commission, *Daily Report — Foreign Radio Broadcasts*, January 18, 1943, F18.

for these firms."

"Japanese investors in various subsidiary companies of the giant holding company have become direct shareholders of the Central China Promotion Company, and the authorities now stress the necessity of incorporating all Chinese shareholders into the company on an equal and cooperative basis with the Japanese.

"In this connection the Central China Electricity and Waterworks Company recently transferred all its Japanese shares to the Central China Promotion Company and the Central China Mining Company. The Central China Silk Company is also contemplating a similar step in the near future."

Meantime, Domei reported from Shanghai on October 21, 1942 to the effect that, [1]

"marking the first large-scale participation of Chinese capital in cooperation with Japanese concerns, the Central Reserve Bank of China will shortly grant a 50,000,000 yuan loan to Japanese companies under control of the Central China Promotion Company. The loan will be used for the production of coal, iron, salt and other essential raw materials, while transportation and communication enterprises will also benefit by the loan."

In another Japanese broadcast on December 25, 1942, it seems that

---

[1] FCCP A177, Tokyo(Domei) in English at 6:30 a.m. to the world, quoting text from Shanghai dated October 21, 1942.

the CCPC, in addition to the 13 subsidiary companies it has controlled since its establishment, it now "supervises 10 other companies registered under enemy nationals in Central China. "① For the year 1943 extensive plans are scheduled by the CCPC and various Sino-Japanese joint industrial enterprises, including restoration of normal railway service along the Chekiang-Kiangsi line by the Central China Railway Company, development of new fluor spar mines by the Central China Mining Company, establishment of a soda factory and other industries. The Central China Railway Company's construction plan for the Chekiang-Kiangsi line already is launched in the Hangchow-Kinhua area and is expected to be completed by the end of 1943. Development of new fluor spar production by the Central China Mining Company already has started on a small scale with a regular output expected in the near future. The company also is planning creation of a large-scale mineral refinery at Shanghai. A salt company by the Central China Salt Company in scheduled to be opened at Haichow in northern Kiangsu Province. ②

C. Program of Development — Plans and Results

The scope of enterprise of the CCPC, according to the Japanese Diet Bill for the 73rd Session held in March 1938, shall be to "invest in and

---

① Broadcast from Tokyo to Latin America and Eastern USA, English language, December 25, 1942, 9:30 p. m. EWT.
② *Foreign Radio Broadcasts*, October 21, 1942, H7.

finance the following business: (1) transport enterprise, (2) communications, (3) electric power, gas and water supply, (4) mining, (5) aquatic products, and (6) other enterprises relating to public utility and industry." These enterprises are being carried out by the CCPC, although on a much smaller scale than those financed by the NCDC. Thus, by the end of the fourth year of establishment on November 7, 1942, the CCPC had a total capital investment in its subsidiaries of 221,000,000 yen, which was only one-half of that for the NCDC amounting to 434,837,000 yen. Several factors are responsible for this disparity. In the first place, the Japanese military were active in the exploitation of North China resources even before the outbreak of the Sino-Japanese war no the seventh of July, 1937. Kochu Koshi, or China Development Company, was organized in 1935, as a subsidiary of the SMR to exploit the major resources in North China including coal, iron ore, salt, cotton and power, and had thus already paved the way for the NCDC into which Kochu Koshi was incorporated as one of the 30 subsidiary enterprises. Meantime, the SMR itself had been active in surveying the possibilities for railway expansion in North China. Secondly, political and military developments in North China had by 1937 already reached a stage similar to those in Manchuria before the Japanese occupation of Manchuria in 1931; whereas in Central China Japan still had to cope with strong Chinese resistance, first in Shanghai in the fall of 1937, and later in Nanking and Hankow along the Lower Yangtze Valley until the end of 1938. After 1938 the Chinese guerrillas have been active in engaging the Japanese military in Central China. Finally, so far as the resources themselves are concerned, these in North China gear in more closely with the needs of Japan's wartime economy than those in Central (including South) China. In North China are to be found seven-tenths of China's pre-war railways, three-fourths of China's pre-war coal output, and over one-half of China's pre-war salt and cotton output. In other words, under prevailing circumstances conditioned by earlier economic, political and military penetration, as well as by greater abundance and accessibility of strategic raw materials essential to Japan's wartime economy, Japanese military through the medium of the two development companies has devoted greater energy and resources to the economic exploitation of North than Central and South China.

1. Transportation. In the field of transportation four subsidiary companies have been established by the CCPC, two special corporations in railway and steamship transportation, and two ordinary corporations in steamship and bus transportation. The paid-in capital by the end of 1940 amounted to ￥33,815,000 for railways, ￥17,094,000 for steamship transportation, and ￥2,264,000 for bus transportation.

Railways. Railways in Central China suffered the severest damage during the China Affair. Some 60 bridges were destroyed on the Nanking-Shanghai and Shanghai-Hangchow-Ningpo lines alone. The ferry service from Pukow to Nanking was destroyed by the Chinese. A major portion of the Chekiang-Kiangsi line was dismantled by the Chinese before retreat, so also was that of the Canton-Hankow line.

Through the organization of the Central China Railways Company, a subsidiary of the Central China promotion Company, rapid progress has been made in the rehabilitation of the existing lines and the extension of the Hwainan line. The company, organized as a special corporation under the Chinese law in May 1939, had an authorized capital of ￥50,000,000, of which ￥31,500,000 was allocated to the Central China Promotion Company, ￥8,500,000 to the Japanese business interests, and ￥10,000,000 to the puppet Chinese government consisting mainly of the value of railway property taken over by the Japanese military, and later on turned over to the Company. By the end of 1939 the Company was reported to be operating the following lines with a total length of 705 kilometers, namely, Shanghai-Nanking, Shanghai-Woosung, Shanghai-Hangchow, and Nanking-Wuhu. In addition, the Pengpu-Pukow section of the Tientsin-Pukow line was operated by the company, as well as the Hwainan line (292 kilometers), of which the reconstruction of the northern section was completed in October 1940. Consummation of the Hwainan line helped to provide, in addition to transportation by water, another means by which to ship coal from the Hwainan (or Wainan) coal fields and from the Shanyuan coal yards. With the mines operating at full capacity, one-third, or 700,000 tons, of the coal consumed annually in Shanghai was expected to be supplied by the Hwainan mines in 1941. ①

The lines now operated by the Company reach 2,094 kilometers, as shown in Table 22:

---

① *Finance and Commerce*, September 27, 1939, p. 264; May 8, 1940, p. 434; *Oriental Economist*, November 1940, p. 654.

Table 22. Railways in Central China under Control of the Central China Railway Company, 1942 (In kilometers)

	Main Line		Branch Line	
	Operating	Total	Operating	Total
Partially operating lines*	295	2,062		24
Canton-Hankow (Wuchang-Yochow)	225	1,101		
Chekiang-Kiangsi (Hangchow-Chuchi)	70**	961	–	24
Operating lines	1,773	1,773	26	26
Tientsin-Pukow***	313			
Shanghai-Nanking	311		13	
Shanghai-Hangchow-Ningpo	274		13	
Nanchang-Kiukiang	128			
Hwainan	292			
Kiangnan****	172			
Soochow-Kashing	78			
Canton-Kowloon	35			
Hsinhui-Tushan	128			
Chiaohsien-Swatow	42			
Total in operation	2,068		26	
Total length		3,835		50

* Names in brackets refer to the operating sections of the lines.

** Estimated. The section between Hangchow and Kinhua is expected to be completely rehabilitated by the end of 1943.

*** Refers to the section between Tientsin and Pukow.

**** From Nanking to Wuhu and Sungkiapu.

A new ferry for the trains, constructed at the Kiangnan Dockyard in Shanghai with a total displacement capacity of 2,600 tons, a length of

101 meters and a width of 27.2 meters, has been installed for regular service between Pukow and Nanking since April 6, 1942.① For the year 1943 the Company is scheduled to begin reconstruction of the Chekiang-Kiangsi railway — to restore operation for the section between Hangchow and Kinhua.

The Company also operates motor freight and bus service on 1,000 kilometers. Technical operation of the various railway and bus lines of the company is strictly supervised by the Japanese staff of 2,600 in its service.

According to the financial result for the year ending March 31, 1941, the Company had a gross income of ¥3,726,000 and an expense of ¥3,854,000, thus suffering a loss of ¥128,000. However, for the years 1940 and 1941 it paid a sum of 819,000 yuan to the Ministry of Finance of the puppet Nanking government, as dividends on government shares and the first rental payment.

According to a Domei dispatch from Shanghai dated December 4, 1942, investments in the CCPC's subsidiaries reached 221,000,000 yen, of which 105,000,000 yen has been invested in the Central China Railway Company.

Steamships. In steamship navigation, there are now two companies affiliated to the CCPC, the one a special China corporation operating in the interior and along the coast, and the other an ordinary China corporation operating in the vicinity of Shanghai. The special corporation, the

---

① *Peking Chronicle*, April 17, 1942.

Central China Steamship Company, was established in February 1940 with an authorized capital of ￥30,000,000, of which ￥16,000,000 represented Chinese share (largely property of the China Merchants Steam Navigation Company, a semi-governmental Chinese concern, and some private Chinese shipping concerns). ￥8,540,000 Japanese private interests, and ￥5,460,000 subscription by the CCPC. The paid-up capital in 1941 amounted to ￥17,094,000, with ￥2,736,000 from the CCPC.

The business of the Company consists of coastal and interior shipping, as well as wharfing and warehousing, with the special privilege of having access to non-treaty ports. Its assets consist of wharfing facilities which had belonged to the former China Merchants Steam Navigation Company, ships that were in the possession of the Toa Shipping Company and two Chinese steamship companies, and cash investments by the CCPC and the Toa Shipping Company. The Company in May 1940 took over the inland shipping business from the Toa Shipping Company, its operation being limited to the lower reaches of the Yangtze River. It was reported in 1941 to be operating seven routes instead of the former five. In keeping close touch with the Toa Shipping Company, it has been carrying on its policy of developing new routes and augmenting the number of vessels. For the fiscal year ending September 1940, the company had a gross income of ￥1,117,000 and an expense of ￥1,005,000, with a prefit of ￥112,000.

The Shanghai Inland River Steamship Company was established on July 28,1938 as an ordinary Chinese corporation with an authorized capital of ￥2,000,000, of which ￥600,000 was subscribed by the CCPC, ￥1,000,000 by the Japanese shipping interests, and ￥400,000 by the puppet Nanking government. The company has the exclusive monopoly to operate steam launches on inland waterways of Shanghai hinterland. In 1940 the company was reported to have owned 83 steamships, hired 11 and chartered 56 — a total of 150. One thousand boats were, in addition, used for passenger and cargo trade. During January 1940 the volume of cargoes carried totalled 37,000 kg., and passengers 77,000. Cargoes carried were three times, and passengers eight times greater than during the corresponding period of 1939. Wharfs, storehouses and repairing shops, as well as an increase in the fleet, were on the program for 1940. The company has had favorable business since its establishment, and was thus able to increase its dividend by 4 percent to 10 percent for the business year of 1940.

Bus Transport. The Central China Urban Motor Bus Transportation Company was established as an ordinary Chinese corporation on November 5, 1938, with an authorized capital of ￥3,000,000, of which ￥1,448,000 was subscribed by the CCPC, ￥1,500,000 by the Japanese syndicate, and ￥12,000 by the Chinese (￥10,000 "in kind", and ￥2,000 in cash). The paid-up capital in 1941 amounted to ￥2,264,000, with ￥744,000 from the CCPC. The Company has the monopoly to operate bus and transportation services in East Central China. It operated bus lines in six cities in Central China in 1940, the average number of passengers carried being 90,000 daily.

The gross income of the Company for the year ending October 1940 reached ￥3,428,000, and the expense reached ￥3,318,000, thus leaving a profit of ￥110,000. A dividend of 6 percent was declared.

2. Communications. For the control of electrical communication, the Central China Tele-communications Company was established as a special Chinese corporation on July 31,1938, with an authorized capital of ￥15,000,000, of which the CCPC contributed ￥6,000,000, the International Communications Company of Japan and Japan Electric Communications Corporation contributed ￥4,000,000, while the remaining ￥5,000,000 represented allocation "in kind" for plant equipment seised from the Chinese. The Company has monopoly on all telephones, telegraph, radio and other forms of tele-communications services in East Central China. It maintains an international broadcasting station at Chenju, and an international receiving station at Liukiahang, both in the suburb of Shanghai. Radiograms can be sent via the "CCPC" to America (up to December 7, 1941), Europe, and nearly all places in East Asia, including Japan, Manchuria (Dairen), Occupied China (Tientsin, Tsingtao, Nanking, Soochow, Hangchow, Hankow), Hongkong, the Philippines (Manila), Thailand (Bangkok), and Japanese ships. Telephoto service is maintained between Shanghai and Tokyo, and direct radio telephone service between Shanghai and Japan and "Manchoukuo". There are city telephone exchanges in about ten cities in East Central China, such as Greater Shanghai, Nanking, Soochow, Hangchow, Wukiang, and Changsueh. In 1940 the company had 59 offices, handled 5,160,000 telegrams, had 10,561 telephone instruments and 6,500 telephone subscribers. The gross income for the business year ending

October 1940 was ￥9,828,000, and the expense ￥7,684,000, leaving a profit of ￥2,144,000. The company increased its dividend rate from 4 percent on commercial shares only in 1939, to 6 percent on commercial and government shares in 1940.

3. Power and Other Utilities. In the field of public utilities, there are three companies, — two special Chinese corporations for electricity and waterworks and real estate, and one ordinary Chinese corporation for gas, with an authorized capital respectively of ￥43,000,000, ￥20,000,000 and ￥3,000,000.

Electricity and Waterworks: The Central China Hydroelectric Company, established on June 29,1938, as a special Chinese corporation, had an authorized capital of ￥25,000,000, of which ￥15,000,000 was in the form of property assets provided by the Chinese and ￥10,000,000 in the form of Japanese capital investment (￥7,500,000 by the CCPC and ￥2,500,000 by the Central China Electrical Industry Association). The assets contributed by the Chinese, which were assessed by the Valuation Commission appointed by the Industry Ministry of the puppet Nanking government, consisted of what remained of the plants and equipments of seven Chinese companies in Shanghai as follows: Nantao Electric Company, Chapei Waterworks and Electric Company, Nantao Waterworks Company, Hsiang Hua Electric Company, Chenju Electric Company, Pootung Electric Company, and Pootung Water Supply Bureau(officially managed). The Japanese investment was provided by the Central Electrical Industry Association which had been formed with the Electric Power League of Japan as its center. The restoration of the Chinese undertakings began with their operation, as far as possible, under military supervision. The Kochu Koshi, a subsidiary of SMR, was placed in charge of these undertakings until June 30, 1938, when they were entirely turned over to the present company upon its establishment. [1]

The Company, which has monopoly of all electrical enterprises and waterworks in East Central China, started by repairing the existing light and water supply systems in the area outside the International Settlement of Shanghai, and building new ones. It plans to combine and rehabilitate similar systems throughout Central China, and place the power enterprises in the entire area under its unified control, including power generation, transmission and distribution. It also proposes to provide "drinkable fresh water" by improving present systems and adding new ones. In 1940 the new company consolidated the electric and water service undertakings in the principal cities of Central China and placed them under uniform control. Sixteen power plants having a total generating capacity of 108,492 k.w. are being operated by the company in 15 cities in East Central China. During the half year period ended April 30, 1940, it generated 112,312,000 k.w.h. for 86,397 households and 3,456 factories. Eight waterworks furnished 5,518,630 cubic meters of water per month.

Simultaneously, the capital was increased by ￥20,000,000, of which ￥8,510,000 in cash was provided by the CCPC, ￥2,870,000 in cash by the electric power industrialists in Japan, and the remaining

---

[1] *Oriental Economist*, September 1938, p. 603.

¥8,620,000 by the Chinese power companies in the form of properties. ① For the business year ending September 1940, the company had a total authorized capital of ¥43,000,000, of which ¥29,390,000 was paid-up. By November 1940, the Company increased its capitalization from ¥43,000,000 to ¥50,000,000. It completed its initial electrification program by building five power plants in Nanking, and purchased the T'aichao power House in Changpe, the Wuti plant in Ch'angchow and the Suchow (Soochow) plant. In addition, 12,500 kilowatt power house had been installed in Chapei and another 10,000 kilowatt unit in Nanking. ② It had a gross income of ¥9,098,000 and an expense of ¥7,899,000, leaving a profit of ¥1,199,000. According to the *Oriental Economist* (October 1941, p. 519), "all the enterprises have been restored to their 'pre-China Affair' status. The company is expected to declare its initial dividend for the business term which ended in March of this year."

Gas. The Greater Shanghai Gas Company was established as an ordinary Chinese corporation in November 1938, with an authorized capital of ¥3,000,000, of which ¥1,500,000 was subscribed by the CCPC, ¥1,000,000 by the Japanese private interests, ¥200,000 by the puppet Nanking government, and ¥300,000 by the Chinese in cash. The paid-up capital amounted in 1941 to ¥900,000, of which one-half came from the CCPC.

---

① *East Asia Economic News*, April 1940; *Oriental Economist*, May 1940, p. 294.
② *Oriental Economist*, November 1940, (p. 655)

The Company has as its function the supply of gas to Greater Shanghai. The construction of gas works, at cost of Yuan 1,400,000, started in February 1940, and production of gas began during 1941. The plant has a producing capacity of 7,000 cubic meters of gas daily, with an annual producing capacity of 25,000 Imperial gallons of coal tar by-products. The output for the first six months of 1941 was stated to be 1,874 metric tons. For the business year ending October 1941, the company had a gross income of ¥5,000 but an expense of ¥118,000, thus suffering a loss of ¥113,000. *Oriental Economist*, October 1941, thus remarked, "The Greater Shanghai Gas Company has completed the installation of distributing tubes in consonance with city planning, but its business results are not worth mentioning as yet." (p. 519)

Real Estate. The Shanghai Real Estate Company was established on September 1, 1938 as a special Chinese corporation with an authorized capital of ¥20,000,000, of which ¥5,000,000 was subscribed by the CCPC, ¥5,000,000 by Japanese interests, and ¥10,000,000 representing contribution "in kind" from the puppet Nanking government. The paid-up capital amounted in 1941 to ¥15,000,000, with ¥2,500,000 from the CCPC.

The Company has in its charge Shanghai City plan and various port and harbor improvement plans. It fell heir to the land and building of the former Shanghai City Government, located in the Kiangwan area, including the modern Jukong Wharf development. The land area covers 40,000,000 square meters. Before the Pearl Harbor Incident, the company concentrated its efforts on the port and harbor improvement works, deferring non-urgent enterprises. For these reasons the company kept its dividend stationary at 6 percent for the business term ending September 1940, although business has been consistently favorable since its establishment. The gross income for the year ending September 1940 reached ￥1,195,000 and the expense ￥734,000, leaving a profit of ￥461,000.

4. Iron and Iron Ore. In the Yangtze Valley provinces, the iron ore reserves are estimated by the Chinese Geological Survey as shown by Table 23. The iron resources in the Yangtze Valley provinces, 111.8 million tons, are small as compared with 174.6 million tons in North China and 883.5 tons in Manchuria. But their immediate importance from point of practical utilisation far exceeds the size of their reserve. Before the China Incident, all of the iron ore production from principal mines in China Proper, 950,000 tons, was derived from the iron mines located in the Yangtze Valley provinces of Hupeh and Anhwei, with the exception of 18,000 tons from Yangchuan in Shansi Province. [1]

Table 23. Iron Ore Reserves in Central China
(In 1,000 metric tons)

Province	Reserves	
Hupeh		39,640	
Hanyehping Company, Tayeh	10,500		
Hsiangpishan, Tayeh	8,800		
Linhsiang	6,340		

---

[1] *General Statement on the Mining Industry*, fifth issue, 1932 – 34, Geological Survey of China, Nanking, Tables 78 – 79.

continued

Province	Reserves	
O-Cheng	10,000	
Itu	4,000	
Anhwei		19,864
Tungkuanshan	4,921	
Chikuanshan	4,000	
Tangtu	6,298	
Changlungshan	4,645	
Kiangsu		4,437
Fenghuangshan	4,437	
Kiangsi		15,179
Chengmenshan	6,300	
Lienhua	6,299	
Pinghsiang	2,000	
Tungtengshan	580	
Hunan		26,550
Yuanling	1,050	
Anhua	2,160	
Hsikuangshan	3,600	
Chaling	3,900	
Ninghsiang	11,840	
Yiuhsien	4,000	
Chekiang		5,130
Changhsing	5,130	
Szechuan	1,000	1,000
Total Yangtze Valley		111,800
Total North China		174,604
Total China Proper		322,916
Total Manchuria		883,521
Total China and "Manchuria"		1,206,437

Table 24. Iron Ore Production in China, Excluding Manchuria, 1934 (In tons)

	Principal Mines	Native Mines
Yangtze Valley		
Hupeh	452,000	
Hanyehping Company	382,000	
Hsiangpishan	70,000	
Anhwei	480,000	5,000
Taochung	280,000	
Paohsing Company	80,000	
Fulimin Company	120,000	
Chekiang	–	300
Hunan		12,800
North China		
Shensi		180
Shansi	18,000	180,000
Honan		25,000
Other		186,300
Total	950,000	409,580

It is thus natural that Japanese attempt to exploit the iron ore resources in Central China should be confined to the two provinces of Anhwei and Hupeh where modern mines could be found, and to a lesser extent to the adjoining provinces in Chekiang, Kiangsu and Kiangsi. A report in the summer of 1939 by Dr. Wong Wen-hao, Minister of Economic Affairs in Chungking, indicated that the Japanese interests had already begun to take ore from deposits in Tayeh, Hupeh; in Maanshan, Anhwei; and in Kiangsu north of the Yangtze, and that their objective was to draw five million tons per annum from these sources. Such takings since 1938 have not been recorded in China's export statistics, and for strategic reasons have also been withheld from Japanese import statistics. But developments tend to support Dr. Wong's fears to a certain extent.

Among the iron ore mines in Central China, the best ore comes from those in Tayeh. It is both hematite and magnetite, and the run of the mine hematite in the past has shown 58 percent iron. The Japanese are, therefore, anxious to get it. The Tayeh mines, seized by the Japanese upon the fall of Tayeh on October 20, 1938, were turned over to the Japan Iron Manufacturing Company for operation, 200,000 to 300,000 tons of iron ore in stock were captured by the Japanese military upon occupation, although the Chinese troops in retreating had destroyed two modern blast furnaces with a producing capacity of over 200 tons of pig iron each just completed in September 1938, and had taken away all the railroad locomotives and ore cars, and virtually all the rails on the 18-mile track between Shihweiyao, location of the blast furnaces, and the mines. ①

Beginning May 1939, the Japan Iron Manufacturing Company started to work the Hsiangpishan and smaller iron mines in the Tayeh area — some 40 kilometers inland from the port of Shihweiyao on the Yangtze, with a monthly production of 10,000 tons of ore. Railway from Tayeh to Shihweiyao was again put to use, and transported ore to the Yangtze to be loaded on ocean-going steamers for direct shipment to Japan. In low-water season, ore was shipped to Wuhu on lighters and tugs and thence to Japan. Many permanent brick buildings were erected at Shihweiyao

---

① *Trans-Pacific*, December 22, 1938.

and Tayeh, to replace the destroyed ones. In August 1941, the American Consul at Hankow reported that 4,000 laborers had been recruited for work at the Tayeh mines and that production was at the rate of 15,000 tons a month and was expected soon to reach 20,000. Recent report from reliable Chinese sources indicates that the Japanese are employing 30,000 workmen at the Hanyehping Iron Mines at Tayeh, and that production of iron ore in the first half of 1942 was about 590,000 tons, or at the rate of 98,000 tons a month.① If the average monthly rate reported for the first half of 1942 were maintained throughout the year, production for 1942 from Tayeh mines would have amounted to 1,180,000 tons. The Chinese report gave the production for the Hanyehping mine alone and not for the other producing mines near Tayeh, but it is probable that the estimate actually covers total production in the Tayeh area.

Next to Tayeh, the more important iron ore mines in Central China are to be found in Anhwei and Kiangsu, with Wuhu on the Lower Yangtze as the port of export. The mines in Anhwei, Kiangsu and Chakiang were

---

① This figure, although high, is not totally unreasonable. In the first place, if these 30,000 workmen were assumed to have the same output per man achieved by the 4,000 in August 1941, the monthly rate would be 112,500 tons, compared with the 98,000 given by the Chinese intelligence. Secondly, the magnitude of this production does not seem unreasonable in the light of the production of earlier years. The Hanyehping mine in 1920 produced at the rate of 69,000 tons a month, although in 1935 and 1936 production was nearer 50,000 tons a month. Thirdly, a December 16, 1942 dispatch from American military attache states that the Japanese have reconditioned the railways in the Tayeh mining area, and that three trains are dispatched daily from the mines and a total of 2,000 tons of ore are being moved. This information would thus indicate the possibility of an annual movement of 730,000 tons.

taken over by the Japanese military during the early part of 1938. These mines, about 20 in number, had an aggregate reserve of more than 20 million tons, and their values were assessed by an engineering party from the South Manchuria Railway Company over a period of three months. ① Immediately afterwards the Central China Mining Company was established to take over the operation of the mines in the Wuhu area. The Company, an ordinary Chinese corporation, had an authorized capital of 20,000,000 yen, of which 4.5 million was subscribed by the Central China Promotion Company, 3 million by the Japan Iron Manufacturing Company, and 2.5 million by other Japanese business interests, the nominal 10 million yen of Chinese capital representing not subscriptions but the value of the mining properties or, properly speaking, the ore deposits "given" to the Central China Mining Company. Since then, the Company's investment has been increased to finance the expanding activities. By the end of 1942 it was reported that a sum of 52.3 million yen, out of a total investment of 221 million yen of the Central China Promotion Company, has been earmarked for the Central China Mining Company. ②

On March 28,1940, a statement made by the Chairman of the Central China Promotion Company at a shareholders' meeting in Tokyo indicated that the Company's mining subsidiaries in Central China — referring to the iron ore mines around Wuhu — were then producing 50,000 tons of iron ore monthly from four mines, and that two additional mines

---

① *Oriental Economist*, September 1938, p. 602.
② D. W. B. dispatch, Shanghai, December 4, 1942.

were to open shortly. If that level of production were maintained throughout 1940, the year's total would have reached 600,000 tons. ①

According to the *Oriental Economist*, October 1941,

> "all the mines under the management of the Maanshan and Taochung Mining Stations (in Anhwei Province) which constitute the main pillars of the Company's business are operating very favorably. Of the Company's new mines, the one at Fenghuangshan (in Kiangsu Province) has been operating in full owing since the latter part of last year (1940) while the Tungkwanshan mine (in Anhwei Province) is nearly ready for operation. The output of the mines under the management of the Company today surpasses the peak attained in the years prior to the China Affair, and the fact presages that those mines, as a great supply source for Japan's iron and steel industry, will make a further remarkable expansion in the future."

(p. 518)

Among the Gripsholm prisoners returning to the United States in the fall of 1942, one missionary from Anhwei Province reported considerable Japanese mining activity in the Wuhu district and shipment of large quantities of "iron ore and scrap iron" to Japan since the occupation.

From these sources, it may be reasonable to conclude that the output of Wuhu mines may have reached the pre-war total of 725,000 tons

---

① China and "Manchuria" as sources of iron ore, pig iron and scrap iron for Japan, prepared by A. Bland Calder, Assistant Commercial Attache, American Consulate General, Shanghai, January 29, 1941.

of iron ore per year.

Taking Tayeh production of 1,080,000 tons and Wuhu production of 725,000 tons together, the total estimated iron ore production available to Japan may thus be placed at 1,805,000 tons.

5. Coal. Coal reserves in Central China are distributed, according to the China Geological Survey, as follows:

Table 25. Coal Reserves in Central China
(In 1,000,000 metric tons)

		Amount		%
China Proper		232,559		95.44
Central China	2,109		0.86	
Hupeh	440		0.18	
Anhwei	360		0.15	
Kiangsi	992		0.40	
Chekiang	100		0.04	
Kiangsu	217		0.09	
Manchuria		4,610		1.89
Sinkiang		6,000		2.46
Chinghai		500		0.21
Total China & "Manchuria"		243,669		100.00

The five Central China provinces have a total coal deposit of only 2,109,000,000 metric tons, or 0.86 percent of the total coal deposit of China including Manchuria. In coal production in China proper before the war, 20,797,273 tons in 1934, the five provinces supplied only 1,940,230 tons or 9.2 percent of the total coal production of China excluding Manchuria.[①]

For the exploitation of coal resources, the CCPC established in June 1939 the Hwainan Coal Company as an ordinary Chinese corporation with an authorized capital of ￥15,000,000, distributed as follows:

Japanese	
Central China Development Company	￥4,150,000
Mitsui and Mitsubishi interests	5,000,000
Chinese	
Chinese interests	
"In kind"	2,500,000
In cash	1,500,000
Nanking puppet government "in kind"	1,850,000
Total	15,000,000

The Company's paid-up capital in 1941 amounted to ￥9,675,000, of which ￥1,038,000 came from the CCPC. The Company, with a Chinese president and a Japanese general-manager, is entrusted with the operation of the Hwainan collieries in Central China, said to have a total coal deposit of 200,000,000 tons. The collieries are located about 60 kilometers west of Pengpu, on the Tientsin-Pukow Railway, along the Hwai River, and comprise the Tatung, Chiulung and Tungshan mines. The mining equipment was destroyed by the Chinese before Japanese troops penetrated into Anhwei Province. According to *Trans-Pacific* of March 30, 1939,

"the Tatung mine is now being exploited by technicians and

---

① *General Statement of the Mining Industry*, fifth issue, tables 1, 27.

workers dispatched by the Iizuka Coal mine, of the Mitsuhishi interests. At present the mine is yielding 120 tons of coal, but the output is to be increased to 3,000 tons next summer. Preparations are being made by the Mitsui interests to develop the Chiulung mine. It is estimated the daily output of the three mines will be increased to 5,000 tons a day late this year. This amount would be enough to satisfy Central China's present demand for coal. "

According to the *Oriental Economist*, October 1941 (p. 518), "with rapid progress witnessed in the reconstruction and extension works for the Kinlung and Tatung coal mines, the company last year set up a system for the active participation of its business. " For the business year ending September 1940, the company had a gross income of ¥2,351,000 and an expense of ¥2,005,000, thus leaving a profit of ¥346,000. It declared an initial dividend of 6 percent for the year.

In 1939 under Japanese operations the company's output of coal from the Hwainan mines was stated to be about 1,000 tons daily. Japanese reports state that with the mines operating at full capacity, one-third or 700,000 tons of the coal consumed annually in Shanghai could be supplied by the Hwainan mines in 1941.

6. Salt. The Central China Salt Company was established as a special Chinese corporation on August 21,1939, with an authorized capital of ¥5,000,000, of which ¥2,000,000 was subscribed by the CCPC, ¥500,000 by the Japanese Dai Nippon Salt Company, and ¥2,500,000 in cash by the Nanking puppet government. The paid-up capital amounted in 1941 to ￥1,250,000, of which ￥500,000 came from the CCPC. The company in entrusted with the operation of the Lianghwai salt field in the region north of the Hwai River and at Haichow, and presumably also the Sungkiang field in southern Kiangsu and the Liangche field in Chekiang. It has charge over sale of salt in Central China and its export to Japan.

Salt production for the fields under the company's control for 1937, as compared with that for the five years 1932 – 36, has declined, as shown below:

Table 26. Salt Production in Central China, 1937
(In metric tons)

Salt Field	average, 1932 – 36	1937
Kiangsu— North(Lianghwai district)	494,813	411,904
South(Sunkiang district)	20,400	19,846
Chekiang(Liangche district)	234,845	174,973
Total	750,058	606,723

The company sustained heavy losses in 1939 as some of its important salt fields were washed out by high water. From November 1,1939 to October 31,1940, business conditions improved and no less than 180,000 tons of salt were supplied to different companies and provinces. For the business year ending September 1940, the Company had a gross income of ￥2,400,000 and an expense of ￥1,868,000, leaving a profit of ￥532,000 and paying a dividend of 8 percent.

7. Raw Silk. [1] To control the production and sale of silk for export, the Central China Sericultural Association was established in June 1938. Five filatures in the city of Wusih and one in Soochow, with a combined total of about 2,000 basins, began operation under the association's control. Two months later the Central China Raw Silk Company (Kachu Sanshi Kaisha), of which the above association was the parent body, was organized under joint Sino-Japanese management with capital of ¥8,000,000, of which ¥2,000,000 was invested by the Chinese in the form of plant equipments and ¥6,000,000 by the Japanese sericulturists in cash. Its capital was soon increased by another ¥2,000,000, of which ¥1,000,000 was contributed by the Chinese in the form of plants and ¥1,000,000 was subscribed by the general public in Japan and China. In this capital increase, all necessary factory equipment and facilities including approximately 10,000 basins were furnished by the Chinese. Of the ¥6,000,000 originally invested by the Japanese, half was offered by Katakura & Company, the Ounze Filature Company and the Kanegafuchi Spinning Company, and another half by others interested in the industry.

The fundamental aim of the company is to control the sericultural in-

---

[1] For the published materials on the Central China Raw Silk Company, see "The Central China Sericultural Company", *Oriental Economist*, May 1939, pp. 310 – 13; Barnett, Robert W. : *Economic Shanghai: Hostage to Politics, 1937 – 41*, Institute of Pacific Relations, New York, 1941, pp. 96 – 100; *Finance and Commerce*, October 9, 1940, p. 310; December 4, 1940, p. 302; January 1, 1941; February 12, 1941; April 2, 1941, p. 327; June 11, 1941, p. 579.

dustry of Central China, including the production and distribution of silkworm eggs, the raising of cocoons, the buying, selling and disposal of raw silk, and all affairs relating to the management of the industry. To provide a basis for thoroughgoing control, the Industry Ministry of the "Reformed Government in Nanking" enforced the provisional legislative act for control of the Central China sericultural industry as from October 1, 1938, in accordance with which the licensing system was adopted for silk production, machine silk reeling and cocoon transactions. Thus, the business of the company is entirely monopolistic.

According to the company's business development plan, the number of filatures under its management is to be increased in three years to 53, operating a total of 10,956 basins and with an estimated yearly output raised to 32,400 piculs, as is explained in the accompanying table. After this plan has been carried out, no further development is contemplated.

Table 27. Production Program of the Central China Raw Silk Company

	No. of filatures	No. of basins	Estimated yearly output	
			Raw Silk	Cocoons
			(In piculs)	
1st year	–	3,300	6,600	82,000
2nd year	–	6,000	19,400	242,000
3rd year	53	10,956	32,400	403,000
4th year and thereafter	53	10,956	32,400	403,000

As the company holds the privilege of monopolising the sericultural industry of Central China, it will act to adjust the relations between the sericultural industries of Japan and China by fixing the quantities of silk to be produced and marketed and also by carrying out a policy that will define the field of production. Under this policy, in order to minimise any ill effect upon the sericultural industry of Japan, Japanese products will be used principally for manufacturing high-grade stockings of 13 – 15 denier thread for export to Europe and America; Chinese silk is to be used mainly for manufacturing silk fabrics of 20 – 22 denier thread partly for domestic consumption, which will be actively promoted, and partly for export; while surplus yarns produced both in Japan and China will be allocated for the manufacture of mixed wool cloth and other new purposes.

Actually, however, the company's plan went through two stages of development: (1) carrying out successfully its original goal set for cocoon and raw silk production through control over cocoon production and marketing up to the summer of 1940, and (2) yielding to the broaded considerations of the program of Japanese army and navy to substitute raw cotton for raw silk production in Central China, and to preserve the silk interests in Japan as against the Japanese, Sino-Japanese and foreign silk interests in China after the summer of 1940.

With the monopolistic power of control over the sericultural industry in Central China which was implemented by the control regulations promulgated by the Industry Ministry of the puppet Nanking government, the Company went ahead smoothly with its program of production during the first stage. By the end of September 1938, 11 filatures with 3,332 basins had been opened, including eight in Wusih, two in Soochow and one in Hangchow. The total quantity of silk produced up to September

25, 1938 was 2,233 bales, thus evidencing a recovery of the industry in Central China after its almost complete suspension since the outbreak of hostilities in Shanghai on August 13, 1937. Between September 1938 and the end of January 1939, three more filatures in Wusih and three in Hangchow were established, bringing the number of basins to approximately 5,000. The progress since then had been slow. By the summer of 1940 the company had brought into operation in Central China 19 filatures, which had 6,276 basins with a productive capacity of 25,000 bales of raw silk per year.

In the course of this monopolistic control the silk filatures in Shanghai and elsewhere not affiliated with the Company were gradually squeezed out of existence due to difficulty of obtaining cocoon supplies. The company's filatures were provided with cocoons purchased from Chinese growers in a market where prices were controlled and where Japanese buyers frequently paid in military scrip; while other filatures were able to obtain them from areas of Free China only after they had been taxed by guerrillas and transported through Japanese-occupied regions where they were taxed again. Chinese national authorities permitted this trade on condition that the foreign exchange accruing from it be placed at the disposition of government banks. However, the progressive tightening of Japan's coastal blockade in the spring of 1940, hostilities in Chekiang, and persistent guerrilla activities involving periodic mopping-up campaigns in the Shanghai hinterland practically closed this breach, so far as Chinese filatures in Shanghai were concerned.

In April 1940 Kenji Kodama, president of the Central China Promotion Company, had announced that the silk-reeling subsidiary, having already been permitted by the Nanking regime to take over 18 operating plants, would increase its number of filatures to 53 as planned. Observers noted, at the same time, that the Central China Raw Silk Company had begun to stimulate additional cocoon production by extending loans of ¥6,000 per farm unit to farmers in Chekiang and Kiangsu, paying in advance on mulberry leaves up to five yen per picul. The company claimed, moreover, that in the spring of 1940 there had been a 30 percent increase over 1939 in the number of silkworm sheets distributed. Those varied activities enabled the Company to declare a 10 percent dividend and to assert that during 1939 its business had yielded a huge profit.

Beginning with the summer of 1940, a change of policy in respect to silk by the Japanese military in China took place. Restriction of silk production and export from China was said to have two objectives in view, first, the encouragement of silk farmers to grow raw cotton in order to meet the growing shortage of the cheaper fibre, and second, the elimination of Chinese competition with Japanese silk industry. The restriction was exercised through several channels. First, an export tax of 110 yuan per bale on raw silk was levied by the Silk Reconstruction Bureau in August 1940, which was increased to 480 yuan per bale on the first of December 1940. As a result, silk export from Shanghai for the four month period from June to September 1940 declined to 16,574 bales, as compared with 21,492 bales for the corresponding pariod in 1939 — a decrease of 4,918 bales. Second, in January 1941 the Japanese sponsored government Silk Testing Bureau, located in the Japanese controlled area of Hongkew district in Shanghai, refused to accept silk for conditioning and to issue the necessary export papers. No official notification was given to exporters, and inasmuch as only silk acquired through non-Japanese sources of supply was affected, the reasons for this rather high handed attitude could well be surmised. Representations by the Shanghai Raw Silk Exporters' Association yielded no practical result, although the Government Silk Testing Bureau in conjunction with the Nanking puppet regime endeavored to come to an understanding with the Japanese army and navy with a view to allowing unhindered passage of all silk from the International Settlemnet to the Bureau in Hongkew, and *vice versa*. Finally, by refusing to issue permits for the transport from interior to Shanghai of all silk destined for America in September 1940, the Japanese military put an end to the silk export to America. This was said to be due to the falling of American demand for Far Eastern silk and the consequent drop in silk prices on the New York market. The ban was intended to reduce Chiness silk supply and thus to bolster prices for the silk industry in Japan.

The program of Japanese army and navy to reduce silk production and export affected, however, all silk interests alike, including those of the Central China Raw Silk Company. During the winter months of 1940 many filatures of the Company were closed down or operated on a curtailed basis. By June, the Company, realising that the development of the silk industry in Central China would be impossible under such circumstances, made arrangements to commence operation for the first of its silk and wool weaving mills, located in the Yangtzepoo district in Shanghai.

After the enforcement of the freezing order by the United States and the United Kingdom on Japan, silk export came to an almost complete suspension. *New York Times*, October 16, 1941, published a cable received the day before from the Raw Silk Exporters' Association in Shanghai as follows:

> "All silk business and shipments suspended for reason that military refused delivery of export permits unless foreign exporters instead of cash payment could arrange to import for their military account wheat, oil, gasoline, or other essential materials, which for obvious reasons cannot be done. Future uncertain."

As a result, 15,000 bales of silk were held up in Shanghai godowns, one-third of which belonged to the Central China Raw Silk Company. The latter had in 1941 started to operate several silk weaving mills in Shanghai and Hangchow, but only a few hundred bales of silk could be utilised by these mills, while demand in Occupied China was negligible. *Finance and Commerce*, in its October 29, 1941 issue, remarked,

> "As may be imagined, the outlook, in these circumstances, for all engaged in the silk industry, including the many farmers and filature workers, is well nigh desperate, and to make matters worse the Chinese are absolutely in the dark about what should be done regarding the spring crop of 1942. The livelibood of thousands of people has been jeopardized. It is true that many have turned to cotton growing, but families who for generations have looked to silk

as their main support cannot easily change their traditional occupation. They are hoping against hope for some improvement but cannot see from what direction it may come. Those who understand how China's world famous industry is being sacrificed to Japan's own economic needs do not see hope from any direction."

8. Marine Products. The Central China Marine Products Company (also known as the Central China Fishery Company) was established as an ordinary Chinese corporation on November 6, 1938, with an authorized capital of ￥5,000,000, of which ￥2,770,000 was subscribed by the CCPC, ￥1,700,000 by the Japanese interests, and ￥530,000 by the Chinese (￥330,000 "in kind" and ￥200,000 in cash). The paid-up capital amounted in 1941 to ￥3,165,000, with ￥1,385,000 from the CCPC.

The Company controls the marine products industry including supervision and management over the marketing of marine products in Central China, distribution of fishing nets, manufacture of ice, and cold storage and refrigeration of fish for transportation. It has a new fish market developed in Shanghai yielding in 1939 an operating revenue of Yuan 1,500,000 per month, and a smaller one in Nanking. Besides, it has 24 motor-boats of 250 tons each, and is said to have brought in 10,000 Japanese fishermen to help. At Tinghai on the Chushan Island near the coast of Chekiang Province, storage bouses have been erected.

Prior to 1937 there were 360,000 persons engaged in tne fishing industry in Chekiang and Kiangsu provinces, with 21,400 fishing boats and a catch in 1936 valued at Yuan 97,000,000.

The Company during the business year ending October 1940 had a gross income of ¥2,001,000 and an expense of ¥1,279, yielding a profit of ¥722,000. The dividend for the year was increased from 4 percent to 10 percent.

Appendix 1. North China Development and Affiliated Companies, March 31, 1941 (In 1,000 yen)

Company	Year established; kind of organization; main office	President	Capital authorized	Capital paid-up	Revenue	Expense	Profit	Dividend
North China Development Co.	Nov. 1938; Japan special; Tokyo	Okinori kaya	350,000	218,461	18,303	15,356	2,947	6%
Hsingchung Co. (Kochu Koshi)	Dec. 1935; Japan ordinary; Peking	Tsuneo Yamanishi	10,000	10,000	67,130	63,409	3,721	6%
North China Transportation Co.	April, 1938; China special; Peking	Kanji Usami	300,000	239,700	220,414	220,223	191	—
Taku Transportation Co.	Feb. 1937; Japan ordinary; Tientsin	Eiji Yokota	6,000	6,000	2,070	1,863	207	6%
Tsingtao Wharf Co.	Sept. 1938; Japan ordinary; Tsingtao	Sakujiro Tsunoda	2,000	2,000	2,612	2,136	476	6%
North China Telephone & Telegraph Co.	July, 1938; China special; Peking	Otohiko Inouye	35,000	20,500	16,364	14,463	1,901	6%
North China Electric Co.	Nov. 1939; China special; Peking	Chu Hsing	100,000	49,750	4,916	3,781	1,135	5%
Inner Mongolia Electric Co.	May, 1938; Inner Mongolia special; Kalgan	Susumu Masuda	18,000	18,000	1,692	1,264	428	4%
Chiaokiao Electric. Co.	May, 1937; China ordinary; Tsingtao	Chang Chung-ho	8,000	8,000	2,313	1,612	701	12%

continued

Company	Year established; kind of organization; main office	President	Capital authorized	Capital paid-up	Revenue	Expense	Profit	Dividend
Tsinan Electric Co.	Feb. 1939; China ordinary; Tsinan	Chuang I-fu	4,000	2,000	1,010	678	332	8%
Chefoo Electric Co.	March, 1939; China ordinary; Chefoo	Chang Pen-cheng	2,000	1,200	784	649	135	6%
Tatung Coal Co.	Jan. 1940; Inner Mongolia special; Kalgan	Hsia Kung	40,000	33,750	6,152	9,691	-3,539	—
Chinghsing Colliery Co	July, 1930; China ordinary; Peking	Tsao Ju-lin	30,000	20,100				
North China Coal Sales Co.	Oct. 1940; China ordinary; Peking	Nobuo Yamamoto	20,000	10,000				
Inner Mongolia Mineral Sales Co.	July 1939; Inner Mongolia semi-special; kalgan	Tsuneyoshi Iwasaki	2,000	500				
Shantung Mining Co.	May, 1937; Japan ordinary; Tsingtao	Yoshishige Miyazawa	5,000	2,250	1,270	650	620	6%
Lungyen Iron Mining Co.	July, 1939; Inner Mongolia special; Kalgan	Lu Ching-ju	20,000	14,983	3,303	2,759	549	—
North China Alumina Mining Co.	Dec. 1939; China ordinary; Peking	Takuji Ogura	5,000	3,800	3,350	3,123	227	6%
North China Gold Mining Co.	April, 1938; Japan ordinary; Peking	Tatsuo Samejima	4,000	4,000	9	76	-67	—

continued

Company	Year established; kind of organization; main office	President	Capital authorized	Capital paid-up	Revenue	Expense	Profit	Dividend
North China Salt Co.	August, 1939; China ordinary; Tientsin	Keizo Uchida	25,000	16,250	5,845	4,821	1,024	5%
Shantung Electric Chemical Co.	Jan. 1941; Japan ordinary; Tsingtao	Tetsuji Kondo	800	800				
North China Raw Cotton Co.	March, 1938; Japan ordinary; Tientsin	Kunizo Sasaki	3,000	1,500	426	226	200	5%
Total capital of subsidiary companies:			639,800	465,083				

Appendix II. Central China Promotion Company and Subsidiaries, March 31, 1941 (In 1,000 yen)

Title	Year established; representative	Forms of organization	Capital subscribed capital paid-up	Latest business term ending	Gross income	Expense	Profits	Dividend rates
Central China Promotion Co.	November, 1938 Kenji Kodama, president	Special corp'n under Japanese law	100,000 45,000	December, 1940	3,419	2,582	837	6%

continued

Title	Year established; representative	Forms of organization	Capital subscribed capital paid-up	Latest business term ending	Gross income	Expense	Profits	Dividend rates
Central China Mining Co.	April, 1938 Koryo Isotani, chairman	Ordinary corp'n under Chinese law	20,000 20,000	October, 1940	7,332	6,050	1,282	8% for ordinary shares. 2% for special shares
Central China Hydro-Electric Co.	June, 1938 Tang Cheng-Po, chairman	Special corp'n under Chinese law	43,000 29,390	September, 1940	9,098	7,899	1,199	dividend passed
Shanghai Inland River Steamship Co.	July, 1938 Kyutaro Sugimoto, managing director	Ordinary corp'n under Chinese law	2,000 2,000	October, 1940	7,465	7,264	201	10% (excluding investments in kind)
Central China Telecommunication Co.	July, 1938 Ko Fukuda, chairman	Special corp'n under Chinese	15,000 15,000	October, 1940	9,828	7,684	2,144	6%
Central China Raw Silk Co.	July 1938, Kakusaburo Suzuki, managing director	Ordinary corp'n under Chinese law	10,000 6,500	October, 1940	80,409	77,496	2,913	10%

continued

Title	Year established; representative	Forms of organization	Capital subscribed capital paid-up	Latest business term ending	Gross income	Expense	Profits	Dividend rates
Shanghai Real Estate Co.	September, 1938 Chen Shao-nai, chairman	Special corp'n under Chinese law	20,000 15,000	September, 1940	1,195	734	461	6% (excluding Gov't shares)
Central China Urban Motor Bus Transportation Co.	November, 1938 Yang-Hsiao-tseng, chairman	Ordinary corp'n under Chinese law	3,000 2,264	October, 1940	3,428	3,318	110	6%
Central China Marine Products Co.	November, 1938 Chojiro Taguchi, managing director	Ordinary corp'n under Chinese law	5,000 3,165	October, 1940	2,001	1,279	722	10%
Greater Shanghai Gas Co.	November, 1938 Michi Ichiara, managing director	Ordinary corp'n under Chinese law	3,000 900	October, 1940	5	118	−113	dividend passed
Central China Railways Co.	May, 1939 Makoto Den, president	Special corp'n under Chinese law	50,000 33,815	March, 1940	3,726	3,854	−128	dividend passed
Hwaian coal Co.	June, 1939 Lu Yao, chairman	Ordinary corp'n under Chinese law	15,000 9,675	September, 1940	2,351	2,005	346	6%

continued

Title	Year established; representative	Forms of organization	Capital subscribed capital paid-up	Latest business term ending	Gross income	Expense	Profits	Dividend rates
Central China Salt Co.	August, 1939 Chang Chung-Chou, chairman	Special corp'n under the Chinese law	5,000 1,250	September, 1940	2,400	1,868	532	8%
Central China Steamship Co.	February, 1940 Su Yang-wen, chairman	Special corp'n under Chinese law	30,000 17,094	September, 1940	1,117	1,005	112	dividend passed
Combined capital of subsidiary companies			221,000 156,053		—	—	—	—

Appendix Ⅲ.

Fundamental Principles Governing the Development of North China Adopted by the North China Policy Committee Consisting of the Officials of the Japanese Planning Board, the Army and Navy, the Finance and Foreign Ministers, and the Manchurian Affairs Bureau, on December 24, 1937.

1. A special corporation will be established so that all the essential industries of North China may be effectively controlled.
2. The corporation will be formed under a scheme involving Sino-Japanese cooperation.
3. The North China development undertakings to be placed under the control of the special corporation will include railways, harbor and port construction, construction of highways, general transportation facilities, telephone and telegraph systems, the electric power industry, and the mining industry (including coal, iron, gold). Enterprises in the spinning industry, cotton growing and all other similar industries are to be free to private concerns.
4. The control corporation will be a holding company, under which many subsidiary corporations will be established under the Sino-Japanese joint plan in various lines.
5. Foreign capital will be invited to take part in these subsidiary corporations.
6. Regarding railway business in China, the proposed special corporation will obtain a franchise from the "Provisional Govern-

ment of the Republic of China", and, if necessary, a subsidiary railway company may be established in which the South Manchuria Railway may be allowed to invest. The authorities will arrange for the S. M. R. to offer technical and other assistance to the corporation, although the S. M. R. will not be allowed directly to operate any lines.

7. The coal mining industry will be partially operated by the railway company.

8. No definite decision has been made so far regarding the China Development Company, a subsidiary of the S. M. R., but it is understood that all investments of that company in the electric industry and development works in North China will be taken over by the control Corporation. Naturally, the China Development Company will have to be dissolved and all employees of the company will be transferred to the special control corporation.

Source: Tokyo dispatch by Reuter of December 20, 1937 published in *North China Herald*, Shanghai, January 5, 1938.

Appendix IV.

Organic Law of the North China Development Company Law No. 81

(Japan, 1938) Promulgated April 30, 1938

I. General Organization

1. The North China Development Company is a limited company established for the purpose of accelerating, controlling, and coordinating the economic development of North China.

The Head office of the company shall be in Tokyo.

2. The capital of the North China Development Company shall be ¥350,000,000, which may be increased at any time with the approval of the (Japanese) Government.

3. The (Japanese) Government shall invest in the North China Development Company to the extent of ¥175,000,000.

   The government investment may be in kind.

   The payment for the government shares may differ from that of the other shares.

4. The first payment for the shares subscribed shall not be less than one-sixth of the value of the shares, and the Government may, after the second installment, pay for its shares all in kind.

5. The capital of the company may be increased even before the original shares have been paid up.

6. The shares of the company shall be registered in the names of the holders.

7. The name of the North China Development Company shall not be imitated or used by any other company or commercial enterprise.

8. Changes in the articles of organization may only be made with the approval of the majority of shareholders at a meeting at which over half of the entire shares of the company are represented.

Ⅱ. Personnel

9. The North China Development Company shall have a governor, two deputy-governors, five or more directors, and two or more supervisors.

10. The governor represents the North China Development Company and exercises general control over the affairs of the company.

In the absence of the governor, one of the deputy-governors shall act in that capacity.

The deputy-governors and the directors assist the governor and, in accordance with the articles of the company, assume various duties or participate in the management of the company.

The supervisors supervise and examine the affairs of the company.

11. The governor and the deputy-governors shall be appointed by the (Japanese) Government with the approval of the Emperor.

The governor and deputy-governors shall hold office for five years.

The directors shall be elected by the shareholders for a period of three years.

12. The governor, deputy-governors, and directors holding active positions in the company shall not hold any concurrent positions or conduct other commercial enterprises.

13. The company may appoint a number of advisers.

The advisers shall offer opinion at the request of the governor.

The advisers shall be appointed by the company with the approval of the Government.

III. Scope of Enterprise

14. The company shall invest or advance money towards the following enterprises and shall also control and coordinate their func-

tions:

(a) Enterprises relative to communications, transportation, and harbor establishments.

(b) Telephone and telegraph enterprises.

(c) Electric power enterprises.

(d) Mining enterprises.

(e) Salt and relative enterprises.

(f) Other enterprises contributive to the economic development of North China which require special control and coordination.

IV. Debentures or Company Loans

15. The company shall have the privilege to issue debentures to the extent of five times the actual paid-up capital.

    When new debentures are being issued the above limit shall not apply but the old debentures must be refunded within one month after the issue of the new debentures.

    When issuing debentures the company need not be bound by Article 209 of the Commercial Law.

16. The approval of the Government must be obtained for the issuance of debentures by the company.

17. The Government shall guarantee the payment of the principal and interest of the company debentures.

18. The holders of the debentures of the North China Development Company shall enjoy priority rights in respect of the assets of the company in the redemption of the debentures.

V. Reserves

19. The company shall set aside for every fiscal year 8 percent of the profits as reserve capital and another 2 percent as a special reserve fund for the equalization of dividend returns.

VI. Government Supervision and Assistance

20. The functions of the company shall be supervised by the Government.

21. The company shall apply for government approval before issuing any debentures.

22. Decisions in regard to changes in the articles of organization, amalgamation or dissolution shall not be effective unless approved by the Government.

23. The company shall not dispose the profits unless with the approval of the Government.

24. The company shall compile budgets for investments and loans for every fiscal year and submit them one month before the beginning of the fiscal year to the Government for approval. In case important changes in the budget are to be made during a fiscal year the same procedure shall be followed.

25. The Government may issue necessary orders in regard to the supervision of the company's business enterprises or in regard to the coordination and adjustment of the company's enterprises in their relation to (Japan's) national defense and the economic development of North China.

When orders necessary in point of national defense are proclaimed by the Government in accordance with the foregoing provision, such losses as the company may sustain shall be compensated by the Government.

The aforesaid compensation payable by the Government shall not exceed the limit set by the Imperial Diet.

26. The Government shall appoint a government inspector to oversee the business of the company. The government inspector shall have the right to inspect the treasury and books, documents, and other articles of the company.

The Government inspector may order the company to submit reports and figures regarding the business conditions of the company should be deem it necessary.

The government inspector has the right to attend shareholders' meetings and other conferences and to present his opinion.

27. The Government may invalidate the decisions of the company or discharge the staff members of the company in case the decisions or actions should be found to have contravened the law or other measures or regulations based in law.

28. In case the profits of the company for any fiscal year should be insufficient to pay a dividend of 6 percent on private-owned shares, no dividend shall be paid on the government shares.

29. In case the profits of the company should fall below 6 percent for any fiscal year, the (Japanese) Government shall for the first five years undertake to make up the difference in the amounts obtained as follows:

(a) The amount resulting from the total of commercial shares as multiplied by the difference between 6 percent and the percentage of profit mentioned above.

(b) The amount obtained from the total of debentures as multiplied by the difference between 5 percent and the percentage of profit mentioned above.

In the distribution of profits if the dividend for the commercial shares should exceed 6 percent, the excess amount should be uesed for the purpose of refunding the Government for the money advanced in the above connection.

The calculation of profits received from the total investment and the portions of commercial shares and debentures (company loans) of the total investment shall be determined by a separate Government order.

30. In case the profits for the commercial shares should exceed 6 percent and in case the distribution of the excess profits could not be equalized between the government and commercial shares, the distribution shall be made on the basis of five to one.

31. The company shall be exempt from income and business taxes for ten years as from the first year after the year in which the company begins to do business.

32. The company shall be exempt from the local taxes of Hokkaido and other local administrations within the period specified above.

33. When registration taxes are to be collected at the time of the or-

ganization of the company, of the increasing of the capital, of an amalgamation or of the registration of paid-up capital after the second installment, the unit of impost shall be one-third of the actual amount of paid-up capital or of the actual amount of the paid-up capital increased or of the actual amount paid each time towards the shares.

Ⅶ. Penalties

34. In case the company should have been found to have violated these articles of organization or such other orders or measures promulgated by the Government on the basis of this law, fines of one hundred yen to two thousand yen shall be imposed on the governor or the deputy-governor acting for or in the capacity of the governor. In matters relative to the duties of the deputy-governor or directors, similar penalties shall be imposed.

Article 206 - 208 of the Law Governing Procedures in Non-contentious Matters shall apply in the imposition of the penalties above-mentioned.

Source: *The Chinese Year Book, 1938 - 39*, Council of International Affairs, Chungking, 1939, pp. 244 - 247.

Appendix Ⅴ.

Summary of the Diet Bill for the Central China Promotion Company Submitted to Lower House on March 18, 1938

1. General

The Company shall be organized as a joint-stock company for the purpose of investing in, and financing, enterprises relating to the public welfare and the promotion of industrial development of the region. The company shall have its main offices in Shanghai.

The company shall be capitalized at ¥100,000,000, half of which will be subscribed by the Japanese Government. Part of the Government holdings may be invested in kind. This company may increase its capital on approval by the Government.

2. Officers

The company shall have one governor, one vice-governor, three or more directors and two or more auditors. The governor and vice-governor shall be appointed by the government, and directors and auditors shall be elected from among shareholders, the election of directors being subject to official approval. Directors will function for four years.

3. Business

The company shall invest in, and finance, the following business:

(1) Transport enterprises;

(2) Communications;

(3) Electric power, gas and water supply;

(4) Mining;

(5) Aquatic products;

(6) Other enterprises relating to public utility and industry.

Under special circumstances, the Government may manage the aforementioned enterprises.

4. Debentures

The company may issue debentures, subject to official sanction, to the value of five times the paid-up capital.

The Government may guarantee payment of interest on and the principal of the debentures.

5. Official Supervision and Assistance

The Government may place a supervising official at the company.

The company may contract loans and dispose of profits on approval of the Government. (Other provisions resemble those of the North China Development Company).

Source: *Monthly Circular*, Mitsubishi Economic Research Bureau, Tokyo, April 1938, pp. 19 – 20.

WAR-TIME ECONOMIC
RECONSTRUCTION IN CHINA

I

Two years of prolonged war have brought about fundamental changes in the social and economic structure of China. The retreat from the coastal provinces to the interior is economic as well as military. As a result of foreign economic penetration China had, since the forties, concentrated her economic development rather artificially along the coastal regions and the Yangtze Valley, leaving the interior provinces untouched by modernizing influences. The necessities of the war compelled a reconsideration of this anomalous situation. The industrial, commercial and financial centers along the coastal belt and the Yangtze River had been largely occupied by enemy forces. The interior provinces, it was realized, must be rapidly developed in order to reinforce the military requirements. This shifting of the center of China's economic development calls for a new consideration of the aims towards which China's new economic order must strive and of the methods by which it can be attained. China can no longer consider the aim of "people's livelihood" as the primary objective;

she must now first develop her national ressources, both human and material, with a view to strenthening her national defence and increasing her economic self-sufficiency. Both aims cannot be realized without increasing the exercise of governmental control over the nation's economic activities; nor could they be carried out if these activities be not closely coordinated. The new economic order that is emerging in the interior provinces at present will, therefore differ from that of pre-war days both in the aims to be pursued and in the methods to be followed. In the present article a brief survey of developments in these respects will be given.

II

For the reinforeement of national defence the first task in an undeveloped region must be the introduction of a modern system of transportation, especially railways and highways. Up to the end of February 1939. China, though she had lost 6,500 of her 9,700 kilometers of railways, was building under the Ministry of Communications about 6,000 kilometers of new lines in the interior provinces of the southwest, covering Hunan, Kwangsi, Yunnan, Szechuan, and Kweichow. Two lines, Yunnan-Burma and Szechuan-Yunnan, are designed to provide international outlets for China, leading to Haiphong in Indo-China and Rangoon in Burma. Other railway lines, including the Hunan-Kwangsi, Hunan-Kweichow, Kweichow-Kwangsi, and Chengtu-Chungking, will serve the double purpose of military mobilization and economic development.

The construction of railways is a slow and costly process, and must proceed side by side with the building of highways for meeting the emergency needs of the war. From 1931 to 1937 China built 110,000 kilometers of highways. Since the war began, the Central Government has built 4,700 kilometers of roads in addition to those constructed by the various provincial governments, of which Kiangsu alone contributed 2,000 kilometers for military purposes. Besides, existing roads in the southwestern and northwestern provinces, with a kilometrage of 14,700 have been improved upon, the most important being the Yunnan-Burma Road with a length of about 1,000 kilometers; while new roads, having a kilometrage of 3,000 in the same regions, are now under construction.

The building of heavy industries is another fundamental measure from the viewpoint of national defence. True, China had a number of arsenals for the manufacture of ammunitions and other war supplies; but these arsenals depend mainly upon imported materials and are in a position to produce only rifles, machine-guns, bombs, and bullets, instead of field guns, tanks and other heavy pieces. Attemps to build the heavy industries can be traced back as early as the nineties (when the Hanyehping Iron and Steet Works was first established in Hankow); and shortly before the present war, the ammonium sulphate plant had already started operation in the vicinity of Nanking. These attempts were, after all, half-hearted, as the Chinese government did not have a comprehensive plan for developing the heavy industries until a year before the war. In July 1936 a three-year plan for heavy industries, calling for an annual production of 2,000 tons of ferro-tungsten, 300,000 tons of iron, 300,000 tons of steel, 3,600 tons of copper, 5,000 tons of lead and zinc, 1,500,000 tons of coal, 25,000,000 gallons of gasoline, 50,000 tons of ammonium sulphale, as well as power machinery and electrical supplies, was proposed by the National Resources Commission, requiring a total capital outlay of $230,000,000 to be derived from appropriations by the National Treasury and from foreign investments. The plan was in full swing in various parts of China, particularly in the three provinces of Hunan, Hupeh, and Kiangsi, when the war broke out. An immediate removal of the heavy industries from threatened areas was deemed imperative. The work involving 2,000 staff members, 80,000 laborers, and a considerable loss of time, equipment and buildings, was effected after July. Today, many of the mines and industrial plants have resumed operation in various parts of Szechuan, Yunnan, Kweichow and other provinces; and are producing a variety of war supplies including coal, iron, steel, copper, ammunitions, elelctric power and supplies, and substitutes for gasoline.

III

A second objective towards which China is striving is that of self-sufficiency. Although an agricultural nation, China has become less and less self-sufficient since her contact with the West in the forties. Her unfavorable balance of trade has tended to increase; in terms of million Haikwan taels, it was 1.5 in 1868; 3.6 in 1878; 32.4 in 1888; 50.5 in

1898; 117.8 in 1908; 166.9 in 1918; 204.6 in 1928; and 317.3 in 1934. This increase in import excess is doubly serious for an agricultural nation, in view of the mounting percentage which agricultural products claim in total imports. The percentage for the two groups of agricultural imports — food, drinks and tobacco as well as raw materials and partly manufactured goods — has increased from 14.21 in 1868 to 16.94 in 1931, a three-fold increase within less than sevety years.

In view of the increasing strain on the nation's finance since the outbreak of the war, import excess must no longer be allowed to take its own course. The regulation over China's foreign trade, with a view to reducing the import excess, constitutes therefore the first step towards the establishment of a self-sufficient economy. True, import excess has already shown a downward trend since the Shanghai War of 1932, falling successively, in terms of million dollars, from the peak of 867 in that year to 734 in 1933, 494 in 1934, 343 in 1935, and 236 in 1936. It remained at 123 during the first half of 1937, but with the outbreak of the war in July, an export excess of 8 million dollars was witnessed during the second half of the year. A similar situation occurred in 1938, when the import excess stood respectively at 121 and 4 million dollars for the first and the second half-years. The returns for the first quarter of 1939 gave an import excess of 78 million dollars, as compared with 97 and 31 million dollars for the same periods in 1937 and 1938. Thus, throughout the 21 months of a nation-wide war, China has been able to maintain its lowest level of import excess reached before the war broke out, despite her vastly increasing needs for foreign manufactured supplies to meet war demands, including such articles as cotton goods and wheat flour (the factories for the manufacture of these products have been largely destroyed by the war), machinery and tools, motor trucks, and gasoline. This favorable situation should be attributed chiefly to the war-time measures adopted to regulate China's foreign trade and exchange. Control over imports has been effected through regulations over the sale of foreign exchange by the Central Bank since March 14, 1938. In respect to exports, measures have also been adopted with a view towards acquiring foreign imports or exchange resources with which to pay for the imports. The Foreign Trade Commission has been entrusted with the two-fold task of acquiring foreign exchange from commercial export and of exporting staple commodities in exchange for foreign imports or foreign exchange. During 1938, the Commission approved commercial exports to the extent of $86,000,000; and exported during the year $45,000,000 worth of commodities on its own account, a part of which was disposed of on a barter basis.

Another step towards the establishment of a self-sufficient economy, more positive in character, is that of increasing the nation's productive power. In agriculture, an effort is made to increase the production of food and clothing crops for military and civilian needs, and of export crops for the acquisition of foreign exchange. The National Agriculturat Research Bureau extended during 1938 60,000 *mow*[①] of land for rice cultivation

---

① One *mow* is equivalent to 0.1518 acres.

in Hunan; 50,000 *mow* in Szechuan, 240,000 *mow* in Kwangsi and 700,000 *mow* in Kweichow for wheat cultivation; 70,000 *mow* in Szechuan and 52,000 *mow* in Yunnan for cotton cultivation. In Hunan 760,000 *mow* formerly devoted to the cultivation of glutinous rice was used for non-glutinous rice production; as glutinous rice, being a luxury crop for wine distilling, should be curtailed in output as much as possible during a time of war. Besides, main export crops such as raw silk in Szechuan, Yunnan, Kweichow and Kwangtung; tea in Anhwei, Kiangsi, Chekiang, Fukien, Hunan, Hupeh and the four southwestern provinces of Szechuan, Yunnan, Kweichow and Sikang, were improved upon and extended in area of production. In the financing and marketing of agricultural production, much work has been done by another governmental organization, the Agricultural Credit Administration. During the year 1938, it established 22 cooperative banks in Szechuan, 16 in Kweichow, 11 in Hunan, 17 in Kwangsi, 2 in Hupeh, and 17 others in the Japanese-occupied areas; 22 agricultural warehouses in Szechuan, 3 in Hunan, and 1 in Kweichow. Production loans were granted for farm irrigation in Szechuan, Sikang, Yunnan, Kweichow, Kwangsi and Shensi; for food production in Szechuan, Kweichow, Kwangsi, Kwangtung, Hunan, Hupeh, Honan and Shensi; and for cash crops (including tea, silk, ramie, raw cotton, wood oil and sugar cane) in Szechuan, Kweichow, Kwangtung, Anhwei and Hunan. The Administration also purchased, to serve military and civilian needs, large quantities of rice and wheat in Szechuan, Shensi, Hunan and Kwangsi; and raw cotton, cotton yarn and cotton cloth in Shensi, Hunan and Kwangsi; and raw cotton, cotton yarn and cotton cloth in Shensi, Hunan, Hupeh, Chekiang, Shanghai, Hankow and Hongkong.

In mining, production is being increased with two objects in view: the supply of basic minerals for war-time domestic needs and the export of minerals for the acquisition of foreign exchange. Both tasks are entrusted to the National Resources Commission, which is operating or planning to operate the following mines in various provinces: coal in Kiangsi, Hunan, Kwangsi, Szechuan, Yunnan, Kweichow, Hunan, Shensi and Kansu; mineral oil in Szechuan, Shensi and Kansu; iron in Szechuan, Yunnan and Hunan; copper in Szechuan, Sikang and Yunnan; lead and zinc in Hunan, Sikang and Yunnan; mercury in kweichow; gold in Chinghai, Szechuan, Honan, Sikang, Hunan and Kwangsi; tin in Yunnan, Kwangsi and Hunan; tungsten in Kiangsi, Hunan, Kwangtung and Kwangsi; and antimony in Hunan. Among these minerals, gold, mercury, tin, tungsten and antimony are designated largely for export.

In industry more than in mining reliance has to be placed for the moment more upon native handicrafts than on machine production, in view of the destruction of most of the modern industrial centers along the coast and the Yangtze Valley. Two governmental organizations have been at work in attempting to increase industrial production, in addition to the National Resources Commission mentioned above. The Industrial and Mining Adjustment Commission has been in charge of the removal of factories and mines from areas near military operations to the rear, and their rehabilitation through provision of financial and technical assistance.

Factories were at first removed from Shanghai, Wusih and other centers along the Lower Yangtze to Hankow and Chungking but, before the Japanese occupation of Hankow in October 1938, another removal to the further interior was imperative. In all, 341 factories, with machinery and equipment of over 100,000 tons, were removed to the following provinces, 142 to Szechuan, 110 to western Hunan, 20 to Shensi, 15 to Kwangsi and 54 to other provinces. The machines removed included 32,600 tons for textile factories, 8,000 tons for metal-working factories, 3,300 tons for electric supplies factories, 3,400 tons for porcelain factories, 2,200 tons for chemieal factories, and 8,600 tons for coal mines, in addition to the equipment of the Hanyehping Iron and Steel Works. Loans were made to 135 factories; and 5,300 tons of materials and supplies ware ordered for use by the removed factories.

Another organization, the Association for Chinese Industrial Cooperatives, was organized, with an appropriation of $5,000,000 from the Executive Yuan, in August 1938 at Hankow, and was removed to Chungking in January 1939. The principal function of the Association is to organize and finance small handicrafts after the cooperative pattern for wartime industrial production. Up to the end of March 1939, five branches have been established in the northwest, southwest, southeast, Szechuan-Sikang, and Yunnan districts, with 34 sub-branches, 432 cooperative societies, and 5,721 members, in the metallurgical, metal and machinery, chemical, building materials, clothing, food, vehicles, and other industries.

IV

The change in aims necessarily entails a corresponding change in method. In order to attain the new aims for China's war-time economy, military preparedness and self-sufficiency, new methods must be employed in place of the old. These methods call for a fundamental reorganization of the governmental machinery on the one hand, and a thorough-going improvement of private undertakings on the other.

In the fall of 1937, immediately after the outbreak of the war, three Adjustment Commissions on Agriculture, Industry and Mining, and Foreign Trade, and two Ministries on People's Econemy and on Heavy Industries were set up under the National Military Council to look after economic needs of the nation during the war. These commissions and ministries, it may be noted, existed side by side with the four Ministries on Industries, Finance, Railways, and Communications, the National Economic Council, and the National Reconstruction Commission of the National Government, as well as the National Resources Commission of the National Military Council. Soon it was discovered that much duplication in personnel and work had made the task of war-time economic mobilization difficult. Unless a reorganization were effected, the existence of two sets of organizations, respectively of the National Military Council and of the National Government, would have made smooth functioning impossible. This unhappy situation was probably unavoidable during the early stages of the war when the attention of the Government was centered primarily on military rather than economic and political activities. But after the occupation of Nanking by enemy forces in December 1937 and the subsequent removal of the capital to Chungking, events began to take a new turn. In Hankow, actually the seat of the Government until its fall in October 1938, the Government was thoroughly reorganized on a war-time basis. The two Ministries of the Military Council were abolished, while the three Adjustment Commissions, together with the National Resources Commission, were amalgamated with the two Ministries of Economic Affairs and Finance under the Executive Yuan of the National Government. The Ministry of Railways was absorbed by the Ministry of Communications, so also the Highway Bureau of the National Economic Council. A new ministry, that of Economic Affairs, was created, in order to take over the old Ministry of Industries, as well as the remaining Bureau of Hydraulic Engineering of the National Economic Council, the National Reconstruction Commission, the National Resources Commission, the two Adjustment Commissions on Agriculture and on Industry and Mining. The Foreign Trade Adjustment Commission of the Council was reorganized as the Foreign Trade Commission of the Ministry of Finance. In this way, a logical boundary line was set between the National Military Council and the Executive Yuan of the National Government. The Council became at once essentially a military organ engaged in military operations including military transportation, as well as the manufacture and provision of munitions and war supplies; while the Yuan, with its various Ministries, remained a civil body undertaking governmental activities not directly related to war operations. The Ministry of War belonging simultaneously to the Council and the Yuan, serves as a liaison between the two bodies. As the war develops, other organs have been added, including the Liquid Fuel Control Committee of the Executive Yuan and the Fuel Control Administration of the Ministry of Economic Affairs for the control of the supply and consumption of gasoline and coal; the Agricultural Extension Committee of the Yuan for agricultural extension, the Association for Industrial Cooperatives of the Yuan for the promotion of small industries; the Land and Water Transport Committee of the Yuan for the coordination of land and water transport; the Cooperative Administration of the Ministry of Economic Affairs for the promotion of cooperative organization; and finally, the Planning Commission of the Supreme National Defence Council for the examination and approval of all plans, whether economic or otherwise, related to war-time reconstruction.

The increasing control exercised by the Government over the nation's economic activities is a logical development of the War, especially in China where the basic economic structure has not been all too healthy. The Government, in imposing control from above, must have due regard to the improvement of the vast number of economic units below, whether agricultural, industrial, or commercial. At this juncture, the rapid development of rural cooperatives is especially encouraging. The Central Government has recently established a Cooperative Administration in the Ministry of Economic Affairs, while in the various provincial governments cooperative committees had been established in some cases even before the war. The Agricultural Credit Administration, engaged primarily in organizing cooperative banks and warehouses for agricultural financing and marketing, has played an important role in promoting the organization of agricultural cooperatives through its manifold activities, while the more recently organized Association for Industrial Cooperatives is attempting to do in the field of industrial cooperatives in towns and villages. In the field of industry and commerce, the Ministry of Economic Affairs has worked out a set of regulations governing the organization of trade associations for merchants, manufacturers and exporters, promulgated on July 13, 1938. These three types of trade associations are to constitute the basic units by means of which government economic control in towns and cities can be exercised from top to bottom. Their organization for "important" branches is compulsory whenever a certain number of members can be found in each locality; and members of trade associations are simultaneously members of the Chamber of Commerce in the locality. Counly or municipal Chambers are to unite in the organization of a provincial Chamber, and provincial chambers are to unite in the organization of a national chamber. In this way, a network of economic cells can be set up, vertically by geographical gradation and horizontally by trade for urban commerce and industry, just as the agricultural and industrial cooperatives constitute the basic economic units for peasants and craftsmen in the villages and market towns.

V

Whatever might be the outcome of the war, the new economic order that has been emerging for more than a year in the interior provinces will continue to develop. The vast area that these provinces cover cannot be simultaneously exploited, and the factors to be considered in their exploitation must include availability of raw materials, facility of transport, the supply of motive power, and the accessibility to markets. In the six southwestern provinces of Hunan, Kwangsi, Yunnan, Kweichow, Szechuan and Sikang, and the northwestern provinces of Shensi, Kansu and Chinghai, ten centers have been chosens for economic development and industrialization by the Ministry of Economic Affairs, after a careful consideration of the above-mentioned factors. Of these centers the most important are the Chungking-Chikiang area in central Szechuan; the Tokiang-Minkiang area in southwestern Szechuan (surrounded in the south by the Yangtze River, in the west by the To River, and in the east by the Min River, with the famous Tseliuchin salt district and the Weiyuan iron district as the northern boundary); the Kunming-Yimeng-Lufeng area in central Yunnan; and the Yuanling-Shunch'i area in western Hunan; the other areas are the Sian-Paochi area in central and western Shensi; the Kweilin area in northeastern Kwangsi; the Wanhsien-Changshaw area in eastern Szechuan; the Kweiyang area in central Kweichow; the Kanting-Taining-Taofu area in eastern Sikang; and the Kansu-Chinghai area.

The extent to which the new economic order may succeed depends upon many factors, some of them are hard to foretell. Aside from the vicissitudes of war and international developments within the immediate future — both of which will undoubtedly have considerable bearing upon any attempt at reconstruction — man-power, resources, and organization must be given the primary consideration. The supply of technical ability to plan and to direct new enterprises, as well as the availability of skilled and unskilled labor to carry them out, have assumed increasing importance with the progress of economic development. The great demand for college graduates and technical ability of a higher order at present is a hopeful sign but it indicates the existence of the important question of an insufficient supply of trained personnel to undertake the work of reconstruction. After two years of prolonged warfare, China, bound by centuries of custom and tradition, has not as yet resorted to woman labor to replace the men in the front for large-scale productive employment. The shortage of labor is nevertheless a universal complaint among manufacturers mine-owners, and other classes of entrepreneurs. As to natural resources, the southwestern and northwestern provinces, although fairly richly endowed, are less opulent in comparison with the areas now occupied by the Japanese. Coal and iron, the key minerals to any large-scale industrialization, are deficient in these areas; and, owing to the greater dependence on land rather than on water transport, the cost of transportation in these areas is prohibitive. In respect to organization, a great deal has been achieved in bringing about close coordination and greater efficiency since the outbreak of the war, but much still remains to be desired. Duplication of organization and the overlapping of authority on the part of the Governmental agencies necessarily result in delay and waste; while the task of crystallizing the numerous economic cells in agriculture, industry and trade is always an immense one in a country where village and town economy has continued to prevail for ages.

In short, China is decidedly entering upon a new epoch—Under the effective leadership of Generalissimo Chiang Kai-shek, a new page has been turned in the history of China. The moment for China's rejuvenation has at last appeared, but no one will deny that the task ahead is replete with difficulties and uncertainty. "Simultaneous Resistance and Reconstruction" is the aim towards which every Chinese is striving, though the obstacles to its attainment are tremendous.

今日西南各省之衣的问题

方显廷　毕相辉

民生四大要素，衣居其一焉。衣之原料，就吾国一般情形而论，当以棉织布匹为主，其他丝织、麻织、毛织等品，虽亦为民用所需，然普遍性远不如棉布。试以西南各省之情形证之，西南制丝与丝织品大抵以供输出，产量微小，消费有限；毛织绝少生产，消费尤限于特殊用途或特殊阶级；麻织布匹如夏布则不仅产量不多，且服用亦为季节所限。然观棉纺织品，则平时不仅有巨量之自产，且有巨额之输入，以供民衣，其普遍之程度可想见矣。以普遍程度之不同，故因供需失调所影响于社会民生与夫市场经济之动态者，棉布遂又远较其他衣被原料为严重。是故抗战以来，西南各省，因棉布之消费增加，供给呆滞，或原料短缺，衣被之供给遂成为战时问题之一，本文目的，即以棉布为范围，略论今日西南各省之衣的问题及其解救之途径。

吾人估计西南棉布消费量，不能以全国人民平均棉布消费量为基准。盖西南偏处一隅，社会经济地位落后，人民购买能力较低，加以民风朴俭，气候和暖，当地土织棉布，坚韧耐用，凡此皆有使西南人民之棉布消费量降在全国平均数以下之可能性。按照严中平氏之精密估算，在抗战前夕，全国人民每人消费机织棉布（十二磅布）四码，消费手织棉布十码，共十四码。若将手织棉布亦换算为十二码布，则全国人民平均每人消费十二磅布九.九码。由是言之，西南平均棉布消费量，当在九.九码以下。

计算一地棉布之消费数量，应根据：一、当地棉布之历年产销数量；及二、当地棉布之历年净输入数量。而欲求当地棉布之产销数量，又应根据：一、当地历年棉花产销数量；二、当地历年棉花净输入数量；三、当地历年棉纱产销数量；及四、当地历年棉纱净输入数量。根据此数种基本数字，然后以其他必要资料（如棉絮消费量，织布以外之棉纱消费量等等）相互考核，吾人对于棉布消费始可获得详实之计算。以西南各省统计资料之缺乏及今日收集资料之困难，欲循此理想之途以从事研究，实难收功。今兹所述，仅就可能收集之资料为近似之推算而已。

吾人根据四川渝万两关之花纱布输入统计及四川省政府建设厅之川省棉产统计计算二四至二六年度该省每年棉纱进口为二六一，七五六公担，棉布进口为九八，七四四公担，棉花进口为二，五四四公担，棉花生产为二三八，一八五公担，以此为基准，抗战前夕川省棉布之需求量可以推算而得。一、以输入棉布之重量折纱，更以纱量折合十二磅布（长四十一码，宽三五吋，纱重一一.二磅）为一，九〇四，八一六匹。二、自输入棉纱总量核减织布以外之棉纱消耗量，同样折合十二磅布为四，五〇八，三八三匹。三、自生产及输入皮棉总量，核减棉絮消耗，折合纱量，更以纱折成十二磅布为二，〇五二，二六五匹。总计川省平时输入及生产棉布共为八，四六五，四六四匹，相等于此项布匹所需之棉纱为二二五，七四五包。西康布匹需求，大体仰赖于四川之供给，故上项数字可视为川康两省平时纱布需求量。

贵州生产皮棉年仅四万余市担，输入几绝无，此少额自产皮棉，除供给当地人民棉絮消费之外，当更无手纺棉纱之生产。更根据黔省各路纱布输入统计，每年输入棉纱约一七，五八〇包，输入各种大小不同之布匹共二，一四八，三九六匹。自输入棉纱总量核减织布以外之棉纱消费，以之折合十二磅布，约为五七六，八四三匹。（按该省建厅统计，自产布匹为二，二〇九，一八五匹。但其中除少量宽幅布之外，每匹重量至高不过二市斤，约二.三磅；今以吾人所计算十二磅布之数量，折合建厅所发表之轻量布匹，其数差相合符。）至于输入布匹总量按其大小轻重换算为十二磅布，约为八四三，三一〇匹。总计贵州输入及自产布匹（合十二磅布）为一，四二〇，一五三匹，相当棉纱三七，八七一包。

更言广西，根据有关方面之报告，平时该省每年棉纱净输入三七，六〇〇包，棉布按十二磅布核计八八八，一四九匹，输入皮棉三，四〇〇市担，自产皮棉三二，三六四市担。计输入棉纱核减织布以外之消耗外，约可织十二磅布一，二二六，〇七二匹；输入皮棉与生产皮棉合计，核减棉絮消费，约可织十二磅布一八，四八六匹。总计广西省输入及自产布匹（十二磅）凡二，一三二，七〇七匹，相当于此项布匹之棉纱五六，八七一包。

云南花纱布供需情形，吾人迄无资料足资参证，若根据上述各省棉布需求数字估计，则平均川康黔桂四省每人消费十二磅布六.四码，衡诸云南人口，则云南棉布需求量应为（十二磅布）一，七八六，五五九匹，相当棉纱四七，六四一包。

综观以上情形，吾人对于平时西南各省纱布需求可以窥得其轮廓，即西南五省人口八八，九三三，三一九人，平时每年消费棉布总量约为十二磅布一三，八〇四，八八三匹，相当棉纱三六八，一二八包。若就织而言，川康黔桂四省，自产八，三八二，〇四九匹，占四省布匹需求量之六九%；若就纺织而言，则川康黔桂四省自纺自织布匹凡二,〇七五,七五一匹,占四省布匹需求量之一七%。易言之,川康黔桂四省棉纱之自给率仅有一七%,而棉布之自给率则达六九%。

西南平时棉布及其原料之供需情形,略如上述。抗战已还,西南人口增加,棉布需求数量自亦随之增大,关于战时西南人口异动,迄无准确之调查,据各方估计,西南五省战时人口增加净数(即减去因战事外移者)至多为一百万人。以平时棉布消费量(每人平均六.四码)衡之,一百万人之棉布需求为一六三,四一四匹,相当棉纱约四,三五六包,为数尚不甚巨。但西南战时棉布供给上之较大负担实尚不在此,而在军用布匹之供应。迄今为止,战时全国全年军用布匹为数达十四磅布与十六磅布共三百万匹,折合十二磅布约三,四八二,一四三匹,即以西南五省负担其半数而论,亦达一,七四一,〇七二匹,相当棉纱四六,四二九包,此盖战时新增之主要棉布需求。总计西南战时棉布之新增需求凡一,九〇四,四八六匹,相当棉纱五〇,七八五包。以之与平时需求量合计,则为棉布一五,七〇九,三六九匹,相当棉纱四一八,九一三包。

供应此项棉布需求,端赖自产与输入。依吾人推算西南四省(川康黔桂)平年有产布八,三八二,〇四九匹之手织能力,设使酌增效率将织造能力提高三〇%,且就五省而言,每年手织出布一〇,八九六,六六四匹,似属可能。此外合计内迁、新设、旧有之动力织机,开足全工,约有一千台左右。按普通生产速率,其每年产额,亦有达八〇〇,〇〇〇匹之可能。所剩须赖输入供给之棉布约四,〇一二,七〇五匹。然为实现此一千余万(一一,六九六,六六四)匹之本地生产,必须供给棉纱三一一,九一〇包。西南今日所有棉纺工业设备,包括内迁、新增、旧有各纱锭,假定其于二十九年六月底全部开工,为数仅近一七〇,〇〇〇锭,即依其全部生产能力计算,每年所能供给之棉纱亦不过二五,〇八一包。此外西南民间土纺照平时川桂二省生产能力增产三〇%计算,亦有纺造棉纱七一,二三八包之可能。两共一八六,三一九包,为西南棉纱生产能力之供给量。其不足供应西南织布能力者尚达一二五,五九一包之巨。同时为供应西南全部棉纺能力之消耗,必须有皮棉七七一,八九五市担,西南五省生产皮棉除供给必要之棉絮外,能用作棉纱原料者,为数仅一九〇,二六三市担。故为供应棉纺能力,尚须输入皮棉五八一,六三二市担。总之如以保持并利用西南现有之花纱布生产能力为标准,而求西南战时棉布需供之平衡,则亟待设法解决者有棉花不足额五八一,六三二市担,棉纱不足额一二五,五九一包,棉布不足额四,〇一二,七〇五匹。西南衣的问题之是否严重化,大体上亦以能否输入上述数量之花纱布为断。

不过尚有数种情形亦应予计及者:一、吾人对于西南棉布生产能力之计算,系以乡村或家庭工业型之手织为主,此项蕴藏之生产能力,历年以来,实已走上衰落之途,其技术较机织低下,品类亦极陈旧不入时式,设使不加以适当之鼓励与改良,则维持战前旧有水准且不易,遑论增产三〇%。二、吾人对于西南棉纱生产能力之计算,系按现有厂纺设备之最高限度及尽量利用土纺而言。纺纱工人技术一项吾人完全未予计及。同时现下开工锭数亦且距最高限度甚远。以本年五六月间之情形而论,西南五省开工锭数不过一万五千枚,能否于廿九年六月全部开足,尚成问题。而土纺能力之尽量利用,必需鼓励改良始可达到目的,情形与手织相同。设若棉纱棉布之生产能力未臻预定之程度,则棉花之输入量虽可较上列数字略减,然棉纱棉布输入量势须更增。例如以二十八年之情形而论，假设手织土纺之生产能力已各顺利获得三〇％之增产效率，然厂纺之实际生产能力不过一万余包，机械之实际生产能力亦不过二〇〇，〇〇〇匹，因纺纱能力之低，虽输入棉花一四六，九六三市担即已敷用，然棉纱输入因此势须增至二一二，四一二包，棉布输入势须增至四，六一二，七〇五匹（棉布应输入量，以本年军用布匹曾于去年有充足之储存，约可减少一百万匹，故实际应输入棉布量约为三，六一二，七〇五匹。为数之巨，仍属可观）。

是故就纱织能力已达到现有设备之最高限度而言，则需要输入巨量棉花，就目下纱织能力水准而言，则需要输入巨量棉纱，同时无论纺织能力若何，均需输入巨量布匹。无疑，设使吾人一旦能扩充织布生产能力使增产四，〇一二，七〇五匹，扩充纺纱生产能力使增产一二五，五九一包，更推广棉田棉产使增产五八一，六三二市担，则供需既得平衡，自无赖乎输入。然而吾人从多方面推算，欲达到西南花纱布之完全自给，必须于西南五省改良现有棉田，使其产量能自五八九，九四〇市担增至七九六，二七六市担，必须推广棉田五，五七二，一一二市亩，使能增产皮棉一，三七一，九〇三市担；必须添置动力纱锭四四六，一八六枚，使西南五省有总锭数六一五，一八六枚，藉以生产一五，七〇九，三六九匹棉布所需之棉纱四一八，九一三包，必须增加织造能力使增产棉布四，〇一二，七〇五匹。为达到此项目的，如以动力机计算，尚需推广五，〇一六台，如以手织机计算，尚需推广约一四，〇〇〇台。吾人为避免动力机器设备之巨费，甚可从推广手织机着手，以求易举，如是则于西南五省旧有手织基础之上更推广布机一万余台，其事尚非过于艰巨。至于增置纱锭四十余万枚及推广棉田五百余万市亩，则其工作之艰难，殆将超过今日轻言增产者所能想像矣。

综而观之，吾人欲解决西南棉纱织品之供需失调，增产问题固为迫切，然根据目前事实，则输入问题，实同一重要。就增产之难易言之，花纱远较严重于棉布；然若就输入之难易言之，则以棉纱生产能力低微，致棉花需求量缩小，而棉纱需求量增大，遂使棉纱输入之需要亦增，同时随棉纱之供给减少，棉布之输入非益复增加不可，故棉布问题遂转较严重于棉纱，棉纱问题又转较严重于棉花。此皆上举二十八年度供需数字之所能切实证明者也。

花纱布输入问题之臻于严重，今日西南运输之困难，当为主要原因，而输入来源之限制，外汇价格之浮动，及汇水之高额，亦均有以促成之。关于今日西南运输能力之分析，与乎抗战后西南花纱布实际运入之数量，本文皆未遑为具体之剖述。惟根据经营棉纺织业之专家估计，二十八年中西南棉花输入，约可达六十万市担，此对于一年内棉花实际需求，已形超过，故大致本年度棉花之供给不成问题。然棉纱则二十八年度内约只能输入六万包（每日五千包）；棉布约只能输入三十六万匹（每月三万匹），前者视二十八年度需要输入数量（二一二，四七二包）不足十五万包，后者以棉纱输入之减少，其供给不足程度更将由前述三百六十余万匹增为八百余万匹，以与可能输入三十六万匹相抵，不足额将达七百余万匹之巨。不过上年关于运输能力之估计固未必十分详确，同时西南运输设备亦迄在不断改进中，故纱布可能输入数量，势可因而增大，抑更有一点吾人尤须特别注意者，即布匹需求，原富于极大之弹性，时至今日，或因购买能力降低，或因价格高涨，工资昂贵，或因迁徙频仍，生活不安，或因货质低下，不合消费心理，凡此均足招致消费之减少。盖衣被非破敝不堪御体，则新物之添置，殊有伸缩之余地故也。设使战时因上述各种原因，致使棉布需求减少于平时四分之一，则前述西南战时棉布需求以人口及军用增加而视平时之一三，八〇四，八八三匹增为一五，七〇九，三六九匹者，势且将减少为一二，二一七，二九五匹（军用布匹未照减），如是，则即使按照上文估计之运输能力，西南棉布问题实已大见缓和。故实际上本年度花纱布不足额之估计，犹有待于更精确之材料，本文所言，仅就平时消费基准作比较而已。然自另一方面言之，此种基于需求弹性所发生之消费减少现象，其本身实已表示消费欲望之受限制，与夫供给减少现象之存在。自此种意义言之，战时西南衣的问题之严重，固仍未消灭也。

吾人试观二十七年一月以来重庆市花纱布市价之变动：计棉花二十七年一至七月之四〇~五〇元，涨为八月之七七元，更涨为十月以至今年四月之百元左右，迨后（五六两月）虽略反跌为约九十元，但七月以来又复涨至四月之水准，棉纱（二十支四品达）自二十七年一月之三八五元涨至五月之四八〇元，更涨为七月之七八〇元，自九月以迄今年四月，则徘徊于八八〇元左右，五月以后，更复突破一千元关，逐涨至七月之一，二〇七元，最近尤达一，三〇〇~一，四〇〇元之高峰。布匹以白市布为例，则自二十七年一月之十七元渐涨至今年四月之三十八元，五月以后迄目前为止更逐步高涨为五〇元左右，其他布匹市价在同期间之涨风亦类似。按其逐步狂涨之情形，则今后各项价格尤其纱布价格将犹有更高峰出现，可以预测。西南衣被问题之严重，于此显然可见。

在西南花纱布增产未遑之今日，衣被问题之重心，尤系于输入之困难已如上述。欲解除此种困难，势必待运输技术与设备之改良增进，货品来源之开辟，与夫汇价汇水关系之稳定。至于如何增进运输能力，开辟货品来源，则不属本文范围，于此无待细述。惟有二事足以提供解决棉布供给问题之参考者：

第一，布匹之需求既富弹性，吾人为谋供需关系之改善，既可利用此种伸缩性而为之有计划地统筹分配与供给，使需求限于必要，供给得其平均。第二，棉纱质地之相当降低，不但不妨碍布匹之消费，反可节省原料，增产成品，如限制十六磅布减为十四磅乃至十二磅，固于消费无损，而原料之消耗则藉以节约甚多。凡此二端皆可以人力促成，而有待乎吾人之努力者。

吾人固非弃置增产问题不谈。反之，吾人以为设法统筹供给，同时即应设法进行增产。关于花纱布增产计划，时论多抒高见，吾人于此不加赘述。惟有一点敢促时贤注意者：第一，增产应勿以区域自给为准，若就各省省境限际以为自给之筹谋，是显与经济原理相背。例如吾人深知西南棉产之改进与推广，事实上有种种障碍，然西北固为我棉产丰富适宜之区，则如何拟具统一之增产计划，互相调剂。其事转较强求西南棉花自给为切实。第二，吾人今日一方面深感动力机械费资庞巨，设备艰难，而另一方面民间劳力技术复有过剩与弃置，故吾人设能将手织土纺推广于民间，则不仅纺织品克以增产，同时农民之工艺技术亦得藉以提高，农村工业化亦得藉资推进，此亦设计增产时所不可忽视者也。

论粮食统制

经济统制,战时较平时重要;粮食统制,尤为战时经济统制之要图。此观乎二次欧洲大战之经验,尤属信而有征,无待申论。

我国抗战,已逾一战,经济统制,虽因种种困难,进展较缓,然究有相当之推动,独于粮食统制,则直至最近始加注意。我国粮食生产,素告缺乏,平时既赖入超以资调剂,战时因海口先后被敌封锁,及生产因兵祸与兵役而备遭摧残,其供需之失调,更见严重。在此情形之下,粮食统制之进行反见落后,宁非怪事?此种矛盾现象,一经分析,自然不难发现其存在之理由:第一,我国缺米省份如浙闽粤等,大都沦陷敌手,故洋米仍可源源输入,以资调剂。第二,后方西南西北各省,对于粮食生产,过去类多自给自足,不虞匮乏。

然自今春以来,后方粮食问题,亦渐见其严重,滇越滇缅两路被封以后,宜昌又告失守,交通路线相继断绝,货物来源,渐感枯竭,益以禁烟之影响,于是后方游资,遂有集中于粮食囤积之势。昆明米价暴涨,于客冬已开其端;本年夏季,复以雨水不调,致川省稻米,亦呈歉收之象。加以空袭频仍,损失至巨,米商裹足不前,而造成七八九月间渝蓉两市米价之飞涨。九月初旬渝市米价三日间竟自每旧斗(约合二.八市斗)二十二元涨至三十元左右,磁器口一带且全无米可买。至此粮食统制之呼声,始随米价之高涨,而遍闻于后方川滇等省。中央开设全国粮食管理局于行政院隶辖之下，八月一日开始办公。八月十四日该院决议禁止囤积居奇，并通过统一缉私办法。九月十一日，委座发表告川民书，谓□实施粮食管理，"具有比执行禁烟与剿匪还要严格的决心"，且订定捐助军粮奖励办法："凡是缴纳谷子捐助军粮在一千担以上的，给一等奖章，九百担以上的给二等奖章，如此逐段推到捐助在一百担以上的，就给予第十等奖章；至于一百担以下的捐户，也分别给予奖状。"九月十四日，重庆市政府复颁布各镇临时米店及临时联合米市组织办法及社会局奖励购运食米办法。十月一日，渝市粮食管理委员会成立，四日在全国粮食管理局领导之下，全川分区举行粮食会议。川黔粤等省之粮食管理局，遂亦相继成立。至十七日重庆《大公报》在"从粮食管理得来的教训"社评中，至谓："最近粮食管理，实行并不久，可以说才在创始的初步，然而现在业已有了确实的成效。就陪都说，来源充畅，而市价稳跌，社会上无形的忧虑，因而一扫。这一点初步的成功，在抗战建国全局上，其意义却十分重大。我们对这一点，认为是极可宝贵的教训，值得特别表扬。"由此以观，三年来未经注意之粮食统制，遂一跃而为全国上下所重视之中心问题矣。

粮食统制之真谛，在粮食素具入超之我国，自治本言，不外促进生产；自治标言，不外调剂供需。促进生产之方法，举其要者有二：即（一）增加种植面积；（二）增加每亩产量。增加种植面积之道分：（甲）开垦荒地；（乙）利用冬季休闲，或将原种其他农作物土地改种粮食。增加每亩产量之道分：（甲）改良品种，防制病害；（乙）增辟蓄水池塘，防制旱灾并利农田灌溉；（丙）改良农具，应用机械，俾使大规模生产。上述办法，在平时固可不计速效，逐步推行，在战时则非择要施行不可。如垦荒为积年累月之大计，非一蹴可几,改种尚可于短期内付诸实行,改良品种与增辟池塘,亦为久长之计,至应用机械,以提高产量,则更非抗战期间所能举办。委座于告川民书中虽谓:"政府鉴于今年粮价的失调,现在力谋各种粮食作物生产的增加,并决定增加农田灌溉的贷款,改善蓄水的方法,限制不必要农产的种植,从种植方法增加产粮的地亩",然而欲期上述办法早日收效,则尚有待于切实之努力。

治标之方在调剂供需,俾后方粮食,得畅流无阻。考后方粮食,本应不虞匮乏。据中央农业实验所之推测,去年我国米谷生产,后方十五省共计约七万五千万市担,至本年米谷收获时为止(十月),计共消费至多不过七万万市担,则所余者尚有五千万市担,再加前年余存至少亦约五千万市担,合计约有一万万市担以上,足可维持食用至今年年底(见八月二十三日重庆《大公报》)。其所以缺乏之原因,不外下列四端:(一)经济上原因:乡民不愿粜谷得钱,因(甲)各种日用品价格过昂,有无物可买之势;(乙)现在存款利息过低,存钱不如存谷,不致受货币膨胀之损失。(二)运输上原因:乡村劳力除服兵役及从事工业外,现正农忙,故劳力供给,颇成问题。(三)加工上原因:乡村无暇碾米供给都市,而都市自身之碾米能力,复极不足。(四)心理上原因:一般农民见都市缺米,遂各图自保,于是产米者既不出售,需米者复思多存备用,同时奸商乘机囤积,企图谋利。综上四因,遂造成目下乡村有米都市无米之畸形现象。至补救办法,据全国粮食管理局所拟定,有以下三种:(一)米粮登记,余粮管理。各乡村除留其自身足用之米外,所有余粮,人民有出售之义务,如不出售,则政府当加以征购,倘有规避征购者,应予以最严厉之处罚。(二)划分区域,调整产销,以消费区域为中心,根据其平时米粮来源之路线,划定来源县份。如重庆市场已指定十九县为其来源县,其他各米粮消费市场亦将照办;至集散市场,一方面指定其应供给之消费市场,一方面指定其来源地区,如此层层指定,层层联系,以直达出产者为止。如各层供需,能照指定进行,固无需政府加以强制,否则某层出问题,即由某层施行管理,强制出售或予以征购。(三)平抑粮价。在较广范围内施行,如某一地区粮价较其四邻为高,则米粮必大量集中;如某一地区粮价较其四邻为低,则米粮来源势必断绝,必须各地粮价保持水平,则米粮供需始可维持正常。上述三项办法该局方在分途进行中。如为实施米粮登记则于九月八日颁行"川省粮食调查暂行办法大纲",调查下列事项:(一)人口;(二)粮食消费;(三)粮食输入输出之地点及数量;(四)现存陈粮数量;(五)今年收获数量;(六)今年粮食之余额及不足数量。川省如此,其他各省市如黔粤及重庆等,亦在闻风兴起,分别组织省市粮食管理委员会。同时,委座于告川民书中明切训示:(一)"一定要责成拥有粮食的人家,按照政府规定,将自食有余的粮食,在定期以内陆续运到市场出售,如果不遵法令,逾越限期而藏积不售,必予强制征购,在征购的时候,就只能按市价发给半价,那时若再规避征购,即将其应售之粮食全部没收,并得科以照价加倍的罚金";(二)"川省各县稍有财力的富户,藏积一年两年前陈粮者必不在少。现在抗战时期,需要军粮,我们民间既有丰富的积粮,与其任其日久耗蚀,何如自动捐助出来,贡献国家,充作战士的粮食。从前卜式输财,弦高犒军,历史传为美谈,我们四川同胞爱国明理,向不后人,也该仿照前人的好榜样,因此,我要在四川省先提倡捐助军粮的运动。"(奖励办法见上述)

我国粮食统制,为时虽短,成效则已可观。惟统制工作,在经济落后之我国,素感困难,粮食统制,自难例外。吾人愿就管见所及,略陈数端,想为粮食统制当局所乐予采纳。

（一）定期统计与情报制度：统计数字,为管理粮食之基础,故全国粮食管理局于成立之始,即颁行"川省粮食调查暂行办法大纲",从事于粮食统计之搜集。此种办法,虽指全省而言,然以限于人力资力,闻拟先从江巴两县入手,渐次推及他县。惟各年粮食生产之丰歉,参半决于天时,则本年之统计,自难凭作来年统制之根据,故粮食调查,势非逐年举行不可。再者,粮食统计之搜集,其目标不尽在测知收获以后之实际产量,而尤着重于收获以前之可能产量,庶施政当轴得依据预测,对粮食供需之调剂,作未雨绸缪之措施。欧美各国,对于主要农产——特别粮食,有农情预测之办法,每年按期举行。其在我国,中央农业实验所亦已采行有年。吾人切望粮管局能利用中农现有之机构,更扩大而充实之,务使情报所得之数字,能作统制之科学根据,则于调剂盈亏之时,自能将运销数量之多寡,方向之改变,以及价格之变动等完全控制,有时可不必作实际之转移,即可收到统制之效果。

（二）民众组织与运储设备：粮食统制范围广大,自大都会以至穷乡僻野之民众,莫不为统制之对象,则民众组织必须严密,始克收效,自无待言。我国民众组织向极散漫,保甲制度虽已行之有年,然以人口未经普查,组织因乏科学根据,难臻严密。如是,粮管局于实施统制时,虽有缜密之统计与妥善之办法,而此种办法是否能自上而下,逐步实施,实成问题。委座于告川民书中洞鉴此中困难,故于详示调查产销数量及出售余粮等管理办法之后,曾谓："上面所说的办法,仍然是采用市场交易和有价买卖的方式,与世界各国战时施行的通例比较起来,仍然是十分宽大。"然为长期统制之有效起见，则自宜以民众组织之健全化为前提也。

欲求粮食供需调剂之有效，民众组织，固宜设法健全，运储设备更应亟谋完备。盖无运输设备则粮食生产因地理上分布之不均，即无法调剂。无仓储便利，则粮食生产因时间上分配之不均，亦不易融通。前者有赖于交通建设之推进，为整个建设之一部，非粮管局所能单独为力。后者可由农本局会同其他农业金融机关，广建合作农仓，经营粮食以及其他农产品等之储押放款，以资补救。

总观上述，粮食统制头绪纷纭，战时统制在谋供需之平衡，平时统制尚待生产之促进。两者俱以国家全部经济统制息息相关，必须通盘筹划，始克奏效，决非头痛医头脚痛医脚之枝节办法所能收效者也。

川康棉纺织工业之固有基础

一　区域

据川省府二十五年调查,全川出产土布者,凡四十七县,兼有纺纱者凡三十三县。其时宁雅二属,尚未划归西康,而宁属如西昌、宁南、会理、盐边各县,年辄自昆明输入棉纱五千余(五,二〇〇)包以从事织造,可知此所谓全川四十七县,实包括今日川康两省范围。

兼有纺纱之三十三县,同时必为产棉县区。此据四川省棉作试验场二十六年棉产调查,二十九县以纺纱为副业之农户同时皆为棉农,足以为证。此二十九县中,以纺纱为副业者,其所占棉农户数百分比,以仁寿、射洪、三台、遂宁、盐亭各县为较高,各占三〇~四五%,而此等县份,适亦为川省棉产最丰之区。论棉田面积各在五千亩以上;论及棉产额,遂宁、射洪二县(以二十六年产额为例)各达六万市担,为全省最高纪录,仁寿达三万市担,三台近二万五千市担,盐亭一万余市担,在棉产量上均占高位。二十九纺纱县区中,其皮棉产额较微者为内江、隆昌、井研各县,各不足一百市担,而此等县区之纺纱户所占棉农户数之百分率遂亦最低,各为一〇%,处于商品市场组织扩大化之今日,棉花盛产区域,原不必即为土纺盛产区域,但就三十九县之情形而论,此种比例关系固仍甚密切,而以涪沱二流域间各区为尤然。

至于棉纺区域之布分,应以所用原料种类之不同而殊别。其以土纺作原料者,一以取给原料近便之故,一以历史相沿成习关系,大抵皆与土纺工业同地并存,或与土纺市场取得极密切之联系。例如前举二十九土纺县区中,遂宁县为棉产最丰之区,同时土纺工业亦较发达,因此以土纺作原料之棉织业,遂亦有旺盛之时期,其所产土布之市场分布,曾远及滇黔湘鄂各边区,价额达十余万元以上。其他土纺县区如仁寿县之富加镇,富顺县之胡家镇暨戴家寺,各为土纺布主要产地市场。又如南充、资阳、南溪、犍为、资中、隆昌,各县盖皆为土纺区域而同时亦为出产土纱布之县区。

以土纱织布之区域,即分布于土纺区域,观上例可明。然而就自今情况而言,此种依附于土纺之土纱织布区域盖已失去其独立存在之地位。盖自机纱倾销,益以布匹内外销市场组织扩大,昔日依附于当地原料之小生产,或已全部转化为利用外来原料之较大生产,或部分利用外来原料而维持固有之小生产,凡此均使原来土纺织布区域中同时有机纱织布存在,而后者或且转占优势,前举遂宁县原为土纺织布最盛之县区,然近来土纺布之外销数额已自十余万元急缩为二万元,同时资本数十万之洋纱匹头帮则跃为新兴势力,此即足以为证。故今日即使尚有独立存在之土纺织布区域,其在今日八十织布县区中,必占极小比率,则为无疑。反之,机纱织布区域,除与土纺织布区域并存之外,其独立存在者,或且已较并存区域为广,此种独立存在之机纱织布区域,固为旧日土纺织布区域所蜕化而成,然同时亦随原料来源之变化及商品市场之扩大,遂脱离旧日生产交易中心，而转移于交通运输便利地带或大中心城市，今日重庆、成都各市区之棉织工业，即为此类动态之说明。以重庆而言，二十四年共有铁轮机一，〇七三台，木机八八三台，前者每年消耗机纱二，二七九包，后者每年消耗机纱一，八〇六包，共四，〇八五包。以言成都，二十四年纺织洋布之机房共有大小五百余家，每日用机纱织造花白布二千五百匹。此外如西康原宁属各县，其所以有织布工业之存在，主要盖亦因机纱输入之便利。

要之，今日川康棉织工业之区域分布，除棉纺工业分布于涪沱二流域棉产丰盛县区如仁寿、射洪、三台、遂宁等三十余县之外，棉织工业则不仅分布于同上棉纺区域，而同时亦随机纱与成品之输运便利，逐渐密集于与较大商业中心或与消费市场（而非与棉产市场）接近之区，计两者共达川省近八十县之范围。

二 原有产量与技术

关于川省（康省无棉纱出产）棉纱之产量，迄无统计可稽，仅能根据皮棉数字作近似之估计。按川省二四～二六共三年间平均皮棉产量为四七六，三六九市担，同期间输入皮棉数量为二，五四四市担。此项皮棉，除去川康二省人民絮棉消耗约共二七一，〇三四市担之外，余额二〇七，八七九市担合二四，一九五，一二九磅，约即为纺造土纱之需。以土法纺成棉纱，废棉率仅有五％，故推知川省棉纱（土纱）产量约为二二，九八五，三七三磅，以机纱单位计算（每包四二〇磅），共为五四，七二七包。

以言棉布产量：据四川省府二十五年调查，全川土布出产数量共为八六,六一六,二二六匹,为数之巨,殊难尽确。惟此处所指匹数,初无一定标准。例如重庆、成都织布工业固已渐跻于工厂制造之阶段,而所产布匹之种类,尚且长度多只五六十尺,最重不过六斤半,成都所产布匹,宽度有仅一尺而重量不足一斤者。以此推测农村家庭工业产品,则如隆昌所产长度二十余尺,宽度不足一尺,重量不足一斤者,殆为普遍情形(表一)。以此种布匹标准上之漫无规律,遂益证前举八千余万匹之数字,盖不足以为凭。而欲探究川产布匹之实际数量,尚须从棉纱消费量上为近似之估计。

表一 川康布匹种类之例举

布匹名称	长(尺)	宽(尺)	重(斤)	产地
市布	52.00	2.40	3.68	重庆
胶布	52.00	2.00		重庆
花布	50.00	2.00		重庆
冲毛呢	52.00	2.20	3.75	重庆
宽面布	100.00		6.50	成都
木机布	64.00	1.20	3.13	成都
中琢	16.00	1.10	2.25	成都(行销最广)
纱布	46.00	1.00	0.63	成都
改良布	64.00	1.20	2.63	成都
二八布	21.00	0.80	0.63	隆昌
中布	24.00	0.80	0.63	隆昌
改良布	25.00	0.80	0.75	隆昌
台布	25.00	0.80	0.75	隆昌

川省自产棉纱(土纺)五四,七二七包,已如前述。根据渝万两关棉纱入口数字,则二四~二六共三年平均输入棉纱二六一,七五六公担合计一三七,三九八包。此项输入机纱,尚须减去约总数八分之一供杂项织物消费,其余一二〇,二二四包,始为纯用于织布

之原料。总计自产土纺与输入供织布用之机纱合计,共为一七四,九五一包,若以之一律织成长四十一码,宽三十五时,实重一一.二磅之十二磅布,易言之,即以此项十二磅布为计算标准,则前者可织布二,〇五二,二六五匹,后者可织布四,五〇八,三八三匹,共为六,五六〇,六四八匹。以此种十二磅布一匹平均合川产土布四匹计算,应有匹数约为二千六百万匹(表二)。

表二　川康棉纱棉布之平时产量

按棉纱分类	棉纱产量(包)	棉纱输入(包)	以十二磅布作标准之布匹产量(匹)	以十二磅布一匹合川产土布四匹计算之布匹产量(匹)
土纺	54,727		2,052,265	8,209,060
机纱		120,224*	4,508,383	18,033,532
总计	54,727	120,224	6,560,648	26,242,592

* 输入机纱总数为137,398包,供杂织原料者约占八分之一,相减之后为120,224包。

生产上述土纺概系应用最陈旧之手摇机纺,通常由农村家庭老妇幼女从事操作。若按每年每架土纺机平均工作十一个月,即三三五日及每架土纺机每日出产量棉纱〇.三磅即每年出产一〇〇.五磅计算,川省三十余县年出产棉纱五四,七二七包,合二二,九八五,三七三磅,应有土纺机二二八,七一〇架,事实上每年每架工作或不足十一个月,每架每日产量或不足〇.三磅,则土纺机架数或犹驾乎二十二万余架以上。亦未可知。

至于织造土布,农村家庭工业型之生产技术,限于手工业者且不论,即后起之城市"工厂",其技术亦无有应用汽力或电力者。单以织布机一项而言,例如重庆市(包括南岸江北)于最盛时期共有织机四,一六七台,其中木机共二,二七四台,占五四.五%,其余四五.五%合一,八九三台则为铁轮机。及至二十四年,织机总数自四,一六七台减为一,九五三台,其中木机虽骤减为八八三台,然犹占总数之四五.二%,以重庆市推测农村可知木机之存在,对于铁轮机尚占优势地位。若按铁轮机之实际生产率每年合十二磅布一〇〇匹计,则生产前举之六,五六〇,六四八匹布,即应有布机六五,六〇六台。然木机之生产能力远在铁机以下,故实际布机总数又必在十万台左右。

三　原有组织

就大势而言,川康纺织二类生产机关之组织情形,系与整个棉纺织业之演化过程相适应。一方面由于棉产区域保持较多之旧技术(如土纺机与木织机),因而家庭工业型之组织形式遂亦于农村占优势,而另一方面,随棉织业之逐渐脱离棉产区域以向商业中心移动,于是工厂型之组织形式,亦渐代之而兴。关于家庭工业型之组织,其单位数与从业人员数以及一般业务情形,大抵随市场纱布价格之涨落而异,且其变动至速,初无一定规模可言。至于工业型之组织,虽采用雇佣劳动而技术基础则仍为手工业规模。此"工厂"以川建厅调查二十五年之事实为例,其较著者川省共有九十七家,分布巴县、江北、成都、宜宾、万县等四十八县九十七家中,其资本数额以自一千元至六千元之间者为最多,共有五十一家,最高者达十万元,最小者仅六十元,皆属特例。工人数在十八至五十之间者为最多,达五十家,最高数达七百四十四人,最低不足五人,亦属例外。若按县区单位计算,则以巴县有此种工厂家数最多,达二十一家;其次为璧山、内江二县,前者达十一家,后者达八家;其他除少数县区有二三家外,大抵只有一家;论平均资金数额,则以江津为大,达八万余元;成都、富顺、鄠都居其次,各为一万元;其余皆在数千元之间,而井研、江北、宜宾、涪陵、彰明各县在千元以下,论平均工人数,则以富顺、鄠都、开县、梁山、南充各县为多,各在百人以上;成都、简阳、巴县、江津、綦江、璧山、高县、大竹、邻水、垫江、蓬安、遂宁、射洪、安县、德阳各县均在五十至百人之间,余则在五十人以下。全省平均每家有资金五千四百二十一元,有工人五十六人(表三)。

表三　四川省手工织布工厂概况

区县	手织工厂家数	每家平均资金(元)	每家平均工人(人)
成都	1	10,000	61
灌县	1	2,300	25
崇庆	1	3,000	36
资中	1		
内江	8	1,925	24
简阳	2	5,235	78
井研	1	60	27
巴县	21	82,708	86
江津	1	85,000	82
江北	3	466	31
荣昌	2	1,450	40
綦江	1		98
璧山	11	2,891	56
铜梁	2	4,100	37
洪雅	1	3,000	26
乐山	1	2,000	20

续表

区县	手织工厂家数	每家平均资金(元)	每家平均工人(人)
宜宾	3	536	44
高县	2	9,200	54
长宁	1		36
富顺	1	10,000	112
合江	2	3,000	17
涪陵	2	900	13
鄿都	1	10,000	122
万县	1	4,000	38
开县	1	2,500	100
忠县	1	2,000	16
云阳	1	8,000	34
大竹	1		80
渠县	1		
广安	1	6,000	29
梁山	1	5,400	198
邻水	1	3,600	56
垫江	1		62
南充	1	3,000	124
岳池	1	8,000	34
蓬安	1	4,000	59
西充	1	1,000	25
遂宁	1	2,800	58
蓬溪	1		40
射洪	1		57
广汉	1	3,000	30
安县	2	2,800	62
德阳	1	3,000	50
金堂	1	1,002	24
罗江	1	1,536	19

续表

区县	手织工厂家数	每家平均资金(元)	每家平均工人(人)
阆中	2		2
彰明	1	600	25
开江	1	5,700	25
总计48县	97	5,421	56

四　平时纱布供需量

如前所云，川省自产土纱共五四，七二七包，此外更输入机纱专供织布者共一二〇，二二四包，两项共计一七四，九五一包，除利用此项棉纱可织十二磅布六，五六〇，六四八匹之外，尚有布匹自外埠入口，根据渝万两关贸易统计，二四～二六共三年布匹输入数字平均为九八，七四四公担，按十二磅布实际重量计算约为一，九〇四，八一六匹。与自产布匹合计，共为八，四六五，四六四匹。此即为川康两省平时棉布需求量，相当于此项棉布之棉纱需求量则为二二五，七四五包。以川康平时人口总数(五四，二〇六，八五四人)平均，计平时每人布匹需求量为六.四码，每人棉纱需求量为一.七五磅。单就布匹而论，平时全国人口平均每人需求量为九.九码，较川康超出三.五码。此则内地农村经济衰落购买能力低微，而人民节朴程度较深以及气候之和暖与土织布匹之坚牢耐用，有以致之。

五　抗战以后之新事态

自抗战以来，川康棉纺织工业即发生两种有巨大影响之新事态，其一为机械纺纱工业之内迁，随而展开川康棉纱织工业史上之新时期，其二则为原料供给之断绌，随而使已有生产陷于停顿是也。

如前所言，川康共有手织布机十万台（以铁轮机生产率计算合六五，六〇六台），此项布机，合消耗棉纱一七四，九五一包，其中五四，七二七包为本地出产土纺，其余一二〇，二二四包则有赖于输入。及至武汉、广州相继沦陷，输入益发困难，棉纱输入数量遂不足以供应全部手织机之消耗而使已有织布业之规模因部分布机之停顿而转形缩小。以二十八年而论，全年约可向川康输入棉纱四万五千包。以此数与内迁纱厂自产机纱一万包合计不过五万五千包，则缺额棉纱达六五，二二四包之巨。按铁轮机每年消耗棉纱一，一二〇磅（合织布一〇〇匹）计，则缺额棉纱六五，二二四包即足使布机二四，四五九台限于停业。设使土纺一旦能增产输入之缺额，则织机之停业问题自可解决，然以皮棉产额、皮棉输入及土纺原有设备之限制，欲使土纱一旦自五四，七二七包，增至一一九，五九一包，盖为不可能之事，而各内迁纱厂多附设有动力织布机，设使此项布机同时开工，则手织机之停业者应尚不止此数。故抗战后虽一方面以机械纺织工业内迁而展开川康棉纺织工业新时期，然另一方面则川康棉纺织工业之环境固转趋于恶劣。

与上述两种事态并存而互相关联者，则战时川康纱布供需关系之剧变是也。试仍以二十八年为例，如上所言，除土纱照常供给五四，七二七包之外，尚能供给自产机纱约一万包，便能输入棉纱四万五千包合计一〇九，七二七包。以此项棉纱可织十二磅布四，一一四，七六三匹。估计二十八年内约可能向川康输入棉布二十七万匹。与自产布匹合计为四，三八四，七六三匹。此即为战时川康棉布供给之数量。按战时川康人口，约增加净数五十万人。战时全国士兵衣被所需棉布约十四磅布三百万匹之半数（以十二磅布折计）约合一，七四一，〇七二匹，亦须仰赖于川康棉织业之供给。若除去军用布匹之外，余数二，六四三，六九一匹以供战时川康民用之需，平均仅可供给每人一.九八码，合棉纱为〇.五四磅。以与平时供给量相较，各占平时之三一%。因战事之发生，遂骤使川康民用纱布需求较之平时缩减七〇%，此即衣的问题之所以为今日川康民生问题之重心也。

THE PROSPECT FOR CHINA'S INDUSTRIALIZATION

WITH the spread of Western culture and civilization, industrialization has assumed a phenomenal growth in many parts of the world. In the West, notably in Northwestern Europe starting with the British Isles, industrialization began a century and a half ago. In these countries coal and iron, together with capital accumulated mainly from maritime and colonial commerce, could be found in abundance. Historically, it is evident that industrialization acts not only as a spontaneous, unconscious, and self-generating factor for nation-building, but also transforms itself at once into a deliberate, conscious, and planned policy of all governments, in the hands of far-sighted statesmen.

China is no exception to this general trend of development. Here the need for industrialization is no less urgent than in any other country. Both economic poverty and military decadence have contributed to the demand for industrialization. Under a predominantly agricultural economy China's poverty is characterized by an unfavorable man-land ratio, which gives rise to the perennial struggle of an overcrowded population for the limited supply of cultivable land; while her military decadence increased through the successive defeats which she suffered at the hands of industrialized Powers for almost a whole century following the Opium War of 1841 – 42.

Attempts at China's industrialization were launched as early as the reign of Emperor Tung-chih after 1862. Under the leadership of Tseng Kuo-fan, Tso Tsung-tang, and Li Hung-chang, the statesmen responsible for the revival of the Manchu dynasty after the Taiping Rebellion, several factories were established for the manufacturing of ammunition. This period, lasting from 1862 to 1877, was followed by commercial product manufacturing during 1878 – 1894, influx of foreign enterprises from 1895 to 1902, cancellation or repurchase of foreign concession rights from 1903 to 1911, industrial prosperity under Chinese initiative from 1912 to 1931, depression and attempts at recovery from 1931 to 1936, and finally the retreat towards the great interior since 1937. Throughout this long period of eighty years, China's feeble attempts at industrialization have been thwarted at many points by civil war on the one hand, and by foreign invasion on the other. The achievements to date, although meagre when judged by Western standards, represent nevertheless considerable departures from the economy known to China since the dawn of her history four thousand years ago. In assessing, with lessons of history, the prospects of China's industrialization, the task here is merely to point out the main factors that have facilitated or retarded the progress of industrialization. The problem as to what are the principal fields in which lie the future of China's industrialization will have to be reserved for discussions some other time.

INDUSTRIALIZATION begins with the possession of capital. In the West the accumulation of capital had taken place for many centuries before industrialization set in during the second half of the eighteenth century. In England, the birthplace of industrialization, the expansion of foreign trade from the fourteenth century onward resulted in an accumulation of capital which provided the basis for industrial development. In China capital accumulation is insignificant for many reasons. Here foreign trade is almost negligible when compared with her enormous population. Trade has all along been domestic; such trade is likewise limited because of the self-sufficient character of her national economy. The predominance of agriculture over industry and trade ties up whatever meagre capital she may have accumulated in the form of investment in land which is immobile. The time-old family system calling for equal division of property among the descendents is a deterrent to large-scale accumulation of wealth, which probably accounts for the necessary provision of capital by the state when the first factories were started in the early sixties under the Manchu dynasty. Today, after a period of eighty years, modern industrial capital amounts to only 3,808 million dollars (prewar value, approximately equivalent to 1.3 billion U. S. currency) which, estimated on the basis of a population of 450 millions, gives a per capita share of less than nine dollars. [1] It must also be noted that small as the total industrial capital is, the share for domestic capital reaches only 987 million dollars or 26%; the rest, 2,821 million dollars or 74%, being foreign capital invested in China.

---

[1] Estimate by Koh Tsung-fei in an unpublished article to which the present writer is kindly given access.

The problem of capital looms larger when it is remembered that a good part of modern industrial capital in China today has been destroyed in the course of the past four and a half years of war. Much of China's modern industrial capital is located in areas now occupied by the Japanese, while in "free China," mainly in southwestern and northwestern regions, modern industrial capital is only a recent development. Before the Sino-Japanese War southwestern and northwestern China did not possess more than, at the best, one-tenth of China's modern industrial capital. When the war came, a large part of the modern industrial capital in the "occupied" areas was abandoned or destroyed; while the rest was removed, first from Shanghai, Wusih, and Nanking to Hankow and Changsha, and later thence to Chungking, Chengtu, Sian, Kweilin, Kweiyang, and other places. Meantime, in the rear provinces, new factories were erected; so were workshops under the impetus given by the Chinese Industrial Co-operative Movement, popularly referred to as "Indusco."[①] All in all, modern industrial capital in "free China" today has increased over that in prewar days, but in aggregate it cannot have reached, as a rough approximation, two-tenths of the modern industrial capital in prewar China. The sum is thus altogether inadequate for China's industrialization even on a moderate scale, and naturally gives rise to the question as to sources of capital supply once the present war is over and the all-embracing blockade is lifted.

[①] For a detailed and sympathetic account see Nym Wales, *China Builds for Democracy: A story of co-operative industry*, Hongkong: Kelly & Walsh, 1941.

As stated elsewhere, modern industrial capital in China is divided in ownership, three-quarters being foreign and one-quarter Chinese. Foreign industrial capital in China, which increased greatly after the conclusion of the Treaty of Shimonoseki with Japan in 1895, granting under it the right to erect factories on Chinese soil to foreigners, has all along been an important factor in China's industrialization, and will undoubtedly continue to be so once China decides to rebuild her industrial areas upon the conclusion of the present war. Two problems will then present themselves in connection with the utilization of foreign capital. The first is political, that of separating foreign investment from foreign political control. In the past, foreign investment had been a means toward the acquisition of foreign rights and interests — the so-called foreign "spheres of interests." Of this the most notable example is that of the South Manchuria Railway. This company, as has been well remarked by a recent writer, "deserves to rank with the East India Company and the Hudson's Bay Company as one of the great semi-governmental economic organizations of history. Founded after the Russo-Japanese War with a modest capital of 200,000,000 yen, part of which consisted of the damaged and depreciated properties which had been taken over from the Russians, it has grown on a truly imperial scale and is today far and away the largest corporation functioning in East Asia. Receipts of 12,500,000 yen in the first year of its operation had increased to 302,000,000 yen in 1935 - 36. Besides operating what is probably the most efficient railway system in Asia, the South Manchuria Railway is a heavy investor in almost all the major industrial enterprises of "Manchoukuo", in Fushun coal, Anshan steel, the new chemical company, and many other mines, mills, and factories."① China, when the war is over, will be greatly depleted of her meager capital stock, and must inevitably look toward the creditor nations, especially the United States, to finance her industrial development. The separation of investment from political control will then have to depend on the extent to which China can satisfy the minimum demand of her foreign creditors, namely, peace and order which is indispensable to profitable investment.

The second of these two problems is economic. When Dr. Sun Yat-sen, founder of the Chinese Republic, advocated in 1922 in his *International Development of China* foreign investments for Chinese industrial development, the world was confronted with the problem of excess industrial capacity arising from the cessation of the First World War. The Second World War now in full swing is far more extensive in area, as well as intensive in capital destruction. When it comes to an end, it remains a problem whether the excess industrial capacity arising from the cessation of war will be diverted to rehabilitation at home by the various foreign governments or to overseas investment. It is certain, however, that the United States, as the world's leading nation in possession of an excess capital seeking investment, will, despite the financial drain which she may have to sustain on account of her recent war against Japan, Germany, and Italy, have sufficient capital seeking for investment in foreign

---

① Chamberlain, W. H., *Japan over Asia*, Boston, 1938, pp. 45 - 46. [In recent years some of the industrial enterprises in "Manchoukuo" have been removed from the aegis of the South Manchuria Railway. —Ed.]

countries after the war is over. Now that she has thrown in her lot in common with China, Britain, and the Dutch East Indies in the Far East — the ABCD Alliance — and has definitely committed herself to the defeat of the Axis Powers including Japan, a nation noted for its "brilliant feat of deception," ①her interest in Chinese postwar industrial development is no longer purely economic, but also highly political. For it is only if China is free and independent and given opportunity to industrialize with foreign financial and technical aid that she may serve as a stabilizing factor in Far Eastern politics. ② Already not a few people have advocated a long-range industrial development project akin to the Tennessee Valley Authority (TVA) to be launched in postwar China, which will embrace a program of comprehensive industrial development with American capital and technique covering the basic needs of postwar China for modern means of transport, scientific agriculture, and large-scale manufacturing. ③

The possibility of raising capital from among the Chinese themselves is twofold, namely, from the Chinese at home and from the Chinese over-

---

① Phrase used by President Roosevelt in his speech to the American nation broadcast on the evening of December 9, 1941.

② Peffer, Nathaniel, *Prerequisites to Peace in the Far East*, New York: Institute of Pacific Relations, 1940, Chapter VI.

③ Lack of space does not permit us to enter into a detailed discussion of the transfer problem arising from foreign investment, but suffice it to say that in the course of industrialization China in a new postwar world of closer economic cooperation, even though confined only to the democratic nations, will have her contribution to make once her existing and potential resources are better developed and utilized.

seas. Capital within China is derived from credit expansion, as well as excess of production over consumption. Under a unified fiscal policy the four government banks — Central Bank, Bank of China, Bank of Communications, and Farmer's Bank — can expand their credit, reduce the rate of interest, and thus encourage investment in China's postwar industrial development. Income from these investments when saved but not consumed will be available for further investments, and thus the process tends to become cumulative and an expanding capital fund may be created for the purpose of financing China's postwar industrialization.① The process of raising capital through excess of production over consumption is less hopeful than that of credit expansion. The low standard of living in China, which has been much reduced on account of the war, cannot be expected to sustain still further encroachments. Thus consumption cannot be reduced through a lowering in the standard of living, although with better income distribution there may still be margin for economy. Production, on the other hand, cannot be much increased unless accompanied by mechanical improvements that will have to come through industrialization. However, the capital that has fled abroad in course of the war, estimated to be US $200,000,000,② and blocked since July 25, 1941, at the request of the Chinese Government by the Governments of the United States and Great Britain to which most of the Chinese capital in flight has gone, should be placed with due compensation in the hands

---

① See Keynes, *General Theory of Employment, Interest and Money*, New York, 1935.
② The actual total is reported to have been larger, approaching US $300,000,000.

of the Chinese Government for postwar industrial development.

A second source is the investment by the overseas Chinese, who in the past have contributed a fair share toward Chinese industrial development in textile, chemical, and other enterprises. But with the imposition of restrictions on capital export by most of the governments to which overseas Chinese are subject on the one hand, and the narrowing of opportunities of profit-making and capital accumulation for the overseas Chinese in recent years on the other, the prospect for capital investment by overseas Chinese in China's postwar industrial development has apparently become more uncertain during and immediately after this period of upheaval.

The gifts of nature—that is, land or natural resources—are no less important than capital as factors of industrialization. These resources, although varied, fall generally under two divisions, mineral and agricultural. Mineral resources play a far more important role than agricultural under present technological arrangements. Of these, the leading items include coal, iron, mineral oil, and copper, from the viewpoint of industrialization. Coal, oil, and copper are indispensable to the generation and transmission of motive power, [1] while iron supplies the basic mineral for

---

[1] The potential water power resources are estimated at 20,000,000 h. p. for China, or 0.05% of the world's total (i. e. ,444,574,000 h. p.), and is thus negligible. The utilized water power resources reach only 1,650 h. p., also 0.05% of the world's total (i. e., 32,963,950 h. p.) See *Power Resources of the World*, World Power Conference, London, 1929, Table XX. According to a German estimate, China's potential water power resources reach 31 – 40 million h. p. (See *The Chinese Year Book, 1935 – 36*, Premier issue, pp. 997 – 8.)

machine culture. ① China is deficient in mineral oil and copper, not so in coal and iron. In England where coal and iron were found in abundance in the northern and midland districts, industries began to move northward and toward the midlands from the west, the south and the east. In other countries of Northwestern Europe, concentration of industrial developments also took place around the favored regions of coal and iron like the Ruhr district. In China, unfortunately, coal and iron abounded in districts where industrial development failed to occur. Shansi and Shensi, with 189,077 million metric tons of coal reserve, or 82% of the total for China including the Four Northeastern Provinces (i. e., 243,699 million metric tons), have not been developed industrially even up to the present. The provinces where modern industries first developed lie mostly along the coast or the Great Yangtze, namely, Liaoning, Hopei, Shantung, Kiangsu, Kwangtung, and Hupeh.

Coal And Iron Ore Deposits in Relatively Industrialized Provinces of China②
(In million metric tons)

	Coal	Iron Ore
Liaoning	1,836	872.2
Hopei	3,071	42.2

---

① Increasing importance of wood as a substitute for steel is recognized in a recent article on "The World's Greatest Wood Magicians," *Readers' Digest*, October 1941, pp. 72 – 75.

② *Statistical Abstract of the Republic of China, 1940*, Directorate of Statistics, National Government of China, Chungking (in Chinese).

	Coal	Iron Ore
Shantung	1,639	14.3
Kiangsu	217	7.4
Kwangtung	421	8.0
Hupeh	440	39.6
Total	7,624	983.7

These six provinces possess a coal reserve of only 7,624 million metric tons, or 3% of the total for China. In respect of iron ore deposits, there is a closer correspondence between location of reserves and industrial development. Liaoning, possessing 872.2 million metric tons or 60% of China's total (i. e., 1,452,778 million metric tons), is a relatively industrialized province; but Sikang, Szechuen, and Chahar, ranking second, third and fourth in importance, with respectively 120.1, 117.2 and 91.6 million metric tons of iron ore, are little developed industrially (Szechuen being developed only during the last three and half years owing to war demands). This failure to develop modern industries near the areas of coal and iron ore deposits accounts partly for the slow progress of industrialization in China. It can be explained by the fact that whereas in England, for instance, industrial development came spontaneously of its own course, and as an outcome of economic evolution, in China it was fostered primarily by foreign initiative and enterprise. The foreign Powers, reinforced by a desire to facilitate intercourse of trade with the vast interior of China's hinterland, decided upon the choice of port cities accessible to steam navigation as the centers for early industrial and economic penetration, while neglecting the more inaccessible interior provinces which, however, from viewpoints of resources and security, would have been better alternatives for industrial development to the Chinese. Today, with the occupation of Liaoning and Chahar by the Japanese, the prospect of China's industrialization is further reduced, temporarily at least, by the loss of her great iron ore reserve. The two coal provinces of Shensi and Shansi remain poorly developed and are affected by war hostilities. Except for the narrow-gauge railway in Shansi (The Tungpu Railway) and the western terminus of the Lunghai Railway, means of communication in these two provinces for the transport of bulky commodities are prohibitive if not totally absent.

As to agricultural resources, the greatest setback to industrial development is sporadic, unorganized production. Industrial crops, such as raw cotton, wool, and wheat, are not graded or standardized. As a result, any manufacturer in China would have to double or triple his purchases before a satisfactory assortment can be made to suit his production needs. It is thus not unfamiliar for Chinese manufacturers under such handicaps to prefer foreign to Chinese raw materials—for example, to use Australian instead of Honan wheat in Tientsin mills. Chinese agricultural production, which is heterogeneous, irregular, and uncertain, has failed to give due consideration to the needs of Chinese industries, while Chinese industrial production has similarly neglected to make known its requirements to Chinese agriculture. The failure to co-ordinate agricultural development with industrial has its serious repercussions on national production, and it is only recently that attention has been drawn to this aspect of Chinese economy. It is proposed that in order to meet the raw material needs of modern industries operated on a large scale, the small-scale agricultural producers be united into Co-operatives for the attainment of uniform and quantity production through control over seed standardization and crop marketing. [1]

The scarcity of industrial labor in an agricultural country like China is another factor that retards her industrial development. Industrial labor requires not only skill, but also discipline. In England, the two waves of labor immigration, the Flemish during the fourteenth and the Huguenots during the sixteenth century, laid the foundation for the development of her premier industry, namely, cloth manufacture. Alien labor found a congenial home in England because of the similarity in culture and standard of living. China, in the course of her industrialization, could not afford to rely on foreign labor, as her standard of living prohibited the employment of high-priced western industrial workers except for filling the managerial and technical positions. Chinese labor, primarily agricultural, did not possess the necessary skill for the operation of complicated machines and tools imported from abroad. Again, accustomed as Chinese labor has been to the traditions of guild or domestic industries, it lacks the very discipline which is indispensable to successful production under the factory system — a phenomenon not uncommon among the handloom weavers of England in the early years of her Industrial Revolution. The

---

[1] See my article on "The Relationship Between Agriculture and Industry", *Southwest Industrial Bulletin* (in Chinese), March 1940.

port cities where factory industry was first introduced, for example Canton and Shanghai, were naturally faced with the problem of industrial labor supply earliest. After decades of development these cities began to build up a reserve of industrial labor to which other centers looked for supply. Thus many of the factory workers in Tientsin and Tsingtao cotton mills, in North China, had to be drawn from these cities in the south.

Today the Japanese occupation of these areas has forced many of the industries to migrate from south and central China to the Great Southwest, and with this migration have also been transferred the industrial workers of Shanghai, Wusih, and even Hankow. These workers now constitute the nucleus through which a new army of industrial labor has to be recruited and trained from the agricultural population in the Southwest. The quantity immediately available for factory employment is inevitably small and insufficient for the purpose of large-scale industrial development. Industrial factory labor in China as a whole did not amount to over a million even before the present war; with the destruction of the war and the dispersion of such labor in the course of the war China must feel more keenly than before the shortage of industrial labor supply. Unless an extensive program of industrial training be launched by government or industry, the scarcity of industrial labor may constitute another stumbling block to China's extensive industrialization, whether during the war or after its conclusion. On the other hand, given freedom of development after the abolition of the "unequal treaties" referred to in a subsequent section, scarcity of industrial labor may hasten the need for semi-manual mechanization, as has already been the case during this wartime to some extent.

The scarcity of managers, entrepreneurs, engineers, technicians, and other members on the directing staff is another weakness in China's industrialization. In England early managers of factories and industrial enterprises were largely successful merchants engaged in foreign trade. The term "merchant manufacturer," so commonly employed in England's cloth industry, refers to the merchant who gives out woolen yarn to the outworking weavers for weaving into cloth on wage basis, and it is largely from this class that early managers in woolen mills were recruited. In China the early factories, being financed as well as operated by the state, were organized after the *yamen* pattern. While the engineer might be a foreigner of second-rate ability (for in these days there was not sufficient attraction to engage men from abroad of first-rate training and caliber), the managerial staff was filled with big or petty bureaucrats as the case demanded. In the course of time these bureaucrats, seizing the opportunity for profit-making in certain remunerative branches, began to leave these factories and managed to raise funds among friends, relatives or colleagues for financing new enterprises of their own. Meantime, factories financed by foreign capital and staffed by foreign managers and engineers usually employed Chinese assistants on account of linguistic difficulties. These assistants, commonly known as "compradores," began to operate factories themselves once they had acquired sufficient wealth from their profession as middlemen and learnt the secrets of trade from their foreign superiors. In other words, it is from three classes that managers and entrepreneurs for Chinese industrial enterprises were recruited, namely, foreigners, bureaucrats, and compradores. Gradually, three more sources of supply were added. Overseas Chinese, having made a fortune from business enterprises abroad, returned to China to establish new undertakings in various fields of industry, and usually became managers as well as proprietors. Again, as the need for trained personnel became more keenly felt in the course of China's industrialization, the Chinese Government began to send students abroad, first to Japan, later on to Europe and America, for advanced study in theoretical as well as applied aspects of various branches of the sciences. Upon completion of their study abroad, some of these "returned students" came back to assume managerial and technical posts in different industrial enterprises. Finally, through cooperation with the League of Nations, the National Government of China has availed itself of the services of various technical experts in the state plants engaged in the production of minerals, iron and steel, machinery, and electrical apparatus.

The most important source, however, remains that of graduates from the Chinese colleges and universities. Here a large number of recruits are being drawn year by year into active industrial service. It is difficult to estimate the number of graduates annually available, but judging from the number of graduates for the prewar year 1936 - 37 from universities, colleges and technical schools, namely, 4,330, [1] the recruits entering in-

---

[1] *Statistical Abstract of the Republic of China*, *1940*, p. 194. Another recent source is the influx of refugee Jews into Shanghai and parts of "free China" from the Nazi-dominated Europe.

dustrial fields could not have been too large in view of the rapid spread of industrialization in China during these years. Now, during wartime, the Chinese Government has been stressing scientific and vocational education in various schools. ①

THE above-mentioned factors, capital, land, labor and management, are the four factors of production which relate especially to the internal economies of individual industrial enterprises. Among the most prominent factors affecting external economies must be included, in the first place, transportation, and in the second, government policy. In England, the first stage of the Industrial Revolution was marked by improvements of roads and canals, while the second occurred side by side with the introduction of railways and steamships. Just as mechanical inventions in industry brought about the Industrial Revolution, so their application to transport ushered in the Commercial Revolution. Indeed, the role of transport in industrial development cannot be overestimated. No country in history could expect to transform its industrial life without simultaneous revolution in transport. To a continental country like China mechanical transport is indispensable to industrialization, as was the case of the United States after the Civil War, or of the Soviet Union after the Novem-

---

① Another source, mainly a wartime development, is that of enterprising refugees drifting under conditions of wartime inflation into business enterprises. Starting out oftentimes with meager capital at their disposal, they sometimes come to acquire considerable gains from trading operations, and thus jump overnight from petty traders into wholesale dealers or owners and managers of industrial works engaged in the production of articles whose supply has been cut off by the enemy blockade. These refugees range all the way from janitors, workmen, clerks, chauffeurs, school teachers, to university professors.

ber Revolution in 1917. But transport in China has been in a most backward condition. With a population of 450 millions and an area of 11,000,000 square kilometers, she had only 17,400 kilometers of railways and 85,000 kilometers of motor highways before the war. Much traffic, therefore, is local, and handled by such primitive means of transport as wheelbarrows, mulecarts, junks, pack-horses, and coolie labor. The cost is often prohibitive, and the service most uncertain. The conditions prevailing even today in the interior parts of the country are reminiscent of England during the early days of the Industrial Revolution. Young, in his *Six Months Tour through the North of England* (1768, published 1770), considered the main road between Preston and Wigan as "infernal," to be avoided by travellers "as they would the devil."① Experience of this sort can be easily repeated in China, even in the vicinity of leading industrial centers like Tientsin. ②Under such conditions of transport it is but natural that China's industrial enterprises before the war were mostly located along the coastal ports and other cities easily accessible to railways or steamship navigation. Indeed, Chinese industrial centers developed like a crescent around the coast from Antung in Liaoning southwestward to Pakhoi in Kwangsi, while with the exception of Hankow the great hinterland remained untouched by modern industrializing influences.

Finally, the failure of the Government to adopt a persistent policy for

---

① Quoted in Fay, *Great Britain from Adam Smith to the Present Day*, 1940, p. 175.

② See my monograph on *Rural Weaving and the Merchant Employers in a North China District*, Nankai Institute of Economics, Tientsin, 1935.

the protection and encouragement of industry has considerably impeded the course of China's industrialization. It is an undeniable fact that China, on account of the encroachments upon her sovereignty under the bondage of "unequal treaties" concluded with foreign Powers in uninterrupted succession since the days of the Opium War of 1841 – 42, is in the words of Dr. Sun Yat-sen, "everywhere becoming a colony of the Powers.... China is the colony of every nation that has made treaties with her, and the treaty-making nations are her masters. China is not the colony of one nation but of all."[1] As a "colony" in fact if not in name, China was bound to leave her industries unprotected. She had thus in the early forties of the last century given away her tariff autonomy, a very important instrument for industrial protection, until its recovery in 1929; and according to Dr. Sun, had consequently sustained an annual loss of $500,000,000 (prewar value) through invasion of foreign goods. Nay, she had to stand a further loss of industrial protection under the 1895 Treaty of Shimonoseki, according to which foreigners were allowed to erect factories on Chinese soil, thus evading the payment of a stipulated tariff of five percent *ad valorem* altogether. In other respects, the foreign manufacturer enjoyed superior advantages over the Chinese. Greater financial backing, easier access to shipping facilities in Chinese waters because most of them were owned and operated by foreign companies, better technical staff and equipments, surer protection against illegal levies and

---

[1] *San Min Chu I* (*The Three Principles of the People*), trans. by Frank W. Price, Commercial Press, 1929, p. 38.

exactions by provincial and local warlords afforded by the system of extraterritorial rights, all these and other advantages enjoyed by rivals placed the Chinese manufacturers under serious handicaps in the race for their foreign business. Not "protection to infant industries," but "protection to foreign industries" carried the day; except for the temporary relief afforded to the Chinese manufacturers, especially cotton mill owners, during the World War of 1914 – 18, Chinese industries could not have prospered the way they did during those years. With the return of foreign imports after the cessation of the First World War, Chinese industries, whose growth during the war years was indeed rapid but very unsound in finance and organization, had immediately to undergo a prolonged period of depression. The appreciation of silver currency following the abandonment of the gold standard and the adoption of the American silver purchase policy in the early 'thirties brought about a deflation in China, and Chinese manufacturers had to join hands with world industrialists in their common fate until the establishment of a managed currency in China in 1935. They were tending toward recovery under the National Government, when another catastrophe wiped out a large part of China's modern industries painfully built up in the course of the last eighty years. The titanic struggle against Imperial Japan, which began on July 7, 1937, closed a chapter in the economic history of China.

It also opened a new one. The years that have elapsed since the outbreak of the Sino-Japanese War are pointing toward a new era of industrial reconstruction for China. China is truly emerging as a full-fledged independent nation in the course of the war. The retreat to the great interior hinterland has enabled China to carry out a program of industrial reconstruction unshackled by any restrictions imposed upon her by the "unequal treaties." In this great hinterland — China's southwest and northwest — she is alone in the field, and can do what she deems to be in her best interest. Both Soviet Russia and Germany — the former as a policy and the latter due to defeat in the First World War in which China was also a participant — have already relinquished their extraterritorial rights in China; on May 31 and July 14, 1941, the United States and Great Britain had announced respectively their readiness to surrender these rights at the conclusion of the war. The way is thus open for China to exercise her sovereign rights as a full-fledged independent nation, and in respect of industrial reconstruction to adopt a policy that will, besides serving her best interests, not conflict with the fundamental objectives of a stable economic order in a postwar world.

THE prospect for China's industrialization depends upon a number of factors, some of which have been outlined in the brief survey above. These factors, embracing capital, land, labor, management, transportation, and government policy, are not all too favorable to China's rapid industrialization in the near future, but hopeful signs are nevertheless not entirely lacking. One outstanding evidence of these is the heroic effort being made by the Chinese Government at wartime industrialization. The attempts being made have already brought industrial production in "free China" to an unusually high level — unusually high in view of the immense difficulties which have been encountered thus far, including among others the completeness of the enemy blockade and the absence of adequate means of modern transportation and industrial production. Recent statistics for the first three or four years of war in "free China" have shown, for example, a several-fold increase of many industrial products for the satisfaction of both military and civilian requirements. Coal production has increased during this interval (1937-40) from 3,600,000 to 5,700,000 tons, pig iron from 31,000 to 100,000 tons, crude copper from 400 to 1,000 tons (in addition to 1,200 tons of scrap copper being acquired by purchase within Szechuen province), and mineral oil from 34,000 to 440,000 gallons; while during 1938-40 alcohol production has increased from 1,800,000 to 4,500,000 gallons, machine-spun cotton yarn from 30,240 to 54,100 bales (of 400 lbs. each), flour from 1,710,000 to 3,400,000 bags (of 50 lbs. each), soap from 99,000 to 309,000 boxes (of 100 pieces each), matches from 7,000 to 11,700 cases (of 7,200 small boxes each), and paper from 600 to 1,800 tons. The rate of increase for these ten commodities, essential for military and civilian needs, has varied from the highest of 12.9 times for mineral oil to the lowest of 1.5 times for machine-spun yarn. It is the trend and not the absolute level of output which is here significant.

The decisive consideration determining the prospect for China's industrialization, however, must be the eventual outcome of the present war against China's aggressor. Victory will not only reinforce Chinese political unity, which constitutes the most elementary prerequisite to the successful realization of any program of industrialization, but will also place at her disposal the rich natural resources, notably iron ore and coal, now found in unlimited quantities in the Manchurian province of Liaoning and the North China provinces of Chahar and Shansi. Furthermore, victory under a strong and united government in China will undoubtedly enhance Chinese prestige and credit in the family of nations, as the four and half years of her unabated resistance to her aggressor has already succeeded in doing, and will thus offer to the postwar world, presumably democratic, the surest guarantee to political and economic stability in the Far East. Victory will bring with it unprecedentedly favorable conditions for a new era in the industrialization of China.

Harvard University, December 1941

图书在版编目(CIP)数据

方显廷文集. 第 6 卷/方显廷著. —北京：商务印书馆,2022
ISBN 978-7-100-21725-5

Ⅰ.①方… Ⅱ.①方… Ⅲ.①方显廷—文集 ②工业发展—中国—民国—文集 Ⅳ.①C53 ②F429.06-53

中国版本图书馆 CIP 数据核字(2022)第 170865 号

权利保留,侵权必究。

方 显 廷 文 集
第 6 卷

方显廷 著

商 务 印 书 馆 出 版
(北京王府井大街 36 号 邮政编码 100710)
商 务 印 书 馆 发 行
北 京 冠 中 印 刷 厂 印 刷
ISBN 978-7-100-21725-5

2022 年 11 月第 1 版	开本 880×1230 1/32
2022 年 11 月北京第 1 次印刷	印张 16 插页 2

定价:110.00 元